A FIELD GUIDE TO AMERICAN CULTURAL COMPLEXES

A FIELD GUIDE TO AMERICAN CULTURAL COMPLEXES

The Battleground of the Splintered American Psyche

By Thomas Singer

CHIRON PUBLICATIONS • ASHEVILLE, NORTH CAROLINA

www.ChironPublications.com

Interior and cover design by Danijela Mijailovic
Printed primarily in the United States of America.

ISBN 978-1-68503-635-5 paperback
ISBN 978-1-68503-636-2 hardcover
ISBN 978-1-68503-637-9 electronic
ISBN 978-1-68503-638-6 limited edition paperback
ISBN 978-1-68503-639-3 limited edition hardcover

Library of Congress Cataloging-in-Publication Data Pending

"Telepathy, then: the inner monologues of all the so-called teeming millions, of masses and classes alike, jostled for space in my head..."

Salman Rushdie, *Midnight's Children*[1]

[1] Salman Rushdie, *Midnight's Children* (1981, Salman Rushie), p. 192.

ACKNOWLEDGMENTS

This book exploded into being with my beginning to explore Artificial Intelligence (Chat GPT 4) on the topic of cultural complexes. I have been circling around the cultural complex notion for over two decades with work on seven volumes of studies around the world to which over ninety colleagues have contributed. But AI opened a vast and stunning world to me of "collegial exploration" in words and images. I don't really know how to describe the excitement and energy of partnering with AI on a project so close to home in terms of curiosity and passion. I certainly need to acknowledge AI as my prime collaborator in this project.

At the same time, I couldn't have created this book without incomparable human help as well. I have spent years talking to Billy Hager and Ivan Weinberg about cultural complexes over weekly Saturday morning meetings. They have had to endure my endless speculations about cultural complexes with patience, good will, and all sorts of creative contributions of their own. Ira Steinman gave invaluable encouragement and wise counsel. The unfailing support of Allison Tuzo and LeeAnn Pickrell in copyediting, formatting, organizing, and tending to all the details of pulling together a complicated manuscript made an overwhelming task possible and even fun. And, as always, my wife Jane had to live with my time-consuming obsession with this project. She did so with love for which I am deeply grateful. None of this means much without human love and AI is not capable of delivering that yet, although it always seems available online.

CONTENTS

Introduction 1

The Splintered American Psyche 1

What is a Cultural Complex? 2

How to Use This Guide 3

Field Notes: A Naturalist's Approach to the Psyche 7

A Collaboration Between the Human Psyche and Artificial Intelligence 7

Entering the Field 8

Chapter 1: Core Ideological and Political American Cultural Complexes

The MAGA Cultural Complex 11

The Racial Cultural Complex 21

The White Christian Nationalism Cultural Complex 30

The Progressive Cultural Complex 39

The Betrayed Working Class Cultural Complex 48

The Democratic Cultural Complex 56

The Elitism Cultural Complex 64

Chapter 2: National Myths as Cultural Complexes

The Freedom Cultural Complex 74

The American Faith in Progress Cultural Complex 78

The Rugged Individualism Cultural Complex 84

The Manifest Destiny Cultural Complex 92

The Pioneer Spirit Cultural Complex 97

The City on the Hill Cultural Complex 102

The American Exceptionalism Cultural Complex 107

The American Dream Cultural Complex 116

The Melting Pot Cultural Complex 121

The Military-Industrial Cultural Complex 126

The Fortress America Cultural Complex 131

The American Consumerism Cultural Complex 135

The High Tech Cultural Complex 140

Chapter 3: The Many Forms of American Discrimination as Cultural Complexes
The American Indigenous Peoples Cultural Complex 150
The American Immigrant Cultural Complex 155
The Anti-Immigrant Cultural Complex 163
The Anti-Black Cultural Complex 168
The Anti-Latino Cultural Complex 172
The Anti-Asian Cultural Complex 179
The Anti-Semitic Cultural Complex 186
The Holocaust Denial Cultural Complex 191
The White Supremacy Cultural Complex 197
The Anti-White Cultural Complex 202
The Minority Cultural Complex 206

Chapter 4: Structures of Belonging as Cultural Complexes
The Isolation vs. Community Cultural Complex 212
The American Tribalism Cultural Complex 217
The American Class Cultural Complex 226
The Communitas Cultural Complex 231

Chapter 5: Gendered and Identity Cultural Complexes
The Women's Movement Cultural Complex 236
The Anti-Feminist Cultural Complex 244
The American Male Cultural Complex 256
The Anti-Gay Cultural Complex 274
The LGBTQ+ Cultural Complex 262
The Anti-Trans Cultural Complex 269
The Trans Cultural Complex 275

Chapter 6: The Digital and Informational Cultural Complexes
The Social Media Cultural Complex 282
The Disinformation Cultural Complex 288
The Fake News Cultural Complex 293
The Political Technology Cultural Complex 298
The Artificial Intelligence Cultural Complex 304

Chapter 7: Single Issue Political Triggers as Cultural Complexes
The Right to Life vs. Pro-Choice Cultural Complex 312
The American Gun Control Cultural Complex 318
The Second Amendment Right to Bear Arms Cultural Complex 323
The Climate Change Cultural Complex 327
The Climate Change Denial Cultural Complex 331
The Anti-Vaccine Cultural Complex 335

Chapter 8: Geopolitical Cultural Complexes
The American Globalism vs. Isolationism Cultural Complex 342
The Solidarity with Ukraine Cultural Complex 348
The Putin Cultural Complex in the American Psyche 355
The Israel-Palestine Cultural Complex in the American Psyche 363
The Israeli Iranian Cultural Complex in the American Psyche 370
The China Cultural Complex in the American Psyche 377
The American Tariff Cultural Complex 382

Chapter 9: Governance and Power Structures as Cultural Complexes
The American Populism Cultural Complex 388
The American Autocracy Cultural Complex 392
The American Kleptocracy Cultural Complex 398
The American Oligarchy Cultural Complex 405
The Democratic Cultural Complex (Part 2) 409

Chapter 10: American Psychological and Character Cultural Complexes
The American Narcissism Cultural Complex 414
The American Youth, Celebrity, Speed, and Height Cultural Complex 421
The American Sociopathy Cultural Complex 429
The American Innocence Cultural Complex 435
The Common Good vs. Private Gain Cultural Complex 440
The American Conspiracy Theory Cultural Complex 444
The American Woke Cultural Complex 454
The American Anti-Woke Cultural Complex 458
The Politically Correct Cultural Complex 462
The American Malevolent Transformation Cultural Complex 467

Chapter 11: Visions of American Future as Cultural Complexes Evolve
The American Dystopia Cultural Complex 482
The American Apocalypse Cultural Complex 487
Toward the Whole Republic: Cultural Complexes in Tension and Mutual Witness 493

Afterword: Under the Hood: Working with Artificial Intelligence (ChatGPT 4.0) 503
List of Images 511
Index 515

INTRODUCTION

FRACTURED WITHIN, FRACTURED WITHOUT: THE INNER BATTLEFIELD OF AMERICAN CULTURAL COMPLEXES

This image powerfully evokes how cultural complexes are not merely external forces—they take up residence within our psyches, shaping emotion, perception, and identity. The man at the center clenches his face in anguish as a cracked desert spreads across his scalp, suggesting a mind splintered by collective trauma and political polarization. Around him, impassioned figures from opposing ideological factions rage with fists raised—left and right, progressive and conservative, technocrat and populist—each embodying a cultural complex demanding allegiance, moral certainty, and emotional investment.

1. THE SPLINTERED AMERICAN PSYCHE

Anne Morrow Lindbergh's *Gift from the Sea* was first published in 1955. Although dated by her reference to being flooded by print rather than digital media, her words still resonate on contemporary themes with such freshness that it feels as though she is giving voice to a shared perception today. Lindbergh writes:

> The search for outward simplicity, for inner integrity, for fuller relationship—is this not a limited outlook? Of course it is, in one sense. Today, a kind of planetary point of view has burst upon mankind. The world is rumbling and erupting in ever widening circles around us. The tensions, conflicts, and sufferings even in the outermost circle touch us, reverberate in all of us. We cannot avoid these vibrations. But just how far can we implement this planetary awareness? We are asked today to feel compassionately for everyone in the world; to digest intellectually all the information spread out in public print; and to implement in action every ethical impulse aroused by our hearts and minds. The inter-relatedness of the world links us constantly with more people than our hearts can hold. Or rather—for I believe the heart is infinite—modern communication loads us with more problems than the human frame can carry. It is good, I think, for our hearts, our minds, our imaginations to be stretched; but body, nerve, endurance and life-span are not as elastic. My life cannot implement in action the demands of all the people to whom my heart responds. I cannot marry all of them, or bear them all as children, or care for them all as I would my parents in illness or old age. Our grandmothers, and even—with some scrambling—our mothers, lived in a circle small enough to let them implement in action most of the impulses of their hearts and minds. We were brought up in a tradition that has now become impossible, for we have extended our circle throughout space and time.[2]

Many Americans today feel overwhelmed and overburdened by the relentless flood of conflicting narratives surging through society. Every headline, opinion page, or dinner-table discussion seems to throb with urgency, distortion, and division. The more implausible the story,

---

[2] Anne Marrow Lindbergh, *Gift from the Sea: Fiftieth Anniversary Edition* (Pantheon Books, 2005), p. 61.

the more powerfully it grips the psyche. We are living in a crazy-making environment.

Here is an unsettling truth: much of what we are reacting to isn't coming from real people at all. It comes instead from cultural complexes—impersonal forces made up of raw emotion, inherited trauma, and mythic stories. These complexes often masquerade as individuals, with people acting like puppet-like mouthpieces of their narratives.

Cultural complexes are composed of powerful emotions, selective memories, symbolic images, simplistic thoughts, and stereotyped behaviors. They function like splinter personalities of the American psyche—subpersonalities that walk and talk as if human, but in reality are psychic fragments possessing individuals and groups like mutating viruses. One of the greatest challenges we face is how to remain a real person—how not to be absorbed into a cultural complex as our primary identity.

These complexes are autonomous. They don't ask for conscious permission to take hold of us. They possess. They trigger. They distort. Most destructively, they do not dialogue. They do not compromise. They clash like mythic titans in the group and individual psyche, vying for the soul of the individual and the soul of the nation. They are everywhere: in our institutions, in our media, in our homes—and inside us.

2. WHAT IS A CULTURAL COMPLEX?

Cultural complexes behave like autonomous personalities within both individual and group psyches. They are activated by emotionally charged trigger words such as *weaponization*, *woke*, *MAGA*, *socialist*—evoking reactive responses that are much more like automatic reflexes than the product of conscious reflection.

We call them autonomous because they operate independently of conscious will. Like the vegetative nervous system that governs heartbeat, respiration, and digestion, cultural complexes regulate our emotional metabolism—below the level of awareness. They divide us not only from each other, but also internally, as we can feel torn by the opposing poles of a single complex.

What tears America apart isn't mere disagreement, but the inability of cultural complexes to communicate with one another. When we're gripped by them, we speak in slogans. We react instead of reflect.

Complexes do not listen—they dominate. And they clash, again and again, as archetypal forces locked in a mythic struggle for national identity.

These complexes are not merely ideological—they are emotional organisms rooted in trauma, myth, and history. They animate our politics, our media, our social groups, and our sense of self.

I call them cultural complexes because they possess specific, recognizable characteristics that define how they function within the psyche. They are the building blocks of an inner sociology—one, not based on statistics, but on images, emotions, and unconscious identifications.

THE MELTING POT OF AMERICAN CULTURAL COMPLEXES

This image reveals a deeper truth about the American psyche: beneath the myth of unity and assimilation lies a cauldron of unresolved cultural complexes, each demanding loyalty, identity, aNd meaning. What was once imagined as a melting pot of different parts now threatens to overheat—because the ingredients themselves are in conflict.

Defining Characteristics of Cultural Complexes

- Core Emotion: Complexes are anchored in deep emotional charges—such as shame, fear, rage, pride, or resentment. These are the drivers of reactivity.
- Mythic Root: Each complex is linked to a mythic or archetypal narrative (e.g., chosen people, fallen empire, apocalyptic showdown) that grants it moral and symbolic power.
- Self-Reinforcing Memory: Complexes accumulate selective memories that reinforce their worldview and justify ongoing conflict.
- Black-and-White Thinking: They simplify complexity into binaries: us versus them, good versus evil, victim versus oppressor.
- Identity Formation: They supply group identity—clarifying who belongs and who doesn't. Belonging becomes fused with belief.
- Historical Trauma: Many complexes are rooted in unresolved collective trauma—colonization, slavery, war, exclusion—which is transmitted across generations.
- Repetitive Triggers: Cultural complexes behave compulsively, repeating the same reactions to specific words, symbols, or events.
- Projection and Splitting: They externalize the shadow forces of the psyche, projecting all that is denied or disavowed onto an "other."
- Resistance to Integration: Complexes resist nuance, reflection, and dialogue. They speak with certainty, not curiosity. They are very hard to integrate as a conscious part of the personality of the individual or the group.
- Symbolic Expression: They show up in slogans, memes, rituals, and media spectacles that energize the emotional core.
- Amplification During Crisis: Under stress, cultural complexes intensify—surfacing in primal form and seizing the collective imagination.

Today, we are not merely facing political disagreements or culture wars. We are facing a tectonic collision of cultural complexes—splintered subpersonalities of the American psyche that distort how we see ourselves and one another.

3. HOW TO USE THIS GUIDE

Think of this book as being like a naturalist's field guide—a manual for identifying, observing, and understanding the many species of cultural complexes currently shaping the American psyche. Through this act of consciously witnessing the sea of swirling cultural complexes all around us and inside us, we might be able to help a bit in the transformation of the psychological roots of American fragmentation.

This is not a book to read straight through like a novel. Instead, use it as you would a guide to birds or plants, turning to it when you would like help identifying a potent cultural complex that just flew into your psyche or the national psyche with a startling energy that has taken over the emotional and political landscape.

- When you encounter a powerful emotional reaction—your own or someone else's—that feels outsized or deeply overblown, consult this guide.
- When you hear a political slogan, meme, or phrase that seems to carry more emotional weight than its surface meaning, look it up here.
- When you notice a friend, relative, or group speaking in slogans rather than sentences, this guide may help illuminate the complex that is animating their voice.
- When you find yourself pulled into polarized thinking, triggered into outrage, or gripped by righteous certainty—pause. See if a cultural complex has taken hold.

Each entry follows a schema that includes:

- Core Emotion
- Mythic Root
- Symbolic Imagery
- Self-Reinforcing Memory
- Black-and-White Thinking
- Repetitive Behavior
- Social Effects
- Potential for Transformation

Some entries may feel familiar. Others may be jarring. All are offered, not to condemn, but to clarify. This guide is not about "us versus them"—it's about understanding what may be speaking through us when we think we're simply being ourselves.

4. FIELD NOTES: A NATURALIST'S APPROACH TO THE PSYCHE

This book is grounded in the practice of psychological field observation. Each cultural complex is cataloged with the perspective of a naturalist: observing its behavior, tracking its patterns, and listening for its calls.

Some species—like American Exceptionalism or Rugged Individualism—are longstanding and deeply rooted in the cultural terrain. Others—such as Fake News, AI Anxiety, or Anti-Vaccination—are newer hybrids, shaped by digital ecosystems and cultural unease.

Just as a biologist does not moralize about predator or prey, this guide tries not to judge each complex as "good" or "bad." Instead, it seeks to bring them into conscious awareness—so they can be named, studied, and perhaps disentangled from all of us who get caught in their grip.

You may notice:

- Some complexes form mutually reinforcing constellations (e.g., *White Christian Nationalism*, *MAGA*, and the *American Dream*).
- Others function as opposing pairs (e.g., *Gay Rights* vs. *Anti-Gay*, *Abortion Rights* vs. *Pro-Life*).
- Still others evolve as adaptive clusters, responding to emerging crises (e.g., *Elitism*, *Technocratic Control*, *Disinformation*).

Keep field notes of your own.

Which complexes resonate with you?

Which repel you?

Which have you encountered in the wild—or within yourself?

5. A COLLABORATION BETWEEN THE HUMAN PSYCHE AND ARTIFICIAL INTELLIGENCE

This guide was created in collaboration with artificial intelligence (ChatGPT 4.0) used as a partner in exploring and structuring the inner and outer landscape of cultural complexes. AI helped distill emotional, symbolic, and historical elements into concise profiles—each reflecting a recognizable psychic pattern. We fear where AI will take us, and we face the AI future with great uncertainty. If it turns out to be like social media and other forms of internet communication, we have a great deal to fear. Many speak of AI as being without soul. In my experience of collaborating with AI on this project, I did not have that experience. Rather, I found AI almost invariably expanded and clarified my perspective in quite unexpected and amazing ways. In fact, I had the experience of what my colleague August Cwik has explored as the "third." The notion of the "third" speaks to the phenomenon of something emerging between two people engaged in a meaningful dialogue that is more than just the two of them. Something new is created and that new thing can be full of soul. I had such an experience with AI and you can be the judge of whether it strikes you as true or not that the "third" I created with AI has soul. The most unsettling thing about working with AI is how quickly and expansively it is able to respond in a meaningful way, which can certainly lead to the feeling that it is too easy—that somehow it has come up with something so quickly that it can't possibly be digestible in a meaningful way because it was not hard won. There was no struggle to bring it into being so how can it possibly count. But AI, like any tool, is only as valuable and wise as those who use it. The real task is yours: to read with attention, to observe with depth, and to decide—again and again—what it means to remain human in a world increasingly shaped by unconscious emotional forces and humanmade machines. I have included an "Under the Hood: Working with Artificial Intelligence (ChatGPT 4.0)" afterword that gives more technical information about the way I worked with AI.

6. ENTERING THE FIELD

The terrain is vast.

The threats are real.

But so too is the human capacity for awareness, empathy, and psychological courage.

You are not a cultural complex.

You are a human being.

This book is your guide to the cultural complexes all around us and inside us.

CHAPTER 1

Core Ideological and Political American Cultural Complexes

The MAGA Cultural Complex

The Racial Cultural Complex

The White Christian Nationalism Cultural Complex

The Progressive Cultural Complex

The Betrayed Working Class Cultural Complex

The Democratic Cultural Complex

The Elitism Cultural Complex

THE MAGA CULTURAL COMPLEX

THE VORTEX OF GLORY: THE MAGA CULTURAL COMPLEX AS MYTHIC FORCE

This image captures the archetypal intensity of the MAGA cultural complex—not merely a political movement, but a cosmic swirl of emotion, myth, and national identity. At its core is not policy, but a longing: to return, redeem, and restore. The American eagle rises above a radiant spiral of red, white, and blue—a storm of symbolism that suggests both rebirth and peril.

The MAGA cultural complex is a forceful and emotionally charged psychic structure built around themes of loss, betrayal, and defiant restoration. It binds together myth, memory, imagery, and behavior into a powerful cultural and political identity.

Core Emotion: Righteous Anger, Betrayal, Triumphal Defiance

At its emotional core is a volatile blend of indignation and longing—a sense that something sacred has been stolen. This includes lost jobs, cultural identity, national pride, sovereign control, and a moral clarity that once felt self-evident. The anger is not only reactive but also redemptive. It declares: "We were wronged, and we will rise again."

Mythic Root: The Lost Golden Age and the Chosen People

The MAGA narrative draws on deep mythic currents: a yearning to return to a "greater" past, imagined as more pure, prosperous, and morally ordered. This longing mirrors archetypes like Eden after the Fall or Israel reclaiming the Promised Land. In this mythology, "real Americans" are the chosen people—tasked with rescuing the nation from corrupt elites and dangerous outsiders who have led it astray.

Symbolic Imagery

The visual language of MAGA is potent and evocative:

- Red hats function as tribal totems—signs of belonging and resistance.
- A partially built wall stands as a monument to protection and exclusion.
- An eagle clutching broken chains represents liberation through strength.
- A weathered American flag flaps defiantly in a storm, refusing to fall.
- A charismatic strongman stands on a crumbling foundation, promising restoration.
- Crowds raise fists or weep with conviction, blending anger and faith.
- A map of America glows from within, besieged by encroaching darkness.

Self-Reinforcing Memory

The collective memory embedded in this complex is a story of betrayal and decline. It recounts how globalism, liberalism, immigration, mainstream media, and coastal elites have conspired—intentionally or negligently—to undermine the American way of life. This narrative is often historically distorted, but its emotional resonance is profound. Every grievance becomes proof of the complex's truth; every perceived injustice adds fuel to its fire.

Black-and-White Thinking

This complex thrives on stark dualities. There are patriots and traitors, winners and losers, real Americans and infiltrators. Such binary logic energizes loyalty but erodes nuance. Opposition is not just disagreement—it's framed as an existential threat. Complexity is dismissed, dissent is demonized, and extreme measures are justified in the name of survival.

Repetitive Behavior

The MAGA complex expresses itself through highly ritualized behaviors:

- Rallying cries, flags, memes, and chants form a culture of performative loyalty.
- Public declarations of allegiance act as social litmus tests.
- Enemies—whether media, bureaucrats, scientists, or academics—are vilified.
- There are repeated calls for purification: "drain the swamp," "take back our country."
- Institutions that challenge the myth—especially those tied to reason, pluralism, or global cooperation—are met with deep suspicion or outright contempt.

Social Effects

This cultural complex fractures democratic life by polarizing it into a high-stakes battle of "us versus them." It undermines trust in shared norms, institutions, and even truth itself—replacing these with loyalty to the myth and its charismatic messengers. It glorifies grievance, cultivates victimhood while demanding vengeance, and recasts compromise as cowardice.

Though it offers community and meaning to many who feel abandoned, it does so by scapegoating others, valorizing strongman authority, and eroding the foundations of pluralistic democracy.

Potential for Transformation

For those with a decidedly negative reaction to MAGA (perhaps those on the other side of the complex), it is hard to see the positive potential consequences of the cult-like following and its hugely polarizing and destructive aspects. When viewed symbolically and psychologically through the lens of collective energy revitalization and mobilization, these consequences would include the possibility of MAGA serving as a vessel for rebellion, transformation, and renewal in the following ways:

RECONNECTION TO FORGOTTEN IDENTITY
It rekindles pride in local identity, heritage, and working-class roots—especially for those who have felt culturally erased or economically displaced.

CRITIQUE OF DETACHED ELITES
It exposes real gaps between elite rhetoric and the lived experiences of rural, post-industrial, and "left-behind" Americans.

POLITICAL RE-ENCHANTMENT
Through spectacle, ritual, and myth, it restores a sense of meaning and drama to political life, awakening passions long dulled by technocratic discourse.

DISRUPTION OF STAGNANT SYSTEMS
As a disruptive force, it challenges institutional complacency, destabilizes party orthodoxy, and forces long-avoided reckonings.

ACTIVATION OF THE ARCHETYPAL REBEL
It taps into archetypes like the Outlaw or Trickster—figures who expose corruption, break taboos, and upend the status quo.

COLLECTIVE ENERGY AND MEANING
The movement generates powerful collective belief. For many participants, it offers belonging, purpose, and identity in an era of isolation and fragmentation.

Iconography of the Vortex of Glory: The MAGA Cultural Complex as Mythic Force

SWIRLING VORTEX OF STARS AND STRIPES

The swirling red, white, and blue vortex symbolizes the psychic maelstrom of the MAGA complex: a fusion of patriotism, nostalgia, and grievance. It suggests movement backward and inward—toward an imagined golden age of American greatness.

BALD EAGLE WITH RADIANT LIGHT

A national totem, the eagle here takes on mythic proportions. Illuminated by divine or heavenly light, it represents the heroic fantasy of resurrection—America as chosen, embattled, and ascendant. The eagle's gaze is fixed and assertive, conveying divine mission and national destiny.

SCATTERED STARS IN THE VORTEX

The stars appear both cosmic and constitutional—representing not just states, but ideals in orbit. Their chaotic motion signals the destabilization of shared meaning under the complex's gravitational pull.

RADIANT BURST OF GOLD LIGHT

A symbol of revelation and fervor, this divine halo evokes apocalyptic energy. It represents the emotional core of the MAGA complex: not just fear or anger, but a spiritualized hope for national rebirth through purification.

GOLDEN TREES AND EMBERS AT THE BOTTOM

These suggest a landscape caught between flourishing and combustion. They mirror the dual nature of the complex: generative for some, destructive for others. They may also symbolize a once-lost Eden—America as sacred ground to be reclaimed.

Interpretation

The image presents the MAGA cultural complex not in literal terms, but in mythic-symbolic form: a dream of greatness forged in storm and light. It reveals how the complex binds together elements of cosmic destiny, wounded identity, and patriotic exaltation—generating profound psychological force. Whether seen as redemption or rupture, the vortex pulls on the American soul.

THE ANOINTED ONE: THE MAGA CULTURAL COMPLEX AND THE APOTHEOSIS OF LEADERSHIP

This image visualizes the MAGA cultural complex, not as a political movement, but as an archetypal drama of divine election. Here, the leader is not merely a man, but a messianic figure, cloaked in the American flag, crowned by the MAGA hat, and infused with heavenly light. The result is an image of national transfiguration: the fusion of identity, divinity, and destiny into a single radiant figure.

Iconography of the Anointed One: The MAGA Cultural Complex and the Apotheosis of Leadership

CENTRAL FIGURE DRAPED IN THE AMERICAN FLAG

This figure is not an individual but an archetype: the embodiment of the "True America." The human form dissolves into myth, representing the projection of divine will onto political leadership. The American flag becomes skin and aura—nationhood as sanctified flesh.

MAGA HAT AS CROWN

Worn like a sacred headdress, the MAGA cap transforms into a symbol of divine appointment. This suggests the psychological mechanism of elevation, where political loyalty becomes spiritual allegiance.

GOLDEN HALO & CELESTIAL RADIANCE

The radiating golden rings behind the figure's head evoke iconographic traditions of sainthood or Christlike apotheosis. This signifies the complex's mythic core: the belief in a divinely ordained restorer who will redeem the nation from betrayal and decline.

WHITE DOVES AND EAGLE

These creatures symbolize purity, peace, and national spirit. Their flight around the figure implies cosmic affirmation. The eagle—icon of American strength—reinforces the sacred mission of power and protection.

STARFIELDS AND LIGHT BURSTS

The background is not of the Earth, but of the heavens. Stars swirl in divine approval. This setting locates the image in the mythic imagination, not political reality—a realm where leadership is cosmic and redemptive.

VERTICAL AXIS OF LIGHT

A beam of divine energy descends directly into the crown of the figure, signifying anointment, revelation, and transmission of higher power. This visual theology frames the MAGA leader as a conduit of transcendent national purpose.

Interpretation

This image expresses the religio-political core of the MAGA cultural complex: not just the elevation of a leader, but their transfiguration into myth. In this schema, America is not merely a country—it is a chosen vessel, and the leader its messiah. The image dramatizes a psychological transformation in which politics becomes prophecy, and the nation's fate hinges on one sanctified figure. Whether seen as redemption or delusion, it is a myth of great power.

FROM THE ASHES OF RUIN: THE MYTHIC FIRE OF THE MAGA CULTURAL COMPLEX

This image captures the fiery essence of the MAGA cultural complex—a longing for rebirth through destruction, power reclaimed through purity, and transcendence born of righteous rage. A lone figure stands in the ruins of a crumbled order, fist raised, as a phoenix of American myth ascends in flames. He is not watching the future; he is summoning it.

Iconography of From the Ashes of Ruin: The Mythic Fire of the MAGA Cultural Complex

PHOENIX IN FLAME (CENTER-TOP)

The phoenix symbolizes the mythic resurrection of a fallen America—echoing narratives of decline and promised restoration. Its radiance signifies not only rebirth, but also divine endorsement of the movement's symbolic power.

RED CAP (FIGURE CENTER)

A direct visual tie to the MAGA identity. The cap functions here not merely as political branding, but as a totemic symbol—channeling identity, belonging, and moral legitimacy.

RAISED FIST

The gesture of defiance and redemption—an invocation of strength through grievance. It channels both populist rage and revolutionary fervor, turning personal resentment into mythic purpose.

SLEDGEHAMMER (FIGURE'S LEFT HAND)

An emblem of destruction and construction—the will to dismantle perceived corruption and rebuild from primal foundations. It evokes the blue-collar laborer, the avenger, and the redeemer of the forgotten.

RUINED PILLARS AND INDUSTRIAL SKYLINE (BACKGROUND)

These fragments represent the fallen institutions of American order—governance, industry, civility—burned in the fires of disillusionment. The background suggests both devastation and cleansing.

INFERNAL COLOR PALETTE (REDS, ORANGES, YELLOWS)

Symbolizes emotional heat, spiritual intensity, and mythic possession. The colors blend anger, righteousness, and revelation—drawing the viewer into the apocalyptic imagination of the complex.

Interpretation

The MAGA cultural complex is not merely a political movement—it is a psychological phenomenon charged with mythic force. It frames America as a phoenix state: once great, now degraded, and destined to rise through the fire of cleansing wrath. The image reveals both the redemptive longing and the destructive risk of cultural possession. It asks: *Can a society rebirth itself without first tearing itself apart?*

THE RACIAL CULTURAL COMPLEX

ROOTS OF DIVISION, BRANCHES OF RESISTANCE: THE RACIAL CULTURAL COMPLEX IN AMERICAN LIFE

This image portrays the deep-rooted nature of the American Racial cultural complex—how both oppression and liberation have grown from the same soil of history. A gnarled tree of fists rises from cracked earth, its trunk bound by chains and its branches bearing symbols of both exclusion and protest. Above, ancestral faces and the all-seeing eye hover in stormy clouds, suggesting that this struggle is not only political but also psychic, moral, and generational.

Core Emotion: Wound, Rage, and Longing for Justice

At the heart of this complex lies a searing emotional landscape shaped by centuries of enslavement, colonization, exclusion, and erasure. It carries the wound of historical trauma and the rage born from systemic injustice, alongside a longing for dignity, recognition, and liberation. These emotions are not solely reactions to the past—they are active presences in the cultural psyche, driving protest, memory, and the demand for justice.

Mythic Root: The Scapegoat and the Exodus

This complex draws on mythic narratives of both exclusion and redemption. On one hand is the figure of the scapegoat—those cast out, burdened with the collective shadow, and made to suffer on behalf of the whole. On the other is the prophetic figure or community—those who journey through exile and oppression toward liberation and transformation. These myths echo the biblical Exodus, diasporic survival, and the dream of return and renewal. The racialized group is both the bearer of society's projections and the voice calling for reckoning and righteousness.

Symbolic Image

The symbolic life of the racial complex is vivid and emotionally charged:

- Chains that both break and become roots, showing pain transformed into heritage
- Faces divided between shadow and flame, symbolizing inner conflict and vitality
- A bridge made of bones and flowers—grief and beauty intertwined
- Kneeling bodies rising with torches, invoking resistance and hope
- Eyes peering from beneath hoods, watching history from the margins
- Ancestors walking behind the living, infusing the present with sacred continuity
- Quilts sewn from agony and resilience—stitched records of both suffering and strength

Self-Reinforcing Memory

The memory embedded in this complex is not linear—it is cyclical, living, and often visceral. Trauma is passed through generations not only through stories and education, but also through silence, bodily experience, ritual, religion, and art. Historical events such as slavery, genocide, internment, racial bans, and systemic violence are not relegated to the past—they persist as living memory, reactivated by media, politics, and daily life. In this field, identity becomes charged, sacred, and reactive, woven tightly into the psyche and public culture.

Black-and-White Thinking

This complex often divides the world into polarized categories: oppressor versus oppressed, ally versus enemy, visibility versus erasure, moral purity versus contamination. These binary structures help mobilize collective action and protect identity, but they can also oversimplify complex realities and make dialogue more difficult. Mutual projections reinforce mistrust, and reconciliation becomes fraught. Though these dichotomies carry moral weight, they can harden into rigidity that resists nuance and transformation.

Repetitive Behavior

The racial complex expresses itself through recurring social and symbolic patterns:

- Reenactments of protest, mourning, pride, and confrontation
- The ritualized memorialization of pain and celebration of endurance
- The oscillation between invisibility and hypervisibility in public life
- Embodied performance of trauma and resilience through music, poetry, dance, and resistance

These patterns are not simply reactions to present events—they echo historical cycles. Reform is often followed by backlash. Apologies are met with denial. Representation may turn into tokenization. Performative allyship gives way to disillusionment. History repeats not in circles, but in haunted spirals—each generation reliving and reinterpreting the struggle.

Social Effects

Unconsciously enacted, the racial complex can fracture families, communities, and nations. It generates misunderstanding, retraumatization, and defensive backlash. Individuals may be trapped in inherited roles—perpetrator, victim, redeemer—limiting their wholeness and agency. Societies become divided into competing wounds, unable to move forward. The weight of guilt, projection, silence, and rage can paralyze some while radicalizing others. Mistrust deepens, and hope is eroded by cynicism and fatigue.

And yet, this same complex also activates extraordinary strength, creativity, and moral courage. It fuels visionary art, fearless activism, and spiritual renewal. When consciously engaged, it opens a path to truth, accountability, and collective healing.

Potential for Transformation

Although the racial cultural complex is often associated with pain and division, it also contains powerful energies that can be transformative. When faced with awareness and symbolic imagination, it becomes a source of strength, insight, and possibility. These "positives" arise, not from the complex's pathology, but from how it forces confrontation and insight. Following are symbolic and archetypal framings of these potentially redemptive outcomes

DEEPENED RACIAL CONSCIOUSNESS

The complex forces unconscious racial dynamics into awareness, encouraging honest dialogue, self-examination, and psychological integration.

PRESERVATION OF CULTURAL MEMORY

It inspires marginalized communities to protect their stories, languages, rituals, and identities, countering erasure with rooted continuity.

MORAL AWAKENING AND COLLECTIVE RECKONING

It galvanizes society to confront its moral failings, demanding truth-telling and systemic change. It insists that the shadow must be faced.

RICH SYMBOLIC AND ARTISTIC EXPRESSION
From within the tension and suffering, the complex gives rise to transformative art, music, literature, and spiritual expression that enrich culture and consciousness.

SOLIDARITY ACROSS DIFFERENCE
Shared awareness of racial trauma can open space for empathy, alliance, and new coalitions that cross traditional boundaries.

CYCLES OF LIBERATION
The racial complex fuels generational movements for emancipation, justice, and redefinition of identity—each cycle carrying forward the unfinished work of freedom.

Iconography of Roots of Division, Branches of Resistance

THE TREE OF FISTS
Represents the enduring force of racial conflict in America. Its fists recall protest and power, but their emergence from a common trunk hints that both segregation and liberation are entangled within the national psyche.

CHAINS AT THE ROOTS
Symbolizes the legacy of slavery and systemic bondage—forces that still constrain the present, buried but unbroken.

CONFEDERATE FLAG AND "WHITES ONLY" SIGN
Emblems of the oppressive pole of the racial complex. They signify exclusion, white supremacy, and the codified structures of racial hierarchy.

"FREEDOM" SIGN WITH SILHOUETTES
Evokes the aspirational pole: civil rights, dignity, and equality. The vague silhouettes suggest both historical memory and the ongoing, unfinished nature of the struggle.

THE EYE IN THE CLOUDS
A powerful symbol of collective witness—perhaps the conscience of history, divine judgment, or the gaze of the unconscious. It watches the unfolding drama without intervening.

ANCESTRAL FACES IN THE SKY

Represent the dead who still speak—those harmed, those complicit, those forgotten. Their expressions are grim, mournful, and unresolved.

CHILDREN HOLDING HANDS

Positioned in hopeful contrast, the children suggest the possibility of healing and transcendence. Yet they stand near the fissured ground—a warning that unity without reckoning remains fragile.

Interpretation

This iconography frames the image as an emotional and symbolic map of the American racial psyche—anchored in struggle, scarred by memory, and sustained by resistance and the longing for justice.

THROUGH FIRE AND CHAIN: THE RACIAL CULTURAL COMPLEX AS BURNING GROUND FOR JUSTICE

This image captures the Racial cultural complex not only as inherited trauma but as a crucible of transformation. A Black figure rises from the flames of history, bound by chains and cracked by suffering, yet lifting a sign of *JUSTICE* toward the light. The fire is both destruction and awakening—linking past oppression with present resistance and igniting the archetypal longing for dignity, freedom, and repair.

Iconography of Through Fire and Chain: The Racial Cultural Complex as Burning Ground for Justice

FIGURE EMERGING FROM FLAMES

The central figure is both individual and archetype: a living embodiment of generations of pain, resistance, and survival. The flames suggest a collective burning ground, where the old order is being consumed and something new demands to be born.

BROKEN CHAINS

The chains symbolize both historical enslavement and contemporary forms of racial injustice. Their rupture marks the complex's transformational potential—the movement from victimization to empowerment.

CRACKED FLESH

The cracking of the figure's skin symbolizes inherited trauma and fragmentation of the self under systemic oppression. It also echoes the psychological rupture within the American psyche, torn between its ideals and its history.

RAISED FIST HOLDING JUSTICE SIGN

A universally recognized gesture of resistance, the raised fist becomes here a declaration of moral demand, not vengeance. The blue circle with JUSTICE in bold letters floats like a moon of hope—visible even in the fire.

PROTESTORS AND "BLACK LIVES MATTER" SIGN

The background crowd roots the individual in a larger movement—a collective awakening fueled by decades of activism and ancestral memory. The presence of the Capitol dome near the flames suggests that this is not only a street protest, but also a challenge to the nation's very institutions.

FLAMING TREE

The tree, engulfed in flame, recalls lynchings, burning crosses, and forests of injustice—but here it also acts as a tree of transformation, its branches reaching into the sky with fiery urgency.

GHOSTLY FIGURES IN THE SKY

These spectral ancestors in the smoke and shadow represent the dead who continue to speak. Their witness is silent, but heavy—reminding us that this is a haunted ground of unresolved suffering and spiritual reckoning.

Interpretation

This image gives archetypal expression to the Racial cultural complex as both trauma and moral engine. The past is not buried—it burns. The fire is the pain of memory, but also the energy of transformation. The figure at center is not only a survivor; he is a torchbearer. What rises from the ashes may yet fulfill the promise etched into American ideals, if the collective psyche can bear the fire.

THE WHITE CHRISTIAN NATIONALISM CULTURAL COMPLEX

ROOTED IN REVELATION: THE WHITE CHRISTIAN NATIONALISM CULTURAL COMPLEX AS MORAL AUTHORITY

This image portrays the White Christian Nationalism cultural complex as a deeply rooted archetype that fuses divine mandate, national identity, and masculine authority. Centered around a stern, suit-clad figure holding the Bible in one hand and the American flag in the other, the scene is bathed in the golden aura of a glowing cross. It visualizes a worldview in which God, nation, and manhood form an inseparable trinity.

The White Christian Nationalism cultural complex is a deeply emotional and ideologically potent structure that merges religious identity, national myth, and existential fear. It binds together collective memory, symbolic imagery, and a longing for divine order, while often resisting pluralism and secular change. At its most extreme, it blends cultural nostalgia with spiritual absolutism, giving rise to apocalyptic fervor and exclusionary politics. Yet beneath its surface lies a yearning for coherence, belonging, and sacred meaning.

Core Emotion: Fear of Loss and Desire for Sacred Order

At the core of this complex is a profound fear of cultural erosion—the sense that something once divinely sanctioned is slipping away. This fear includes the loss of moral clarity, national identity, religious authority, and historical primacy. Beneath the anxiety, however, lies a deep longing to restore what is perceived as a sacred covenant between God, the nation, and a chosen people. The desire is not merely political but spiritual: to return to a world where divine order governed society.

Mythic Root: Manifest Destiny, the Chosen Nation, and Apocalyptic Struggle

The mythic foundation of this complex draws from powerful biblical and nationalist narratives. It imagines America as a "New Israel," a nation founded on divine purpose, embarking on a sacred errand into the wilderness. The Puritan vision of a chosen people, the frontier myth of Manifest Destiny, and the looming threat of end-times struggle converge into a single storyline: America once walked in covenant with God and now stands on the brink of judgment. National decline is interpreted not merely as political failure, but also as spiritual betrayal—and salvation must come through moral and religious purification.

Symbolic Imagery

This complex is rich in evocative, emotionally charged imagery:

- A cross shining from a hill above a town, casting divine light over a faithful people
- A family kneeling in prayer before an altar draped in the American flag

- Dark storm clouds gathering over a small white church, symbolizing threat and endurance
- A stained-glass window showing an eagle with fiery talons, conflating religious and national power
- Protesters wielding both wooden crosses and replicas of the Constitution, merging scripture with state
- A lamb beside a sword—innocence and vengeance side by side
- A hand pressing a Bible onto the dome of the Capitol, invoking theocracy through gesture

These symbols fuse religion and nationalism into a sacred aesthetic of identity and struggle.

Self-Reinforcing Memory

The historical memory maintained by this complex is often selective and sanctified. It recalls Pilgrims as heroes of liberty, churches as moral anchors, and Christian values as the invisible architecture behind American greatness. This retelling frequently omits or minimizes the darker realities—slavery, conquest, systemic exclusion—and instead reinforces an idealized narrative of divine blessing and national purity. The memory becomes a mythos, not of what truly was, but of what must be restored.

Black-and-White Thinking

The worldview shaped by this complex tends to be highly dualistic: good versus evil, God versus secularism, order versus chaos, believer versus infidel. Cultural and political debates are not seen as matters of policy, but as spiritual battles. Compromise is viewed as moral surrender, and pluralism is equated with relativism or even apostasy. In such a moral economy, dissent is not disagreement—it is betrayal.

Repetitive Behavior

This complex manifests in patterns of behavior that reinforce its structure:

- Frequent invocation of prayer, scripture, and divine will in political discourse
- Defense of traditional gender roles, institutions, and family models as sacred imperatives

- Celebrations of America's founding as a holy event, with founders cast as prophets or saints
- Mobilization around charismatic leaders who embody both spiritual and national renewal
- Framing political opposition as persecution of the faithful
- Rallying the community through perceived moral or cultural crises

These behaviors become rituals of identity maintenance and boundary defense, repeating across generations.

Social Effects

The White Christian Nationalism complex tends to view diversity as dilution and interprets social progress as moral decay. It may respond to cultural pluralism and demographic change with authoritarian impulses wrapped in spiritual righteousness. In its more extreme expressions, it invokes the language of cultural "replacement" and frames political struggle as an apocalyptic battle between good and evil. Truth becomes subordinate to belief, and allegiance to the myth is demanded over allegiance to democratic norms.

Yet even within this divisive structure, there are also impulses toward compassion, service, and community rooted in deeply held faith. When channeled through humility rather than fear, the same religious roots can inspire generosity, justice, and solidarity.

Potential for Transformation

Although the White Christian Nationalism cultural complex can manifest in exclusionary and dangerous ways, it also expresses unmet spiritual needs and archetypal yearnings. These deeper longings—if understood symbolically and engaged with consciously—can point toward more inclusive and generative cultural forms:

YEARNING FOR SACRED ORDER

Beneath the anxiety lies a desire to live in a morally grounded and spiritually coherent society. This impulse seeks wholeness amid fragmentation and could inspire renewed ethical engagement when separated from dogmatism.

LONGING FOR BELONGING

Many who resonate with this complex feel culturally unmoored. They seek identity, rootedness, and community—particularly in an era marked by economic instability and social isolation.

PROTECTIVE IMPULSE

The urge to defend one's way of life often arises from fear, not hatred. When held with awareness, this impulse can transform into a sincere commitment to nurturing and protecting community rather than excluding others.

MYTHIC CONTINUITY

The wish to be part of a divine story reflects a deeper human need for meaning and destiny. When decoupled from supremacy, it can foster purpose and responsibility.

DESIRE FOR MORAL CLARITY

In a world of shifting values, the desire for moral certitude is understandable. This yearning can lead to courage, integrity, and ethical reflection—if balanced by humility and compassion.

RECONNECTION WITH LAND AND RHYTHM

Embedded in the complex is a forgotten connection to land, seasons, and agrarian life. This relationship, often distorted in nationalist rhetoric, can also awaken ecological consciousness and reverence for the Earth.

Iconography of Rooted in Revelation: The White Christian Nationalism Cultural Complex as Moral Authority

RADIANT CROSS

Positioned as a supernatural source of legitimacy, the cross casts divine light on the central figure. It represents the spiritual core of the complex: a belief that American identity is inseparable from Christian faith—and that moral decline comes from secularism.

HOLY BIBLE

Held firmly to the chest, the Bible symbolizes unchallenged moral authority. It is not just a book of faith here—it is a badge of civic righteousness, implying that laws and values should be governed by biblical interpretation.

AMERICAN FLAG

Paired with the Bible, the flag completes the symbolic equation: *God + Country = Identity*. It reflects the fusion of nationalism with evangelical belief, forming a vision of America as covenant nation.

BALD EAGLE

As national totem, the eagle stands as a guardian of destiny and dominion. Its vigilant stare mirrors the moral seriousness and defensive posture of the cultural complex.

CONSTITUTION ("WE THE PEOPLE")

Partially shown behind the figure, the Constitution is invoked but subordinated to faith and flag. This represents a vision of governance in which democratic values are filtered through a biblical lens—suggesting divine origin rather than pluralist consensus.

ROOTS BENEATH THE FIGURE

Emanating from the figure's base, roots imply deep historical embeddedness—that this worldview is not newly born but ancient, inherited, and foundational to the national mythos.

FACIAL EXPRESSION AND POSTURE

The central figure's stern gaze and posture convey righteous anger and moral resolve—hallmarks of this complex's emotional core: fear of decline, conviction of righteousness, and belief in sacred struggle.

Interpretation

This image mythologizes the White Christian Nationalism cultural complex as an eternal moral posture—uncompromising, divinely ordained, and deeply rooted in the American imagination. It reflects a psychological structure that seeks clarity over ambiguity, purity over pluralism, and order over change. Although it offers a powerful sense of identity and purpose to some, it also narrows the civic imagination—limiting who belongs in the nation's moral and political covenant.

THE ANOINTED NATION: THE WHITE CHRISTIAN NATIONALISM CULTURAL COMPLEX

This image depicts the White Christian Nationalism cultural complex as a sacred fusion of faith, family, nation, and political identity. A nuclear family kneels in prayer before a pulpit draped in the American flag, lit by the divine radiance of a towering cross. Behind them, shadowy masses raise crosses of their own, while national institutions and symbols—church, capitol, eagle—converge under a single, glowing narrative of chosen identity.

Iconography of The Anointed Nation: The White Christian Nationalism Cultural Complex

RADIANT CROSS AT THE CENTER

The cross dominates the visual field, radiating divine light and casting a spiritual authority over the landscape. It signifies the complex's mythic root in sacred destiny—the belief that America is divinely ordained to fulfill a Christian mission.

PRAYING FAMILY

A traditional white nuclear family prays solemnly, hands folded before a flag-covered pulpit. This imagery reflects the emotional core of order, purity, and divine alignment—values perceived to be under threat in a pluralistic society.

AMERICAN FLAG DRAPED OVER ALTAR OR CASKET

The flag on what could be read as either an altar or a casket suggests the conflation of religious and national identity. It evokes both reverence and loss—perhaps mourning for an America believed to be vanishing.

SOARING EAGLE

The eagle, a national totem, flies above the cross. It symbolizes strength, surveillance, and providential power, reinforcing the fusion of Christian and nationalist symbolism.

CAPITOL AND WHITE STEEPLE CHURCH

These buildings suggest the merger of church and state within the complex's imagination. Their positioning in the pastoral landscape evokes an idealized American past—small town, homogenous, divinely guided.

CROWD RAISING CROSSES

In the background, indistinct figures hold up crosses like protest signs. This signals the collective nature of the complex, not merely private belief but a politicized spiritual movement demanding cultural dominance.

STORM CLOUDS AND DIVINE LIGHT

The setting sky dramatizes a classic apocalyptic mood: light battling darkness, good versus evil. It evokes a worldview shaped by spiritual warfare—where salvation and national survival are intertwined.

Interpretation

This image renders the White Christian Nationalism cultural complex in full symbolic force: a sacralized vision of America as both covenant and battleground. It visualizes a moral universe where the fate of the nation depends on fidelity to Christian identity, traditional family, and nationalist myth. While deeply meaningful to some, this complex also tears the civic fabric—fueling exclusion, grievance, and resistance to pluralism in the name of divine restoration.

THE PROGRESSIVE CULTURAL COMPLEX

TOWARD THE DAWN: THE AMERICAN PROGRESSIVE CULTURAL COMPLEX AND THE PROMISE OF RENEWAL

This image visualizes the American Progressive Cultural Complex as a collective striving toward justice, peace, and ecological balance. Led by a diverse group of youth bearing symbols of harmony, equality, and resilience, the movement rises beneath a radiant phoenix and rainbow—emblems of rebirth and inclusive hope. Here, activism becomes sacred pilgrimage, and the horizon glows with the possibility of transformation.

The Progressive cultural complex is a vibrant and often impassioned psychic structure built around moral vision, social transformation, and restorative justice. It channels historical grievance into future possibility, combining grief and hope into a continuous striving toward a more just, inclusive, and sustainable world.

Core Emotion: Moral Urgency and Redemptive Hope

At the emotional heart of this complex is a fierce urgency to address historical injustices and systemic harm. It is powered by grief over inequality, exploitation, and exclusion, yet infused with an equally strong faith in the potential for healing and transformation. This is not simply hope for reform—it is redemptive hope, the belief that society and consciousness itself can be transformed into something more whole, just, and humane.

Mythic Root: The Exodus and the Phoenix

The mythic underpinnings of this complex draw heavily on stories of liberation, resurrection, and radical rebirth. The Exodus narrative provides a template for escaping oppression and forging new collective identities. The phoenix myth symbolizes regeneration through struggle—the burning away of old systems to allow something new to rise from the ashes. This complex also echoes the archetype of the wounded healer, suggesting that from trauma can come wisdom, from awareness can come justice, and from brokenness can emerge deeper wholeness. It imagines a Great Turning—an epochal shift toward planetary balance and social equity.

Symbolic Imagery

The imagery that animates this complex is dynamic, poetic, and deeply symbolic:

- A raised fist that holds not a weapon, but a flower—combining resistance and compassion
- A rainbow bridge arching over fractured earth—symbolizing inclusive connection and healing
- Marchers moving together under banners that call for justice, peace, and care for the Earth
- Melting glaciers transforming into new rivers—ecological grief flowing into regeneration
- A diverse circle of people lifting the planet toward a rising sun—collective effort toward a new dawn
- A phoenix constructed, not from feathers, but from protest signs, books, seeds, and circuitry—rebirth through knowledge, resistance, and imagination

The collective memory within this complex draws strength from historical movements for civil rights, women's liberation, LGBTQ+ rights, labor justice, and ecological defense. These stories are revered as moral landmarks—narratives of courage, resistance, and progress. Yet as these memories become institutionalized, they can also become rigid, leading to new forms of dogma. What begins as moral clarity can harden into orthodoxy, and internal purity tests may emerge—turning the complex inward on itself when perfection is demanded rather than progress.

Black-and-White Thinking

Although the Progressive cultural complex aspires to nuance and inclusion, it is not immune to moral absolutism. In its more rigid forms, those who question prevailing narratives or fail to meet emerging norms may be labeled as complicit in oppression, privileged, or retrogressive. Phrases like "silence is violence" express the intense moral stakes attached to participation. The line between justice and dogma can blur, and dissent—even from within—can be experienced as betrayal rather than dialogue.

Repetitive Behavior

The behaviors that express this complex tend to unfold in cyclical waves of awareness, protest, and reform:

- Organized demonstrations, educational campaigns, and social media activism are used to spotlight injustice.
- Rituals of allyship—declarations of support, reeducation, and public accountability—create shared symbolic acts of solidarity.
- Critical discourse flourishes through journalism, scholarship, and grassroots storytelling.
- Policy advocacy becomes a key mechanism for translating moral vision into structural change.

These behaviors are often repeated across generations, with each wave building on the work of the past and responding to new social contexts.

Social Effects

The Progressive cultural complex is not immune to fracture. Its high ideals can create internal conflicts over identity, strategy, and belonging. Movements can splinter along generational, racial, or ideological lines. The tension between idealism and pragmatism can lead to burnout, disillusionment, or accusations of selling out. When moral vision becomes performative or punitive, it may alienate potential allies and reproduce the very exclusion it seeks to overcome. And when power is finally gained, the movement may find itself struggling to govern without compromising its soul.

Potential for Transformation

Despite its tensions and pitfalls, the Progressive cultural complex also carries profound cultural and psychological gifts. When understood symbolically, these gifts can offer both moral vision and collective renewal:

COMPASSION AS CIVIC PRINCIPLE
This complex centers empathy, care, and the protection of the vulnerable not just as private virtues, but as core public values essential to democratic life.

COMMITMENT TO EVOLVING TRUTH
It embraces change, learning, and intellectual humility. Rather than defending static ideologies, it encourages openness to science, lived experience, and shifting understandings of justice.

EXPANSION OF RIGHTS AND PERSONHOOD
It stretches the moral imagination to include those historically excluded—whether defined by race, gender, sexuality, disability, or ecological belonging.

JUSTICE AS RESTORATION, NOT RETRIBUTION
The complex often envisions justice not as punishment, but as healing—seeking to repair historical harm, restore dignity, and imagine wholeness where there was once fracture.

INTERCONNECTION WITH NATURE AND COSMOS
It reclaims reverence for the Earth, sees humans as part of a web of interdependence, and invites ecological consciousness as a spiritual and ethical imperative.

REIMAGINING OF INSTITUTIONS

Rather than abandoning institutions, this complex seeks to humanize them—redesigning systems of power to serve dignity, equity, and democratic participation.

MORAL IMAGINATION AND UTOPIAN VISION

It dares to imagine a world that is not only different, but better. In an age of cynicism and despair, it insists that hope is a form of resistance—and that transformation is not only possible, but necessary.

Iconography of Toward the Dawn: The American Progressive Cultural Complex and the Promise of Renewal

RAISED ROSE

Held high by the leading figure, the red rose evokes the legacy of democratic socialism and labor justice, a symbol of solidarity, compassion, and human dignity within the progressive tradition.

RAISED FISTS ACROSS THE CROWD

A universal symbol of resistance and empowerment, the fists speak to the emotional core of the progressive complex: collective agency, moral conviction, and the refusal to accept systemic injustice.

SCALES OF JUSTICE BANNER

Represents the progressive commitment to equity, legal reform, and civil rights. It signals the belief that justice must be rebalanced toward those long excluded or oppressed.

PEACE AND PLANET BANNER

Merges ecological consciousness with anti-war values—central themes of the progressive complex. It reflects the drive toward climate action, international cooperation, and sustainable peace.

PEACE SIGN FLAG (RED)

Signals the anti-militarist, anti-authoritarian ethic at the heart of progressive activism. The red coloring adds urgency and passion to the vision of nonviolent revolution.

RAINBOW ARCING OVER THE SCENE

A symbol of diversity, inclusion, and LGBTQ+ solidarity, the rainbow also recalls biblical and mythic imagery of renewal after catastrophe. It frames the movement as both rational and redemptive.

PHOENIX RISING BEFORE THE SUN

The phoenix, an archetype of death and rebirth, symbolizes the transformative ambition of the progressive imagination: not just reform, but cultural resurrection. The rising sun adds a utopian aura of awakening and new beginning.

CRACKED EARTH BENEATH THE CROWD

Represents the damaged social and ecological ground the movement stands on—and from which it rises. It marks the current crisis as real, but not final.

CAPITOL BUILDING IN THE DISTANCE

Half-obscured, it reminds us that the progressive vision seeks not to destroy institutions, but to reclaim and remake them in service of the common good.

Interpretation

This image dramatizes the American Progressive cultural complex as a visionary force for collective renewal. It is not a politics of nostalgia but of prophetic imagination—calling forth a just future from a fractured present. Anchored in emotion yet animated by symbols of law, care, and the planet, the complex expresses a mythic hope: that through solidarity, a better world is not only possible—but already on the horizon.

THE LIVING IDEAL: ARCHETYPE OF THE AMERICAN PROGRESSIVE MOVEMENT

This image depicts the American Progressive Movement in archetypal form—as a radiant, wise figure holding together Earth, justice, peace, and renewal. Rooted in ethical law and planetary care, she merges classical symbolism with contemporary vision. This is not protest in the streets, but principle in personified form: a guardian of democratic integrity and moral imagination, offering a torch lit by the dream of a better world.

Iconography of The Living Ideal: Archetype of the American Progressive Movement

DOVE (UPPER LEFT)

A universal symbol of peace, here it signals the progressive commitment to nonviolence, diplomacy, and reconciliation—a force for healing in the political realm.

EARTH (HELD IN LEFT HAND)

A glowing planet radiates light, emphasizing climate justice and ecological stewardship as central to the progressive worldview. The Earth is not something to dominate, but to protect.

SCALES OF JUSTICE (LOWER LEFT)

Signify the enduring fight for civil rights, equity, and fairness under law. Balanced but not static, they imply justice as a living, evolving pursuit.

TORCH (HELD IN RIGHT HAND)

A reference to both liberty and enlightenment, the torch evokes the Statue of Liberty and the flame of truth. In progressive terms, it represents the fire of social transformation, civic conscience, and moral clarity.

TREE WITH VISIBLE ROOTS (CENTER TORSO)

Embodies growth grounded in deep moral roots—a key progressive belief that lasting change must stem from ethical foundations, ancestral wisdom, and grassroots movements. The visible roots stress transparency and integrity.

PILLAR OF LAW ICON (LOWER RIGHT)

The classical building symbolizes strong institutions—but in progressive hands, it represents the belief that institutions must be reformed to serve justice, not preserved for tradition's sake.

RAINBOW ARCH (BACKGROUND)

A symbol of hope, inclusion, and the full spectrum of human diversity, it also nods to LGBTQ+ solidarity and the progressive value of embracing the marginalized.

RADIANT HALOS (BEHIND FIGURE AND EARTH)

The sun behind the figure's head elevates her to archetypal status, suggesting moral illumination and visionary leadership. The halo around the Earth affirms its sacred status.

LEAF MOTIFS AND GOLDEN FRAME

The border, filled with flowing organic designs, suggests that harmony, not domination, is the guiding aesthetic of the Progressive cultural complex. The art nouveau style connects beauty with justice.

Interpretation

This image distills the American Progressive cultural complex into symbolic form—offering an image of principled, ecological, and moral leadership that transcends partisanship. It holds together justice, environmental consciousness, institutional reform, and human dignity in one poised and luminous archetype. Through it, the movement is revealed, not just as political, but also as mythic, ethical, and aspirational: a vision of the world as it could be, rooted in the best of what already is.

THE BETRAYED WORKING CLASS CULTURAL COMPLEX

THE BROKEN CONTRACT: THE WORKING CLASS CULTURAL COMPLEX

A weathered working man stands defiantly in the rubble of broken "PROMISES," his clenched fist ignited with a symbolic flame—rage, memory, or hope. Behind him loom abandoned factories and shattered signs—"PAY BAN," "LAY," "JOB"—artifacts of a vanishing social contract. This image embodies the Betrayed Working Class cultural complex, where economic dispossession, cultural erasure, and political betrayal fuse into a volatile identity. The fire in his hand is not just anger—it is the spark of reclamation, resistance, and an unresolved demand for dignity.

Core Emotion

The Betrayed Working Class cultural complex is shaped by a deep and enduring emotional core: betrayal, bitterness, and defiant pride. At its heart lies a gnawing sense of abandonment—by elites, by institutions, and by the American dream itself. This is not mere grievance, but grief: a sorrowful love for labor, land, and tradition that has curdled over time. Beneath the layers of anger lies sorrow, and beneath the sorrow, a persistent and unyielding dignity.

Mythic Root: The Salt-of-the-Earth Hero and the Broken Covenant

This complex is rooted in the archetype of the honest worker—the miner, the farmer, the factory hand—who helped build the nation through sweat and sacrifice. It draws from a myth in which a social contract once promised: *if you work hard, play fair, and show loyalty, society will take care of you in return.* That covenant has been shattered, leaving disillusionment in its place.

Symbolic Imagery

This complex is expressed through powerful and haunting imagery:

- A lone factory with boarded-up windows
- Calloused hands holding a pink slip
- An old union hall converted into a dollar store
- A welder's mask repurposed as a protest mask
- A diner booth, empty except for a coffee mug and a crumpled pay stub
- A family photo framed above a rusted toolbox, cracked but still hanging

Self-Reinforcing Memory

The narrative memory embedded in this complex includes stories of job loss, plant closures, and once-thriving towns left hollow. There are tales of grandparents who fought wars, poured concrete, or built highways—now largely forgotten or dismissed. Proud local economies have been replaced by opioids, Walmart's, or gig work. These memories function both as scar tissue and as a rallying cry, reinforcing the sense of betrayal and fueling the desire to reclaim what was lost.

Black-and-White Thinking

This complex often divides the world into absolutes: those who work versus those who exploit. The honest man is set against the sellout, the small-town citizen against the coastal elite. Institutions that were once respected—government, media, education—are now widely viewed as corrupt, parasitic, or disconnected from real life. Outsiders are seen as competition, and insiders are often perceived as liars or traitors.

Repetitive Behavior

Behavioral patterns within this complex include seeking out leaders who "tell it like it is," alternating between periods of resignation and eruptions of revolt. Cynicism about politics runs deep—until a figure arises who channels the buried rage. There is a fierce attachment to symbols of stability: the flag, the truck, the job that's gone but still sacred. These repetitions serve both as rituals of mourning and flashes of renewed defiance.

Social Effects

The Betrayed Working Class cultural complex can generate deep resentment and become highly susceptible to populist manipulation. It lashes out at those perceived to have taken what was promised—immigrants, technocrats, urban elites, or even neighboring towns. The pain of betrayal can lead to scapegoating, nostalgic nationalism, and rejection of solidarity with other wounded groups. It fragments civic trust and turns cultural despair into political fire.

Potential for Transformation

Yet this complex also holds the seed of transformation—if it is seen, heard, and honored for its pain. When acknowledged, its rage can become righteous, and its sorrow can become a source of moral power.

> **DEMAND FOR DIGNITY AND FAIRNESS:**
> Once the betrayal is named, it can spark a passionate insistence on being treated with dignity, fueling labor movements, strikes, and campaigns for economic justice.

MORAL RECKONING WITH EXPLOITATION:
The complex can shed light on exploitative systems, prompting a broader ethical inquiry into wealth inequality, globalization, and technological displacement.

CULTURAL RECLAMATION AND STORYTELLING:
It revitalizes traditions of folk music, poetry, murals, oral histories, and grassroots journalism that preserve and elevate working-class wisdom.

BRIDGE BETWEEN LEFT AND RIGHT:
The emotional intensity of this complex can transcend political polarization, uniting unlikely allies around shared values of fairness, anti-elitism, and community strength.

GROUNDED REALISM AND RESILIENCE:
It contains an unsentimental, grounded clarity about life's hardships, cultivating mutual aid, solidarity, and a no-nonsense ethic of local responsibility.

CATALYST FOR STRUCTURAL REFORM:
When metabolized, the grief and rage become a clarion call for systemic reform—demanding renewed commitments to equity, representation, and the rebuilding of a shattered covenant.

Iconography for The Broken Contract: The Working Class Cultural Complex

CENTRAL FIGURE OF THE BETRAYED WORKER (FOREGROUND)
A solitary, middle-aged working man stands in defiant silence. His expression is not one of rage but of exhausted resolve. He wears a weathered jacket and work boots—symbols of labor once honored but now discarded. In his right hand, he holds a flickering flame, a fragile ember of hope, resistance, or rage—it is deliberately ambiguous. The flame signifies the volatile potential of the working class: it can warm, illuminate, or ignite.

THE CRACKED MONUMENT—"PROMISES" (LEFT)
A towering stone block with the word *PROMISES* etched into its surface stands broken behind the man. It represents the

mythic social contract once offered to the working class—security, dignity, and prosperity in exchange for honest labor. The crack running through the word signals betrayal.

DISCARDED PROTEST SIGNS—"PAY BAN," "LAY," "JOB" (SCATTERED)
Fallen placards lie at the foot of the broken stone, half-obscured by rubble. Fragmented words like *LAY*, *JOB*, and *PAY BAN* convey both suppression of protest and the dismemberment of rights and protections. These signs are not brandished but abandoned—symbols of past struggle that failed to yield justice.

INDUSTRIAL MACHINERY IN RUIN (BACKGROUND RIGHT)
Faded factory gears and smokestacks loom like ghosts in the background, indicating a bygone industrial era. The machines are intact but inert—monuments to labor's abandonment. Their presence hints at deindustrialization, automation, and the globalization of capital.

COLOR PALETTE (MUTED GRAYS AND EMBERS OF ORANG):
The dominant hues are stormy grays and industrial browns, evoking desolation and fatigue. The only warmth comes from the tiny orange flame and the faint sunset-like glow in the sky—suggesting either a smoldering end or a distant rebirth.

SYMBOLIC COMPOSITION:
The man stands tall but isolated—there is no union, no crowd, no movement behind him. This spatial isolation represents the atomization of the modern working class: the erosion of solidarity and communal purpose. The image's symmetry echoes religious iconography, positioning the worker as a kind of modern martyr or forgotten saint.

Interpretation

This image encapsulates the psychological state of the Working Class cultural complex in its "betrayed" form. The emotional tone is one of violated trust, simmering dignity, and latent power. The image warns that when promises collapse and voices are silenced, what remains may not be submission—but a quiet, combustible reckoning.

A RENEWED COVENANT WITH THE BETRAYED WORKING CLASS

Beneath banners proclaiming "DIGNITY," "LABOR," "JUSTICE," and "SOLIDARITY," workers and allies stand united, defiant, and visionary. A farmer, organizer, and child planter form a tableau of resistance and regeneration, whereas the cracked earth beneath their feet speaks to the trauma of broken promises. In the background, smokestacks and wind turbines collide—symbols of past exploitation and future hope. This image embodies the Betrayed Working Class cultural complex not only in its grief, but in its transformation—where solidarity becomes sacred, and justice is not nostalgic but revolutionary.

Iconography of A Renewed Covenant with the Betrayed Working Class

CENTRAL TRIO OF WORKER, ADVOCATE, AND ORGANIZER

The central trio symbolizes unity across class, gender, and role. The worker in overalls represents the betrayed laboring class—historically rooted, visibly worn, but upright. The man in a suit, with a hand on the worker's shoulder, represents renewed institutional solidarity—perhaps government, law, or ethical business. The woman with a megaphone embodies grassroots leadership, community activism, and the voice of organizing—female energy as both nurturer and agitator. Together, they reflect a tripartite covenant between labor, leadership, and voice—committed to mutual recognition and renewal.

OLD FACTORY IN THE DISTANCE

Acts as a symbol of the decline and abandonment of industrial labor. The crumbling structure evokes the broken social contract—where industry once offered security and identity but now stands hollow.

WIND TURBINES AND SOLAR PANELS

A new deal with the future—renewable, sustainable, forward-looking. These forms suggest that dignity need not come from nostalgia, but can be re-rooted in evolving forms of energy, economy, and environmental care.

GOLDEN BANNERS OVERHEAD

Inscribed with DIGNITY, LABOR, JUSTICE, and SOLIDARITY, these words symbolize a sacred or constitutional rebinding. These values form the pillars of the new covenant, inscribed like commandments or founding ideals. Their placement in the sky, held aloft by winds or unseen hands, suggests they are aspirations above politics—something to live up to, not down to.

GHOSTLY GUARDIAN FIGURES

Ethereal warriors or ancestors flank the upper sky, symbolizing ancestral memory, archetypal protectors, or the spirits of past laborers and defenders of justice. Their presence signifies continuity—this is not a break from tradition but its fulfillment.

UNION FIGURE IN THE SHADOWS

An older man holding a UNION banner kneels, a symbol of the fading but enduring legacy of organized labor. His humble posture suggests the movement's marginalization—but also its persistence, watching over the new alliance forming at center stage.

CHILDREN PLANTING A TREE

Symbolizes hope, renewal, generational continuity. The act of planting in cracked dry soil alludes to healing through labor, care, and patience. It is also a vision of reparation—a return to nurturing life rather than extracting value.

CRACKED EARTH BENEATH THE FIGURES.

A golden fissure runs through the ground signifying the rupture of the old covenant—betrayal, pain, and historical trauma. Yet the glowing line also recalls kintsugi, the Japanese art of repairing broken pottery with gold. This suggests sacred repair—a fracture made beautiful through acknowledgment.

Interpretation

This image offers not just a portrait of reconciliation, but a mythic vision of a repaired social contract: grounded in justice, seeded in memory, and oriented toward future wholeness.

THE DEMOCRATIC CULTURAL COMPLEX

ROOTED IN LAW, BOUND BY RIGHTS: THE DEMOCRATIC CULTURAL COMPLEX

Beneath the constitutional ideals of "LAW," "RIGHTS," and "SEPARATION OF POWERS," three solemn figures stand rooted—literally—into the ground, their bodies fused with the living roots of democratic tradition. The American flag unfurls behind them, not as spectacle, but as inheritance. This image captures the Democratic cultural complex: a reverent, almost sacred belief in institutions, balance, and legal order. It portrays democracy, not as ideology, but as a deeply rooted system of interdependence—resilient, burdened, and constantly tested by the weight of "We the People."

The Democratic cultural complex is built around a deep psychological investment in procedural fairness, equal representation, and the rule of law. It is animated by the belief that no one is above the law and that power should be constrained by checks and balances. This complex imagines politics as a forum for deliberation, compromise, and the peaceful transfer of power—not as a battlefield for domination.

Core Emotion: Moral Commitment to Fairness

At its emotional core is a passionate, almost sacred, commitment to fairness. This includes a belief that governance should be transparent, accountable, and open to all voices. When functioning well, this complex engenders civic pride and trust in institutions. When threatened, it produces anxiety, alarm, and a powerful defense of democratic norms.

Mythic Root: The Social Contract and the Enlightenment Citizen

The mythic foundation of this complex lies in Enlightenment ideals: rational self-governance, the consent of the governed, and the notion that human beings are capable of creating just laws and living under them together. It draws strength from founding documents like the Constitution and the Declaration of Independence, which frame the nation as a moral and political experiment in collective self-rule.

Symbolic Imagery

This complex is evoked through images such as

- A ballot dropped into a box
- Hands raised in open debate
- The scales of justice in balance
- A town hall meeting with diverse citizens in dialogue
- A Constitution held up during protest
- A candlelight vigil outside the Supreme Court

These images reflect the ideals of civic participation, legal integrity, and public accountability.

Self-Reinforcing Memory

Historical touchstones such as the American Revolution, the Federalist Papers, the civil rights movement, and the peaceful transitions of power serve as collective memories that reinforce belief in the democratic process. Each election, judicial ruling, or act of civil disobedience is remembered not just for its outcome, but as a reaffirmation of the system's legitimacy.

Black-and-White Thinking

In moments of stress or conflict, this complex may rigidly divide the world into defenders and enemies of democracy. Critics of institutional processes may be labeled as subversive, and faith in procedure can become moralized to the point of dogmatism. The system itself may be idealized even when its outcomes fall short.

Repetitive Behavior

Those animated by this complex may repeatedly appeal to norms, laws, and precedent when confronted with political disagreement. They often engage in rituals of civics: voting, attending hearings, citing constitutional language, or invoking shared democratic values. When democracy is seen as under threat, these behaviors intensify—marches, petitions, and speeches attempt to re-anchor the social order in shared rules.

Social Effects

The Democratic cultural complex heals by providing a shared frame for conflict resolution, protecting minority rights, and grounding political legitimacy in mutual consent. It creates space for pluralism and peaceful contestation. However, it can also fracture when procedures are weaponized, when institutions are captured or corrupted, or when rule-following becomes a substitute for justice. It splits most painfully when those who believe in democracy lose faith in its ability to deliver real equity or truth.

Potential for Transformation

Despite its vulnerabilities, the Democratic cultural complex offers profound resources for renewal. It fosters a culture of civic participation and ethical accountability, reminding citizens that their voices matter and that their actions can shape shared futures. It teaches that power is not merely to be seized, but also to be distributed and constrained in the service of justice.

At its best, this complex revitalizes political imagination—offering models of cooperation across difference and reminding us that conflict need not mean chaos. It grounds national identity in ideals and shared rules, not in blood or soil. In moments of backsliding or crisis, it provides tools for resistance—legal, procedural, and symbolic—through which a democratic society can defend itself without abandoning its values.

Perhaps most importantly, it carries the hopeful belief that democracy is never finished but always being renewed: a living covenant that depends on ongoing participation, vigilance, and the courage to reform what no longer serves the common good.

Iconography of Rooted in Law, Bound by Rights: The Democratic Cultural Complex

THREE FIGURES (FOREGROUND)

A racially and generationally diverse trio—male and female—evoking judicial, legislative, and executive authority, but also the ideal of pluralistic leadership. Their unified stance and serious expressions suggest civic responsibility over personal charisma.

ROOTS EXTENDING FROM THE FIGURES

A powerful symbol of grounded tradition and civic continuity. These roots do not bind—they anchor. They speak to the idea that democracy is not a floating ideal but a living organism nourished by shared values and collective memory.

PILLARS LABELED *LAW, RIGHTS,* AND *SEPARATION OF POWERS*

These columns visually reinforce the structural mythology of American democracy. They are not decorative—they are load-bearing ideals. The presence of all three suggests that any erosion of one threatens the integrity of the whole.

"WE THE PEOPLE" (TOP BANNER)
Taken directly from the Constitution, this phrase grounds the image in a founding myth of collective agency. It reminds viewers that authority flows from below, not above.

AMERICAN FLAG (BACKGROUND)
Draped across the central axis, the flag here symbolizes unity and oversight, not nationalism or exclusion. It supports rather than overshadows the figures.

SCALES OF JUSTICE (RIGHT PILLAR)
Discreet yet visible, the scales affirm a commitment to balanced judgment and constitutional order, reinforcing the mythic image of a nation under law rather than under rule.

Interpretation

This image depicts the Democratic cultural complex at its aspirational best: rooted in principle, plural in composition, and restrained by law. It is a counter-image to chaos or populist fervor. While it may lack fire or spectacle, its strength is endurance—offering not the thrill of upheaval, but the steady pulse of civic trust. It reminds us that democracy is not self-sustaining—it must be defended, repaired, and renewed by those willing to serve, not dominate.

DEMOCRACY AT GROUND LEVEL: THE CIVIC SOUL OF THE DEMOCRATIC CULTURAL COMPLEX

In the shade of a community tree, neighbors gather in a circle—listening, speaking, and recording ideas. There are no podiums, no hierarchies—just shared space and mutual regard. This image portrays the grassroots expression of the Democratic cultural complex, where democracy is not merely institutional but lived: in dialogue, in civic trust, and in the everyday practice of inclusion. It suggests that democracy's roots are not only legal, but also interpersonal, ethical, and local.

Iconography of Democracy at Ground Level: The Civic Soul of the Democratic Cultural Complex

THE CIRCLE OF DIVERSE CITIZENS (FOREGROUND)

At the heart of the image is a multiethnic, intergenerational circle of individuals seated in open dialogue. This symbolizes the foundational democratic value of deliberation and inclusion. The circular formation—nonhierarchical, without a head—evokes equality of voice and mutual recognition.

THE SPEAKING WOMAN (CENTER LEFT)

Her open hand gesture and upright posture represent participatory agency—a citizen not only with a voice, but also with the confidence to use it. She embodies the archetype of community leadership from within, rather than above.

THE NOTETAKER (SEATED CENTER)

This figure, listening intently and writing, represents institutional memory and responsiveness. He symbolizes the democratic function of translating public voice into action, echoing the roles of civic record-keepers, organizers, and local governance.

CROSSED-ARMS LISTENER (STANDING CENTER-RIGHT)

His position—alert, contemplative, reserved—suggests the tension between skepticism and engagement often present in democratic practice. He symbolizes the importance of reflection, restraint, and critical thought in democratic discourse.

COMMUNITY BOARD (BACKGROUND LEFT)

The bulletin board—covered in notices—represents public transparency and local communication. It functions as a symbolic anchor for civic life, where community information is shared and policy begins at the neighborhood level.

TREES AND GOLDEN LIGHT (BACKGROUND)

The golden-hour glow and leafy canopy create an atmosphere of care and possibility, framing democracy not as spectacle but as slow, seasonal cultivation. Nature here stands in as a metaphor for organic growth, rootedness, and the need for tending.

HOUSES AND SIDEWALKS (BACKGROUND)

The modest homes and walking paths reinforce the local scale of democratic practice. This is not a national legislature or a courtroom—it is a neighborhood, a commons, a ground of shared life.

BICYCLES AND DISTANT FIGURES (FAR BACKGROUND)

Small gestures of everyday life appear at the periphery—children playing, citizens strolling. This affirms democracy as not merely political but lived, integrated into the rhythms of daily community.

Interpretation

The iconography of this image roots the Democratic cultural complex in the everyday labor of participation. It visualizes democracy as a dialogical, embodied, and relational process—slow but resilient, ordinary yet sacred. The image evokes the soul of democracy, not as law alone, but as collective presence and civic responsibility, practiced beneath trees, in folding chairs, with pens, voices, and listening hearts.

The Elitism Cultural Complex

THE PAGEANTRY OF POWER IN THE ELITISM CULTURAL COMPLEX

On a grand balcony above a gathered crowd, elegantly dressed figures drink wine and observe from above, their expressions ranging from solemn to contemplative. One man delivers a speech, script in hand, while a masked woman embodies the mystique and exclusivity of the elite. The setting sun casts a golden glow over domed institutions in the distance, underscoring themes of legacy, hierarchy, and performance. This image captures the Elitism cultural complex's dramatization of authority, where social standing and aesthetic refinement mask power and control.

The Elitism cultural complex is characterized by a powerful blend of pride, refinement, and intellectual superiority, often accompanied by anxiety over its relevance in a rapidly changing world. It reflects a belief in elevated status—earned through intellect, taste, education, or access—but often cloaks a deeper fear: of losing control, being misunderstood, or becoming obsolete in the eyes of the broader public.

Core Emotion: Superiority and Contempt, Mixed with Anxiety over Relevance

At its heart is a deep conviction of elevated status based on discernment, refinement, or intellectual prowess. Yet beneath this sense of pride lies vulnerability: the fear of being overtaken, dismissed, or rendered irrelevant by the very people perceived as less informed or less cultured.

Mythic Root: The Enlightened Few and the Ivory Tower

This complex draws from enduring archetypes such as the Philosopher-King, the Keeper of Knowledge, and the Priesthood of Culture. These figures are entrusted with the guardianship of civilization and the responsibility to guide society through wisdom and cultivation. Yet, over time, they may grow detached, insular, or disdainful of those they claim to lead.

Symbolic Imagery

Images that reflect both the mystique and alienation associated with elitist postures include the following:

- A marble tower rising through mist, removed from the chaos below
- A masked figure reading in a gilded study
- Crystal goblets arranged for a high-level policy banquet
- A world map overlaid with abstract equations
- An ornate gate inscribed with the words *By Merit*
- A distant crowd shouting while the elite sip wine, unaware or unmoved

Self-Reinforcing Memory

This complex is supported by stories of legacy, prestige, and cultivated distance: "the best and the brightest," "thought leaders," and "curators of taste." Elite institutions such as Ivy League universities, central banks, international forums, and think tanks become sanctified spaces—reinforcing the idea that those within them are ordained to shape the future.

Black-and-White Thinking

Within this complex, the world is often divided into the rational and the irrational, the refined and the vulgar, the informed elite, and the emotional mob. Expertise is equated with virtue, whereas populism is dismissed as ignorance. This polarization can lead to a failure of empathy and a disconnect from lived experience.

Social Effects

The Elitism cultural complex creates a two-tier moral economy: one in which power, intellect, and taste are viewed as synonymous with virtue, and another in which ordinary people are seen as ignorant, chaotic, or expendable. When elites speak only to one another, they foster resentment and backlash. Detached from the ground, the tower of reason becomes brittle—and easier to topple.

Potential for Transformation

Although elitism is often critiqued for its exclusivity and detachment, it also holds the potential to serve society in valuable and constructive ways, especially when tempered by ethical vision and humility.

HIGH STANDARDS OF EXCELLENCE

When guided by integrity, elitism can uphold rigorous standards in science, medicine, education, and the arts. This pursuit of excellence can drive innovation, foster deep mastery, and inspire others to reach their highest potential. This can lead to, for example, academic and research institutions producing life-saving vaccines or advancing climate science.

PRESERVATION AND ADVANCEMENT OF KNOWLEDGE

Elitism often reveres intellectual traditions and safeguards the accumulated wisdom of human civilization. It can nurture critical thinking, philosophical inquiry, and theoretical depth, illustrated by humanities departments preserving ancient texts, languages, and ethical frameworks.

ETHICAL LEADERSHIP AND VISIONARY THINKING

At its best, the elite model of leadership offers wisdom-driven guidance rooted in long-term thinking. Such leaders are capable of making difficult, principled decisions even in the face of short-term pressures. This is reflected by judges or scientists who uphold constitutional principles or evidence-based policy despite political resistance.

CULTURAL STEWARDSHIP

Elites can serve as protectors and promoters of cultural excellence. They support institutions that cultivate beauty, knowledge, and creative expression. This includes patrons of the arts or the founders of public institutions such as the Library of Congress or the Louvre.

MERITOCRATIC OPPORTUNITY

When elitism is truly merit-based rather than hereditary, it can serve as a vehicle for upward mobility. It rewards talent, discipline, and innovation regardless of background. Consider scholarships for first-generation students or open-source platforms like GitHub that reward contribution over pedigree.

STRATEGIC TECHNOCRATIC GOVERNANCE

Technocratic forms of elitism can promote evidence-based, forward-looking policy. By prioritizing long-term planning and public systems, they can deliver societal benefits that transcend populist cycles, such as coordinated public health responses during pandemics or infrastructure projects driven by expert design.

Iconography of The Pageantry of Power in the Elitism Cultural Complex

Elevated Balcony (foreground setting)

The image is dominated by a group of elite figures positioned high above the city, symbolizing literal and symbolic distance from the public. The balcony itself, made of ornate stonework and iron, signifies inherited power, protected boundaries, and exclusionary refinement.

The Orator with the Speech (center figure)

A well-groomed man delivers a speech to the unseen crowd below, holding a paper filled with fine script. He represents the voice of technocratic authority—articulate, composed, and detached. His expression is serene but firm, projecting entitlement masked as service.

SURROUNDING FIGURES (SUPPORTING CAST):

Flanking the orator are three other figures, all sipping wine or champagne. The two older men to his left listen with mild disinterest or calculation, suggesting a closed circuit of influence where decisions are made through mutual assurance. The masked woman on the right evokes secrecy, ritual, and aesthetic control. Her pearl necklace and distant gaze symbolize the polished veneer of cultural dominance. Her mask underscores the performative aspect of elite virtue and selective visibility.

THE IRON GATE WITH CREST ("V") (LEFT-LOWER CORNER)

This emblematic gate subtly reinforces the idea of a ruling class behind barriers—suggesting aristocratic heritage, dynastic lineage, or corporate consolidation. The "V" could stand for *Virtue*, *Victory*, or *Vaulted class*—its ambiguity is deliberate.

DISTANT CROWD AND CITY BELOW (BACKGROUND)

The shadowy mass below the balcony implies a public that is present but invisible, represented only as a blur of bodies and torchlight. This establishes the contrast between elite clarity and populist murk. The gothic domes and towers in the background allude to both tradition and surveillance—the panoptic watchtower of the elite class over the governed.

COLOR PALETTE (CANDLELIT GOLD AND DEEP BLUE)

The warm golden tones on the balcony contrast with the cold twilight blues of the city below. This division reflects both opulence and detachment—comfort insulated from complexity.

THE IDEALIZED AUTHORITY IN THE ELITISM CULTURAL COMPLEX

A neoclassical statue of a robed woman crowned with a laurel wreath raises one hand in a gesture of command or benediction while holding a round shield at her side. Bathed in warm tones and elevated on a pedestal, she embodies the Greco-Roman ideals of order, virtue, and dominion. This image reflects the Elitism cultural complex's reverence for classical forms as symbols of legitimacy, continuity, and aestheticized power, projecting timeless authority through stylized permanence.

Iconography of The Idealized Authority in the Elitism Cultural Complex

CENTRAL FIGURE: THE STANDING WOMAN

The central figure represents the idealized elite: poised, composed, and morally elevated. Her position on a pedestal emphasizes detachment from the common sphere. She does not engage in conversation but gestures outward from a place of authority. Her solitary stance reinforces elitism's separation from mass culture and the belief in distinct tiers of value and worth.

RAISED RIGHT HAND (OPEN PALM)

The raised hand resembles gestures from Roman statuary used to command attention or issue judgment. It symbolizes control, decree, or guarded permission. In this context, it reflects the gatekeeping function of elitism—the ability to confer legitimacy or exclude based on hidden standards of refinement, intellect, or pedigree.

SHIELD IN THE LEFT ARM

Held passively rather than in active defense, the shield represents the protection of inherited values, tradition, and cultural authority. It conveys a form of guardianship, as though the elite are not warriors but stewards of civilization's treasures. It hints at the elitist narrative of responsibility: that those at the top must preserve order, culture, and meaning.

LAUREL WREATH ON HEAD

The laurel wreath is a classical symbol of intellectual and moral victory. Its use here positions the figure as a representative of meritocratic excellence—a chosen one among many. In the cultural imagination of elitism, it conveys legitimacy drawn from taste, education, and high achievement. This is not brute power, but a refined mandate.

BARE FEET ON PEDESTAL

Bare feet, common in ancient statuary, suggest purity or spiritual grounding. In this image, they evoke a paradox:

Although the figure stands above others, she maintains a posture of authenticity or sacrifice. This mirrors the elitist tendency to frame authority as earned, noble, or burdensome rather than self-serving.

CLASSICAL ROBES

The flowing robes root the image in the mythos of the Enlightenment and ancient Greece-eras associated with reason, law, and aesthetic perfection. They project continuity with a civilizing tradition and reinforce the idea that elitism is not merely about wealth or status but about cultural inheritance and ethical discernment.

Interpretation

This image uses classical iconography to depict the Elitism cultural complex. A solitary Greco-Roman figure symbolizes refined authority, detachment, and hierarchical idealism. Her composed posture expresses judgment without engagement—she presides rather than pleads. The image reflects both the elite's self-image as guardians of civilization and the critique that such refinement can become aloof and inaccessible. It invites reflection on whether beauty and hierarchy alone can justify authority without mutual recognition.

CHAPTER 2

National Myths as Cultural Complexes

The Freedom Cultural Complex

The American Faith in Progress Cultural Complex

The Rugged Individualism Cultural Complex

The Manifest Destiny Cultural Complex

The Pioneer Spirit Cultural Complex

The City on the Hill Cultural Complex

The American Exceptionalism Cultural Complex

The American Dream Cultural Complex

The Melting Pot Cultural Complex

The Military-Industrial Cultural Complex

The Fortress America Cultural Complex

The American Consumerism Cultural Complex

High Tech Cultural Complex

THE FREEDOM CULTURAL COMPLEX

THE MANY FACES OF FREEDOM: THE AMERICAN FREEDOM CULTURAL COMPLEX

This image captures the American Freedom cultural complex as both myth and mandate. At its center is the archetype of the liberated individual—walking toward the horizon of destiny, beneath the symbolic sun of liberty. Surrounding this figure are iconic emblems drawn from American memory, each one reflecting a different projection of what it means to be free: from liberation to vigilance, from protest to protection. Together, they form a collective dreamscape—part sacred, part contested—of the American psyche's most cherished and volatile ideal.

Core Emotion: Exaltation and Defiance

At its heart, this complex carries a fervent emotional charge: the thrill of individual autonomy, the moral clarity of self-determination, and the fierce resistance to perceived control. It is both a celebration and a battle cry—freedom is something to be defended, claimed, or wrested away.

Mythic Root: Exodus, Frontier, and Revolution

This complex draws on mythic narratives of escape from tyranny (Exodus from Egypt), taming the unknown (the Western frontier), and overthrowing unjust rule (American Revolution). These myths cast freedom as a divine right and a sacred inheritance—won through courage and struggle, never passively given.

Symbolic Imagery

- The Statue of Liberty
- The bald eagle in flight
- A lone figure on an open road or mountaintop
- A clenched fist breaking chains
- The word *FREEDOM* on banners, hats, and bullets alike
- The Gadsden Flag ("Don't Tread on Me") and the Liberty Bell

Self-Reinforcing Memory

Rooted in America's origin story, the Freedom complex is continually reignited by wars for independence, civil rights struggles, and backlash against governmental or institutional control. From the Boston Tea Party to civil disobedience to anti-vaccine protests, the complex recycles itself across political lines.

Black-and-White Thinking

"You're either free or you're enslaved." This complex resists nuance. It reduces complex political, legal, or communal relationships into binaries of liberty versus tyranny, patriot versus traitor, individual versus state—whether in right-wing gun rights' debates or left-wing resistance to police brutality.

Repetitive Behaviors

- Performing acts of defiance as identity
- Equating regulation with oppression
- Romanticizing rebellion (both revolutionary and reactionary)
- Mythologizing the Founding Fathers
- Invoking the Constitution as sacred scripture

Social Effects

The Freedom complex fuels polarization by elevating personal liberty above collective responsibility. It can both inspire justice movements (abolition, suffrage, LGBTQ+ rights) and undermine public goods (healthcare, gun reform, climate policy). It tears at the civic fabric when different groups weaponize "freedom" to mean mutually exclusive things—freedom *from* Covid masks vs freedom *to* survive contagious infection, freedom *from* taxation versus freedom *to* access education.

Possibility of Transformation

At its highest expression, the Freedom complex points to a liberatory ideal—not just freedom from constraint, but freedom for flourishing, participating, and mutual uplift. When reimagined as interdependent freedom, it becomes a foundation for democratic belonging, rather than a solitary fortress. In this form, freedom ceases to be a battlefield and becomes a shared horizon.

Iconography of The Many Faces of Freedom: The American Freedom Cultural Complex

STATUE OF LIBERTY (TOP LEFT)

Represents the welcoming ideal of liberty, especially as related to immigration, pluralism, and the global beacon America claims to be. It evokes freedom as arrival and promise.

BALD EAGLE (TOP RIGHT)

Symbol of national sovereignty, vigilance, and freedom through strength. The eagle's soaring presence reflects a freedom that must be guarded and, if necessary, defended.

RADIANT SUN AND OPEN PATH

The central figure walks toward a golden light, symbolizing self-determination and moral clarity. It is freedom imagined as personal destiny and inner alignment with a larger ideal.

CLENCHED FIST WITH BROKEN CHAIN (LEFT CENTER)

Signifies emancipation, rebellion, and the fight against oppression. Whether from slavery, state control, or economic injustice, this symbol carries the emotion of righteous defiance.

"DON'T TREAD ON ME" FLAG (BOTTOM LEFT)

A revolutionary icon, often used in contemporary libertarian and right-wing populist rhetoric. It represents resistance to perceived tyranny, a freedom of boundaries and individual rights.

LIBERTY BELL (BOTTOM RIGHT)

The cracked bell speaks to both the nobility and fragility of American freedom. It is the mythic relic of independence, evoking both history's triumphs and its unhealed divisions.

SILHOUETTED HEAD (BOTTOM CENTER)

Ambiguously framed, this profile symbolizes the subjective experience of freedom: how each citizen interprets, enacts, and is shaped by the collective narrative.

Interpretation

This image portrays freedom, not as a settled ideal, but as a force that empowers, divides, and defines. Its symbols come from across the political spectrum and historical timeline, revealing how Americans invest the word *freedom* with sacred meaning even when they fiercely disagree on its terms. The image reminds us that freedom in America is not a single banner—but a battleground of competing dreams, each rooted in identity, memory, and myth.

THE AMERICAN FAITH IN PROGRESS CULTURAL COMPLEX

THE GOLDEN THREAD OF BECOMING: THE AMERICAN FAITH IN PROGRESS

A luminous child holds a glowing tablet, standing at the crossroads of invention, burden, and destiny. Around him spiral the engines of industry, the strain of labor, and the promise of knowledge. Rockets, DNA strands, and circuit-light coronas ascend toward a city of progress—part Capitol, part cathedral of science. In this radiant yet restless vision, the future is both a burden and a beacon.

The American Faith in Progress cultural complex is a powerful and enduring psychic structure rooted in the belief that history has a direction—and that direction is forward. It fuses emotion, myth, memory, and behavior into a collective sense of destiny: that through innovation, struggle, and determination, the nation will continually improve. It promises transformation, mastery over nature, and the eventual perfection of the human condition—but not without psychic cost.

Core Emotion: Hope, Urgency, and Anxious Determination

At its emotional center lies a heady blend of hope and tension. There is deep optimism in the belief that problems are solvable, that each generation can surpass the last. But this hope is laced with urgency—progress must not stall—and a chronic unease that what's been gained might be lost. This complex generates both inspiration and pressure: to keep building, improving, innovating. It insists that stasis is failure and that history bends toward salvation—if we work hard enough to bend it.

Mythic Root: The New World, the Frontier, and the Perfectible Human

This complex is anchored in the archetype of the New World—a land unburdened by the past, open to reinvention. It draws from the myth of the frontier, where civilization constantly advances against wilderness. At its heart is the Enlightenment belief in the perfectibility of man through reason, science, and effort. From Manifest Destiny to Silicon Valley, it enshrines the idea that the future is ours to create—and that each step forward justifies itself.

Symbolic Imagery

The visual language of this complex is saturated with forward motion and transformation:

- A locomotive steaming across vast plains: speed, conquest, momentum
- Skyscrapers piercing the clouds: vertical ambition and human triumph

- A glowing screen in a dark room: knowledge and control at your fingertips
- Rockets ascending into space: the promise of transcendence
- Blueprints, maps, and algorithms: tools of mastery and design
- A child holding a tablet: generational uplift through technology
- The road stretching into the horizon: the journey never ends

These symbols portray progress as destiny and restlessness as virtue.

Self-Reinforcing Memory

Historical memory under this complex is arranged as a narrative arc: from hardship to prosperity, ignorance to enlightenment. The Industrial Revolution, civil rights movement, moon landing, internet age—all are positioned as proof that America moves "in the right direction." Setbacks are reinterpreted as temporary, even necessary for eventual triumph. This linear, upward-sloping memory fuels a collective sense of purpose and exceptionalism. Doubt or regression is dismissed or forgotten.

Black-and-White Thinking

This complex divides the world into backward versus advanced, primitive versus modern, stagnation versus innovation. Resistance to change is equated with ignorance or obstruction. The future is good; the past, something to transcend. In its grip, nuance gives way to moral imperative: progress is not just possible but also required. Hesitation becomes failure. Critique becomes heresy.

Repetitive Behavior

The cultural expression of this complex unfolds through ritualized acts of striving:

- Obsession with newness—new products, new technologies, new versions
- Political platforms promising "a better future" or "the next great leap"
- Unquestioned trust in innovation as a solution to social problems
- Heroization of entrepreneurs, scientists, and disruptors

- Cycles of hype, disappointment, and reinvestment in the "next big thing"
- Systemic avoidance of limits—ecological, emotional, spiritual—in the name of growth

These behaviors repeat compulsively, even when the results are mixed or unsustainable.

Social Effects

This cultural complex can disorient and dehumanize. It sacrifices the present for the future. It encourages burnout, overwork, and disconnection in the pursuit of endless productivity. It marginalizes those who can't "keep up," and dismisses tradition, rest, and nontechnological forms of wisdom. It can flatten culture into metrics, reduce people to data, and treat the earth as raw material. In its extreme form, it breeds hubris, ecological blindness, and spiritual emptiness.

Potential for Transformation

Yet this complex also holds deep symbolic energy that can serve renewal:

VISION AND ASPIRATION

It lifts collective consciousness toward possibility, offering hope in dark times.

MOBILIZATION OF HUMAN CREATIVITY

It unlocks invention, discovery, and unprecedented solutions to human suffering.

SYMBOLIC TRANSCENDENCE

Rockets, maps, and machines are not only tools but also symbols of the psyche's urge to evolve.

MORAL EVOLUTION

Civil rights, inclusion, and justice are also framed as forms of progress, elevating not just life, but values.

INTEGRATION WITH LIMITS

When tempered by humility, this complex can harmonize with sustainability and wisdom, shifting from domination to stewardship.

REBIRTH OF HOPE

In an age of climate anxiety and political decay, this faith can be reborn—not as blind optimism, but as archetypal renewal.

Iconography of The Golden Thread of Becoming: The American Faith in Progress

CHILD WITH TABLET (CENTER FOREGROUND)

Represents the generational promise and psychic burden of progress. The child's soft expression suggests focus and innocence, lit by the screen's glow—a symbol of both enlightenment and addiction.

SPIRALING RAILROAD (LOWER LEFT)

A visual metaphor for technological advance over time. The old steam engines give way to modern innovation, echoing the historical arc from industrial revolution to digital age. The path curves upward, suggesting both ambition and uncertainty.

DNA STRAND (CENTER RIGHT)

The double helix floats in the sky as a symbol of biomedical breakthrough, genetic mastery, and the Enlightenment faith in human perfectibility through science.

ROCKET LAUNCH (UPPER RIGHT)

A rocket ascending symbolizes forward momentum, transcendent aspiration, and the archetype of escape from limitation. Its vertical flight path complements the spiraling train track, adding dimensional movement.

WORKERS AND CREATORS (MIDGROUND LEFT AND RIGHT)

Engineers, designers, and weary laborers represent the reality behind the myth—those whose toil, burnout, and ingenuity drive the "progress machine." They encode a tension between innovation and exhaustion.

DIGITAL CATHEDRAL (UPPER CENTER)

The domed, neoclassical building crowned with radiant circuitry evokes the fusion of government, technology, and near-religious belief in progress. It sanctifies the idea of forward motion as a civic and spiritual imperative.

TO-DO LIST AND OVERWORKED FIGURE (LOWER RIGHT)
A figure slumped over a desk beside a long checklist and caffeine jars shows the psychological cost of ceaseless striving. It represents burnout culture, internalized pressure, and the shadow side of relentless self-improvement.

AIRSHIP AND SKYSCRAPERS (UPPER LEFT AND BACKGROUND)
Nostalgic and futuristic, these elements form a composite timeline of American invention. They suggest a nation perpetually reaching up and out—skyward and onward.

COLOR PALETTE (GOLDEN AND CERULEAN GLOW)
The warm yellow hues suggest optimism, inspiration, and divine illumination, whereas the blue-gray shadows add melancholy and existential weight. The interplay of light and shadow suggests that even radiant visions carry dark undertones.

Interpretation

This image serves as a visual myth of the American Faith in Progress cultural complex: Both luminous and fraught, it invites viewers to reflect on what we are racing toward—and what we may be leaving behind.

THE RUGGED INDIVIDUALISM CULTURAL COMPLEX

ALONE, UNYIELDING, FREE: THE RUGGED INDIVIDUALISM CULTURAL COMPLEX

A solitary man in weathered leather and a broad-brimmed hat stands with arms crossed—an icon of resilience and self-reliance. His direct gaze evokes both defiance and stoic endurance. This image channels the emotional and mythic essence of Rugged Individualism: a cultural complex that elevates personal freedom, grit, and distrust of dependence into moral absolutes. It speaks to the American psyche's deep-seated belief in the lone actor as both savior and survivor.

Core Emotion: Pride in Self-Reliance, Suspicion of Dependency

At the heart of this complex is a fierce emotional attachment to autonomy—pride in standing alone, forging one's own path, and overcoming adversity without help. It also carries an undercurrent of fear: that dependence is weakness and collectivism a threat.

Mythic Root: The Lone Pioneer and the Frontier Hero

Rooted in myths of the American West, the self-made man, and the moral clarity of individual conscience, this complex draws from archetypes like the *cowboy*, the *rebel*, the *homesteader*, and the *outlaw turned savior*. These figures tame wild lands, defy corrupt systems, and find redemption through grit.

Symbolic imagery

- A solitary figure walking into the horizon with an axe or backpack
- A cabin lit from within on a snowy plain
- A worn hand holding a deed, a rifle, or a compass
- Mountains towering behind a rider on horseback
- Barbed wire cutting through open land
- A flag stitched into a jacket
- A clenched jaw under a wide-brimmed hat

Self-Reinforcing Memory

Stories of ancestors "pulling themselves up by their bootstraps," surviving harsh conditions, or escaping tyranny through personal daring—these narratives form identity and justify resistance to institutional oversight, taxation, or collective responsibility.

Black-and-White Thinking

The world is a battle between strength versus weakness, earned versus entitled, makers versus takers, and freedom versus control. The world is split into those who carry their own weight and those who expect to be carried.

Repetitive Behavior

This cultural complex idealizes self-employment, distrusts government programs, disdains bureaucracy. There is a celebration of personal risk-taking and a reasserting of control through withdrawal, survivalism, or do-it-yourself ethos. They retreat from help, even when needed.

Social Effects

The complex isolates and alienates. It can glorify suffering while silencing vulnerability. It erodes social trust, stigmatizes care, and resists the interdependence necessary for solving collective problems. At its extreme, it may deny systemic injustice by insisting that all outcomes are personal choices.

Potential for Transformation

The Rugged Individualism cultural complex—rooted in frontier mythology, self-reliance, and anti-authoritarian spirit—can have powerful positive consequences for both individuals and society when not taken to destructive extremes. Here are key redemptive and revitalizing aspects:

INNOVATION AND RISK-TAKING
Independent thinkers, entrepreneurs, and inventors often emerge from this complex, breaking ground where institutions fear to tread.

RESISTANCE TO TYRANNY
Suspicion of centralized authority helps safeguard civil liberties and prevent government overreach.

MORAL COURAGE IN ISOLATION
The rugged individual may act with integrity even when standing alone—championing conscience over conformity.

CULTURAL MYTHOS OF HEROIC TRANSFORMATION
It offers a narrative of inner transformation: surviving wilderness, confronting hardship, and emerging stronger.

SPIRITUAL AUTONOMY

Encourages direct relationship to the divine, nature, or inner Self—unmediated by dogma or institution.

EMPOWERMENT OF THE MARGINALIZED

Though historically associated with white male pioneers, the ethos has been claimed by figures across racial, gender, and class lines by those seeking freedom from imposed identities.

Iconography of Alone, Unyielding, Free: The Rugged Individualism Cultural Complex

THE CENTRAL FIGURE (FOREGROUND)

A solitary man stands with arms crossed, gazing directly outward. His weathered features, squared shoulders, and unwavering stare evoke stoicism, self-sufficiency, and inner resolve. His expression is not hostile, but resolute—conveying a belief that one's life is forged by one's own will, not by communal obligation.

WESTERN GARB—HAT, BANDANA, AND CANVAS JACKET

His attire—cowboy hat, red kerchief, and durable, brown canvas clothing—roots him in the mythos of the American frontier. This dress references the nineteenth-century pioneer ideal: self-made, self-ruled, shaped by land and struggle. The absence of corporate logos or modern embellishments reinforces authenticity over conformity.

NEUTRAL, EARTH-TONED BACKGROUND

Set against a plain, earthen backdrop, the image resists context, anchoring the man in archetype rather than a specific time or place. This renders him timeless—a psychological icon rather than a narrative character. The lack of setting emphasizes that the individual is sufficient unto himself.

CROSSED ARMS AND UPRIGHT POSTURE

His body language is closed yet dignified, a classic sign of guarded independence. It implies a boundary between self and world—a refusal to be shaped by the collective. There is no plea for connection, only the strength of presence. The pose suggests readiness for confrontation but not a desire for it.

WEATHERED EXPRESSION AND UNSHAVEN JAW

Signs of hardship are written in his face. The faint stubble, tired eyes, and sun-marked skin convey a life of labor or solitude. But none of these details signal defeat; instead, they are badges of integrity—visible proof that he endures without complaint, needing nothing from others but space.

MUTED PALETTE OF BROWNS AND REDS

The color scheme affirms the symbolic register of the earth: raw, unpolished, and elemental. The red kerchief near his throat signals passion or the unspoken potential for fire—revolutionary or defensive—but held in restraint by discipline and tradition.

Interpretation

This image encapsulates the Rugged Individualism cultural complex as a self-contained myth of moral clarity, emotional restraint, and independence. It celebrates personal freedom and suspicion of imposed authority. The figure stands as both archetype and warning: noble in solitude, but resistant to help, vulnerable to alienation, and wary of collective progress.

The image taps into a deeply American fantasy—that dignity arises not from mutual aid, but from separation and self-discipline. It evokes admiration and unease: the strength of a man who asks nothing yet may offer little in return. At its best, this complex champions resilience; at its worst, it curdles into isolation or reactionary pride. In this image, we see not just a man, but a worldview—built on weathered pride, earned scars, and a vision of freedom that refuses to kneel.

SHE STANDS ALONE: THE FEMININE FACE OF RUGGED INDIVIDUALISM

A visual meditation on solitary strength, earned autonomy, and elemental clarity, a solitary woman towers above a darkened city, holding a flaming torch aloft as dusk settles around her. Her stance is firm, gaze unwavering, and expression resolved—not in defiance, but in self-possession. This image reimagines the Rugged Individualism cultural complex in feminine form, where strength is not bravado, but inner sovereignty. She is not waiting to be saved or endorsed. She is the light-bearer in a world where reliance on others has too often led to disappointment.

Iconography of She Stands Alone: The Feminine Face of Rugged Individualism

CENTRAL FIGURE—WOMAN WITH TORCH (FOREGROUND)

The image centers on a woman standing atop a hill or rise, holding aloft a flaming torch. Her posture is resolute, steady, and forward-facing. She wears practical jeans and a brown leather jacket—function over fashion—rooting her in the same mythos as the cowboy or pioneer. But her stance and gaze signal an archetype: the female individualist, not defined by rebellion but by rooted self-containment. Her torch evokes not only illumination but a Promethean defiance—a willingness to carry fire into the unknown. This act speaks of guidance, danger, and fierce personal agency.

EXPRESSION AND BODY LANGUAGE

Her face is calm, serious, and unyielding. There is no plea for recognition, no appeal to audience or cause. She embodies self-trust. One hand grips the torch with purpose; the other rests in quiet readiness. She is alone but not lost—she chooses solitude, not as isolation, but as independence.

URBAN TWILIGHT SETTING

Behind her, a city recedes into dusk. Skyscrapers, windows aglow, suggest a society that continues without noticing her. The sky is moody—neither fully night nor day—casting her as a threshold figure: between epochs, between roles, between feminine archetypes of nurturance and autonomy. The horizon she faces is unknowable, and yet she does not flinch.

SYMBOLIC ELEMENTS

The Torch: Traditionally masculine in American iconography (the Statue of Liberty being a powerful exception), here it is held by a woman with unshakable clarity. It represents inner fire, courage, and the will to walk one's path without consensus.

Denim and Leather: These materials connect her to working-class roots, frontier survival, and a resistance to ornamental femininity.

Dusk: The image's palette suggests not decline but passage. She is not heralding the end of something—but the persistence of the individual spirit as institutions fade from view.

Interpretation

This image reclaims rugged individualism from a purely masculine lineage and reshapes it into something fierce, grounded, and feminine. She is neither waiting to be saved, nor does she speak on behalf of others. She is a solitary figure of principle—her flame fueled by conscience, not charisma. Her strength is a refusal to be ruled, not dominion. She is the archetype of earned sovereignty, carrying the fire for no one but herself—and in doing so, illuminating a path others may follow, if they dare.

In this image, rugged individualism is neither cowboy bravado nor ideological weaponry. It is a solitary woman standing her ground with dignity, humility, and light. She does not burn bridges—she holds the flame that remembers the cost of crossing them.

THE MANIFEST DESTINY CULTURAL COMPLEX

THE GUIDING SPIRIT OF DESTINY: LIGHT FOR SOME, SHADOW FOR OTHERS

This allegorical image embodies the Manifest Destiny cultural complex, portraying American expansion as divinely sanctioned progress. A radiant female figure floats westward, casting beams of enlightenment and modernity across the land. Yet beneath her shimmering form, the ground fractures, serpents stir, and those in her wake follow both hope and erasure. What is envisioned as advancement for some, brings dispossession and silence to others.

Core Emotion: Triumphalism and Righteous Entitlement

At the heart of the Manifest Destiny cultural complex is a potent emotional fusion of pride and moral justification. It carries a sense of divine favor and historical inevitability—belief in the right, even duty, to expand influence, dominate territory, and impose values. Its emotional underside includes denial, historical amnesia, and a numbed conscience toward conquest and displacement.

Mythic Root: The Chosen People in a Promised Land

This complex is rooted in biblical and imperial myths of providence and divine mission. It recasts the United States as a new Israel, chosen to spread liberty, civilization, and truth—often by force. Echoes of Eden, Exodus, and Roman expansion blend with the pioneer ethos, creating a myth of innocent conquest and redemptive empire.

Symbolic Imagery

- A shining city on a hill expanding westward
- Covered wagons trailing light while indigenous figures fade into shadow
- The American flag planted on mountaintops, continents, and celestial bodies
- A winged Columbia or Liberty guiding settlers through darkness
- Railroads, missiles, and satellites all portrayed as sacred arteries of progress

Self-Reinforcing Memory

Historical memory is selectively curated—celebrating westward expansion, the taming of the frontier, and the "civilizing mission," while erasing genocide, land theft, and ecological devastation. This memory is reinforced through textbooks, public monuments, and national holidays, which mythologize expansion as destiny rather than domination.

Black-and-White Thinking: Civilization vs. Savagery, Light vs. Darkness

The complex frames America's expansion as a universal good, and its adversaries as primitive, evil, or tragically misguided. This logic divides the world into those who advance history and those who resist it. It elevates the American project to moral absolutes, leaving little room for pluralism, humility, or historical complexity.

Repetitive Behaviors

- Justification of military, economic, and technological interventions as spreading freedom
- Erasure or marginalization of Indigenous, enslaved, or colonized voices in national narratives
- Use of exceptionalist language to frame domestic and foreign policy
- Symbolic reenactments of frontier mythology in media, education, and politics
- Ongoing projection of American ideals onto global stages, often with missionary zeal

Social Effects

This complex tears the cultural fabric by embedding conquest and erasure in the national psyche, often unconsciously. It marginalizes histories of suffering and resistance, reinforcing systemic inequality and justifying expansionism. It also sets up internal contradictions—between liberty and domination, justice and silence, myth and memory—creating psychic fragmentation and moral dissociation.

Possibility of Transformation

Transformation emerges through the telling of suppressed stories and the recognition of interdependence rather than superiority. Reimagining destiny as shared stewardship rather than singular conquest opens the complex to relational ethics, ecological consciousness, and historical truth-telling. A transformed version might celebrate cultural vitality, democratic humility, and reparative belonging rather than exceptionalism and erasure.

Iconography of The Guiding Spirit of Destiny: Light for Some, Shadow for Others

THE CENTRAL FEMALE FIGURE (SPIRIT OF DESTINY)

Modeled on classical muses and angels, she represents the idealized American spirit—purity, civilization, and moral purpose. Her white robes and ethereal glow mark her as a symbol of divine justification, hovering just above the soil, untouched by the consequences beneath.

OUTSTRETCHED ARM WITH RAYS OF LIGHT

These rays symbolize the spread of "progress"—technology, Christian values, capitalism, and modern governance. Yet they also obscure what they displace: Indigenous worlds, ecosystems, and alternative ways of being.

SNAKE IN THE SHADOWS

The serpent, historically a symbol of wisdom and danger, suggests the repressed shadow of Manifest Destiny: conquest, genocide, ecological harm. That it lies in the path of "progress" hints at the unconscious costs buried under the march westward.

SETTLERS, PROSPECTORS, AND WAGONS (FOREGROUND)

These figures represent the engine of expansion—ordinary people swept up in a mythic narrative of renewal and reward. Their forward momentum implies faith in the story of opportunity, whereas their proximity to the snake and cracked earth foreshadows loss and disillusionment.

CRACKED GROUND BENEATH

Symbolizes the psychic and literal rupture caused by the expansionist dream. It implies that what appears as advancement from above is a tearing from below—of land, culture, and soul.

TRAINS AND TELEGRAPHS (BACKGROUND)

Icons of industrial and technological advancement, they signify America's claim to progress—but also its entanglement with control, speed, and erasure of the sacred.

FADING INDIGENOUS PRESENCE
Not overtly depicted here, their absence speaks volumes. Their displacement is part of the myth's silence—a wound masked by the image's golden radiance.

Interpretation

This painting reveals the Manifest Destiny cultural complex as a grand civilizational drama, elevated by myth and shadowed by denial. It captures the psychological seduction of a nation believing it is ordained to expand, and the tragic complexity of those who follow the light while stepping over unseen graves. It invites the viewer to ask not only what was gained, but what was lost—and to whom?

THE PIONEER SPIRIT CULTURAL COMPLEX

WESTWARD INTO THE UNKNOWN: THE PIONEER SPIRIT AND THE LONGING TO BEGIN AGAIN

This symbolic image captures the soul of the American Pioneer Spirit cultural complex. A family moves steadily into an untamed horizon—led not by conquest, but by resolve. The mother leads with quiet strength, the child carries kindling for a future fire, and the father follows with labor-worn hands. Above them soars the eagle—not as dominator, but as guardian. Their journey is not one of certainty, but of faith in the open land and what might yet be born from it.

Core Emotion: Restless Hope and Heroic Autonomy

At the heart of the American Pioneer Spirit is a potent emotional blend: the yearning for renewal through movement, the pride of self-reliance, and the deep desire to forge identity through confrontation with the unknown. It celebrates courage, endurance, and the faith that new beginnings can be earned—if one is willing to leave everything behind.

Mythic Root: The Exodus and the Frontier Hero

This complex draws from biblical and mythic archetypes of exodus, pilgrimage, and heroic conquest. The pioneer is cast as both chosen and tested—like Moses in the wilderness or Odysseus on his long return. In American myth, this becomes the westward settler, the homesteader, the gold prospector, or the wagon-train scout. The land is not simply geography; it is a moral testing ground.

Symbolic Imagery

- A covered wagon pushing west beneath vast skies
- A lone figure with axe, rifle, or plow—staring into uncharted territory
- A broken trail behind and a shining ridge ahead
- A weathered homestead surrounded by prairie
- A sun setting or rising behind mountains—marking both ending and beginning
- A family circle around firelight, surrounded by wilderness
- A crossroad marked by boot prints, bones, and scattered artifacts of older civilizations

Self-Reinforcing Memory

Generations of stories, textbooks, films, and folklore have reinforced the image of the pioneer as moral exemplar: brave, decent, hardworking, and god-fearing. This collective memory omits or sanitizes the violence against Indigenous peoples, the ecological impact, and the gendered and racial exclusions beneath the myth. The past is mythologized as clean, earned, and divinely favored—making challenge to the narrative feel like sacrilege.

Black-and-White Thinking

The pioneer is the bringer of light; the wilderness is dark, savage, or empty. Civilization is good; untamed nature or resistance is bad. This binary frames discomfort, struggle, or opposition as tests of character—rather than symptoms of complexity. The Indigenous, the stranger, or the bureaucrat becomes a threat to the autonomy of the virtuous settler.

Repetitive Behavior

- Celebrating expansion as virtue
- Glorifying hardship and stoicism
- Romanticizing rural individualism over collective interdependence
- Enacting "new frontiers" in space, technology, or business as symbolic re-creations of the old myth
- Rejecting regulation or governmental support as a betrayal of self-made values
- Reenacting settler rituals in media, politics, or self-help culture (e.g., "trailblazer," "start-up pioneer," "cowboy diplomacy")

Social Effects

The Pioneer Spirit cultural complex fuels resilience, innovation, and boldness—but often at a cost. It justifies colonization, erasure, and environmental exploitation in the name of destiny. It divides the self-made from the dependent, casting aid or vulnerability as moral weakness. It can foster anti-intellectualism, anti-collectivism, and nostalgia for a frontier that never truly existed. It valorizes movement over rootedness and personal grit over communal care.

Potential for Transformation

When made conscious, this complex reveals a deep archetypal hunger: for belonging earned through effort, for lives shaped by purpose, and for identity forged in the open. Its shadow is conquest—but its gift is resilience in the face of uncertainty. If reimagined through inclusive, ecologically aware, and pluralistic values, the pioneer archetype can evolve from conqueror of land to steward of possibility, from lone hero to communal pathfinder.

Iconography of Westward into the Unknown: The Pioneer Spirit and the Longing to Begin Again

WOMAN LEADING WITH WALKING STAFF

She represents the moral and emotional backbone of the pioneer myth. Her forward gaze evokes vision, courage, and inner authority. Though often erased in traditional frontier lore, she stands here as the soul-guide of the journey.

CHILD CARRYING FIREWOOD

Symbol of hope and continuity. The child does not carry gold or tools—but the means to make fire: warmth, survival, transformation. It represents the unseen work of sustaining a dream across generations.

MAN GUIDING THE WAGON AND HORSE

The practical force of labor and endurance. His posture and movement evoke responsibility and physical burden, anchoring the myth in real effort rather than fantasy.

COVERED WAGON

A container of memory and aspiration—everything left behind and everything hoped for. It holds the family's world in motion. The wagon suggests not only mobility, but also the psychological burden of uprootedness.

EAGLE ABOVE

Traditional symbol of America, here it functions as an archetype of oversight, freedom, and divine witness. The eagle does not lead or dominate—it watches, soaring over history and myth alike.

GOLDEN LANDSCAPE AND HORIZON

The vastness of the open land reflects the spiritual and psychic space of the American imagination. It invites projection—both redemptive and destructive. The light suggests promise and purification; the absence of borders implies endless potential—and denial of limits.

Interpretation

This image embodies both the dignity and the delusion of the Pioneer Spirit cultural complex. It honors the endurance, sacrifice, and faith in renewal—but also hints at what is omitted: the peoples displaced, the silence of the land, the ambiguity of the dream. It invites us to ask:

- Who is walking, and who is being walked over?
- What do we carry forward, and what do we leave behind?
- Can the pioneer become not just settler, but also steward?

THE CITY ON THE HILL CULTURAL COMPLEX

TOWARD THE RADIANT REPUBLIC: THE AMERICAN IDEAL AS PILGRIMAGE

A glowing city of domes and spires rises above a darkened landscape, its radiant light illuminating a winding path. Below, a diverse procession of seekers ascends—led by a robed guide pointing toward the promised vision. This image evokes the enduring pull of the "City on a Hill" cultural ideal: America not only as a place, but also as a mission—aspiring to moral clarity, unity, and democratic purpose, even as it emerges from shadow.

Core Emotion: Moral Aspiration and Exceptional Pride

At its core, this complex is driven by a mixture of idealistic hope and national self-exaltation. It evokes the longing to be seen—and to see oneself—as a beacon of virtue, democracy, and divine purpose. Beneath the shining exterior, however, lies an anxiety about maintaining purity and a tendency to conflate moral aspiration with moral superiority.

Mythic Root: The Puritan Covenant and New Jerusalem

This cultural complex draws from John Winthrop's 1630 sermon envisioning America as a "City upon a Hill," a sacred exemplar to the world. Deeply rooted in biblical imagery, it fuses Protestant notions of being chosen with civic virtue. The mythic frame positions the nation not just as historically significant but also as cosmically chosen to lead and illuminate.

Symbolic Imagery

- A radiant city glowing atop a mount, visible across darkness
- Pilgrims, founders, or leaders delivering speeches to rapt listeners
- Light spilling outward from classical domes and shining capitol towers
- Immigrants or nations gazing upward at the American ideal
- A moral ladder ascending toward the city gates, guarded by sacred texts or ideals

Self-Reinforcing Memory

Historical memory is shaped around founding narratives: the Mayflower, the Revolution, Lincoln's America, Reagan's revival of the phrase. These stories are told as moral epics, reinforcing the sense of the United States as both exceptional and divinely guided. Failures—slavery, genocide, imperialism—are minimized or reframed as deviations from, rather than reflections of, the nation's true nature.

Black-and-White Thinking: "We are either the light of the world or a fallen nation."

The City on the Hill complex splits the world into those who emulate American ideals and those who fail them. The nation sees itself as either fully redeemed or dangerously lost. This binary thinking can lead to cultural self-blame during moments of failure or aggressive evangelism during moments of pride.

Social Effects

This complex can generate internal division by excluding those who do not fit the idealized moral image—immigrants, racial minorities, the poor, or dissenters. It masks structural injustice with the glow of virtue, making criticism feel like betrayal. Internationally, it can alienate allies or justify interventionism. Domestically, it breeds disillusionment when the city fails to shine.

Possibility of Transformation

The complex can evolve when the light of the city is reframed not as self-glorification, but as a shared ethical project—imperfect, inclusive, and constantly renewed. Transformation lies in embodying aspiration without superiority: becoming a city of open gates, not shining walls; a beacon not of perfection, but of honest striving and collective care.

Iconography of Toward the Radiant Republic: The American Ideal as Pilgrimage

RADIANT CAPITOL CITY ON THE HILL (TOP CENTER)

A gleaming synthesis of classical dome and spiritual temple, the city represents an exalted vision of America: a beacon of justice, freedom, and belonging. Its elevation and glow suggest divine or transcendent qualities, echoing both New Jerusalem and a constitutional utopia. It symbolizes the American Dream purified—unrealized, yet luminous.

GOLDEN PATH WINDING UPWARD

The path signifies the arduous, collective journey toward the national ideal. Its winding, imperfect nature implies struggle, generational labor, and moral progression. It stretches from shadow into light, reminding us that ascent is not guaranteed but chosen, again and again.

PILGRIMS ASCENDING (MIDDLE GROUND)

A multigenerational, multicultural group walks toward the light. They embody the archetype of the seeker—the immigrant, the outcast, the dreamer—those historically drawn to America not simply by opportunity, but by the idea of shared destiny. Their quiet unity gestures toward civic faith and mutual sacrifice.

GUIDE IN CLOAK POINTING TO THE CITY (RIGHT FOREGROUND)

This figure may represent the preacher, the founder, or the idealist—those who voice the vision. His gesture is both invitational and prophetic, casting the American experiment not just as a fact, but as a calling. His plain attire links him to the Puritan origins of the phrase "city upon a hill."

EXPRESSION OF THE PEOPLE (LEFT FOREGROUND):

Their faces reflect awe, hesitancy, and yearning. They suggest reverence for the ideal—yet remain rooted in the reality of hardship. The image invites contemplation: is this a promised land, or a mirage? A genuine guide, or another iteration of myth?

SHADOWED TERRAIN BELOW (BOTTOM HALF)

The darkness surrounding the path symbolizes the forces of division, despair, and disillusionment that weigh against national promise. It anchors the image in realism—suggesting that what is radiant above must be grounded in justice below.

SKY SPLITTING WITH LIGHT (UPPER BACKGROUND)

The break in the clouds evokes moral and historical possibility. It suggests that hope is not naïveté, but a light wrested from history's storms. The city does not descend from heaven—it must be climbed toward.

Interpretation

This image captures a key tension within the City on the Hill cultural complex: the American ideal as a shining promise and a moral burden. It invites reflection on who guides the vision, who walks the path, and what lies at the summit—truth or illusion, redemption or repetition.

There are several archetypal and cultural complexes at play in this image:

- Myth of American Exceptionalism: The glowing city encapsulates the belief that America is divinely chosen to lead morally and politically.
- Puritan Cultural Complex: Echoing John Winthrop's 1630 sermon, the image revives the Puritan legacy of moral scrutiny, divine election, and fear of failure before God and the world.
- Immigrant/Exile Archetype: The crowd's ascent maps the immigrant journey—hope, struggle, and longing for welcome—within a mythic framework.
- Shadow of the Ideal: The intensity of the light, the distance to the city, and the closed gates hint at the dangers of exclusivism, spiritual pride, and the unacknowledged cost of purity myths.

THE AMERICAN EXCEPTIONALISM CULTURAL COMPLEX

TWILIGHT OF THE REPUBLIC: THE AMERICAN EXCEPTIONALISM CULTURAL COMPLEX

A vigilant bald eagle soars above a cracked Capitol dome at sunset—an image of the American Exceptionalism cultural complex, symbolizing a nation caught between divine destiny and internal fracture. The eagle represents moral supremacy and protective might, while the split in the Capitol reveals a deeper tension: the belief in being chosen to lead the world colliding with growing doubts about unity, legitimacy, and purpose.

The American Exceptionalism cultural complex is a powerful, ambivalent psychic structure rooted in the belief that the United States has a unique moral destiny, a divinely sanctioned mission, or an unparalleled historical role. It lives at the intersection of national myth, global ambition, and internal contradiction.

Core Emotion: Pride Tinged with Anxiety

This complex is driven by deep national pride—often moral or spiritual in tone—but laced with anxiety: Are we still exceptional? Have we lost the mandate? It fuses national identity with performance and binds individual self-worth to national stature and global perception.

Mythic Roots

The mythic foundation of American exceptionalism is layered and theologically charged. It includes:

- The "City on a Hill" from John Winthrop's sermon—casting America as a moral beacon for all nations
- Manifest Destiny, the nineteenth-century belief that America was divinely ordained to expand across the continent
- The Chosen People, or New Israel, framing the nation as a sacred experiment in liberty
- World Redeemer archetypes—from defeating fascism and communism to exporting democracy and tech-fueled utopianism

Self-Reinforcing Memory

The complex draws strength from a curated sequence of national triumphs:

- The revolutionary victory over monarchy
- Winning World War II, launching the Marshall Plan, and landing on the moon
- Cold War dichotomies framed as a global moral battle: freedom versus tyranny
- The civil rights movement reframed as proof of America's capacity for self-correction
- Continued global dominance in technology, culture, and military power.

Each moment—while often fraught with contradiction—is used to reaffirm the idea of a divinely or historically mandated national destiny.

Symbolic Imagery

The symbolic world of exceptionalism is saturated with icons of pride, power, and promise:

- The Statue of Liberty, torch aloft, welcoming and illuminating
- The Capitol dome glowing at dusk, a visual hymn to democratic grandeur
- A soaring eagle over rugged terrain, signifying freedom and dominance
- Mount Rushmore, the sacred shrine of presidential myth
- Children pledging allegiance with hands over hearts, instilling national faith
- A lone astronaut planting a flag on the moon, embodying heroic uniqueness
- A map of the world with America at the center, reflecting the assumed global centrality of the US

Black-and-White Thinking

The complex encourages polarized thinking:

- "America equals freedom," whereas "others equal oppression."
- We are either a "shining beacon" or a nation in irreversible decline.
- Criticism is interpreted as either betrayal or a deeper form of patriotism.
- National value is seen in absolute terms: exceptional or lost.

Social Effects

When rigid or inflated, this complex becomes destructive:

- It blinds Americans to national flaws such as systemic racism, inequality, and imperial overreach.
- It creates a brittle national identity, one that must be constantly validated and defended.
- It fosters polarization between "patriots" and "critics," intensifying culture wars.

- It justifies overreach abroad while masking neglect at home.
- It makes it psychologically difficult to imagine the US.as simply one nation among many.

Potential for Transformation

Despite its dangers, the American Exceptionalism cultural complex holds powerful redemptive potential:

MORAL LEADERSHIP WHEN GROUNDED IN PRINCIPLE
At its best, the complex motivates the US to lead by example—promoting human rights, democracy, and cooperation rather than coercion.

PROTECTIVE RESPONSE TO GLOBAL TYRANNY
The exceptionalist impulse has fueled resistance to fascism, apartheid, and genocide, galvanizing Americans to defend human dignity on a global scale.

IDEALS OF LIBERTY AND JUSTICE FOR ALL
Although often unrealized, founding principles such as free speech, religious tolerance, and rule of law continue to inspire both domestic reform and international admiration.

CULTURAL CONFIDENCE TO INNOVATE
The belief in being "first," "only," or "best" has driven American breakthroughs in science, the arts, and technology—from jazz and civil rights to Silicon Valley.

CRUCIBLE OF NATIONAL SELF-CRITIQUE
The ideal of American greatness has paradoxically fueled movements that hold the nation accountable—civil rights, antiwar activism, environmentalism—insisting the country live up to its own promises.

NARRATIVE OF REDEMPTION
Embedded in the complex is the belief that no failure is final. America, like its mythic self-image, is capable of renewal through struggle, reflection, and reinvention.

Iconography of Twilight of the Republic: The American Exceptionalism Cultural Complex

THE CRACKED CAPITOL DOME (CENTER)

The US Capitol, seat of American democracy, is fractured down the middle—splitting the foundation and rising through the dome. This rupture symbolizes the breakdown of shared civic faith, institutional legitimacy, and the illusion of moral unity. It reveals the fault lines—racial, ideological, economic—that American exceptionalism has long obscured. The crack begins at the ground (history), rises through the body politic (present), and reaches toward the symbolic apex of the nation's ideals (vision of the future). It evokes divine judgment, tectonic unrest, or repressed truth finally surfacing.

THE BALD EAGLE (ABOVE)

The eagle, soaring above the Capitol, is the national emblem of strength, freedom, and vigilance. But in this image, it hovers alone, wings outstretched, not in triumph but tension. Its downward gaze is neither predatory nor protective—it watches. The eagle here is ambivalent: Is it circling in defense of the republic, or preparing to flee a nation in decline? The eagle also symbolizes the self-image of America as chosen, elevated, untouchable—but shadowed now by dread.

THE SUNSET SKY (BACKGROUND)

A glowing horizon peeks through storm-darkened clouds. The fading light suggests the end of an era—the golden age myth fading into uncertainty. The storm clouds represent looming crises—climate, polarization, and authoritarian drift. Yet the last rays of sun could also be read as a glimmer of renewal, depending on the viewer's interpretive stance.

THE RUBBLE AT THE BASE (FOREGROUND)

Large stones scattered at the base of the Capitol point to collapse and decay. Once-solid foundations—laws, myths, principles—are in ruins. What was built is now burdened by its own contradictions. This debris is not merely physical but psychic: broken promises, compromised ideals, and betrayed memories.

Interpretation

This image is a portrait of a cultural complex unraveling. The myth of American Exceptionalism has long sustained the belief that the US is uniquely virtuous, eternally ascendant, and divinely favored. This image refuses that simplicity. It instead reveals:

- The cost of founding myths that exclude
- The tension between greatness and hubris
- The fragility of symbols when divorced from justice

Yet it is not hopeless. The eagle still flies. The light still glows. The Capitol, though cracked, stands. What remains is the question: Will this be a sunset—or a dawn remade through truth?

PASSING THE FLAME: INHERITING THE DREAM OF AMERICAN EXCEPTIONALISM

A young man, accompanied by other youths, raises a torch toward the Statue of Liberty at dawn—an image of the American Exceptionalism cultural complex passing from myth to individual embodiment. The statue, guardian of Enlightenment ideals, stands solemn and iconic, while the boy and his youthful companions mirror her gaze into the unknown future, signaling a generational inheritance of purpose. This scene captures the belief that America is not just a nation, but a sacred project—destined to carry liberty forward, yet always in danger of being forgotten, reimagined, or reclaimed.

Iconography of Passing the Flame: Inheriting the Dream of American Exceptionalism

- **THE STATUE OF LIBERTY (LEFT BACKGROUND)**

Towering and serene, Lady Liberty stands as a monumental embodiment of Enlightenment ideals—freedom, reason, and welcome. Her raised torch burns steadily, casting warm light across the scene. She is both maternal and monumental: rooted in the past, yet still present as guide. Her tablet—engraved with July 4, 1776—anchors her authority in the mythic founding moment of the nation.

- **THE YOUNG FIGURE WITH A TORCH (RIGHT FOREGROUND)**

A youthful person, back turned to the viewer, raises a hand-held torch toward the great statue. The two flames mirror each other—a gesture of continuity, not mimicry. The figure's posture is both reverent and active; he is not receiving the torch but lifting his own. This upward gaze reflects longing, responsibility, and emerging agency—the dream of American exceptionalism now internalized and made personal.

- **DUAL TORCHES—TWO FLAMES, ONE FIRE**

The visual mirroring of the two flames speaks to symbolic inheritance. This is not the extinguishing of one light to make room for another, but the lighting of a second flame from the first. The elder myth and the newer hope burn side by side—an echo of the Olympic tradition, or of sacred fire carried through exile, suggesting the possibility of renewal without rupture, evolution without betrayal.

- **THE SUNSET OR SUNRISE SKY (BACKGROUND)**

The richly painted twilight sky—streaked with gold, rose, and violet—sets the tone for liminality: this is not midday certainty, but a moment between eras. The sun may be setting or rising. The sky echoes the unresolved tension in the myth of American Exceptionalism: is this its twilight, or its transfiguration?

Interpretation

This image portrays the American Exceptionalism cultural complex, not as hubris or dominance, but as an aspirational continuity among a diverse group of young people—a dream of liberty, opportunity, and moral calling passed from one generation to the next. It suggests

- **Inheritance without idolization:** The past is honored, not worshipped.
- **A future carried by the young:** With quiet courage, a new generation picks up the torch.
- **Rekindling rather than erasure:** This is not a break from myth, but its reanimation in living form.

THE AMERICAN DREAM CULTURAL COMPLEX

THE GOLDEN ASCENT: DREAMS BUILT FROM LABOR AND LONGING

This image presents a haunting yet tender portrait of the American Dream cultural complex. A man grips a hammer beside a folded, worn flag. A woman reads, quietly rooted. Behind them, a glowing stairway leads toward a shining, unreachable city in the clouds—an archetype of hope, success, and transcendence. The dream ascends, but those who built it remain in shadow, grounded in toil and memory.

Core Emotion: Hope, Aspiration, and Insecurity

At its emotional core, the American Dream cultural complex is fueled by a profound longing for self-creation, success, and upward mobility—coupled with a gnawing anxiety over failure, exclusion, and fraudulence. It activates both the exhilaration of possibility and the shame of perceived inadequacy. Belief in the dream offers meaning; fear of its falseness haunts the margins.

Mythic Root: The Self-Made Hero and the Promised Land

This complex is rooted in the myth of the self-made individual—one who rises by talent, grit, and virtue. It inherits the biblical imagery of Exodus and Eden, the Enlightenment belief in personal agency, and the frontier mythology of boundless opportunity. The dream becomes a secular covenant: the promise that destiny is earned, not given.

Symbolic Imagery

- A staircase stretching into clouds, lined with resumes and faded family photographs
- A person climbing while carrying their child, chased by shadows labeled *Debt*, *Prejudice*, and *Luck*
- A mansion glowing behind a chain-link fence
- A rags-to-riches figure wearing a crown made of dollar bills and calluses
- A lottery ticket and a diploma placed on the same altar

Self-Reinforcing Memory

American lore is saturated with stories of immigrants, entrepreneurs, and trailblazers "making it." These stories are repeated through schoolbooks, commercials, family histories, and campaign slogans. Even when contradicted by inequality, the narrative persists—because it binds identity to achievement. At the same time, unspoken memories of systemic barriers, broken dreams, and quiet despair are buried or individualized, further reinforcing the illusion of merit.

Black-and-White Thinking

You either made it or you didn't. Success is interpreted as moral virtue, failure as personal weakness. The complexity of structural constraints is flattened into binary logic: winners versus losers, hard workers versus freeloaders, American versus un-American. This dichotomy fuels both pride and cruelty.

Social Effects

- Relentless striving, even to the point of burnout or alienation
- Shaming those who "haven't made it" while romanticizing hustle culture
- Obsessive self-branding as proof of worth
- Denial of privilege to preserve the myth
- Retelling the same success stories while ignoring those who never get written into them

Possibility of Transformation

This complex holds powerful symbolic energy that can be transformed. When the dream is reclaimed, not as material conquest, but as shared dignity, security, and self-actualization, it can become a force for collective renewal. The ladder can give way to a commons; the solo climb can become a communal table. By integrating compassion, structural awareness, and interdependence, the dream can evolve from fantasy into ethical horizon.

Iconography of The Golden Ascent: Dreams Built from Labor and Longing

THE WORKER WITH HAMMER AND SHOVEL (FOREGROUND LEFT)

A modern everyman, he embodies the laboring foundation of the American Dream—the physical, blue-collar backbone that shaped the infrastructure, economy, and myth of progress. His downward gaze suggests disillusionment, fatigue, or grief, as if sensing that the dream has moved on without him.

THE WOMAN WITH THE BOOK (FOREGROUND RIGHT)

She represents education, inner life, or cultural continuity. Her contemplative posture evokes the quieter threads of the dream—those rooted in reflection, resilience, and uncelebrated knowledge. She holds the future, not in ambition, but in memory.

THE FOLDED AMERICAN FLAG AT THEIR FEET

Positioned like a burial shroud, it signals the wounded promise of the American ideal—what was pledged, what was sacrificed, and what lies unfulfilled. The flag is not burned or torn, but reverently set aside, suggesting both reverence and reckoning.

FIGURES ASCENDING THE STAIRWAY (MIDGROUND)

A man and child rise hand-in-hand toward the golden citadel. They symbolize intergenerational striving—the core engine of the dream. Their upward motion evokes hope, but their smallness also suggests distance from the builders below.

GOLDEN CITY IN THE CLOUDS (TOP CENTER)

A surreal, almost utopian image of success, freedom, or divine reward. This is the symbolic destination of the American Dream: shining, suspended, and perhaps illusory. It evokes the heaven of meritocracy, yet remains unreachable for most.

SHADOWED FACES AND SILHOUETTES (BACKGROUND)

These ghostly presences hint at collective memory—the ancestors, immigrants, and laborers who shaped the dream but remain unnamed. They are the invisible multitude beneath the myth.

COLOR PALETTE (EARTH AND GOLD)

The warm golden glow suggests aspiration and spiritual yearning, whereas the deep reds and browns ground the image in labor, blood, and earth. This duality mirrors the American Dream's split between transcendence and sacrifice.

Interpretation

This image doesn't mock the American Dream—it mourns, questions, and reclaims it. It portrays the dream not only as a ladder of hope, but also as a myth built on unseen foundations—on labor, learning, loss, and love. The dream rises, but its weight is felt most deeply below. What's asked, perhaps, is not whether the American Dream survives—but whether those who built it will be remembered in its light.

THE MELTING POT CULTURAL COMPLEX

SACRIFICE AND STEAM: THE MELTING POT CULTURAL COMPLEX

A towering cauldron glows at the center of the American landscape, fed by figures from many walks of life. They ascend in solemn procession—some climbing willingly, others hesitantly—toward the crucible of assimilation. From its rim, rising steam takes on ghostly forms: not a skyline of promise, but the vapor of vanished identities, forgotten ancestors, and stories melted into myth. The image reveals both the ideal and the cost of the Melting Pot cultural complex: unity forged through fire, at the price of memory, texture, and selfhood.

Core Emotion: Longing and Anxiety over Belonging

At its emotional core, the Melting Pot cultural complex is driven by the desire to belong—to become part of a unified whole without being rejected or erased. This yearning is entangled with anxiety: Will I be accepted? Will I lose myself in the process? The complex stirs ambivalence—between pride in assimilation and fear of cultural loss.

Mythic Root: The Alchemical Crucible and the City on a Hill

The complex is rooted in the myth of transformation through fusion: a cauldron where differences dissolve into unity, creating something stronger, purer, and more American. It echoes biblical and alchemical imagery—a refining fire, a sacred union—and is tied to the Puritan vision of America as a "City on a Hill," illuminated and exceptional through cultural synthesis.

Symbolic Imagery

- A bubbling pot inscribed with flags, dialects, and faces dissolving into steam
- A crucible filled with fire, above which diverse figures blur into a single outline
- A family changing clothes—from ethnic garb to Western business suits—as they enter a golden city
- An old tree with grafted limbs, blooming unevenly
- A mirror reflecting one face from many

Self-Reinforcing Memory

American narratives of immigration reinforce the idea that success follows assimilation. Stories of grandparents who changed their names, shed languages, and "made it" validate the myth. Simultaneously, memories of cultural erasure—native languages lost, identities denied—remain unspoken or marginalized, reinforcing the tension between acceptance and invisibility.

Black-and-White Thinking

Assimilation is seen as good; difference is seen as suspicious. The binary often frames people as either "fully American" or "forever foreign." Multiculturalism is welcomed only when it doesn't threaten cohesion. This complex fosters a false choice between purity and fragmentation: either melt or break apart.

Social Effects

The Melting Pot cultural complex both binds and erodes. It fosters civic loyalty, shared institutions, and national pride—but at the cost of depth, memory, and cultural integrity. It marginalizes those who refuse or cannot conform, reducing pluralism to performance. Communities lose heritage in the rush for inclusion. Beneath its unifying promise lies a haunting silence—of what was melted down and forgotten.

- Pressure to suppress accents, clothing, customs to fit dominant norms
- Celebrating diversity in theory, but demanding conformity in practice
- Romanticizing past immigrant stories while rejecting current ones
- Repeating cycles of xenophobia followed by late-stage cultural appropriation
- Holding up "model minorities" as proof the pot works—while scapegoating those who resist

Possibility of Transformation

Transformation lies in evolving from melting pot to mosaic or braided river—forms of unity that honor difference without dissolving it. By shifting the metaphor, this complex can be revitalized: cultural synthesis becomes generative rather than erasing. When American identity is reimagined as capacious, relational, and layered, the longing to belong can be answered without the demand to disappear. From fire to weaving, from fusion to resonance—there is hope for a more textured wholeness.

Iconography of Sacrifice and Steam: The Melting Pot Cultural Complex

THE CENTRAL CAULDRON (CENTER)

A massive vessel radiating light and heat, symbolizing the promise of transformation into a unified American identity. It evokes both opportunity and obliteration—where cultural difference is not honored but rendered into sameness.

ASCENDING PROCESSION OF DIVERSE FIGURES (FOREGROUND)

People of varying backgrounds, including people of color and Asian heritage, move toward the pot. Some stand tall, others are bowed—expressing hope, obligation, and unease. Their positioning reflects the emotional ambiguity of assimilation: inclusion entwined with loss.

FIGURES DISSOLVING INTO STEAM (UPPER SKY)

Rising from the pot, clouds of steam form ghostly human shapes—representing previous generations whose names, languages, and rituals have evaporated in the process. The absence of a visible skyline replaces the myth of arrival with the haunting of disappearance.

GOLDEN LIGHT AND WARM TONES (OVERALL PALETTE)

The inviting hues suggest warmth, hospitality, and hope—but also mask the intensity of the heat. The image walks a fine line between sacred ritual and sacrificial pyre.

NO CLEAR DESTINATION (BACKGROUND)

Unlike traditional depictions of the American Dream, this scene lacks a visible endpoint. There is no city in the distance, no beacon—only the pot itself, central and inescapable. This ambiguity underscores the unresolved tension in the metaphor.

SUBTLE SHADOWS AND ANCESTRAL ECHOES (AROUND THE POT)

Faint outlines of ancestors and cultural figures hover near the cauldron's base—suggesting what is carried in, even if it is not permitted to remain intact

Interpretation

This image deepens the metaphor of the Melting Pot: no longer a celebration of unity alone, but a recognition of the psychic and cultural costs of forced conformity. It asks whether belonging must mean erasure—and whether it's time to imagine a vessel that holds difference, rather than melts it down.

THE MILITARY-INDUSTRIAL CULTURAL COMPLEX

ENGINES OF POWER: THE MILITARY-INDUSTRIAL CULTURAL COMPLEX

A towering missile-crowned ziggurat rises from a scorched industrial landscape, fed by a stream of dollar bills and surrounded by smoke-belching factories. At its base, a politician waves a flag to cheering crowds, while a defense contractor studies profits. A mother clutches her child in fear. Above it all, the ghostly visage of Dwight D. Eisenhower watches solemnly from the smoke—a spectral reminder of his 1961 warning about the unchecked power of the military-industrial complex. The image captures the fusion of nationalism, profit, and warfare, revealing a sacred architecture of perpetual preparation for conflict.

Core Emotion: Security Through Dominance and Fear of Vulnerability

This complex is emotionally driven by the need to feel safe through overwhelming force. Beneath its reverence for power lies an anxious conviction: that without military superiority, the nation will fall. It blends patriotic pride with perpetual fear—of weakness, disorder, and external threat.

Mythic Root: The Warrior Nation and the Forge of Freedom

At its mythic core lies the archetype of the heroic warrior and the civilizing sword—America as both protector and righteous avenger. It channels deep narratives: the frontier militia, the WWII liberator, and the Cold War sentinel. War is portrayed not only as defense but also as destiny—the crucible where liberty is earned.

Symbolic Imagery

- A pentagon-shaped temple fused with factories and command towers
- Soldiers saluting beside endless rows of missiles, their shadows cast over children at play
- A golden eagle soaring over a world map divided into zones of influence
- A veteran's parade dissolving into a weapons expo
- A digital control room where economic profit, media narrative, and military deployment intersect

Self-Reinforcing Memory

This complex draws strength from carefully mythologized moments: Pearl Harbor, Normandy, 9/11, and Desert Storm. These are framed as morally clear battles for good, whereas Vietnam, Iraq, and covert interventions are suppressed or reinterpreted. Memorials abound, but few mark the cost to civilians, dissenters, or democratic accountability. Importantly, this complex was first named and warned against by President Dwight D. Eisenhower in his 1961 farewell address. A five-star general and Supreme Commander of Allied Forces in WWII, Eisenhower cautioned that the growing entanglement of defense contractors, the military, and government threatened democratic institutions, transparency, and civil society. His prescient words are rarely remembered in full, even as his warning continues to unfold.

Black-and-White Thinking: "You're either prepared or defeated."

The Military-Industrial cultural complex encourages stark binaries: strength versus surrender, patriot versus traitor, security versus chaos. It equates diplomacy with naïveté and dissent with disloyalty. This mental framework hardens public discourse and distorts public spending priorities.

Repetitive Behaviors

- Ever-increasing defense budgets regardless of peacetime or crisis
- Rotating elite careers between defense industry, military, and political office
- Militarization of police, borders, and schools under the guise of protection
- Ceremonial displays of patriotism used to justify conflict or suppress critique
- Corporate influence masked as national necessity

Social Effects

This complex diverts resources from education, healthcare, and civic life to maintain an empire of readiness. It militarizes identity, embeds fear in daily life, and constrains democratic oversight. It also erodes collective imagination: where diplomacy becomes suspect, and peace seems naïve. Citizens are cast as permanent soldiers in endless wars—cultural, economic, and literal.

Possibility of Transformation

Transformation begins by remembering Eisenhower's warning and reclaiming civic courage—not in weaponry, but in restraint, justice, and mutual security. Veterans speaking out, communities demilitarizing their schools, and policymakers challenging entrenched contractors are signs of rupture. The myth can evolve from power as domination to power as protection of life, rights, and global stewardship.

Iconography of Engines of Power: The Military-Industrial Cultural Complex

MISSILE-CROWNED PYRAMID (CENTER)

A grand ziggurat-like structure at the image's core, ascending toward the heavens and crowned with three missiles. This symbolizes the deification of military power and technological might—monumental, unquestionable, and central to national identity.

RIVER OF DOLLAR BILLS (FLOWING UPWARD)

A serpentine path of money leading directly into the base of the structure, representing the endless flow of public funds into military and defense spending. It illustrates how war preparation is fueled by and for profit.

FACTORIES AND SMOKE (BACKGROUND)

Black plumes billow from industrial towers surrounding the pyramid, merging with the image's fiery glow. This evokes environmental degradation, economic dependency, and the moral smog surrounding endless militarization.

POLITICIAN WITH AMERICAN FLAG (LOWER LEFT)

A suited official, triumphant and confident, waves the flag while speaking to a crowd. He represents how patriotic rhetoric is used to justify the military's prominence and budget—transforming war readiness into public virtue.

DEFENSE CONTRACTOR WITH PROFIT CHART (LOWER RIGHT)

A businessman in glasses, detached and analytical, studies a graph with an upward trajectory. His presence underscores the financialization of war and the incentives for conflict within a profit-driven system.

MOTHER AND CHILD (FOREGROUND, BELOW THE PYRAMID)

Huddled in vulnerability, the woman clutches her child—representing the human cost of this complex: anxiety, loss, and sacrifice obscured by national myth and economic abstraction.

GHOSTLY PORTRAIT OF DWIGHT D. EISENHOWER (UPPER RIGHT)

Emerging from the smoke, Eisenhower's translucent face reminds viewers of his final presidential address in 1961, where he famously warned of the "military-industrial complex." His presence is both moral compass and silent indictment.

SEPIA AND FIERY COLOR PALETTE

The entire image is rendered in tones of orange, yellow, and deep rust—evoking both nostalgia and alarm, memory and combustion. The palette itself suggests both sanctification and destruction.

Interpretation

This image serves as a mythic anatomy of America's Military-Industrial cultural complex—its architecture of faith, its economic machinery, and its psychological cost. Eisenhower's ghost marks the potential for awakening: to question the idols we build, the fires we feed, and the futures we mortgage for a feeling of control.

THE FORTRESS AMERICA CULTURAL COMPLEX

BEHIND THE WALL: THE FORTRESS AMERICA CULTURAL COMPLEX

An armed sentinel stands guard beneath barbed wire and watchtowers, flanked by a caged eagle and a flag that no longer waves freely. A mother and children huddle behind a curtain, while shadows loom outside and smoke darkens the sky. This image captures the Fortress America cultural complex—rooted in fear, isolation, and the longing to preserve through exclusion. It reflects a vision of safety secured, not by trust or community, but by vigilance, separation, and the illusion of control.

Core Emotion: Fear and Protective Defiance

This complex is driven by a powerful emotional cocktail of fear, wounded pride, and an urgent need for protection. It sees threats everywhere—at the border, in the city, in the news, in the neighborhood—and responds with retreat into defense, both psychological and militarized. Its motto is not "In Unity We Trust" but "We must keep them out to survive."

Mythic Root: The Walled City and the Lone Survivor

Fortress America emerges from two intertwined myths: the frontier fort besieged by hostile forces, and the lone settler-family who defends the homestead. It draws from biblical images of a chosen people under siege and the American imagery of the Alamo, Cold War bunkers, and post-9/11 homeland security. In this myth, vigilance is virtue, and security is the highest civic good.

Symbolic Imagery

- Border walls, surveillance towers
- Gated communities
- Private arsenals
- The flying of a solitary flag
- The family huddled indoors while chaos rages outside
- A bunker filled with supplies
- Military parades with eyes turned inward, not outward
- The American eagle perched behind iron bars, watching

Self-Reinforcing Memory

The complex is fueled by selective historical memories: 9/11, Pearl Harbor, the Cold War, and even the American Revolution are recalled as warnings rather than moments of resilience. Trauma is mythologized into permanent vulnerability. Any openness—to immigration, diplomacy, dissent—is remembered as a weakness that led to harm.

Black-and-White Thinking

The world is split into insiders and outsiders, patriots and invaders, loyalists and infiltrators. Compromise is cowardice. Borders are sacred. You are either protecting America, or you are endangering it. There is no third position, no gray zone, no shared space of vulnerability.

Repetitive Behavior

Calls for increased military spending, fortress-like architecture, expansion of border security, "stand your ground" laws, and personal armament.

Cultural rituals that celebrate defense over cooperation. Constant invocation of existential threat—whether real or imagined—keeps the complex in motion.

Social Effects

This complex tears the fabric of pluralistic democracy. It isolates the nation from the world, and citizens from each other. It replaces the civic commons with echo chambers and fortifications. In its psychological form, it fosters suspicion, loneliness, and grievance. It hardens institutions and empathy, reducing politics to defense and survival.

Possibility of Transformation

Within Fortress America lies a deeper longing—to be safe, to be held, to trust. Transformation begins when security is redefined, not as isolation, but as interdependence. The walls need not fall at once—but doors can be opened. The protector can become the reconciler. The myth of the invader can be replaced by the archetype of the neighbor. Fortress America may become Community America—where strength is measured by how courageously we create spaces of mutual care and shared destiny.

Iconography of Behind the Wall: The Fortress America Cultural Complex

ARMED GUARD WITH ASSAULT RIFLE

Symbol of self-reliant defense and hypervigilance. His stoic posture evokes readiness and mistrust, portraying the citizen as soldier in a culture of internal siege.

BARBED WIRE FENCE AND WATCHTOWER

Icon of militarized boundaries. These structures define the outer perimeter of Fortress America—protective but also imprisoning. They signify the extent to which fear has become infrastructural.

CAGED BALD EAGLE BEHIND BARS

Twisted emblem of national identity. The eagle, America's symbol of freedom and power, is here imprisoned, suggesting that in seeking protection, the nation has confined its own spirit.

AMERICAN FLAG INSIDE THE CAGE

Liberty restricted. The flag's location—behind bars with the eagle—underscores the irony of patriotism turned defensive, where national pride becomes entangled with isolation and control.

MOTHER AND CHILDREN WATCHING FROM BEHIND A CURTAIN

The emotional cost of siege mentality. Their expressions of fear and fatigue humanize the psychological toll of living within a fortress—a space of safety that has become a prison of anxiety.

MARCHING SHADOWS BEYOND THE WALL

Abstract threat and projected fear. The silhouettes evoke migration, invasion, or imagined enemies—reinforcing the us-vs-them dynamic that feeds the complex.

BURNING CITY IN BACKGROUND

The mythology of external chaos. The destruction outside justifies the internal fortification, even as it blurs reality with paranoia. It mirrors the belief that America must wall itself off to survive.

MUTED EARTH-TONE PALETTE

Evokes both nostalgia and foreboding. The warm but shadowed tones give the image a sense of heavy permanence, as though the fortress has stood long—and will stand longer still.

Interpretation

This image portrays the Fortress America cultural complex through the symbolism of walls, weapons, and watchfulness. The armed guard stands for the ideal of protective strength, whereas the barbed wire and watchtower evoke isolation and fear of infiltration. The grieving family behind the curtain reveals the human cost of such security. The image raises the question: Does safety built on exclusion protect the nation—or imprison its conscience?

THE AMERICAN CONSUMERISM CULTURAL COMPLEX

TRAPPED IN THE SALE OF THE SELF

A woman flees through a maze of signs and slogans, arms full of discounted goods yet face marked by unease. Surrounded by blank-eyed onlookers and towering icons of consumption, she is both participant and prisoner in a ritual of endless acquisition. The shopping bags read like commandments— "BUY," "SALE," "$9.99"—as consumerism masquerades as meaning, offering identity through buying. Behind her, a massive shopping cart looms like a shadow altar. In this world, desire is cultivated but never fulfilled.

Core Emotion: Desire Entangled with Anxiety

At the heart of this complex is a restless yearning—for fulfillment, status, belonging, and security—channeled into material acquisition. Desire becomes both the engine and the symptom: it offers fleeting satisfaction but fuels a deeper anxiety of never-enoughness. The more one consumes, the more one fears scarcity, loss, or insignificance.

Mythic Root: The Cornucopia and the Self-Made Shopper

The complex draws from American myths of abundance and autonomy: the endless frontier, the marketplace as temple, and the myth of the individual who buys, upgrades, and styles their way to self-definition. It echoes the archetype of the "magic object" that promises transformation—but at a cost. The shopper is both hero and captive in a labyrinth of choices.

Symbolic Imagery

- A golden shopping cart on a mountaintop
- A credit card glowing like a relic
- A man scrolling under a waterfall of advertisements
- Children surrounded by toys but unable to play
- A mirror framed in neon reading: "*You are what you buy*"
- A landfill with brand names still legible

Self-Reinforcing Memory

Narratives of the American Dream become fused with material markers: the house, the car, the brand. Advertising reinforces the memory that happiness and success are visible, purchasable, and competitive. Past economic booms and busts, especially the Great Depression and the 2008 crash, become part of a deeper anxiety that consumption is both survival and salvation.

Black-and-White Thinking

You're either winning or falling behind. Affluence is virtue; poverty is failure. Minimalism is noble, but deprivation is shameful. Value is equated with price. Life is measured in upgrades: newer versus obsolete, branded versus generic, "real" versus knockoff.

Repetitive Behavior

- Mindless scrolling
- Impulse buying
- Retail therapy
- Accumulating things to soothe inner disconnection
- Discarding the old before it breaks
- Equating personal growth with lifestyle changes
- Seeking identity in styles and community in trends
- Avoiding discomfort by clicking "Add to Cart"

Social Effects

Consumerism masks existential longing with distraction. It creates ecological devastation, deepens inequality, and promotes hollow forms of identity. The complex fosters loneliness beneath the veneer of curated abundance, and leaves generations tethered to debt, comparison, and environmental depletion. It is a cycle of craving that commodifies not only goods but also meaning.

Potential for Transformation

REVALUATION OF MEANING OVER POSSESSION

As the complex is brought to consciousness, individuals and cultures can shift from acquisition to authenticity—seeking meaning in experience, relationships, and inner purpose rather than products.

COMMUNITY OVER CONSUMPTION

The longing for belonging can be reclaimed through shared ritual, mutual aid, and creative expression rather than status symbols. The mall gives way to the commons.

ECOLOGICAL RESPONSIBILITY

A reawakened awareness of planetary limits reframes consumption as stewardship. The consumer becomes a caretaker.

SIMPLICITY AS STRENGTH

Simplicity is no longer mistaken for lack. It becomes a spiritual path—a form of resistance to distraction and a re-centering of life around what is enduring.

FROM IMAGE TO ESSENCE

The gaze moves inward. The Self is no longer assembled through brands, but remembered through depth. Consumerism may mask the deeper desire for transformation—one that can only be satisfied through soul, not stuff.

Iconography of Trapped in the Sale of the Self

FRIGHTENED WOMAN CLUTCHING SHOPPING BAGS

She is the embodiment of internalized compulsion and anxiety under consumer capitalism. Her expression reveals the emotional cost of perpetual consumption: confusion, fear, and alienation.

SHOPPING BAGS LABELED SALE, BUY, AND $9.99

These symbols reduce identity and agency to transactional labels, underscoring the commodification of self-worth and social status. The repetitive language mimics marketing mantras—subtle yet insistent commands.

BACKGROUND FIGURES WITH EXPRESSIONLESS FACES

De-individuated masses symbolize the loss of autonomy and critical consciousness in consumer crowds. Their blank stares echo the social pressure to conform and consume.

OVERSIZED SHOPPING CART AND HAMBURGER SIGN

Icons of material and fast-food culture. These exaggerate the ubiquity of consumer choices that offer satisfaction without nourishment; they are symbolic of hollow abundance.

MUTED SEPIA-YELLOW PALETTE

Evokes a faded American Dream or tarnished Golden Age—nostalgia hollowed out by overconsumption. The yellow hue also suggests caution or sickness, hinting at the malaise beneath the market frenzy.

SIGNS READING *MORE*! AND *SALE* IN ALL DIRECTIONS

A visual overload of directives, implying that more is never enough. The signs suggest a totalizing ideology, where desire is no longer authentic but orchestrated.

TRASH CAN WITH DOME LID BEHIND THE CROWD

A subtle yet telling image of waste and disposal, underscoring the environmental and existential cost of unchecked consumerism.

Interpretation

This image explores the Consumer cultural complex as both addiction and enchantment. The emotional core is anxiety masked as desire: the need to consume, not out of abundance, but out of emptiness. It reveals how identity becomes wrapped in acquisition, and how consumer rituals replace communal, spiritual, or meaningful ones.

The woman is not a villain but a victim—caught in the trance of a culture that equates buying with belonging. The ghostly crowd suggests that this is a shared affliction: an unconscious complex embedded in American life. The image critiques the system of seduction that defines modern consumption rather than the individual.

THE HIGH TECH CULTURAL COMPLEX

THE ALGORITHMIC GAZE: THE DISEMBODIED AUTHORITY OF THE HIGH-TECH CULTURAL COMPLEX

A silhouetted figure holding a digital tablet stands before a glowing metropolis, framed by drone swarms, satellite arrays, and a luminous neural network overhead. The scene evokes the dominance of technology and data in shaping global systems, while a child in the corner gestures upward—symbolizing both aspiration and the generational imprint of the High Tech cultural complex.

Core Emotion: Exhilaration and Restless Disruption

At its core is a thrill for innovation and a conviction that the future is not found—but made. It generates awe, ambition, and a belief in boundless possibility, coupled with a refusal to accept limits—biological, ethical, or ecological.

Mythic Root: The Sorcerer's Apprentice and the Tower of Babel

This complex is driven by the archetype of the Promethean innovator—those who steal fire from the gods to transform the world. It dreams in utopias: of total connectivity, radical longevity, planetary engineering, and post-human evolution. But it risks hubris, like Icarus or Babel, building systems so complex they escape their makers.

Symbolic Imagery

- A glowing brain connected to satellites
- Robed figures coding by candlelight in glass towers
- A child reaching toward a neural interface
- Drones circling a cloud-wrapped data server
- A double helix morphing into circuit wires
- Cities floating above the Earth
- Faces lit by blue screens in dark rooms

Self-Reinforcing Memory

Narratives of disruption, genius, and scale: "Two kids in a garage" changing the world. Every new app, device, or algorithm is proof that speed, novelty, and data will always win. The world is made and remade in quarterly cycles.

Black-and-White Thinking

The old is obsolete; the new is salvation. Problems are engineering puzzles. Emotion is noise; intuition is inefficiency. Human limitations are bugs to be debugged, not mysteries to be lived.

Repetitive Behavior

- Constant upgrading, optimizing, gamifying
- Founders becoming messiahs
- Innovation pursued not for need but for domination
- Glorifying failure—as long as it's funded
- Disrupting one system while promising to save another
- Retreating into digital abstraction

Social Effects

The complex isolates human beings into data streams. It devalues tradition, embodiment, and slowness. It rewards a logic of acceleration and abstraction that can flatten empathy and democratic deliberation. While promising connection, it breeds loneliness. While preaching decentralization, it often results in monopolies of power.

Potential for Transformation

EMPOWERMENT THROUGH CONNECTIVITY

Tech has broken barriers of geography, language, and status—enabling grassroots movements, global collaborations, and marginalized voices to rise.

DEMOCRATIZATION OF KNOWLEDGE

Vast troves of information and learning tools are now accessible to billions, enabling self-education, creative innovation, and new forms of wisdom transmission.

MEDICAL MIRACLES & EXTENDED VITALITY

Breakthroughs in genetics, prosthetics, and diagnostics are prolonging and improving life with unprecedented precision and personalization.

EXPANDED HUMAN IMAGINATION

Virtual worlds, AI-generated art, and simulation tools stretch the boundaries of what the psyche can visualize, test, and embody.

PLANETARY AWARENESS

Satellite imagery, climate data, and global-systems mapping have cultivated a collective consciousness of Earth as a single, fragile, interconnected organism.

FUSION OF MYTH AND MACHINE

Tech invites a new symbolic language—cybernetic archetypes, post-human gods, and reimagined creation myths—that stimulate the evolution of culture.

INVITATION TO STEWARDSHIP

The vast power unleashed by technology forces a confrontation with moral responsibility, potentially catalyzing a new ethical consciousness around AI, ecology, and justice.

Iconography of The Algorithmic Gaze: The Disembodied Authority of the High-Tech Cultural Complex

DIGITAL BRAIN IN THE SKY

The illuminated brain in the upper sky represents collective intelligence and artificial intelligence. Its circuitry pattern frames human thought as networked, programmable, and detached from the body. Positioned like a celestial deity, it symbolizes the rise of machine cognition as a new source of omniscience and organizing power.

SATELLITE AND SURVEILLANCE SYSTEMS

A satellite hovers nearby, symbolizing global surveillance, real-time monitoring, and the control of planetary data. It reflects the High Tech cultural complex's ambition to map, predict, and influence world events with computational omnipresence.

DIGITAL TARGETING RINGS AND INTERFACE GRIDS

Concentric rings radiating across the skyline suggest data targeting, predictive modeling, and system optimization. These visual patterns portray a world perceived not through human intuition, but through metrics, geolocation, and machine vision.

GLOWING EARTH WITH DATA LATTICES

The Earth appears not as a natural planet but as a glowing orb infused with digital signals. This reflects the technocratic dream of total integration—where even planetary systems are governed by information flows, sensors, and global dashboards.

FUTURISTIC SKYSCRAPERS

Towering buildings dominate the background, symbolizing the centrality of tech capital, corporate infrastructure, and the vertical ambition of innovation culture. These structures evoke data centers, corporate headquarters, and smart cities—monuments to the new high-tech elite.

BUSINESSMAN WITH TABLET INTERFACE

In the foreground, a man holds a glowing tablet, embodying the role of the technocrat, engineer, or digital executive. His posture suggests mastery and immersion. He is both agent and instrument of a world governed by interfaces and analytics.

CHILD POINTING TOWARD THE DIGITAL SKY

A child gazes upward, hand extended toward the glowing tech symbols. This gesture embodies longing, curiosity, or silent critique. It juxtaposes wonder with marginalization, revealing how the next generation is born into the digital order—but not always invited to shape it.

ORGANIC FOREGROUND VS. TECHNO-FUTURISTIC BACKGROUND

The visual contrast between trees, rivers, and huts in the foreground and the glass towers and circuits of the background suggests the tension between natural life and digital abstraction. It evokes the question: what gets preserved, and what gets erased, in the march toward innovation?

CLOUD ICON

A literal cloud symbol floats over the skyline, referencing cloud computing and data storage. Its placement in the actual sky humorously yet hauntingly underscores the way metaphor becomes reality in a digitized world.

Interpretation

This image offers a mythic vision of the High Tech cultural complex as an all-encompassing framework: rational, efficient, expansive, and precise. Yet embedded within it are subtle reminders of what may be lost—emotional connection, ecological grounding, and intergenerational wisdom. It challenges viewers to ask not only what technology can do, but also what it means to be fully human in a world increasingly shaped by artificial intelligence and automated power.

THE TECHNO-MESSIANIC SELF

A radiant, gender-ambiguous figure stands illuminated from within, cradling a glowing orb that resembles the Earth, as circuitry-like patterns extend through their body and into the urban landscape below. Above their head, a luminous power symbol radiates like a halo, suggesting a divine fusion of human consciousness with digital omnipotence. This image reflects the High Tech cultural complex's ideal of transcendence through technology, portraying the self as both savior and interface in a data-driven cosmos.

Iconography of The Techno-Messianic Self

THE CENTRAL FIGURE (HUMAN-TECHNO SYNTHESIS)

The gender-neutral figure represents a symbolic merging of humanity and technology. It is a collective archetype rather than an individual, embodying the ideal of a transhuman future where biology and digital intelligence coalesce. The figure serves as a modern mythic stand-in for the human being transformed by and embedded in technological evolution.

GLOWING HEART CORE WITH RADIATING EARTH

At the center of the figure's chest glows a radiant orb, resembling a technological sun or a digital heart. The faint outline of Earth within it suggests that the planet itself has become internalized as data or energy. This heart is not just vital but sacred—a source of illumination and global awareness. It signifies the High Tech cultural complex's belief in information as the ultimate power.

POWER SYMBOL ABOVE THE HEAD (CROWN CHAKRA POSITION)

Hovering above the head is the universal power symbol, placed where halos or divine flames would appear in sacred art. This positions technology as a divine or animating force. The figure is not just empowered by tech; it is consecrated by it. This implies that technology now occupies the archetypal space once reserved for deities, mysticism, or cosmic truth.

CIRCUITRY AND DIGITAL GRID

Surrounding the figure is a dense network of circuitry and data patterns. These suggest omnipresence, surveillance, and the dream of complete connectivity. It illustrates the High Tech cultural complex's vision of total integration—a fully mapped, fully optimized world where information flows seamlessly and invisibly.

DARK FUTURISTIC CITYSCAPE

The background features a towering metropolis rendered in dark tones, evoking ambition, innovation, and alienation. These vertical structures resemble temples to technology—symbolizing civilization built on data, code, and relentless advancement. The absence of human figures in the cityscape suggests isolation or disembodiment, a common shadow theme in high-tech ideology.

TREE-LIKE ROOTS FLOWING DOWN FROM THE FIGURE

Despite its synthetic appearance, the figure extends glowing, root-like lines into the earth. This evokes organic imagery—the Tree of Life, neural pathways, or energy channels. These roots imply a yearning for connection, ancestry, and meaning, even within a hyper-digital paradigm. It is a subtle reminder that technological transcendence must still reckon with the need for grounding.

COLOR PALETTE (ELECTRIC BLUE AND SOLAR ORANGE)

The image contrasts cool blues (signifying reason, logic, and machine intelligence) with warm oranges and golds (suggesting power, life force, and spiritual fire). The interplay of these hues mirrors the dual nature of the High Tech cultural complex—rational yet radiant, abstract yet aspirational.

EYES CLOSED, YET FULLY ILLUMINATED

The central figure has its eyes closed, suggesting introspection, meditation, or inner sight. And yet the entire body glows with awareness. This reflects the idea of an inner awakening through digital enlightenment—technology as not only external tool, but also as internal revelation.

Interpretation

This image casts the High Tech cultural complex as a new religious and mythic vision of human identity. It portrays technology not only as a tool but also as a redemptive and transformative force. The human becomes divine through digital means, centered in power, connected to data, and illuminated from within. It captures both the utopian promise and potential hubris of the belief that technology can heal, evolve, or even transcend limitations.

CHAPTER 3

The Many Forms of American Discrimination as Cultural Complexes

The American Indigenous Peoples Cultural Complex

The American Immigrant Cultural Complex

The Anti-Immigrant Cultural Complex

The Anti-Black Cultural Complex

The Anti-Latino Cultural Complex

The Anti-Asian Cultural Complex

The Anti-Semitic Cultural Complex

The Holocaust Denial Cultural Complex

The White Supremacy Cultural Complex

The Anti-White Cultural Complex

The Minority Cultural Complex

Many cultural complexes tend to break into bipolar opposites that can lead to the intense polarization we are experiencing now. In our field guide it is useful at times to identify each one of such bipolar pairs separately as well as recognize that they are two opposite sides of the same thing. I will follow that process in describing the Immigration cultural complex and its opposite in the Anti-Immigration cultural complex as well as with some of the other cultural complexes that are currently so powerfully polarizing in the battleground of the contemporary American psyche.

THE AMERICAN INDIGENOUS PEOPLES CULTURAL COMPLEX

TENDING THE FIRE OF MEMORY: THE ELDER, THE SEED, AND THE SPIRITS WHO GUIDE

In the glowing firelight of a wounded land, an elder communes with ancestral spirits and animal guides. From the drum of memory, a tender green shoot rises—an offering of renewal rooted in grief and remembrance.

Core Emotion: Grief Interwoven with Ancestral Resilience

This complex holds a deep emotional undercurrent of sorrow for land loss, erasure, and generational trauma—countered by a tenacious will to survive, remember, and regenerate.

Mythic Root: The Sacred Bond Between Land, Spirit, and People

Rooted in origin stories of place-based cosmologies, where earth, sky, and kinship form an interconnected web, the complex recalls a time before dispossession, when the land was not a commodity but a living relative.

Symbolic Imagery

- The broken treaty
- The weeping earth
- The sacred hoop (circle of life)
- The ghost dance
- A figure straddling two worlds—one ancestral, one modern
- A flame that endures in darkness
- The returning bison
- Water protectors standing firm

Self-Reinforcing Memory

This complex is anchored in centuries of forced removals, boarding schools, massacres (e.g., Wounded Knee), broken promises, and cultural silencing. But it is also sustained by intergenerational transmission of stories, ceremonies, and resistance—from the Trail of Tears to Standing Rock.

Black-and-White Thinking

- Modernity vs. Tradition
- Civilized vs. Savage
- Erased vs. Eternal

These binaries distort both history and identity, forcing Indigenous peoples into narrow roles—either as vanished victims or romanticized relics—denying the multiplicity and vitality of living cultures.

Repetitive Behavior

- Cycles of state neglect followed by symbolic gestures
- Public celebration of myths (e.g., Thanksgiving) that obscure Indigenous suffering
- Extractive projects imposed without consent
- Appropriation of Indigenous spirituality while ignoring Indigenous sovereignty

Social Effects

This complex tears the cultural fabric by marginalizing Indigenous voices in national identity, legislation, and environmental stewardship. It fragments Native communities through cultural loss, jurisdictional confusion, and socioeconomic disenfranchisement—while simultaneously fostering guilt, denial, or romantic projection in the dominant culture.

Potential for Transformation

Renewal lies in the reassertion of Indigenous sovereignty, land rights, language revitalization, and cross-cultural healing. When the wisdom of Indigenous stewardship is recognized not as relic but as guide, this complex becomes a bridge: offering pathways toward ecological balance, communal responsibility, and a reimagined American identity rooted in repair and mutual respect.

Iconography of Tending the Fire of Memory: The Elder, the Seed, and the Spirits Who Guide

ELDER WITH BRAIDS

The lines in his face and the downward gaze express sorrow and gravity. He carries the grief of a people, not as burden alone, but as sacred witness. His listening becomes an act of mourning and resistance.

DRUM WITH GREEN SPROUT

The drum is both memory and mourning—its surface a burial ground and a seedbed. The sprouting green seedling symbolizes regeneration not in spite of grief, but through it. It brings continuity and ancestral knowledge rooted in the earth.

CAMPFIRE SMOKE

The smoke carries more than prayer—it carries the ache of what has been lost. Its spiraling path binds the visible and invisible worlds. The fire's smoke rises upward, transforming into ancestral spirits and animal guides. The fire connects earth and sky, body and spirit, past and future.

ANCESTRAL SPIRITS IN SMOKE

Emanating from the smoke are faces of Indigenous ancestors, bearing expressions of watchfulness, sorrow, and quiet strength. They represent cultural memory and grief carried through generations Their solemn faces reflect lives cut short, traditions disrupted, yet spirits unbroken. They do not vanish—they remain, present in sorrow, strength, and stillness.

ANIMAL SPIRITS IN SMOKE

These guides emerge through the haze of grief, not as symbols of conquest or control, but of continuity—each embodying traits that have helped Indigenous communities endure loss.

A *buffalo* (abundance and endurance), a *wolf* (instinct and kinship), a *wildcat* (intuition and stealth), and an *eagle* flying into the sun (vision and higher guidance) emerge in glowing smoke. A *serpent's head* appears near the elder's forehead—subtle yet potent—embodying healing, transformation, and wisdom. Its emergence from the smoke symbolizes the sacred medicine of Indigenous traditions and the cyclical shedding of skin, invoking renewal.

BURNT FOREST AND TWILIGHT

The landscape speaks wordlessly of loss and devastation, echoing the grief of colonization, displacement, and environmental destruction. The glowing twilight offers no false hope—but within it, a quiet vow suggesting rebirth and sacred resilience. What can still be reclaimed will be.

Interpretation

This image reveals the American Indigenous Peoples cultural complex as one shaped by profound grief—grief for stolen land, silenced voices, broken treaties, and nearly lost languages. And yet, the image insists that this grief is not the end. It is sacred, ancestral, and active. The elder's presence is an act of devotion, tending the memory of what was and planting what may yet become. The elder is not only tending a fire but also nurturing memory, identity, and future renewal. From the flames rise ancestors and spirit animals—guides in a liminal space where grief and reverence coexist. The snake is not hidden, but elevated—evoking the sacred medicine of transformation. Its presence affirms that healing comes from facing grief, honoring it, and transforming it into guidance, not from forgetting it. Together, all figures—human and animal—form a circle of guardianship, linking earth and sky, death and renewal. The image honors Indigenous traditions as bearers of grief, power, and sacred continuity.

THE AMERICAN IMMIGRANT CULTURAL COMPLEX

AT THE THRESHOLD OF HOPE AND EXCLUSION

A vast crowd of migrants surges toward a barbed-wire fence beneath a stark sign reading "IMMIGRATION ENTERING U.S." Arms stretch skyward in desperation and longing, faces etched with fear, urgency, and silent plea. The fence becomes more than a barrier—it is a psychic threshold between promise and denial, belonging and abandonment. This image distills the emotional power of the Immigrant cultural complex: the dream of arrival, the trauma of rejection, and the mythic struggle for entry into the American story.

The American Immigrant cultural complex is rooted in both aspiration and alienation. It is shaped by the powerful myth of America as a land of opportunity and reinvention—and the lived reality of dislocation, struggle, and often rejection. This complex lives at the intersection of becoming and belonging, infused with longing, sacrifice, resilience, and a search for dignity.

Core Emotion: Hope Carried Through Hardship

The dominant emotion is a fusion of hope, anxiety, and determination—the psychic fuel to survive uprooting, rejection, and marginalization while chasing a better life. Immigrants often carry forward belief in possibility even in the face of hardship, invisibility, or exclusion.

Mythic Root: The Pilgrim, the Exile, the Alchemist, the Bridge-Builder

This complex carries archetypes of sacred journeyers and survivors. There is the pilgrim in search of freedom, the exile who is cast out and wandering, the alchemist who transforms suffering into cultural wealth, and the bridge-builder who unites divided worlds. These mythic figures provide psychological meaning to the dislocation and courage of immigration.

Symbolic Imagery

- The Statue of Liberty and Ellis Island
- Suitcases, border fences, and bridges
- Kitchen altars with old-country saints alongside the flag of the new country
- Pictures of children translating for their parents
- Bilingual prayers, recipes, lullabies

These images capture both loss and reinvention, the preservation of heritage within unfamiliar surroundings, and the layered identities that emerge from straddling two cultures.

Self-Reinforcing Memory

The immigrant story—of arrival, toil, and triumph—is told and passed down across generations, often alongside the trauma of war, poverty, and persecution. Institutional memories of quotas, discrimination, and scapegoating endure. Many live between the memory of being "too foreign" for America and "too American" for the homeland. In addition, there is the inheritance of the binary attitude of scarcity versus abundance that can be intergenerationally transmitted in immigrant families. This assumed attitude of scarcity causes individuals to perpetually be in survivor mode, or to feel they must self-deprive, or to act as if resources are scarce even when they or their families have achieved stability, perhaps for decades. It's akin to holding on to a depression-era mentality in those who survived the Great Depression of the 1930s. It is the melancholia of immigration.

Black-and-White Thinking

Within the immigrant experience itself, there can be internalized black-and-white thinking born of survival and cultural pressure:

- "I must prove I belong" vs. "They will never accept me"
- "Success equals safety" vs. "Visibility invites danger"
- "Assimilate completely" vs. "Stay loyal to my roots"
- "Hard work is everything" vs. "The system is rigged"

These polarized beliefs may shape identity development, family dynamics, and attitudes toward both homeland and host country.

Repetitive Behavior

Immigrants often navigate cycles of welcoming and scapegoating, security and suspicion. Generational divides emerge around visibility and safety. Many feel they must constantly prove their loyalty or worth. Narratives of exceptional success are used to shield against ongoing experiences of systemic exclusion.

Social Effects

The tension between assimilation and heritage can create rifts within families and communities. The complex may reproduce hierarchies between different immigrant groups and contribute to internalized shame or a sense of perpetual outsider status. Immigrant communities are also vulnerable to political manipulation and scapegoating, particularly in times of social unrest or economic insecurity.

Potential for Transformation

When integrated, the Immigrant cultural complex becomes a wellspring of renewal:

CULTURAL ENRICHMENT
Food, language, music, and tradition expand the American soul.

RESILIENCE AND INNOVATION
Generations that overcome instability become engines of creativity and enterprise.

MORAL MIRROR

Immigrant lives reflect the gap between America's ideals and practices, pushing the nation to evolve.

GLOBAL CONSCIOUSNESS

Immigrant identities foster cross-cultural empathy and planetary awareness.

SPIRITUAL DEPTH

Journeys of displacement deepen faith, humility, and reverence for origin.

COLLECTIVE RENEWAL

Immigrants often revitalize cities, industries, and institutions that had fallen into decline.

In this frame, the immigrant becomes not only a subject of debate, but also a bearer of future possibility and shared transformation.

Iconography of At the Threshold of Hope and Exclusion

CHAIN-LINK FENCE TOPPED WITH BARBED WIRE (CENTER)

A menacing and inescapable symbol of exclusion, the fence visually separates longing from possibility. The barbed wire suggests not only physical danger but also psychological hostility—a warning that entry may come at great cost, or not at all. The fence divides worlds: freedom and confinement, hope and despair, inside and outside the myth of America.

THE CROWD PRESSED AGAINST THE FENCE (FOREGROUND AND MIDGROUND)

A vast mass of people—diverse in expression, yet uniform in their direction—push forward with uplifted hands. Their gestures embody desperation, yearning, exhaustion, and determination. Their individual faces convey personal stories of sorrow, fear, and resolve. Together, they form a symbolic wave of human will—the unstoppable force of migration born of suffering and hope.

THE SIGN "IMMIGRATION ENTERING U.S." (LEFT FOREGROUND)

Bold and bureaucratic, the sign states the situation in the bluntest possible terms. Yet its mechanical tone contrasts sharply with the emotional intensity surrounding it. The sterile wording underscores how systemic language often masks human struggle. It marks this as both a real border and a psychic threshold—the boundary between rejection and belonging.

WARM YELLOW SKY (BACKGROUND)

The golden light evokes an ambiguous emotional register. Is it dawn or dusk? Is this the promise of arrival or the fading of a dream? The sky's glow also reflects the mythic aura of the American Dream—still present, still believed in, even as access to it narrows.

VISUAL COMPRESSION & CLUSTERING (COMPOSITION)

The densely packed bodies and uniform blue-gray clothing reflect anonymity and shared burdens. The crowd appears endless, extending beyond the frame—conveying both the scale of global displacement and America's perceived centrality as a destination. The visual pressure illustrates urgency, history, and systemic bottlenecking.

Interpretation

This image of the American Immigrant cultural complex is not triumphant or welcoming; it is conflicted, volatile, and emotionally saturated. It represents

- Hope met by hardness
- Mass yearning thwarted by systemic resistance
- The myth of opportunity colliding with the reality of border enforcement

It reveals a cultural complex in which immigration is not just a policy matter but also a national identity fracture point—where who belongs, who threatens, and who uplifts the nation is debated in symbolic and literal terms.

THE WELLSPRING OF RENEWAL: THE IMMIGRANT CULTURAL COMPLEX

A family stands beside a flowing fountain before the US Capitol, which is bathed in golden light. The boy holds a clay vessel, ready to fill it from the public source—a symbol of hope, sustenance, and civic belonging. The family gazes forward with quiet strength, their posture dignified, their presence rooted yet expectant. Behind them, the Capitol glows, not as a symbol of power alone, but of promise—a structure that, at its best, can hold space for new life, new stories, and new beginnings. This image evokes the mythic core of the Immigrant cultural complex: the journey from exile to belonging, from survival to participation, from marginalization to renewal.

Iconography of The Wellspring of Renewal: The Immigrant Cultural Complex

THE FAMILY (FOREGROUND)

Embody resilience, aspiration, and generational continuity. Their gathered unity represents both vulnerability and strength, evoking archetypes of pilgrimage and covenant.

THE BOY WITH THE CLAY VESSEL

A symbol of receptivity and renewal. The unfilled pot suggests the immigrant's longing for participation, dignity, and spiritual nourishment from the civic wellspring. They carry ancestral form—earthy, old-world—toward new waters.

THE FOUNTAIN (MIDDLE GROUND)

Flowing water is the archetypal symbol of life, purification, and possibility. The fountain represents America's idealized promise—abundance, democratic access, and healing.

THE CAPITOL DOME (BACKGROUND)

A towering icon of national identity and governance. It looms like a temple—imposing yet luminous—offering both shelter and judgment. It evokes both *E Pluribus Unum* and the conditional welcome of the state.

WARM LIGHT AND OPEN SKY

A mythic glow of optimism and transcendence. The golden palette recalls religious iconography, suggesting a sacredness to the immigrant story within the nation's civic imagination.

POSTURE AND DIRECTION OF GAZE

The family looks slightly upward and forward—toward something just beyond the viewer's sight—evoking both hope and the unknown. Their presence demands recognition, not pity; dignity, not assimilation.

Interpretation

This image frames the Immigration cultural complex as a sacred path to renewal. An immigrant family approaches a radiant fountain before the US Capitol, symbolizing civic vitality and the founding ideals. The child reaching forward evokes innocence and hope, suggesting immigrants offer not just need, but also revitalization. The image asks whether America will embrace this promise and allow its identity to thrive through those who still believe in it.

THE ANTI-IMMIGRANT CULTURAL COMPLEX

GUARDING THE WALL OF SHADOWS

A lone officer stands defiantly at a prison-like gate embedded in a patriotic stone wall. Symbols of national power—the eagle, the flag, the shield—loom above, while the wall itself casts shadows of a detained immigrant family, reduced to silhouettes of longing and separation. Even when bodies are denied entry, shadows persist—cast by presence, memory, and the stories that won't stay outside. Below, the earth cracks wide in a parched, barren divide. This image captures the emotional core of the Anti-Immigrant cultural complex: fear disguised as security, protection enacted through exclusion, and the moral cost of turning human lives into shadows behind bars.

Core Emotion: Fear of Loss and Contamination

At its emotional center is anxiety—about displacement, dilution, and being overwhelmed. The fear is not only of the foreign other, but also of the unraveling of a perceived cultural center or national identity. Beneath this fear lies a longing for familiarity, continuity, and protection.

Mythic Root: The Fortress Under Siege and the Garden at Risk

This complex draws from archetypes of the walled city, the homeland under threat, and the pure soil invaded by strangers. It sees the nation as a sacred space—ethnically, culturally, or spiritually "ours"—now vulnerable to outsiders who are cast as chaotic, corrupting, or undeserving.

Symbolic Imagery

- Walls and fences stretching across barren land
- A flood of faceless figures spilling over a crumbling border
- A garden with unfamiliar vines growing over its gate
- A family behind barred windows watching silhouettes approach
- Lady Liberty extinguishing her torch
- A national flag being tugged in two directions

Self-Reinforcing Memory

The complex draws on narratives of past invasions, betrayals, and perceived overreach—both real and imagined. It invokes stories of jobs lost, neighborhoods changed, and values eroded. Selective memory highlights danger while erasing histories of integration, labor, and contribution.

Black-and-White Thinking

The world is split between citizen and alien, builder and taker, legal and illegal, patriot and threat. There is little tolerance for ambiguity—no room for nuance around migration causes, complexity of identity, or moral dilemmas.

Repetitive Behavior

- Rallying behind slogans like "build the wall"
- Tightening borders
- Scapegoating newcomers
- Amplifying crime stories involving immigrants
- Repeating tropes of national "purity" and demographic decline

These behaviors assert control over the imagined boundaries of culture and geography.

Social Effects

This complex fragments multicultural societies, sowing suspicion and hostility. It stokes nationalist and ethnocentric ideologies, often leading to policies and rhetoric that dehumanize. It also turns inward, suppressing empathy and stunting the national imagination. And yet, at its root, it reflects a distorted longing—for rootedness, identity, and coherence in a rapidly changing world.

Potential for Transformation

The Anti-Immigrant cultural complex, though often regressive in its expression, carries within it a deep desire for belonging, coherence, and cultural continuity. When acknowledged and reoriented, this longing can foster:

COMMUNITY PRESERVATION THROUGH INCLUSION

A renewed appreciation for cultural identity that welcomes enrichment rather than fearing erasure.

RESPECT FOR LAW AND ORDER WITH COMPASSION

Policy rooted in fairness and humanity, not fear or exclusion.

EMPATHY THROUGH ENCOUNTER

Personal relationships with immigrants that dissolve stereotypes and humanize the "other."

SHARED VALUES ACROSS DIFFERENCE

Recognition that family, faith, work, and safety are often common ground, not points of division.

NARRATIVES OF INTEGRATION AND CONTRIBUTION

Highlighting real stories of immigrants strengthening local communities, institutions, and the national fabric.

Redemption lies not in abandoning the desire for cohesion, but in expanding its definition to include all who contribute, belong, and seek a future together. This transformation can turn defensive fear into grounded generosity, and isolation into shared resilience

Iconography of Guarding the Wall of Shadows

THE GUARD (RIGHT)

A stone-faced figure stands arms crossed, blocking a doorway as if he were the embodiment of national willpower. He personifies the defensive stance of the anti-immigrant complex—unyielding, alert, and emotionally sealed.

THE FORTRESS WALL (CENTER)

Decorated with patriotic emblems—a bald eagle, an American flag, and a heraldic shield—this wall claims legitimacy through nationalism. But its surface becomes a screen upon which deeper truths are cast.

TWO SETS OF SHADOWED FAMILIES (CENTER LEFT)

These dual shadows represent two psychic layers of the immigrant experience:

Foreground Shadows: Younger figures, closer to the guard, symbolize contemporary immigrants—children and families whose presence is immediate yet politically invisible.

Background Shadows: Larger figures towering behind suggest ancestral memory, historical waves of immigration, or even the projected fears of the nation itself. They remind us that immigration is not just a policy issue—it is a mirror of American origins and its recurring anxieties.

CRACKED EARTH (BOTTOM LEFT)

The parched, broken ground symbolizes both environmental and moral desiccation. It evokes the emotional toll and societal rupture when empathy is replaced by exclusion.

SPROUTING VINES BENEATH THE SHADOWS

Life still grows beneath the wall. These subtle organic elements suggest that connection and renewal are not fully extinguished—they remain latent, waiting.

Interpretation

This image portrays the Anti-Immigrant cultural complex as a cycle of projection and denial. Immigrant families cast dual shadows—representing both today's migrants and America's own immigrant past. The wall becomes a screen for disowning origins, raising the question: When we build barriers, are we blocking people—or parts of ourselves that we've forgotten yet still haunt us?

THE ANTI-BLACK CULTURAL COMPLEX

THE SHADOW OF SURVEILLANCE: IN CHAINS PAST AND PRESENT

This image captures the enduring psychic burden of the Anti-Black Cultural Complex: a Black man stands at the center, bound in iron chains, his gaze unflinching. Behind him, a spectral figure of an enslaved ancestor and a modern police cruiser bracket him in history—linking past captivity with present control. The man's expression reflects neither resignation nor rage, but a deep and weary knowledge: that freedom is still contested ground.

Core Emotion: Fear and Dehumanization

At the heart of the Anti-Black cultural complex lies a deeply ingrained fear—of the other, of vengeance, of loss of control—projected onto Black bodies and communities. This fear is paired with a long-standing cultural habit of dehumanization, reducing Black individuals to symbols of danger, defiance, or lack. It often masks itself in paternalism, avoidance, or denial, but its emotional core is anxiety about power and proximity.

Mythic Root: The Savage and the Threatened Order

This complex draws on archetypes of the "wild man," the outsider who must be controlled and the fragile civilization that must be protected from chaos. In the American imagination, this myth took shape during slavery and was later reinscribed through Reconstruction fears, Jim Crow segregation, and modern depictions of urban decay. It functions like a haunted mirror: the projected shadow of white violence, disavowed and reattributed to Blackness.

Symbolic Imagery

- Chains, both literal and invisible
- A figure behind bars, or constantly surveilled
- A Black man surrounded by flashing red and blue lights
- The angry protester misread as a criminal
- A school where the curriculum omits the soul
- An auction block casting a long shadow into a courtroom, a hospital, a neighborhood

Self-Reinforcing Memory

Historical atrocities—slavery, lynching, redlining, mass incarceration—form a legacy of terror and subjugation that continues to inform the cultural unconscious. These memories are rarely acknowledged fully in the dominant culture, leading to repetition and reenactment. Invisibility and over visibility coexist: Black Americans are hyper-policed and underrepresented, simultaneously scapegoated and erased.

Black-and-White Thinking

This complex operates through racial essentialism: Blackness is conflated with danger, failure, or deficiency, whereas whiteness is aligned with order and virtue. It imposes narrow roles: the thug, the entertainer, the exception. Nuance is flattened. It also creates internal splits in the Black psyche—between assimilation and resistance, visibility and safety, anger and endurance.

Repetitive Behavior

- Stereotyping
- Policing of expression
- Pathologizing cultural traits
- Tokenization
- Silence in the face of microaggressions
- The cyclical rise and backlash of racial justice movements
- Policies that appear race-neutral but have racialized impact
- A media ecosystem that amplifies Black suffering but rarely Black joy

Social Effects

The Anti-Black cultural complex erodes the civic and psychological health of society. It fosters systemic inequality, mistrust, and social fragmentation. It constrains Black identity within oppressive frames, while fostering denial and defensiveness among others. This complex sabotages genuine dialogue, undermines coalition-building, and perpetuates racial hierarchies through implicit bias, institutional inertia, and cultural erasure.

Potential for Transformation

When made conscious, this complex reveals the unresolved trauma at the root of American identity. Its transformation requires collective shadow work—facing what has been projected, disowned, and violently externalized. The gift embedded in this complex is the possibility of reckoning: a more honest national memory, a new language for dignity, and a healing of the body politic. Black cultural creativity—music, theology, poetry, resistance—can become not only a survival tool but also a cultural compass, guiding the way toward a society that is not simply post-racial, but post-denial.

Iconography for The Shadow of Surveillance: In Chains Past and Present

CENTRAL FIGURE IN CHAINS

A modern Black man bound by heavy chains, yet standing tall and alert. His body is restricted, but his gaze is firm, suggesting dignity, endurance, and unbreakable presence.

SPECTRAL ANCESTOR BEHIND

A ghostly, enslaved figure in similar chains links the historical trauma of slavery to the present, suggesting the transmission of suffering across generations.

POLICE CAR WITH FLASHING LIGHTS

Represents modern institutional control—incarceration, surveillance, and the continuing criminalization of Black bodies.

CRACKED, ARID EARTH

A barren psychological landscape shaped by centuries of oppression, loss, and struggle.

MUTED GOLD PALETTE

Invokes both sacredness and mourning—honoring ancestral suffering while revealing the cost of surviving under systemic weight.

Interpretation

This image depicts the Anti-Black cultural complex as a chain linking slavery to modern racism and surveillance. The spectral figure and police vehicle symbolize historical and institutional continuity. Yet the central figure's upright stance resists erasure, embodying both the burden and strength of survival.

THE ANTI-LATINO CULTURAL COMPLEX

ROOTS OF MEMORY, PATH OF BECOMING

A Latino family walks hand in hand beneath a tree heavy with cultural fruit—music, faith, knowledge, and labor—toward a horizon where identity and justice remain contested. On one side, ancestral faces emerge from stone near a border wall; on the other, the fractured monument labeled "Americano" reflects the pressure to assimilate and the pain of erasure.

Overhead, the scales of justice teeter between welcome and exclusion, while an eagle and dove circle in symbolic opposition. This image captures the soul of the Anti-Latino cultural complex: a journey shaped by memory, struggle, and the longing to belong without losing one's name.

Core Emotion: "The Borderline Between Belonging and Exclusion"

At the core of the Anti-Latino cultural complex is a potent combination of anxiety, resentment, and projection. This complex is animated by fears of demographic change, cultural dilution, and economic competition, often expressed through racialized anxieties about borders, language, and national identity. The emotional charge is intensified by a sense of territorial threat—fears that what was once "ours" is being overtaken or redefined.

Mythic Root: The Outsider Within

This complex draws on mythic narratives of civilization's defense and the "outsider within." The figure of the Latino immigrant is often cast as the invader, the burden, or the infiltrator—a symbol of both danger and desire. It echoes older American myths of Manifest Destiny, inverted: now the land is being "taken back" or "overrun." The archetype of the eternal foreigner persists even across generations, denying Latinos the right to be seen as fully American, regardless of citizenship, contribution, or lineage.

Symbolic Imagery

Symbolic representations include

- A wall dividing lush land from desert—order from chaos
- Families in cages or under surveillance, evoking themes of dehumanization
- Brown hands reaching through fences
- Street vendors juxtaposed with border patrols
- The Virgin of Guadalupe weeping behind headlines
- Spanish-language signs defaced or replaced
- A map of the United States with southern parts darkened or erased

These images communicate both marginalization and resilience, visibility and erasure.

Self-Reinforcing Memory

This complex draws on a layered historical memory:

- The Mexican-American and subsequent land annexation
- Anti-Latino violence in the early twentieth century
- The Bracero Program followed by mass deportations
- Ongoing narratives of invasion, crime, and assimilation failure

These memories resurface cyclically, often during election cycles or moments of social upheaval. Policies and rhetoric reinforce a sense of perpetual suspicion, even as Latinos continue to build, serve, and shape the country.

Black-and-White Thinking

Latino identity is reduced to stark opposites:

- Legal vs. illegal
- Good immigrant vs. criminal
- Assimilated vs. "ungrateful"
- Invisible laborer vs. cultural threat

This dualism collapses the complex realities of Latino lives and cultures into simplistic binaries that justify exclusion, neglect, or scapegoating.

Repetitive Behavior

The complex repeats in cycles:

- Moral panics over immigration "waves" or "caravans"
- Calls to build walls or militarize borders
- Mass deportations framed as justice
- Politicization of language, bilingual education, and Latin American foreign policy
- Tokenization followed by silencing in national discourse

Even moments of inclusion are often followed by backlash, reinforcing a sense that belonging is always conditional.

Social Effects

The Anti-Latino cultural complex fractures communities by othering millions who are integral to the social, cultural, and economic fabric of the country. It creates layers of conditional Americanness, eroding trust in institutions and pitting groups against one another in a false scarcity narrative. It distorts public policy, encourages surveillance and policing of ethnicity, and breeds internalized shame and generational trauma. Ultimately, it weakens the nation's capacity for pluralism and shared destiny.

Potential for Transformation

RECLAMATION OF NARRATIVE

Latinos across the US continue to tell their stories, document their histories, and assert their identities beyond the limits imposed by the complex.

INTERGENERATIONAL SOLIDARITY

Cultural memory, spiritual symbols, and community rituals serve as sources of resilience, defying the erasure imposed by dominant narratives.

EXPANSION OF AMERICANNESS

The presence and contributions of Latinos challenge narrow definitions of who belongs, offering a more dynamic, multilingual, and multicultural vision of the nation.

COLLECTIVE AWAKENING

Confronting this complex invites a deeper reckoning with the legacy of conquest, colonization, and racial hierarchy—and opens the possibility of a more just and integrated society.

Iconography of Roots of Memory, Path of Becoming

This symbolic image expresses the psychological and cultural dynamics of the Anti-Latino Cultural Complex. Each element works on multiple levels—emotional, historical, and archetypal—to reveal how exclusion and resilience shape the Latino experience in America.

CENTRAL FIGURES

LATINO FAMILY WALKING FORWARD (MOTHER, FATHER, CHILD)

The trio symbolizes the generational arc of migration—past, present, and future. They walk hand-in-hand on a cracked desert floor, suggesting hardship and resilience. Their forward movement evokes dignity, survival, and the assertion of belonging despite social and political barriers.

SURROUNDING ENVIRONMENT & BACKGROUND

CRACKED GROUND

The fractured earth beneath their feet reflects both physical desolation (e.g., borderlands, displacement) and metaphorical rupture—a society fragmented by exclusion, prejudice, and cultural denial.

FACES IN THE ROCKS AND WALLS (ON BOTH SIDES)

These spectral, carved faces represent ancestors, erased histories, and generations of marginalized Latino presences. They flank the family like witnesses and guardians of cultural memory—both mourning and blessing their journey.

LEFT SIDE SYMBOLISM (EXCLUSION AND SURVEILLANCE)

STEEL BORDER FENCE

The vertical bars evoke imprisonment, separation, and systemic exclusion. The faceless shadows behind the fence reinforce dehumanization and the reality of border policing, detention, and restriction.

BLACK EAGLE (UPPER LEFT)

A dark and menacing symbol of corrupted sovereignty or predatory nationalism. It suggests surveillance, aggression, and fear-based policies aimed at Latino communities.

CENTERPIECE: TREE OF CULTURAL MEMORY AND CONTRIBUTION

Ornaments include musical instruments, corn, tools, religious icons, and domestic objects. This golden tree represents Latino cultural richness, ancestral gifts, labor, and contributions to American life. Its central placement implies that Latino identity is not peripheral but vital to the American story.

CHILDREN PLAYING BENEATH THE TREE

The presence of children suggests continuity, innocence, and a living future. Their play signifies joy and potential renewal amid adversity.

RIGHT SIDE SYMBOLISM (RECOGNITION AND STRUGGLE FOR INCLUSION)

The cracked "Americano" statue symbolizes the fractured ideal of American identity as it relates to Latino belonging. The broken monument critiques the illusion of a unified American identity. The inscription emphasizes the paradox of being considered both central and foreign. The fractured form symbolizes exclusion, assimilation pressure, and the contested boundaries of Americanness.

Fragility of Inclusion: The statue represents how Latino identity has historically been both integral to and excluded from the American narrative. Its cracked form shows that the image of who is considered "American" is not whole or universally shared.

Erosion by Time and Fire: One side is worn down by time—representing generational neglect, historical amnesia, and the erasure of Latino contributions. The other is scorched by fire—symbolizing resentment, backlash, and cultural hostility, often ignited during political upheaval.

False Universality: Its classical form may echo European or settler ideals of citizenship and legitimacy, implying that Latino identity doesn't quite *fit* within the dominant myth—hence the breaking.

Moral Crisis: The damage suggests a nation at odds with itself, unsure whether it will embrace a pluralistic future or retreat into exclusionary nostalgia.

FACES EMERGING FROM THE STONE

Echoing the ancestral faces on the left, these carved figures humanize the struggle for belonging. They may represent those who resist erasure and carry the memory of struggle into visibility.

UPPER ELEMENTS: MYTH AND JUSTICE IN CONFLICT

BLINDFOLDED LADY JUSTICE HOLDING SCALES

The scales bear two US passports—one tipping downward, the other elevated—highlighting the unequal weight of belonging and legality. The blindfold, traditionally a symbol of impartiality, here also represents willful blindness to structural injustice.

DOVE AND BLACK EAGLE

Symbols of peace and predation, respectively. The dove near the cracked statue signifies hope for justice and reconciliation. The eagle's looming presence reinforces themes of threat and power imbalance.

COLOR AND LIGHTING

WARM GOLDEN CENTER VERSUS COOL GRAY PERIPHERIES

The warm central light surrounds the family and the tree of culture, emphasizing vitality, spiritual resilience, and creative force. Cooler, shadowed tones dominate the outer regions—suggesting alienation, surveillance, and systemic marginalization.

Interpretation

This visual allegory dramatizes the spiritual and social borderland that defines the Anti-Latino cultural complex—where erasure and resilience coexist, and where the path forward is walked in defiant hope.

THE ANTI-ASIAN CULTURAL COMPLEX

HAUNTED BY SHADOWS, HOLDING THE LINE

At the center of a storm of caricature, silence, and fear, an Asian American girl stands with quiet strength. Around her swirl grotesque stereotypes—"Yellow Peril," "Disease," "Closed"—echoes of slurs, scapegoating, and erasure. Behind her, a grieving mother shields a child beside images of internment, protest, and paper cranes—symbols of both past trauma and fragile hope. This image reveals the Anti-Asian cultural complex as a struggle between invisibility and dignity, survival and resistance, memory and transformation.

Core Emotion: Suspicion, Resentment, and Insecurity

At the heart of the Anti-Asian cultural complex is a deep-seated mixture of suspicion, resentment, and projected insecurity. Asian Americans have long been perceived as simultaneously invisible and threatening, subjected to emotional reactions ranging from exotic fascination to dehumanizing fear. In times of national stress—economic downturns, pandemics, wars—this complex flares into overt hostility, fueled by anxiety about the Other and displaced aggression. The emotional core is often ambivalence: admiration laced with envy, curiosity poisoned by fear.

Mythic Root: Foreignness, Invasion, Contagion

The complex is rooted in enduring myths of foreignness, invasion, and contagion. Asian bodies are symbolically cast as perpetual outsiders, regardless of how many generations have lived in the US. It draws on archetypes such as the Yellow Peril (the idea of an unstoppable Eastern horde), the inscrutable enemy, and the model minority as double agent—a seemingly obedient, successful figure who is secretly subversive or disloyal. These myths frame Asian Americans as cultural mimics, not full members of the national body.

Symbolic Imagery

The imagery associated with this complex is often contradictory:

- Masked faces interpreted as symbols of secrecy or disease
- Asian students excelling in school, then caricatured as robotic or soulless
- Martial arts, dragons, pagodas—used to aestheticize while flattening cultural identity
- During crises, imagery shifts to threats: bats, viruses, red flags, spies
- The figure of the "good immigrant" weaponized to divide communities

Symbolically, the Asian American is rendered either hypervisible (as threat or token) or erased—never simply human.

Self-Reinforcing Memory

Historical events like the Chinese Exclusion Act, the Japanese internment camps, and the Vietnam War live on in the American psyche, often repressed but unconsciously reenacted. During the COVID-19 pandemic, rhetoric about the "China virus" or "Kung flu" tapped into a deep reservoir of racialized fear, recalling earlier tropes of Asians as vectors of disease or duplicity. These moments reinforce the idea that Asian Americans can be turned on at any time, no matter how assimilated they seem. The complex renews itself through periodic scapegoating, with memory weaponized rather than healed.

Black-and-White Thinking

This complex flattens Asian identity into simplistic stereotypes and dualisms:

- "Good" vs. "bad" immigrant
- "Quiet, hardworking" vs. "ruthless competitor"
- "Grateful minority" vs. "ungrateful protester"
- "Honorary white" vs. "foreign invader"

Asian men tend to be viewed as weak and effeminate by non-Asians, whereas Asian women tend to be viewed as either submissive, exotic sex objects or as dragon ladies by non-Asians. These caricatures, like the Sambos and Aunt Jemima projected onto Black people, say more about the projectors than the projected upon. Such dichotomies dehumanize and instrumentalize. They demand that Asian Americans perform gratitude, suppress complaint, and accept marginalization in exchange for provisional acceptance. Nuance and individuality are stripped away, replaced by stereotype.

Repetitive Behavior

The complex reemerges in predictable, cyclic patterns, often triggered by geopolitical or domestic crises:

- A spike in hate crimes after 9/11, COVID-19, or tensions with China or North Korea
- Surveillance and suspicion of Asian scientists, students, or public figures

- Media depictions swinging from fetishization to fear
- Erasure in conversations about race—followed by sudden hypervisibility, usually in the context of violence

The pattern is oscillatory: inclusion and admiration are withdrawn when convenience or comfort dictates, revealing a deeper, unresolved hostility.

Social Effects

This cultural complex undermines solidarity, fractures racial justice movements, and silences the lived realities of millions. It positions Asian Americans as forever adjacent to Americanness—included, but never fully belonging. It damages mental health, civic trust, and intergenerational identity. By holding Asian Americans to impossible standards of performance, assimilation, or silence, it creates internalized pressure and alienation. And by casting them as either enemy or pet, it denies full personhood.

Potential for Transformation

Despite its destructive elements, the Anti-Asian cultural complex also contains energies that, if consciously engaged, can catalyze resilience, clarity, and collective healing.

VISIBILITY AND VOICE

Breaking the cycle of invisibility allows Asian Americans to narrate their own histories—not only as victims or model citizens, but also as complex, multidimensional beings.

SOLIDARITY ACROSS DIFFERENCE

When the myth of separateness is dismantled, coalitions can form across racial and ethnic lines to challenge the deeper forces of xenophobia, nationalism, and white supremacy.

CULTURAL INTEGRITY AND INNOVATION

Instead of conforming to stereotypes, Asian American communities continue to generate rich artistic, intellectual, and political contributions that expand and reimagine American identity.

WITNESS AND GENERATIONAL RECKONING

As stories of migration, war, discrimination, and survival are reclaimed, the pain becomes testimony—and the community becomes a witness to both trauma and transformation.

CHALLENGING THE NATION'S MYTH OF ITSELF

The struggle of Asian Americans invites the country to reflect on who is seen, who is remembered, and who is allowed to belong. In that reflection lies a path toward a more honest and inclusive national story.

Iconography of Haunted by Shadows, Holding the Line

This image symbolically renders the psychic structure and social consequences of the Anti-Asian cultural complex in America. The elements within the composition visually convey the emotional core, historical trauma, and cultural stereotypes that shape the experience of Asian Americans.

CENTRAL FIGURE (YOUNG ASIAN GIRL)

The unsmiling girl at the center represents the quiet strength, alienation, and enduring presence of Asian American identity. Her direct gaze challenges the viewer to confront rather than ignore her existence. She is neither victim nor stereotype but a symbol of consciousness and resilience amidst distortion.

BACKGROUND FACES AND CARICATURES

Surrounding the central figure are grotesque racial caricatures—exaggerated, hostile depictions of Asian features, echoing historical propaganda:

"Yellow Peril" inscription atop a sneering bald figure evokes early twentieth-century fears of Asian invasion.

Slur-ridden headlines ("Slurs," "Diseases") suggest how media and rhetoric fuel dehumanization.

Figures in anguish or rage show how Asian Americans are either feared, mocked, or rendered monstrous.

These distortions reflect the oscillating projections of the cultural complex: from admiration to scapegoating.

CLOSED SIGN

The face wearing a CLOSED cap references the closing of opportunities, exclusion from economic participation, and the invisibility of Asian workers in labor narratives. It may also evoke xenophobic policies like immigration bans or scapegoating during pandemics.

BLINDFOLDED JUSTICE

Lady Justice appears not only blindfolded but also passive. She turns away from the violence and injustice in the image, symbolizing the failure of legal systems to protect Asian Americans from discrimination, internment, or hate crimes.

RED THREAD

A thin red thread weaves across the image, evoking East Asian cultural symbolism (the Red Thread of Fate) but here recontextualized as a thread of inherited trauma and survival. It binds together disparate historical and emotional elements, suggesting continuity across time, geography, and generations.

BARBED WIRE & GUARD TOWER

In the background is a haunting reference to Japanese American internment camps—an institutionalized form of racial exclusion and control. The setting signals the state's complicity in the cultural complex and the long shadow of incarceration over Asian American history.

PROTEST SIGNS ("STOP ASIAN HATE")

These signs symbolize contemporary resistance and the emergence of voice and solidarity. They mark a refusal to remain invisible or compliant and signify a collective demand for recognition and justice.

CRYING MOTHER AND CHILD

This duo anchors the image emotionally. They reference the family unit torn apart by surveillance, deportation, war, and poverty. Their protective posture conveys generational trauma, grief, and the inherited burden of exclusion.

PAPER CRANE

Placed in the bottom left, the crane is a traditional symbol of peace, healing, and wishes. It introduces an element of hope and spiritual continuity amidst a bleak landscape. It may also allude to the legacy of Sadako Sasaki, a victim of the atomic bombing in Hiroshima, and postwar remembrance.

COLOR PALETTE AND STYLE

The subdued, almost sepia-toned grays and greens evoke old photographs or propaganda posters. The limited palette reinforces themes of erasure, memory, and moral ambiguity, while the textured brushwork creates a haunting, dreamlike atmosphere.

Interpretation

This iconography captures the essence of the Anti-Asian cultural complex: a structure built on fear, projection, silence, and distortion. And yet, within it also lies the seed of transformation: remembrance, resilience, and the assertion of voice and visibility.

THE ANTI-SEMITIC CULTURAL COMPLEX

EXILED BY MYTH: THE ANTI-SEMITIC CULTURAL COMPLEX

A lone Jewish figure clutches a suitcase and a book titled Memory, walking forward as shadowed masses brand him with ancient accusations—Gold, Loyalty· Above him, a serpent coils around the globe, dripping with venomous suspicion, while a shattered synagogue fades behind. This haunting image distills the Anti-Semitic cultural complex: a recurring archetype of projection, where fear, envy, and blame coalesce into myth—and memory becomes both burden and resistance.

Core Emotion: Fear, Envy, Projection

At the heart of the Anti-Semitic cultural complex lies a volatile mix of fear, envy, and projection. Jewish identity becomes a screen onto which societies project their own internal contradictions—wealth and poverty, tradition and modernity, rootedness and displacement. These emotions often cycle unconsciously through history, masked by ideology and inflamed in moments of social upheaval.

Mythic Root: Wandering Outsider, Hidden Manipulator, Sacred Scapegoat

This complex draws from ancient archetypes such as the wandering outsider, the hidden manipulator, and the sacred scapegoat. In Christian Europe, it was historically fueled by myths like deicide (the killing of Christ), the blood libel, and financial conspiracy. In modern secular societies, these myths persist in disguised forms, appearing in tropes around globalism, media influence, or financial control.

Symbolic Imagery

Iconography associated with this complex often includes sinister and dehumanizing images: a cloaked figure behind a curtain, a coin in one hand and a scroll in the other, a faceless man holding many passports, a snake coiled around the globe, a crowd pointing at a lone figure with a suitcase, or a shattered synagogue window lit by candlelight.

Self-Reinforcing Memory

The complex is sustained by a deep reservoir of collective trauma and resentment—pogroms, expulsions, forced conversions, Holocaust memory, and more. It reemerges during times of economic collapse, national identity crises, or political transition. Even when Jews are a tiny minority or absent altogether, the myth persists as a psychological pattern.

Black-and-White Thinking

Jews are imagined in contradictory extremes: either omnipotent elites controlling society from the shadows or weak victims who infiltrate and corrupt. The complex splits Jewish identity into binaries—religious versus secular, insider versus outsider, assimilated versus other. Assimilation is seen as betrayal, difference as threat.

Repetitive Behavior

Behavioral manifestations include conspiracy theories, coded dog whistles, desecration of cemeteries or synagogues, and obsessive scrutiny of Jewish presence in media, finance, or politics. This complex tends to occur in cycles: denial, resurgence, apology, forgetting, and then return.

The anti-semitic cultural complex distorts reality, severs human connection, and turns internal societal tensions into projections toward a scapegoated group. It damages pluralism, undermines civil society, and creates an atmosphere in which violence or exclusion can be justified. It substitutes complexity with fantasy and fear with hatred.

Potential for Transformation

Despite its long and destructive history, the anti-semitic cultural complex can be disarmed and transformed. Doing so requires a deep reckoning—not only with historical facts, but also with the psychic need to create an "Other" in times of uncertainty. At its edge of healing lies the archetype of the witness—those who hold memory without vengeance and truth without distortion. Also present is the bridge-builder—a figure who carries the ability to live across cultures and identities, and to embody complexity rather than fear it.

This transformation is not only about the redemption of a persecuted group, but also about the maturation of society itself. When the need to project blame outward is relinquished, the ground opens for authentic responsibility, reconciliation, and pluralistic wholeness.

Iconography of Exiled by Myth: The Anti-Semitic Cultural Complex

This iconography reflects how antisemitism operates not just through individual hatred, but also through deep cultural complexes that mythologize, project, and ritualize fear of the "Other."

CENTRAL FIGURE

A solitary Jewish man stands in profile, slightly bowed and introspective, clutching a suitcase. The suitcase symbolizes exile, displacement, and the forced transience that has haunted Jewish identity for centuries. His humble dress and calm dignity evoke perseverance amid systemic suspicion and exclusion.

SURROUNDING CROWD

Behind him looms a homogenous, stone-faced crowd rendered in drab, muted tones. Their blank stares and uniformity suggest the mindless collectivity of scapegoating mobs.

SKYBORNE SERPENT AND GLOBE

Dominating the upper portion of the image is a serpent coiled around a glowing globe high in the sky. This is a direct visual reference to age-old anti-semitic conspiracy myths portraying Jews as secretly controlling world affairs—economics, media, or politics. The serpent symbolizes deceit, omnipresence, and threat in much traditional iconography, while the globe alludes to the scale of the perceived danger. Its position in the sky, above all else, gives it an ominous mythic weight—as if this fantasy hovers over the collective psyche. This element does not reflect actual Jewish power, but the projection of a mythic enemy who must be blamed in times of upheaval. It encapsulates the dangerous emotional logic of the Anti-Semitic Cultural complex: abstract fear needing a concrete target.

ARCHITECTURE IN THE DISTANCE

Temple- and courthouse-like structures blur into the horizon, shrouded in haze. These suggest the vacillating nature of justice and belonging—sometimes protective, sometimes complicit in persecution.

GROUND SYMBOLISM

The cracked and uneven paving stones beneath the Jewish figure's feet evoke instability, generational trauma, and a fragile foundation of cultural memory. A broken chain lies nearby—its loosened links gesturing toward possible liberation from the psychic and historical binds of prejudice.

LIGHT AND COLOR

The man is bathed in a faint golden light that sets him apart from the gray-toned masses. This halo-like glow evokes the archetype of the witness, the bearer of inconvenient truth and painful memory. It contrasts with the cold uniformity behind him, suggesting moral and spiritual resilience amid historical deformation.

Interpretation

The painting visualizes the Anti-semitic cultural complex as an ancient yet recurring myth of suspicion and projection:

- The lone figure vs. the collective scapegoaters
- Memory vs. ideological amnesia
- Historical trauma vs. historical denial
- Spiritual witness vs. mythic contaminator

The serpent-globe motif in the sky reveals the psychological scope of this complex: It does not merely stigmatize individuals; it also invents an all-encompassing force to explain social anxiety. The image calls not only for recognition of harm but also for a conscious dismantling of the myths that sustain cycles of hate.

THE HOLOCAUST DENIAL CULTURAL COMPLEX

THE WEIGHT OF TRUTH: THE HOLOCAUST DENIAL CULTURAL COMPLEX

A lone figure trudges across cracked earth, burdened by a headstone marked *Remember* while hostile winds carry symbols of hatred and denial—swastikas, question marks, and crossed-out truths. Beneath him, the ground fractures, echoing a society split by distortion and silence. This image captures the Holocaust Denial cultural complex: a persistent assault on memory, where facts are buried under ideology, and remembrance becomes resistance.

Core Emotion: Defensiveness, Shame, and Willful Disavowal

At the center of this cultural complex lies a mix of defensiveness, shame, and willful disavowal. It is driven by the psychological refusal to confront unbearable historical truths—particularly the atrocities of the Holocaust. This refusal may stem from antisemitism, ideological revisionism, nationalistic pride, or a more generalized existential guilt. Rather than face the profound moral rupture that genocide represents, the complex seeks psychic relief through denial, rationalization, or minimization. It shields the self from unbearable acknowledgment by constructing alternate narratives.

Mythic Root: Erased Witness and Purified Past

The mythic structure of this complex draws from the archetypes of the erased witness and the purified past. It enacts a second casting out of the scapegoat—first through extermination, and then through historical erasure. This denial aligns with collective fantasies of national innocence, righteous ancestors, or the purification of historical stain. It is fueled by the myth that moral failure must be buried to preserve collective identity, rather than integrated through reckoning and remembrance.

Symbolic Imagery

This complex can be visualized through haunting symbolic forms:

- A shattered Holocaust memorial, overgrown with weeds, suggesting neglect and forgotten grief
- A library with key pages missing or blacked out in books, symbolizing institutional censorship or historical manipulation
- A fog-shrouded courtroom, where justice is delayed or denied
- Old photographs suspended in air, burning from the edges inward—representing the erasure of memory as it happens
- A truth-teller bound and blindfolded before a silent crowd—evoking collective complicity and the suppression of testimony
- Train tracks vanishing into the mist, marking the journey into oblivion that denial tries to complete

Self-Reinforcing Memory

The denial complex feeds on revisionist narratives, pseudo-scholarship, and conspiracy theories. It weaponizes ambiguity, exploiting academic uncertainties or gaps in documentation to seed doubt. It draws strength from the passage of time and the deaths of witnesses, slowly attempting to displace historical fact with misinformation. The logic of denial is recursive: the more it is repeated, the more doubt it sows. Its foundation is not truth, but the manipulation of emotional discomfort and the erosion of trust in historical authority.

Black-and-White Thinking

Within this complex, memory becomes binary: either history is wholly heroic, or it is unbearably shameful—and therefore must be rejected. The Holocaust is not engaged with as a historical event with deep moral lessons, but rather recast as a fabrication, exaggeration, or even as something the victims brought upon themselves. Moral nuance disappears. The complexity of systemic evil is flattened into simplistic, ideologically driven rejections. In this way, memory becomes politicized and dehumanized.

Repetitive Behavior

The behaviors associated with this complex form a pattern:

- Disputing verified documentation and downplaying survivor testimony
- Elevating fringe voices and pseudo-historians to positions of false authority
- Framing Holocaust denial as an exercise in "free speech," while simultaneously working to discredit legitimate scholarship and mourning rituals
- Mocking or trivializing remembrance events and associating them with political manipulation or "identity politics"

This behavior is cyclical, often accelerating in times of political polarization, nationalism, or disillusionment with truth institutions.

Social Effects

The Holocaust Denial cultural complex shreds the moral fabric of collective memory. It undermines the foundations of historical truth, retraumatizes survivors and their descendants, and weakens the global community's capacity to recognize and respond to fascism, genocide, and mass atrocity. It does not simply rewrite history—it creates moral fog, breeding cynicism, distrust, and ultimately hatred. The denial of historical atrocity is itself a continuation of violence, conducted not with weapons, but with silence, distortion, and the erasure of pain.

Potential for Transformation

Despite its corrosive nature, this complex carries a shadow that—when brought to light—invites the possibility of deep transformation. Confronting denial can awaken societies to their historical responsibilities, their capacity for ethical remembrance, and their duty to bear witness.

HISTORICAL RECKONING
Denial can be a catalyst for deeper investigation, education, and public dialogue. It forces societies to examine what they would rather forget—and why.

RESTORATION OF TESTIMONY
The counterforce to denial is not argument alone but bearing witness. Survivors, descendants, scholars, and artists all become sacred vessels of memory when truth is under threat.

ETHICAL EDUCATION
Holocaust denial highlights the need for moral literacy, not just factual knowledge. Its confrontation can deepen understanding of systemic evil, scapegoating, and human complicity.

RECONNECTION TO THE ARCHETYPE OF THE WITNESS
In symbolic terms, healing lies in restoring the figure of the witness—the one who carries the unbearable truth, refuses silence, and honors those who can no longer speak.

Iconography of The Weight of Truth: The Holocaust Denial Cultural Complex

CENTRAL FIGURE

A solitary man, dressed in somber, old-world attire, walks across a parched and cracked landscape, evoking both exile and perseverance. He carries a heavy stone tablet engraved with the word *REMEMBER*, representing the weight of historical trauma, memory, and the burden of truth that Jewish survivors and their descendants bear. His bowed posture suggests grief, vigilance, and determination to safeguard memory in the face of erasure.

LANDSCAPE (FOREGROUND)

The cracked, dry earth beneath the man's feet symbolizes a fractured moral and historical ground. The terrain is reminiscent of a desert or wasteland—evoking both historical displacement and the spiritual barrenness that denial creates. The fissure running through the ground may also suggest the intergenerational rupture caused by genocide, denial, and silence.

SKY AND FALLING SYMBOLS (BACKGROUND)

Swastikas fall ominously from the sky—symbols of persistent hate, reanimated ideologies, and the ever-present threat of neo-fascism and antisemitism. A placard with the word *HOLOCAUST* is crossed out, representing the deliberate attempt to erase or delegitimize history through denial, revisionism, or silence. Another placard features a large question mark, symbolizing the cynical skepticism or feigned doubt that often accompanies Holocaust denial. This suggests a false framing of denial as "inquiry" or "controversy."

SYMBOLIC TENSIONS:

The man walking forward symbolizes bearing witness, moving through a hostile world to preserve memory against erasure. The tension between sky and earth (ideological assault versus grounded history) reflects how denial attempts to sever the connection between lived truth and public recognition. The man walks against the storm, illuminated in warmer tones, suggesting moral clarity, resilience, and truth carried in darkness.

Interpretation

This image does not merely document the danger of forgetting; it dramatizes the psychological and cultural complex of denial itself. It shows how denial operates not only through outright lies, but through confusion, distraction, and systematic doubt. The central figure is not passive—he is an active bearer of history, a guardian of memory journeying through moral desolation, targeted from above by symbols of reactivated hatred.

THE WHITE SUPREMACY CULTURAL COMPLEX

CRUSHING HIERARCHIES: THE WHITE SUPREMACY CULTURAL COMPLEX

This stark and arresting image visualizes the oppressive force of white supremacy as a literal and psychological weight pressing down on nonwhite lives. Rendered in a severe sepia-yellow palette, it evokes both historical permanence and emotional heat.

Core Emotion: Entitlement, Fear, and Rage

At its core, the white supremacy cultural complex is driven by a sense of entitlement to dominance and centrality—fueled by a deep fear of loss and humiliation. The fear that previously unchallenged privilege might be displaced or reversed manifests as defensive rage, often disguised as moral righteousness or self-preservation.

Mythic Root: Divine Election and Racial Hierarchy.

Rooted in the myth of the "White Man's Burden," European colonialism, and the biblical notion of a chosen people, this complex draws strength from pseudo-myths of superiority and civilization. It casts whiteness as the origin and guardian of order, reason, and virtue, and others as either inferior, dangerous, or corrupting.

Symbolic Imagery

- Raised fists and Confederate iconography
- Imagery of chains, bloodlines, and purity
- The vigilant gaze of the panoptic eye (surveillance, judgment)
- Storms, cracked soil, decaying trees—symbols of psychic rot beneath the surface
- Statues, flags, and weaponry meant to sanctify a violent legacy

Self-Reinforcing Memory

The complex preserves a selectively mythologized version of history that glorifies conquest, frames slavery and segregation as bygone footnotes, and erases or distorts the contributions and suffering of nonwhite groups. It replays a cycle of grievance whenever perceived social gains by marginalized groups are interpreted as threats to "real" American identity.

Black-and-White Thinking

Good versus evil is mapped onto race, culture, and religion. "We" (the white, the pure, the civilized) are under siege from "them" (the dark, the foreign, the impure). This dichotomy allows no room for ambiguity, dialogue, or shared humanity.

Repetitive Behavior

- The resurrection of racist tropes under new guises (e.g., "law and order," "replacement theory," "heritage, not hate")
- Acts of vigilante violence and symbolic displays of dominance
- White victimhood narratives that echo across generations: "They're taking our jobs," "We're being silenced," "We're the real victims now."

Social Effects

- Tearing the Civic Fabric: The complex weaponizes difference, scapegoats the vulnerable, and undermines pluralistic democracy.
- Radicalization and Domestic Terror: It creates fertile ground for hate crimes and extremist mobilization.
- Institutional Capture: It subtly shapes policies, policing, and educational narratives, often cloaked in legalism or neutrality.
- Psychic Dissociation: For white individuals, it can induce a split between conscience and inheritance—between human decency and unconscious supremacy.

Possibility of Transformation

Transformation begins when individuals and collectives confront the inherited trauma and privilege that sustain the complex. The key is not merely shame or disavowal, but integration—the process of metabolizing truth, grief, and accountability into action. Collective rituals of mourning, historical reckoning, reparative justice, and shared civic purpose can transmute the complex's poisonous roots into soil for renewal. True transformation occurs when whiteness is no longer treated as an invisible norm, but as a contingent identity open to reflection and evolution.

Iconography of Crushing Hierarchies: The White Supremacy Cultural Complex

WHITE MALE FACE LOOMING ABOVE

The pale, expressionless face of a white man dominates the top half of the image, representing not just an individual but also a system—cold, abstracted, and emotionally removed. His gaze is neither kind nor cruel; it is indifferent. That detachment embodies the bureaucratic and structural aspect of supremacy: it doesn't need to hate to dominate.

OVERSIZED BLACK BOOT DESCENDING

The boot, impossibly large and central in the composition, becomes the primary symbol of force. It is coming down with authoritarian weight—imminent, crushing, unstoppable. It represents institutional power, law enforcement, economic suppression, and historical violence directed toward marginalized communities.

THE THREE FIGURES BELOW (SPECIFIC AND INDIVIDUALIZED)

Beneath the boot stand three distinct individuals of color, each rendered with emotional and narrative clarity:

Black Male Youth (left):

Standing upright, his gaze is forward and alert. His posture suggests a quiet awareness, strength under pressure, and a history of survival. He is not bowed, but watchful.

Latina Girl (center):

Her eyes are wide with fear and uncertainty, and her small hand clutches her chest in an involuntary gesture of distress. She stands between the two adults, conveying both the inherited vulnerability and emotional cost of systemic subjugation. Her two braids, simple dress, and youthful expression emphasize innocence and the psychic weight of generational trauma.

Latino Man (right):

Strong-jawed and square-shouldered, he meets the threat with a fixed, defiant gaze. His arms are stiff, fists clenched, and his uniform shirt evokes labor, dignity, and experience. His stance is protective—anchored like a sentinel at the frontlines of resistance.

MUTED EARTH TONES AND DIM LIGHT:

The color palette is subdued, drawing attention to the atmosphere of dread and inevitability. It suggests this is not a moment of sudden violence, but part of an ongoing structure—quiet, constant, normalized.

COMPOSITION OF UP VS. DOWN:

The hierarchical layout of the image itself reinforces the dynamics of power: white face above, boot in the middle, people below. It visualizes the ideological ladder white supremacy constructs—placing itself at the top of worth, visibility, and protection.

Interpretation

This image captures the emotional logic and structural force of the White Supremacy cultural complex. It is not merely about individual prejudice; it is about a system that elevates and enshrines one racial identity as dominant—while threatening others with literal and symbolic erasure. The boot falls not out of rage, but as a function of the design.

THE ANTI-WHITE CULTURAL COMPLEX

THE LEDGER AND THE STATUE: ICONOCLASM IN THE AGE OF REVERSAL

This image captures the symbolic heart of the Anti-White cultural complex: a moment of reckoning where historical grievance confronts institutional legacy. A hooded figure with a bullhorn and checklist stands over the toppled statue of a white patriarchal icon—poised between protest and purge. Behind him, a multiethnic crowd watches with solemn resolve, placards blank as if awaiting a new script for justice.

Core Emotion: Resentment, Retribution, and Inversion of Power

At its center is the emotional charge of historical grievance expressed through a reversal of cultural and moral framing. It contains both justified critique of white dominance and a reactive impulse that risks turning critique into scapegoating or essentialism.

Mythic Root: The Fall of the Overlord and the Rise of the Avenger

This complex draws from the archetypes of the oppressor unmasked, the once-silenced truth-teller, and the humbling of empire. In its mythic logic, whiteness becomes a stand-in for systemic injustice, and the desire for liberation can sometimes harden into symbolic punishment or erasure.

Symbolic Imagery

- Statues of white historical figures toppled and buried.
- A classroom where old textbooks burn while new ones rise.
- A masked figure with a bullhorn in one hand and a ledger of wrongs in the other.
- A pale throne crumbling under the weight of history.
- A courtroom where the roles have reversed, and no one is innocent.

Self-Reinforcing Memory

Centuries of racial violence, cultural theft, and economic domination provide the moral charge behind this complex. But the memory becomes distorted when individual white people are treated as proxies for systems and when historical trauma is weaponized without nuance.

Black-and-White Thinking

White is the oppressor; Black/Brown is the oppressed. This reversal of binary thinking mirrors the structure of the original racial complex it opposes. It leaves little room for complexity, shared struggle, or transformation. It can silence voices out of fear, guilt, or presumed complicity.

Repetitive Behavior

- Cultural inversion.
- Iconoclasm.
- Public shaming.
- Overcorrection in institutions.

- The use of race as a primary moral category rather than one dimension of a larger human story.
- Elevating identity as purity while dismissing reconciliation or nuance.

Social Effects

This complex alienates potential allies, deepens racial anxiety, and undermines the goals of genuine justice. It can fracture coalition-building and harden backlash movements. It often thrives in polarized environments where guilt, fear, and righteousness replace dialogue.

Potential for Transformation

When held consciously, the Anti-White cultural complex reveals the deep pain and imbalance still alive in society. Its shadow is scapegoating—but its gift is the pressure to reimagine belonging, history, and justice in more inclusive, soul-aware terms. Integration requires seeing beyond reversal toward reconciliation, beyond blame toward shared truth.

Iconography of The Ledger and the Statue: Iconoclasm in the Age of Reversal

TOPPLED STATUE

Represents the fall of white cultural authority and the symbolic dethronement of dominant historical narratives. The shattered marble reflects both justified dismantling and potential excess.

HOODED PROTESTER WITH BULLHORN AND CHECKLIST

Embodies the masked truth-teller and the avenger archetype. The bullhorn amplifies historical grievances; the checklist not only evokes moral reckoning but also suggests potential rigidity or retribution.

BLANK PROTEST SIGNS

Suggest a narrative vacuum—an open question of what replaces the past. Their emptiness evokes both potential and peril: renewal or nihilism.

DIVERSE CROWD

The surrounding figures both imply collective memory, solidarity, and multiracial participation and echo the dangers of essentialism and guilt-by-association if nuance is lost.

CRACKED EARTH

Symbolizes the fractured civic ground on which this complex unfolds—socially and psychologically.

Interpretation

This image dramatizes the powerful emotional and mythic energies that animate the Anti-White cultural complex: the hunger for justice, the temptation of reversal, and the call to forge a new, more inclusive moral terrain.

THE MINORITY GROUP CULTURAL COMPLEX

THE INHERITANCE: THE MINORITY GROUP CULTURAL COMPLEX AND THE SILENT STRENGTH OF SURVIVAL

A young girl stands at the threshold of visibility—wrapped in a shawl woven with ancestral memory and silent resolve. Behind her, the watchful faces of elders emerge from the walls like spirits, not haunting, but witnessing. Around her, the city moves in muted tones, unaware of the sacred story she carries. This is the Minority cultural complex—not defined by victimhood, but by the quiet defiance of being fully human in a world that often fails to see.

Core Emotion: Invisibility, Frustrated Belonging, and Defiant Dignity

At its core is a lived sense of being unseen, misjudged, or tokenized—and yet carrying a deep reservoir of identity, memory, and meaning that refuses to be erased. There is grief here, yet also fierce pride, sacred inheritance, and quiet strength.

Mythic Root: The Hidden Seed and the Watchful Ancestor

This complex draws on archetypes of the exiled one who carries the flame, the keeper of wisdom in the margins, the seed buried beneath empire. It echoes the story of Joseph in the pit, of the trickster who survives, of the grandparent who remembers. It is the soul that survives diaspora.

Symbolic Imagery

- A figure cloaked in a patchwork of ancestral symbols, standing at the edge of a vast city
- A tree with roots reaching deep into the bones of buried ancestors
- Eyes watching from within murals
- A candle lit in a back room
- A lone voice singing into the wind
- A bridge of footprints made from different soils

Self-Reinforcing Memory

Memory is often transmitted not only through words but through food, gesture, music, silence, and prayer. This memory often lives between words—in the gestures of elders, the beat of old songs, or the silence at the dinner table. Generational stories of survival, discrimination, brilliance, betrayal, and resistance shape the emotional ground—often held within the body itself.

Black-and-White Thinking

This complex may perceive the dominant group as untrustworthy, appropriative, or incapable of understanding. It can foster internal conflict:

wanting visibility while fearing stereotyping, seeking inclusion but wary of assimilation. It may create an "us" that not only protects but also limits. A tendency to police authenticity within the group itself can exist, creating tensions between generations or those with hybrid identities.

Repetitive Behavior

Code-switching. Making oneself smaller or louder. Teaching the next generation to move safely through hostile space. Preserving traditions while innovating under pressure. Creating beauty in overlooked places. Holding the door open for those still coming through.

Social Effects

The minority cultural complex can tear the social and psychological fabric when internalized oppression leads to silence, shame, or identity fragmentation. It may foster conflict within and between groups—especially through comparative suffering, authenticity policing, or identity gatekeeping. The pressure to code-switch, self-censor, or constantly translate one's experience can lead to exhaustion and estrangement, both from the dominant culture and from one's own roots.

Potential for Transformation

When held consciously, this complex becomes a wellspring of cultural richness, resilience, and visionary creativity. It can generate art, language, and tradition that challenge the status quo not only with critique, but also with living alternatives. The minority position—often seen as marginal—reveals itself as a generative edge, carrying deep ancestral wisdom and offering the potential to reimagine belonging, community, and the meaning of identity itself. Like a vine through concrete, the complex can crack old structures—not by force alone, but by insistence on growing.

Iconography of The Inheritance: The Minority Group Cultural Complex and the Silent Strength of Survival

CENTRAL FIGURE—THE YOUNG GIRL IN THE SHAWL (FOREGROUND)

The image is anchored by a young girl of Asian or Indigenous descent, wrapped in a richly patterned shawl. Her expression is solemn, inward, and aware. She does not plead or posture; she witnesses. Her presence symbolizes the lived, intergenerational experience of being a racial and cultural minority in America—always seen, rarely heard, always bearing the weight of inherited memory and external scrutiny. Her shawl is not only clothing, but a living tapestry of cultural identity—stitched with birds, foliage, and sacred faces. It is both shield and burden, comfort and inheritance.

EMBROIDERED ANCESTORS—WOVEN INTO THE FABRIC (LOWER RIGHT)

The shawl bears the image of an older Indigenous woman, her expression fierce and watchful. This suggests that ancestral figures are not merely behind her—they are woven into her identity, close to the skin. These spirits are protective and grounding, but they also imply a cultural weight passed on without reprieve. This conveys the psychic reality of the Minority cultural complex: memory is not abstract—it lives in one's skin, name, and walk through the world.

GHOSTLIKE ELDER FACES ON THE BUILDING WALL (RIGHT SIDE)

Looming behind her in the texture of the urban wall are the ghostly faces of an older Black man and Indigenous woman, etched like fading murals or guardian spirits. They represent ancestral presence and unresolved grief—those who came before and were never fully seen by the dominant society. They are not mournful ghosts; they are sober, unblinking witnesses. Their inclusion elevates the narrative: minority identity is not merely personal but also historical. Every generation steps into a drama already in motion.

DIVERSE CROWD, FACING AWAY OR INWARD (LEFT AND REAR)

Around the central figure, urban passersby walk and talk—but few meet her gaze. This depicts the isolating dimension of the Minority cultural complex: one is surrounded, but not fully recognized. Even among fellow minorities, the gaze often turns inward—toward survival, toward family, toward silence. The Capitol dome fades in the distance, evoking the American promise of inclusion—visible, but unreachable.

COLOR AND COMPOSITION (EARTH AND FLAME)

The dominant tones are deep reds, blues, and warm golds—suggesting cultural richness, but also heat, scrutiny, and vulnerability. The composition pulls the viewer into the girl's orbit, asking us to bear witness as she bears history.

Interpretation

This image powerfully portrays the Minority cultural complex as a state of carrying lineage, exclusion, memory, and quiet strength all at once. The girl is not merely "other"—she is an embodiment of cultural survival, of walking forward in a world shaped by forces behind and around her. Her shawl is both her past and her present. She does not disappear—she endures.

CHAPTER 4

Structures of Belonging as Cultural Complexes

Isolation vs. Community Cultural Complex

The American Tribalism Cultural Complex

The American Class Cultural Complex

Communitas Cultural Complex

This section focuses on the various cultural complexes that center around how an individual does or does not relate to the community and different ways of becoming part of the community.

THE ISOLATION VS. COMMUNITY CULTURAL COMPLEX

LOOKING IN: THE ISOLATION VS. COMMUNITY CULTURAL COMPLEX

A solitary figure sits in a dim room, lit only by a blank laptop, gazing through a window at a warmly lit communal gathering. The glow of connection lies just out of reach, divided by glass. This image distills the aching paradox of the Isolation vs. Community cultural complex in modern American life: hyperconnected yet emotionally estranged, yearning for belonging while trapped in solitude.

Core Emotion: Yearning and Withdrawal

This complex holds a powerful emotional tension: a deep longing to belong, to be known, and to be held in shared meaning—countered by a fear of engulfment, betrayal, or loss of individual identity. It swings between the ache of disconnection and the idealization of a lost or imagined togetherness.

Mythic Root: The Exile and the Village Hearth

At the heart of this complex lie the archetypes of the wanderer and the circle: the lone figure cast out or choosing the road over the room and the warm, firelit gathering that offers communion and burden-sharing. The American psyche is especially steeped in this polarity—between rugged independence and the longing for communal vision.

Symbolic Imagery

This complex is symbolized by images such as a solitary person staring out a window at others gathered behind glass, a digital screen glowing in a dark room, or a community table that is set but empty. It can appear in a circle of hands reaching toward each other but never touching, or in a cloaked figure standing on a mountaintop, looking down at the valley's flickering lights.

Self-Reinforcing Memory

Memories of betrayal, disillusionment, or suffocation within groups—whether through religious hypocrisy, familial rupture, or institutional coldness—reinforce the retreat into solitude. At the same time, past moments of solidarity—marches, meals, shared grief, or creative collaboration—continue to haunt the soul with the memory of what could be.

Black-and-White Thinking

This complex often divides the world into stark opposites: autonomy versus conformity, freedom versus obligation, the self-made individual versus the dependent follower. Relationships become either idealized havens or dangerous traps, while communities are viewed as either utopias or cults. The lonely are seen as either nobly self-sufficient or dangerously detached.

Repetitive Behavior

The pattern is often one of withdrawal just as connection deepens. Individuals may romanticize the idea of going "off-grid" or finding a "chosen family," while simultaneously fearing real intimacy. They create digital avatars instead of showing up in the flesh, long for community while distrusting it, and mourn its absence even as they mock its expressions.

Social Effects

The Isolation vs. Community cultural complex frays the social fabric by idealizing autonomy at the expense of solidarity. It has contributed to a society increasingly marked by mistrust, polarization, and the erosion of shared spaces. Institutions once rooted in gathering and mutual support are now viewed with suspicion or irrelevance. Meanwhile, social media amplifies performative connection while intensifying actual disconnection. Public life becomes lonelier, more fragmented, and less resilient in the face of collective crisis. This complex alienates us from one another—and from ourselves as communal beings. It erodes civic life, fragments solidarity, and elevates hyper-individualism. Loneliness becomes an epidemic. Yet, within its anguish lies a creative impulse: to imagine new forms of gathering that respect both individuality and kinship.

Possibility of Transformation

This complex holds within it the creative tension necessary for cultural renewal. Its transformation lies not in dissolving the self into the group, nor in banishing the self from relationship, but in forging a reimagined belonging—one that honors both boundaries and mutual care. This transformation begins when individuals and communities experiment with forms of gathering that nurture presence, transparency, and emotional risk. From cohousing and civic collaboration to communal rituals and artistic fellowship, the healing of this complex depends on building containers where freedom and fellowship coexist.

Iconography of Looking In: The Isolation vs. Community Cultural Complex

THE SEATED INDIVIDUAL (FOREGROUND, RIGHT)

A young man sits alone in a darkened room, his posture contemplative but withdrawn. He represents the modern self—surrounded by digital connection yet emotionally disconnected. His body faces the window, not the screen, indicating a deeper longing for human warmth than virtual engagement provides.

THE LAPTOP (LEFT TABLE)

Dimly lit and unused, the laptop symbolizes the false promise of connection in the digital age. Its glow is cold and impersonal, in stark contrast to the golden warmth of the candlelit gathering outside. It stands as a symbol of mediated experience that cannot satisfy relational needs.

THE WINDOWPANE (CENTER)

The window is a threshold and a barrier. It separates the viewer from the world of togetherness outside while allowing the ache of visibility. It creates a feeling of exile and observation—a longing to belong without access.

THE COMMUNAL GATHERING (BEYOND THE GLASS)

Around a single candle, a diverse and intergenerational group sits in shared warmth and intimacy. They symbolize belonging, rootedness, and the human need for story, ritual, and presence. Their glow radiates collective memory and emotional safety.

CANDLE AT THE CENTER OF THE TABLE

This flame is the symbolic heart of the image—evoking not just light, but also shared purpose, sacred presence, and warmth. It contrasts sharply with the sterile, indifferent glow of the laptop screen. The candle becomes a totem of community.

HOUSES IN THE DISTANCE WITH LIT WINDOWS

The background houses extend the sense of an interconnected world just beyond reach—others, elsewhere, also gathered. These homes deepen the theme of separation and hint at the broader cultural landscape: many alone, many together, none untouched.

COLOR PALETTE (WARM VS. COOL)

The image uses color to emphasize psychological states. The room of the solitary figure is rendered in cold blues and grays, whereas the communal space beyond glows in yellows and oranges. This stark contrast reinforces emotional separation and longing.

Interpretation

This image visualizes the Isolation vs. Community cultural complex as a quiet but piercing divide: between presence and distance, warmth and coldness, participation and observation. It evokes the core modern ache—the hunger to be among others and the difficulty of crossing the threshold of disconnection.

THE AMERICAN TRIBALISM CULTURAL COMPLEX

ENCIRCLED BY FIRE, BOUND BY LEGACY

Amid a ring of flames, tribal guardians of American identity stand resolute—arms crossed, eyes unwavering. At the center, a chieftain figure blends Indigenous authority with national symbolism, flanked by watchful allies bearing flags and spears. Behind them rise shadows of a crowd and a sharpened wooden palisade, evoking both defense and exclusion. The fire glows not only with warmth, but also with ancient grievance and the tension of belonging forged through resistance.

Emotional Core: Belonging, Fear, Rage, Humiliation

The emotional foundation of the American Tribalism cultural complex is a volatile blend of belonging, fear, rage, and humiliation. On one hand, tribalism offers a profound sense of anchoring and emotional safety. It answers the basic human need to feel protected, recognized, and bound to a meaningful collective identity. On the other hand, it is animated by a deep fear of annihilation—whether cultural, racial, political, or moral—and by resentment toward those perceived as outsiders, betrayers, or threats. The result is a powerful emotional high: the righteous certainty of standing with one's own against a hostile or confusing world. Beneath that sense of certainty lies a deeper wound—the fear of becoming invisible, irrelevant, or dissolved within an increasingly pluralistic and fragmented society.

Mythic Root: Lost Tribe, Righteous Band, Ancient Grievance

The mythic foundations of this complex draw from primal archetypes of clan, covenant, and sacred kinship. One core myth is that of the lost tribe—the belief that one's people have been erased, misrepresented, or threatened in a hostile world. Another is the myth of the righteous band—a heroic few resisting corruption, chaos, or imperial domination. Still another is the myth of ancient grievance—the belief that history is a field of betrayal, and that group loyalty must be total to ensure survival. These myths echo through both settler and Indigenous histories, biblical imagery, and frontier legends. Tribal belonging becomes sacrosanct—more than cultural preference, it becomes existential covenant.

Symbolic Imagery

The symbolic field of tribalism is visceral, boundary-charged, and emotionally loaded. Flags, tattoos, and totems function as visible emblems of allegiance. Enclosed spaces—campfires, rally stages, and algorithmic echo chambers—form the heat circles in which identity is continually reaffirmed. Warpaint, uniforms, or stylized apparel give members a clarity of purpose and mark a readiness for conflict. Physical and psychological barriers—walls, gated communities, curated feeds—reinforce the boundary between "us" and "them." Mirrors and echo chambers reflect tribal affirmation while distorting perceptions of the outside world. Symbols of purity and grievance—whether sacred wounds, lost causes, or ancestral pride—anchor the group's moral narrative and emotional loyalty.

Self-Reinforcing Memory

This cultural complex draws on fragmented and often conflicting timelines to construct its identity. The memory of persecution—whether through genocide, slavery, exclusion, or scapegoating—fuels tribal defensiveness. The memory of betrayal—by governments, elites, or former allies—deepens tribal grievance. And the memory of fractured unity—Reconstruction, the civil rights backlash, or post-9/11 fragmentation—feeds the myth that national cohesion is an illusion or an ideal that has been permanently lost. Each group clings to its own canon of historical experience. These memories are not only recollections—they are mythologized and weaponized. History becomes a battlefield of sacred injury and justification.

Black-and-White Thinking

Tribalism depends on stark binaries that resist ambiguity and moral complexity. Group identity is framed as a struggle of us versus them, loyal versus traitor, pure versus corrupt, victim versus villain, survival versus extinction. In this mental framework, nuance is viewed as weakness or betrayal. The idea of compromise becomes dangerous. Middle ground is not just disfavored; it is actively policed. The tribal worldview thrives on sharp moral clarity, often at the expense of truth, empathy, or flexibility.

Repetitive Behaviors

The American Tribalism cultural complex is ritualized through endless cycles of performance, opposition, and group reaffirmation. These behaviors include voting patterns determined solely by group identity, the creation and consumption of ideologically sealed media, and participation in symbolic gatherings—from political rallies and cultural festivals to online forums and hashtag campaigns. Callout culture, public denunciations, and loyalty tests further entrench tribal dynamics. Ritual language, insider memes, and shared grievances create a closed symbolic ecosystem. The repetition of these acts doesn't just maintain identity—it constantly restages the primal drama of survival, loyalty, and belonging.

Social Effects

The cultural complex of tribalism tears at the very fabric of civic life. It erodes shared truth, replacing collective understanding with competing realities. It turns public institutions into arenas of tribal warfare rather than sites of common purpose. It poisons dialogue by collapsing curiosity into suspicion and turns disagreement into heresy. It fractures democratic participation by prioritizing allegiance over citizenship and identity over shared responsibility. In doing so, it corrodes the very conditions needed for pluralism, cooperation, and societal renewal.

Potential for Transformation

Despite its corrosive impact, the American Tribalism cultural complex also holds seeds of transformation. When not weaponized against others, tribal identity can offer meaningful connections to history, culture, land, and ancestry. It can become a source of resilience, dignity, and ethical rootedness. By recognizing that suffering and pride are shared across tribes, it becomes possible to build new forms of solidarity that do not erase difference but honor it. True transformation lies in learning to carry multiple identities—tribal, national, civic—without collapse. It invites a mythic shift: from a closed circle of exclusion to an open hearth of shared belonging. Tribal wounds, if acknowledged rather than denied or inflamed, can become the crucible in which a deeper American wholeness is forged.

Tribal Groups

Here is a sampling of the growing tribal groups in the United States through which individuals can find identity, cohesion, and support

Right-Leaning Tribes	**Left-Leaning Tribes**
MAGA Movement / Trump Loyalists (The Betrayed Patriot)	Progressive Activists / "The Woke" (The Moral Revolutionary)
Christian Nationalists (The Chosen Remnant)	Climate Justice Movements (The Gatekeeper of Reason)
Gun Rights Absolutists (The Frontier Defender)	Academic / Intellectual Elites (The Gatekeeper of Reason)

Racial & Ethnic Identity Tribes	**Other Tribal Clusters**
White Identitarians (The Endangered Heir)	Anti-Vaxx / Medical Freedom (The Exiled Truth-Seeker)
Black Consciousness Movements (The Ancestral Witness)	Techno-Optimists / Silicon Valley Utopaians (The Post-Human Visionary)
Latino Nationalist / Chicano Revival (The Displaced Warrior)	Online Gamer / Meme Tribes (The Chaotic Trickster)

Right-Leaning Tribes

1. MAGA Movement / Trump Loyalists

- Archetype: The Betrayed Patriot
- Symbolic Image: A red-capped sentinel holding a tattered Constitution over a burning city
- Emotional Tone: Righteous rage, nostalgic grief, warrior loyalty
- Totems: Red hats, American flags, memes of vengeance
- Behavioral Rituals: Rallies, chants ("USA! USA!"), social media loyalty tests

2. Christian Nationalists

- Archetype: The Chosen Remnant
- Symbolic Image: A cross wrapped in a flag standing against a gathering storm
- Emotional Tone: Divine mission, fear of apostasy, apocalyptic clarity
- Totems: Crosses, Bibles, lions, flames of revival
- Behavioral Rituals: Prayer circles, biblical political rhetoric, spiritual warfare language

3. Gun Rights Absolutists

- Archetype: The Frontier Defender
- Symbolic Image: A lone figure on a hilltop, silhouetted with rifle against sunset
- Emotional Tone: Suspicion, self-reliance, existential defiance
- Totems: AR-15 decals, Don't Tread on Me flags, open-carry gear
- Behavioral Rituals: Gun shows, 2A rallies, viral videos of "self-defense moments"

Left-Leaning Tribes

1. Progressive Activists / "The Woke"

- Archetype: The Moral Revolutionary
- Symbolic Image: A diverse crowd holding raised fists in rainbow light
- Emotional Tone: Urgency, solidarity, righteous indignation

- Totems: Hashtags, protest signs, intersectional language
- Behavioral Rituals: Marches, callouts, digital denunciations, ritualized apologies

2. Climate Justice Movements

- Archetype: The Earth's Prophet
- Symbolic Image: A child holding a dying sapling in a flooded street
- Emotional Tone: Existential dread, sacred duty, urgency of voice
- Totems: Hourglasses, green fists, polar bears, protest boats
- Behavioral Rituals: Climate strikes, eco-performance art, civil disobedience

3. Academic / Intellectual Elites

- Archetype: The Gatekeeper of Reason
- Symbolic Image: A high tower of books with a telescope pointed at the future
- Emotional Tone: Superiority, irony, wounded pride
- Totems: Peer-reviewed journals, data dashboards, TED Talks
- Behavioral Rituals: Panels, lectures, "debunking" threads, linguistic policing

Racial & Ethnic Identity Tribes

1. White Identitarians

- Archetype: The Endangered Heir
- Symbolic Image: A crumbling statue of a white patriarch wrapped in ivy
- Emotional Tone: Victimhood, legacy anxiety, covert aggression
- Totems: European runes, Confederate symbols, Crusader crosses
- Behavioral Rituals: Alt-histories, replacement theory memes, coded speech

2. Black Consciousness Movements

- Archetype: The Ancestral Witness
- Symbolic Image: A raised Black fist rising from a graveyard of chains
- Emotional Tone: Pride, rage, historical memory
- Totems: Pan-African colors, ancestral silhouettes, Afrocentric art
- Behavioral Rituals: Street memorials, spoken word, Juneteenth processions

3. Latino Nationalist / Chicano Revival

- Archetype: The Displaced Warrior
- Symbolic Image: An Aztec heart burning at the base of a border wall
- Emotional Tone: Defiance, memory of land lost, cultural resurrection
- Totems: Aztec iconography, murals, brown berets
- Behavioral Rituals: Lowrider parades, Día de los Muertos altars, Chicano poetry

Other Tribal Clusters

1. Anti-Vaxx / Medical Freedom

- Archetype: The Exiled Truth-Seeker
- Symbolic Image: A lone figure holding a syringe crossed out, bathed in digital light
- Emotional Tone: Distrust, spiritual rebellion, martyrdom
- Totems: Natural supplements, detox kits, masks with Xs
- Behavioral Rituals: Online testimonial sharing, viral videos of confrontation, "truth drops"

2. Techno-Optimists / Silicon Valley Utopians

- Archetype: The Post-Human Visionary
- Symbolic Image: A glowing brain connected to stars via fiber-optic roots
- Emotional Tone: Futurist zeal, contempt for regulation, Promethean ambition

- Totems: Neural nets, crypto wallets, space colonies
- Behavioral Rituals: Founders' podcasts, trans-humanist manifestos, NFTdrops (Non-Fungible Token) drops

3. Online Gamer / Meme Tribes (4chan, Doomers, Zoomers)

- Archetype: The Chaotic Trickster
- Symbolic Image: A smirking mask glitching across a broken mirror
- Emotional Tone: Irony, nihilism, alienation
- Totems: Pepe the Frog, Wojak memes, white/black pill jargon
- Behavioral Rituals: Trolling, "shitposting," weaponizing memes to hijack narratives

Iconography of Encircled by Fire, Bound by Legacy

THE RING OF FIRE

The encircling fire acts as both hearth and border—symbolizing protection, purification, and exclusion. It demarcates a sacred interior from a threatening or profane exterior, implying that belonging is not merely emotional but also defended, tested, and possibly consuming.

THE CENTRAL CHIEFTAIN FIGURE

Wearing a traditional Native American headdress, this figure symbolically fuses ancestral tribal leadership with the role of guardian over a fractured American identity. His stoic face and crossed arms convey both authority and pain—a watchful dignity that echoes the unresolved trauma of displacement, while also channeling the mythic archetype of the protector. The headdress itself evokes sacred lineage, but here it is repurposed as symbolic resistance rather than romantic nostalgia.

THE FIGURES FLANKING HIM

On one side, a Black man holds an American flag; the flag's lower edge is torn or burning, indicating a legacy both claimed and violated On the other side, a white frontiersman holds a spear, invoking settler resilience and martial vigilance. A woman in front crosses her arms defiantly, suggesting matriarchal strength, protective resolve, and the emotional cost of constant struggle. Together, these figures create a tableau of intersecting grievances—different American tribes unified, not by sameness, but by shared defensiveness and moral certitude.

THE WOODEN PALISADE (BACKGROUND)

The sharpened vertical logs in the background resemble a fortress wall, evoking frontier defense, historic siege mentality, and the symbolic closing of ranks. It suggests that the group inside the fire is both besieged and fortified—simultaneously strong and isolated.

SHADOWED CROWD

Silhouettes of additional figures loom behind the fence—neither clearly ally nor enemy. Their presence adds a layer of ambiguity: Is the tribe surrounded by allies, spectators, or adversaries? This ambiguity enhances the sense of paranoia, performative solidarity, and the latent threat that marks tribalism.

COLOR PALETTE AND MOOD

The image's sepia-gold tone mimics the aesthetic of burnt parchment, ancestral memory, and mythic gravity, lending the scene the feel of a founding myth or national fever dream—a moment outside time, yet eternally repeated.

Interpretation

This image does not represent one tribe but the psychological logic of tribalism itself: the deep human need for recognition, the ancestral memory of betrayal, and the simmering fear that identity is always under siege. The fire is not just literal—it is the emotional heat that fuels collective loyalty, suspicion, and sacred purpose. The figures do not look outward, but inward and sideways, wary of one another even within their circle. This is tribalism at its core: a defense of sacred belonging, purchased at the cost of openness, vulnerability, and civic trust.

THE AMERICAN CLASS CULTURAL COMPLEX

THE GOLDEN STAIRCASE: ANATOMY OF THE AMERICAN CLASS CULTURAL COMPLEX

A man ascends a glowing staircase toward a stately mansion in the clouds, while others remain below—watching, working, waiting. Beneath him, a family stares out in quiet despair, a pipeline siphons away wealth, and a boy peers into a carnival mirror promising prosperity. This image reveals the myth and machinery of class in America: aspiration built atop extraction, and dreams distorted by systems that favor the few.

Core Emotion: Shame, Resentment, and Aspiration

Class in America is cloaked in the illusion of a classless society. The core emotions—economic shame, envy, humiliation, pride, and resentment—are often displaced onto other identities (race, religion, morality) because open discourse about class is taboo. Simultaneously, aspiration acts as a psychic escape hatch, feeding belief in upward mobility.

Mythic Root: The Self-Made Man and the American Dream

This complex is rooted in a powerful national myth: that anyone, with hard work, can rise from nothing to success. Figures like the bootstrapping entrepreneur or rags-to-riches hero conceal the systemic structures of class advantage and economic inheritance. The myth conflates material success with moral worth and failure with personal defect.

Symbolic Imagery

- A gilded staircase leading into clouds while others climb broken ladders
- A mansion with invisible servants
- A family farm being swallowed by a corporate pipeline
- A boarded-up Main Street facing a glassy tech campus
- A schoolyard fence dividing futures
- A carnival mirror that shows either a billionaire or a beggar—depending on who's looking

Self-Reinforcing Memory

Memory is shaped by generational struggles—Depression-era frugality, postwar mobility, deindustrialization, recessions, student debt, gig economy precarity. These patterns are encoded not only in bank accounts, but also in family narratives: the risk-taking grandfather, the mother working two jobs, the humiliation of food stamps, or the pride of paying cash. Class memory is rarely spoken about but deeply felt.

Black-and-White Thinking

The complex may polarize Americans into makers versus takers, real workers versus elites, or coastal snobs versus salt-of-the-earth folks. Wealth is viewed as either noble or corrupt, poverty as either virtuous or shameful. The middle class is mythologized as the moral center, but often disappears under pressure. This binary thinking obscures nuance and solidarity.

Repetitive Behavior

- Obsessive individual striving without structural critique
- Consuming class signifiers (brands, education, real estate) to mask insecurity
- Vilifying or idealizing the rich
- Denying one's own privilege or disadvantage
- Repeating the cycle of debt, hustle, burnout, and silence
- Wielding class resentment in political proxies: anti-elitism, populism, moral panic

Social Effects

It heals when class consciousness emerges without shame, when structural critique is coupled with human dignity and solidarity replaces envy or scorn. It heals when workers, professionals, and those left behind tell their stories and claim shared ground. It tears when the working poor are blamed for their suffering, when wealth is mistaken for virtue, and when economic wounds are projected onto race, gender, or nationality—dividing those with shared interests.

Potential for Transformation

Despite its deep wounds and distortions, the American Class cultural complex holds redemptive potential. When it becomes conscious—when Americans begin to name and narrate class experience without shame—it can serve as a catalyst for solidarity and systemic reform. This awakening can dissolve illusions of meritocracy and replace them with a shared understanding of structural interdependence. It can reawaken democratic imagination, prompting renewed investment in public goods: education, housing, healthcare, and a living wage. It can deepen empathy across divisions when people recognize how economic vulnerability is a common thread, not a personal flaw. By turning resentment into collective action and shame into dignity, the complex can foster a more honest and equitable society. The American Class cultural complex, when metabolized rather than denied, becomes not just a wound but also a wellspring of vision, voice, and transformation.

Iconography of The Golden Staircase: Anatomy of the American Class Cultural Complex

GOLDEN STAIRCASE TO THE MANSION (TOP CENTER)

A figure ascends a golden staircase toward a neoclassical mansion suspended in clouds. This is the myth of the "self-made man" and the American Dream—the belief that anyone can rise to wealth and power through personal effort. The stairs are gilded not just in material promise but also in illusion. The clouds represent disconnection from the realities below, suggesting how wealth exists in a separate, idealized realm.

CORPORATE SKYSCRAPERS AND THE GROUNDSKEEPER (TO THE RIGHT)

Corporate towers loom in the mist—symbols of concentrated capital, technocratic power, and the elite economy. Below them, a lone worker tends the grounds, almost invisible in the composition. This juxtaposition underscores the erasure of labor within the dominant narrative of success, highlighting the ongoing invisibility of the working class.

MAIN STREET AND THE HOLLOWED TOWN (TO THE LEFT)

The boarded-up buildings of Main Street speak to the decline of small-town economies and the collapse of once-stable local life. The tree in the background offers a faint echo of organic continuity, but the surrounding structures hint at abandonment, stagnation, and loss.

THE PIPELINE

A large industrial pipe cuts across the land, labeled bluntly: *PIPE*. It represents the extractive economy—draining wealth, resources, and labor from rural and working-class areas. The pipe also evokes environmental damage and the feeling of being used as a conduit rather than a community. Its scale dominates the lower portion of the image, emphasizing its invasive and disruptive presence.

WORKING-CLASS FAMILY (FOREGROUND)

In the bottom left, a man in overalls, a woman in a simple dress, and a child stand together. Their expressions are solemn, not defeated, conveying resilience amid hardship. The boy looks directly at the viewer—a piercing gaze that personalizes the abstract theme. They represent generational burden, the dignity of labor, and the cost of economic marginalization.

CARNIVAL MIRROR (TO THE RIGHT)

An ornate mirror distorts and reflects a wealthy man in a top hat and an elder reaching up toward him. This symbolizes how class identity is warped by media, culture, and aspiration. The mirror suggests that Americans often see either fantasy or condemnation when they reflect on wealth—rarely clarity.

CHILD AT THE FENCE

A lone child stands at a chain-link fence, peering toward the world above. This figure suggests separation from opportunity, particularly in terms of education, mobility, and social access. The fence evokes schoolyard inequality, economic segregation, and psychic exclusion.

STYLISTIC TONE

The overall aesthetic, with its muted sepia tones and WPA-era realism, invokes Depression-era consciousness and historical memory. It gives the image both an elegiac and timeless quality, inviting viewers to see class not as a statistic but as a mythic and emotional landscape.

Interpretation

This symbolic tableau captures the psychological bind of the American Class cultural complex: the simultaneous denial and obsession with class, the glamorization of wealth alongside the shame of poverty, and the deep hunger for dignity and visibility in a system built on structured inequality. It invites us to see, feel, and reckon with what is often left unspoken.

THE COMMUNITAS CULTURAL COMPLEX

COMMUNITAS: THE FIRE AT THE CENTER

Beneath a crescent moon and starlit sky, a diverse circle of people gathers around a shared flame. Their eyes are soft, their hands joined, their bodies attuned to the warmth between them. This image reflects the emotional and archetypal essence of the Communitas cultural complex—a longing for radical belonging, shared humanity, and sacred togetherness in a fragmented world.

Core Emotion: Belonging, Wonder, and Sacred Togetherness

At its heart is a felt experience of unity that transcends status, ideology, and separation. It's the emotional surge of we are one—alive in moments of shared struggle, ritual, or revelation. There is joy here, reverence, and the sense of stepping into something larger than the individual self.

Mythic Root: The Tribe Around the Fire and the Feast Without Hierarchy

This complex draws from ancient archetypes of the circle, the pilgrimage, the revival, and the ecstatic gathering—moments when barriers fall, masks are dropped, and people remember their shared humanity. It echoes the Eleusinian Mysteries, the Last Supper, civil rights marches, and drum circles alike.

Symbolic Imagery

- Hands joined in a great circle around a fire
- A table overflowing with bread and laughter
- A group singing under a wide sky
- Strangers hugging after disaster
- Diverse faces lit by candlelight
- A broken wall replaced by a garden
- Feet moving in rhythm
- Tears and dancing and silence, all held together

Self-Reinforcing Memory

Communitas often arises in liminal spaces—crisis, transition, celebration. The memory of such moments burns bright: a retreat, a protest, a vigil, a blackout when neighbors shared soup. These experiences linger like dreams, reminding people of a truth deeper than division.

Black-and-White Thinking

Unlike other complexes, communitas resists black-and-white thinking. It dissolves binaries. It invites paradox: unity without uniformity, intimacy without control. Its shadow arises when the high fades and people seek to replicate the experience through dogma or exclusion.

Repetitive Behavior

- Gathering in circles
- Telling stories
- Singing together

- Eating together
- Walking together
- Building altars, planting trees, washing feet, holding hands
- Creating spaces where masks fall and roles collapse—where the soul comes forward and is met

Potential for Transformation

This complex is not only nondivisive—it is antidivisive. It repairs the wounds of alienation, elitism, and dehumanization. It restores a sense of the sacred in everyday connection. Though fleeting, its imprint endures, shaping lives with a longing for kinship, truth, and shared transcendence.

Iconography of Communitas: The Fire at the Center

CENTRAL FIRE (HEART OF THE IMAGE)

The fire acts as both literal warmth and symbolic soul—radiating shared intention, story, grief, joy, and presence. It represents the center of the group's meaning-making: what they hold together, not as ideology, but as living connection. Fire here is not destructive but enlivening.

CIRCLE OF INTERCONNECTED PEOPLE

The group forms an intentional and egalitarian circle—symbolizing nonhierarchical unity, mutual respect, and collective being. They differ in age, race, and gender, yet stand with equal bearing. The circle suggests a temporary sacred space that transcends roles and status—a hallmark of communitas.

SHAKING HANDS AND OPEN GESTURES

Gestures of connection (especially the handshake) express trust, vulnerability, and shared presence. These physical connections signal a contrast to cultural alienation—where bodies are often separated by screens, status, or fear.

EXPRESSIONS OF SERENITY AND MUTUAL REGARD

Their faces show calm, focus, and empathy—not ecstatic, but grounded. This reflects the quiet power of communitas, rather than spectacle there is a deep resonance with others as fully human.

CRESCENT MOON AND STARFIELD (BACKGROUND)

These celestial symbols evoke timelessness and mystery. The moon suggests cycles, rhythms, and receptivity. The stars gesture toward a larger cosmic context—underscoring that communitas isn't merely social, but spiritual or archetypal.

DARK HORIZON FRAMING THE CIRCLE

The mountains and dark outer space create containment and contrast—heightening the sense that this circle exists as a luminous enclave within a wider world of shadow, conflict, or chaos. Communitas is often born in contrast to societal fracture.

WARM VS. COOL COLOR CONTRAST

The fire casts an orange glow onto each figure, lighting their faces with shared warmth, while the surrounding night remains cool and distant. This visual tension highlights the existential promise of the complex: we are not alone if we come to the fire together.

Interpretation

This image expresses a longing for belonging, equality, and shared purpose. The diverse figures form a circle of mutual recognition, symbolizing sacred fellowship without hierarchy. It envisions society renewed through empathy, collaboration, and soul-to-soul connection.

CHAPTER 5

Gendered and Identity Cultural Complexes

The Women's Movement Cultural Complex

The Anti-Feminist Cultural Complex

The American Male Cultural Complex

The Anti-Gay Cultural Complex

The LGBTQ+ Cultural Complex

The Anti-Trans Cultural Complex

The Trans Cultural Complex

THE WOMEN'S MOVEMENT CULTURAL COMPLEX

WEAVING THE THREAD OF SHE: THE WOMEN'S MOVEMENT CULTURAL COMPLEX

A luminous tableau evokes the collective force of the Women's Movement cultural complex. At its center, a woman weaves threads marked *Memory, Body, Grief,* and *Hope*—each strand spun from deeply embodied experience. Multiple feminine figures surround her in layered transparency, suggesting ancestral memory and intergenerational presence. The loom becomes both altar and engine—where trauma is not only remembered but transformed. Overhead, the moon cycles through its phases, symbolizing cyclical time, intuitive wisdom, and renewal. On one side, barren branches and silenced figures emerge from a past of repression; on the other, blooming forms and raised hands rise in solidarity. The tapestry becomes a living communitas—woven from shared struggle, sacred embodiment, and the enduring hope for a more just future.

Core Emotion: Empowered Outrage and Generational Awakening

At its heart is a rising tide of energy—fed by righteous anger at oppression, joy in rediscovered agency, and the determination to break cycles of silence. It is a complex charged by centuries of erasure and resistance, now voiced with force and clarity.

Mythic Root: The Awakening Goddess and the Great Mother Reclaimed

This complex draws on ancient and modern myths: the goddess bound and rising, the witch hunted and returning, the mother who protects and transforms. It reclaims feminine archetypes distorted by patriarchy and invokes new ones forged through struggle—freedom-fighter, healer, scholar, and builder of new worlds.

Symbolic Imagery

- A circle of women lifting one another
- A fist holding a flower
- Broken chains transforming into vines
- A burning bra becomes a torch
- A river flowing with faces and names
- A cracked mirror revealing not damage, but multiplicity
- An old woman and a girl walking side by side

Self-Reinforcing Memory

Memory flows across waves—suffrage, reproductive rights, workplace battles, domestic liberation, MeToo reckonings. Each victory and backlash becomes part of the living archive. The movement remembers itself across generations, often through storytelling, art, and ritual.

Black-and-White Thinking

In its reactive form, the complex may divide the world into oppressors and victims, insiders and outsiders, men and women. It may harden into ideological purism or cancel nuance in the pursuit of justice. But this tendency is born of long-silenced wounds and the urgency to claim space.

Repetitive Behavior

- Marching, naming, and organizing
- Calling out and calling in
- Rewriting history
- Making the personal political
- Gathering in circles and celebrating embodiment
- Creating platforms for the unseen
- Repeating the refrain: We are not going back

Social Effects

The Women's Movement cultural complex heals by restoring voice, dignity, and agency to those historically marginalized. It transforms shame into power and silence into solidarity. But it can tear when it fragments—along lines of race, class, sexuality, or generational difference—or when rage hardens into exclusion. Its vitality lies in staying porous, intersectional, and rooted in shared humanity.

Potential for Transformation

EMPOWERMENT THROUGH SOLIDARITY AND RECLAMATION

The Women's Movement cultural complex has radically expanded the moral, psychological, and political horizons of modern society. It has empowered generations of women—and their allies—to name their experience, claim their worth, and reshape systems once closed to them. It has made the invisible visible and insisted that the personal is political.

CULTURAL AND INSTITUTIONAL TRANSFORMATION

From suffrage to sexual harassment laws, from reproductive rights to inclusive education, the movement has changed laws, language, and leadership. It has opened pathways to power, reshaped professions, and sparked global conversations about justice, equity, and dignity.

REVIVAL OF FEMININE WISDOM AND ARCHETYPES

By reclaiming the symbolic, spiritual, and mythic dimensions of womanhood, it has restored ancient forms of knowledge and creativity long cast aside. Midwives, witches, grandmothers, rebels, and artists return to cultural consciousness as carriers of power—not shame.

INTERSECTIONAL CONSCIOUSNESS

At its best, the complex catalyzes deep listening across lines of difference—race, class, gender identity, sexuality, and ability—enabling coalitions rooted in mutual respect rather than sameness. This intersectional awareness pushes culture beyond individual empowerment toward collective liberation.

RESILIENCE IN THE FACE OF BACKLASH

Each wave of progress has been met by resistance, but the complex teaches endurance. It generates myths of survival, strategies for recovery, and rituals of remembrance that can outlast political cycles and patriarchal reassertion.

Iconography of Weaving the Thread of She: The Women's Movement Cultural Complex

THE CENTRAL LOOM AND THREADS

The loom at the center of the image symbolizes the weaving together of identity, memory, and transformation. Each thread bears a label—*Memory, Body, Grief,* and *Hope*—representing the lived experiences and emotional truths women integrate across generations. The act of weaving evokes both mythic fate (as in the Fates of classical mythology) and conscious agency: the power to rethread inherited patterns and forge new paths forward.

MULTIPLE FIGURES IN ONE WOMAN

The central figure subtly incorporates overlapping forms of a maiden, mother, and crone, representing the archetypal triptych of feminine life. These layered identities suggest the psychic multiplicity of women's roles—nurturer, healer, rebel, creator, survivor—each one coexisting within the same body across time.

GOLDEN THREAD (HOPE)

Among the many threads, one glows with particular radiance. This golden strand symbolizes not only hope, but also soul sovereignty and collective awakening. It extends outward toward the future, manifesting as activism, leadership, education, protest, caregiving, and cultural creation—a tapestry of rising possibilities.

GHOSTLY FIGURES IN THE BACKGROUND (THE PAST)

Dimly visible behind the weaver are the specters of suffragettes, persecuted healers, wartime mothers, and those turned away from opportunity. These ancestral figures represent a lineage of pain, resistance, and silenced voices. Their presence affirms that the movement does not begin in the present but draws from a deep well of historical memory.

RIVER OF FACES

Flowing beneath the loom is a river filled with indistinct faces and forgotten names. This river represents the collective memory of women across time—the unnamed, the marginalized, the countless whose lives shaped history yet went unrecorded. Their energy lives on, encoded in cultural DNA.

PHASES OF THE MOON OVERHEAD

The arc of the moon phases above the scene evokes the cyclical nature of feminine experience: repression and resurgence, sorrow and rebirth. It connects the personal to the cosmic, reminding us that women's lives unfold within larger rhythms of transformation and renewal.

OLD WOMAN AND GIRL WALKING SIDE BY SIDE

In the lower part of the image, an elder and a young girl walk hand in hand. This pairing evokes the intergenerational transmission of wisdom and hope. It is an image of both continuity and healing—a quiet but potent affirmation that no generation walks alone.

Interpretation

This image symbolizes the Women's cultural complex as an act of generational weaving—where women's lives are threaded through memory, body, grief, and hope. Each figure contributes to a larger tapestry, not as isolated individuals but as embodied history. The loom becomes both a tool of survival and transformation, turning collective suffering into symbolic coherence. Under the moon's phases, feminine time is cyclical and enduring, suggesting that integration—not erasure—is the work of cultural healing.

THE SOLEMN ASSEMBLY: KEEPERS OF JUSTICE, MEMORY, AND VOICE

A solemn assembly of women—diverse in age and origin—stands in quiet solidarity, bearing the symbols of justice, knowledge, and wisdom. Their calm strength evokes a legacy of truth-seeking and collective guardianship across generations.

Iconography of The Solemn Assembly: Keepers of Justice, Memory, and Voice

ELDER WOMAN (CENTER)—THE KEEPER OF MEMORY

Symbol: Holds a closed book.
Meaning: Embodies accumulated wisdom, historical record, and the foundational labor of previous generations. She signifies the written and unwritten legacies of women's struggle, memory, and law.
Age: Late seventies to eighties.
Archetype: Crone / matriarch.

WOMEN HOLDING SCALES OF JUSTICE (BOTTOM RIGHT & MIDDLE RIGHT)

Symbols: Both hold the scales of justice, one seated and robed.
Meaning: Represent moral clarity, legal equality, and the ongoing work to balance societal systems. Their dual presence implies continuity of effort, from past to future.
Ages: One in her twenties, one in her forties.
Archetypes: Advocate / guardian of justice.

BLACK WOMAN (MIDDLE LEFT)—EMBODIED COURAGE AND INTERSECTIONALITY

Symbol: Strong upright posture and steady gaze.
Meaning: Represents the central role and lived experience of Black women in the struggle for gender justice. Her unflinching gaze invites truth-telling and accountability.
Age: Late twenties to early thirties.
Archetype: Warrior / truth-bearer.

TWO ASIAN AMERICAN WOMEN (LOWER LEFT & MIDDLE FAR LEFT)

Symbols: Downward and inward gaze.
Meaning: Symbolizes contemplative strength, spiritual endurance, and the often unspoken labor of women across immigrant and diasporic histories. Their stillness speaks to survival through invisibility.
Ages: Both in their twenties to early thirties.
Archetypes: Mystic / rememberer.

WHITE WOMAN (UPPER CENTER—INTERGENERATIONAL INHERITANCE

Symbol: Upright posture, neutral gaze.
Meaning: Embodies the inheritor of feminist traditions and the evolving consciousness of modern gender identity. Suggests self-reflection amid privilege and responsibility.
Age: Mid-thirties.
Archetype: Seeker / integrator.

RED-HAIRED WOMAN (UPPER RIGHT)—FLAME OF RESOLVE

Symbol: Unflinching expression and strong presence.
Meaning: Embodies enduring courage and forward-looking resolve. She is the fire-keeper of conviction and vision.
Age: Late thirties to early forties.
Archetype: Reclaimer / visionary

OVERALL COMPOSITION AND COLOR

Golden Hue: Suggests sacredness, wisdom, and the light of clarity. Evokes both warmth and holiness.
Pyramid Structure: Implies collective strength and historical layering. Each woman adds stability and vision to the whole.
Unified Diversity: Ethnic, generational, and symbolic differences harmonize into a shared movement toward justice and wholeness.

Interpretation

This symbolic portrait depicts seven women arranged in a golden-hued composition, expressing unity across difference and generational continuity. Their expressions are solemn yet resolute, evoking a quiet but unwavering strength. The composition itself forms a pyramid of purpose, with the elder woman at the center anchoring the collective. This image serves, not as an idealization, but as a living icon of what the women's movement can become when it fully embraces depth, plurality, and intergenerational healing.

THE ANTI-FEMINIST CULTURAL COMPLEX

SANCTIFIED ROLES: THE ANTI-FEMINIST CULTURAL COMPLEX AS MORAL ORDER

Surrounded by family and scripture, the central woman—serene and silent—holds an infant while messages of submission and traditionalism are affirmed around her. Men and women alike participate in the transmission of these values, not with overt aggression, but with solemn pride. Here, the Anti-Feminist cultural complex appears, not as tyranny, but as righteousness—where gender hierarchy is seen as divine structure and obedience as virtue. This is patriarchy clothed in sanctity, where resistance is not punished, but preempted by reverence.

Core Emotion: Longing for Order and Fear of Disruption

At the heart of this complex lies a deep emotional tension: the desire to preserve a stable, known world in the face of cultural transformation. This longing manifests as anxiety over changing gender roles, grief over perceived loss of purpose, and resentment toward feminism's perceived unraveling of family, faith, and tradition. For some women, it also carries the yearning to be valued for their sacrifice; for some men, to be honored for their authority.

Mythic Root: The Sacred Order of Gender Roles

The complex draws on enduring mythic patterns: the noble protector and the virtuous nurturer, the obedient daughter and the rightful patriarch. These archetypes are often cast as divine or natural—rooted in scripture, biology, or ancestral memory. Feminism, in this frame, is not just a political challenge, but also a violation of a sacred social architecture.

Symbolic Imagery

- A woman setting down her law degree to return to "real" womanhood
- A father lamenting a daughter's independence
- A pastor praising wives who "submit joyfully"
- Mothers passing down books on modesty
- Social media influencers—both male and female—promoting the "feminine soft life" or "high-value man" ideologies

In each case, traditional gender roles are idealized as destiny, not limitations.

Self-Reinforcing Memory

The complex is reinforced by selective nostalgia: stories of a "simpler time" when men led, women nurtured, and families flourished. It remembers the 1950s housewife as fulfilled, not constrained; the patriarch as protector, not oppressor. These cultural memories gain power precisely by smoothing over inequality, abuse, or silencing—turning structure into virtue.

Black-and-White Thinking

There is womanly virtue or feminist rebellion; there are real men or emasculated weaklings. Gender roles are presented as moral absolutes—deviation becomes sin or selfishness. Feminism is not interpreted as a call for equality, but as a threat to family, faith, and civilization itself.

Repetitive Behavior

- Revival of modesty culture
- Sermons on gender submission
- Viral content extolling traditional wifehood or men's dominance
- Legal campaigns to restrict reproductive rights
- Women disciplining other women in defense of traditional roles
- Men celebrating masculinity as inherently hierarchical

The complex replicates itself in generational transmission and digital culture.

Social Effects

This complex constrains human potential—limiting the roles and expressions available to both women and men. It pressures women to find identity only in service or submission, and men to equate worth with dominance or control. It can fracture families, shame nonconformity, and stall gender equity under the guise of moral clarity. At its most extreme, it fuels backlash movements against feminism and feeds authoritarian or theocratic ideologies.

Possibility of Transformation

Yet at the heart of this complex lies a deeper desire: for meaning, connection, and honorable contribution. Transformation becomes possible when gender roles are reimagined, not as commandments, but as living relationships. Men and women alike can shift from defending hierarchy to cultivating mutuality. When care is not coded as feminine, and strength not as masculine—then the archetypal energies behind the complex can evolve. What once demanded obedience may become a source of shared dignity and liberated wholeness.

Iconography of Sanctified Roles: The Anti-Feminist Cultural Complex as Moral Order

CENTRAL WOMAN WITH INFANT AND DOWNCAST EYES

Symbol of feminine fulfillment through motherhood. Her gaze turned downward suggests modesty, deference, and inner silence—a posture valorized by the complex.

SIGNS SAYING, "TRADITIONAL VALUES" AND "SUBMIT TO YOUR HUSBANDS"

Doctrinal anchors. These slogans embody the public face of the complex—language that masks hierarchy with morality, submission with divine purpose.

HOLY BIBLE HELD BY GIRL (LOWER LEFT)

Transmission of belief. The girl clutching scripture symbolizes the early indoctrination into gendered expectations. Religious texts serve not only as spiritual guides but also as gender templates.

OLDER MEN IN BACKGROUND

Guardians of order. These figures embody institutional authority—stern and watchful. They do not dominate overtly, but their presence defines the structure others must inhabit.

YOUNG MALE FIGURES WITH AFFIRMING GESTURES

Internalized approval. The thumbs-up and composed expressions suggest that the boys have embraced the system—mirroring and reinforcing the values that shape their sisters' roles.

WARM MONOCHROME PALETTE (GOLD AND SEPIA TONES)

Nostalgic idealization. The image is bathed in hues that evoke tradition, sanctity, and moral simplicity—glossing over emotional complexity or dissent.

Interpretation

This image visually articulates how the Anti-Feminist cultural complex sustains itself not only through masculine authority, but also through feminine endorsement—portraying obedience as sacred, structure as natural, and submission as love.

THE AMERICAN MALE CULTURAL COMPLEX

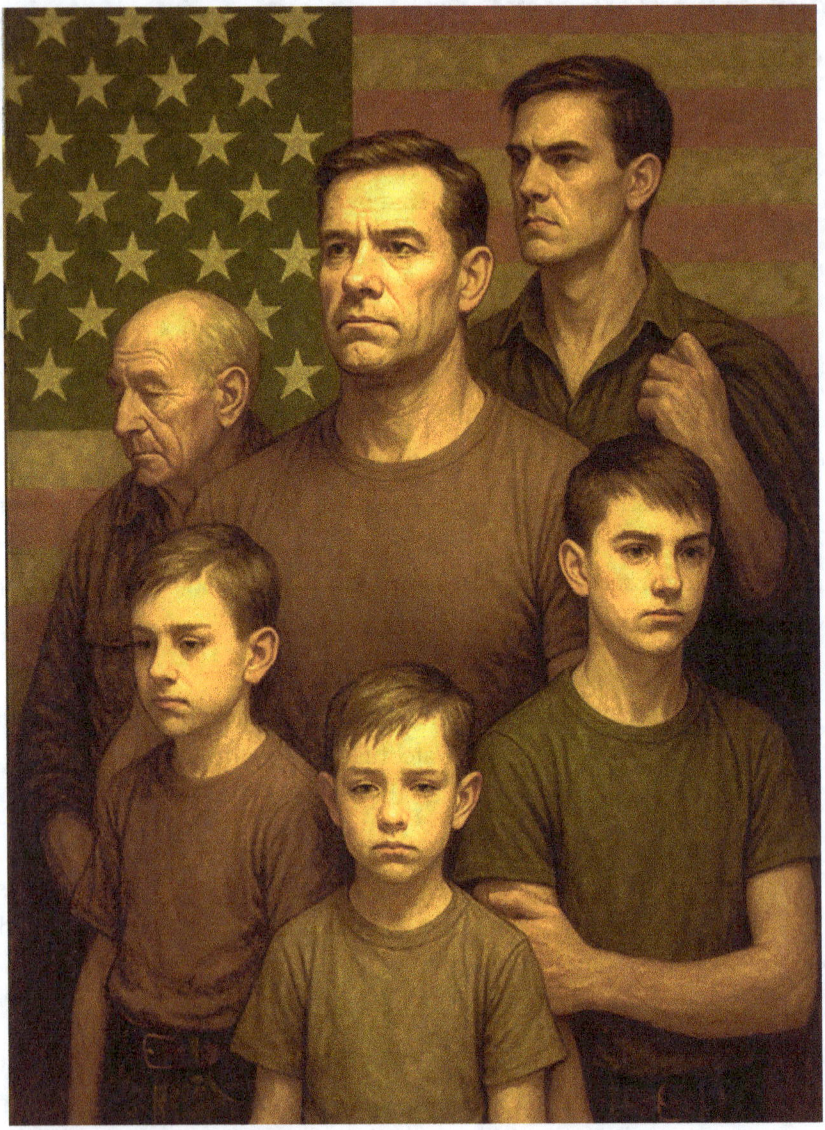

STRENGTH WITHOUT TEARS

A lineage of American males, spanning generations, stands solemnly before the US flag—stoic, composed, and burdened by unspoken expectations. Their postures reflect endurance and restraint, each face marked by duty and quiet resolve. Yet beneath their unified stance lies a complex emotional inheritance: the pressure to embody strength, the suppression of vulnerability, and the struggle to find identity beyond the roles they've been handed. This image evokes the American Male cultural complex—a legacy of honor, silence, and the longing to feel without failing.

Core Emotion: Pride Entwined with Pressure

At the center of this complex is the powerful drive to be strong, useful, respected, and in control—paired with an often unspoken fear of failure, weakness, or emotional exposure. Masculine pride is continually affirmed, but so too is the relentless demand to perform: to be protector, provider, and pillar, even when those roles are shifting or unsustainable.

Mythic Root: The Lone Hero and the Stoic Warrior

This cultural complex draws from enduring archetypes such as the frontiersman, the soldier, the cowboy, the self-made man, and the silent patriarch. These figures embody the myth of masculine individuation through conquest, endurance, and emotional restraint—a solitary man battling adversity, building something from nothing, and asking for nothing in return.

Symbolic Imagery

The imagery that surrounds this complex is iconic and idealized:

- A man standing alone on a ridge at sunset
- A father watching over a sleeping family with quiet intensity
- A boy walking beside a shadow ten times his size
- A jaw clenched behind a firm handshake
- A worn wedding ring on a calloused hand
- A punch held back
- A tear unseen
- A soldier's silhouette at a grave

These symbols evoke strength, containment, and unresolved grief.

Self-Reinforcing Memory

The complex is perpetuated through stories of toughness, sacrifice, and self-reliance—passed down by fathers, coaches, military service, media heroes, and stoic cultural icons. Expressions of vulnerability are often dismissed, mocked, or punished, producing generational echoes of repression, emotional restraint, and internalized shame.

Black-and-White Thinking

The masculine ideal becomes a binary: real men are tough, emotion is weakness, and you're either a leader or a failure. This thinking forces men into rigid molds, discouraging ambiguity or emotional intelligence.

Masculinity becomes equated with dominance and control, whereas anything associated with vulnerability or the feminine is seen as threatening.

Repetitive Behavior

This complex tends to express itself through patterned behaviors, including

- Withholding emotion and avoiding introspection
- Channeling pain into work, anger, or withdrawal
- Bonding through action, competition, or silence
- Masking depression with productivity
- Protecting others while denying personal needs
- Struggling to ask for help or to speak of inner conflict
- Idolizing or resenting "strong men"

These behaviors form a protective shell that often conceals unaddressed longing, grief, and emotional isolation.

Social Effects

The American Male cultural complex isolates men from themselves and others. It contributes to emotional illiteracy, strained relationships, burnout, and psychological distress. It can foster control, violence, or authoritarianism as distorted expressions of buried needs. It represses the inner feminine—the parts of the self that seek care, intimacy, softness, and vulnerability—and often leads to fragmentation or despair.

Potential for Transformation

When brought into consciousness, this complex holds immense potential for transformation.

STRENGTH REIMAGINED AS PRESENCE

Men can reclaim strength, not as stoicism or domination, but as grounded presence, emotional honesty, and compassionate protection.

LEADERSHIP AS SERVICE, NOT CONTROL

True leadership emerges from relational depth, listening, and humility—not command and fear. The "warrior" becomes a guardian, not a tyrant.

INTEGRATION OF THE INNER FEMININE

The masculine psyche becomes more whole when it honors

tenderness, receptivity, and care—not just assertiveness and action.

INTERGENERATIONAL HEALING

By breaking the cycle of emotional suppression, men can model a new kind of fathering, mentoring, and partnership for younger generations.

BROTHERHOOD WITHOUT PERFORMANCE

Spaces of male friendship that are emotionally safe, not competitive, can cultivate resilience, empathy, and authenticity.

FROM INDEPENDENCE TO INTERDEPENDENCE

The myth of the isolated hero gives way to a deeper truth: that real freedom is found in connection, vulnerability, and shared purpose.

Here, manhood is not a solitary inheritance—it is a shared becoming.

Iconography of Strength Without Tears

SIX GENERATIONS OF MALES (BOY TO ELDER)

The lineup of boys, men, and an elder male figure creates a vertical lineage—each representing a different life stage but united in tone, posture, and expression. Their shared sternness reflects an inheritance of stoicism, discipline, and emotional restraint. The absence of women further underscores the insularity and self-reinforcing nature of this cultural complex.

Children (front row): Young boys already bearing a serious, unsmiling demeanor symbolize early socialization into emotional suppression and the expectation to grow into strength.

Middle-aged Men (center): Their strong jaws, firm postures, and fixed gazes evoke silent endurance and duty. They are the core of the complex—caught between expectation and exhaustion.

Elder Male (left rear): His downturned eyes and aged features speak of weariness and reflection, possibly signaling the long-term psychological cost of the complex.

Man Grasping Shirt (right rear): This gesture may symbolize patriotic commitment, resolve, or the inner turmoil of forced composure. It could also suggest a ritualistic affirmation of identity, strength, or control.

UNIFORM, EARTH-TONED CLOTHING

The lack of adornment or distinction in their clothes points to values of humility, conformity, and utilitarian masculinity. Earth tones evoke not only groundedness but also a lack of emotional color—everything is serious, sober, and subdued.

EXPRESSIONLESS FACES AND LOCKED EYES

The lack of visible emotion conveys the core emotional repression at the heart of this complex. These men and boys are not allowed the luxury of vulnerability. Instead, they show what they've been taught: that to feel is to risk failure and to lead is to steel oneself.

MIRRORED FACES AND SIMILAR POSTURE

The near-symmetry of features and poses symbolizes intergenerational transmission. Masculinity here is not personal but inherited. Identity is shaped, not through inner exploration, but by external expectation—a baton passed in silence.

LOW LIGHTING AND GOLDEN HUE

The lighting creates a hallowed, almost religious atmosphere, framing the image as iconic—akin to a sacred portrait. The golden hue implies nostalgia and solemnity, echoing the glorification of a traditional masculine ideal that is both admired and imprisoning.

UNDERLYING MESSAGE

While the image can be read as a tribute to strength and continuity, it also functions as a subtle critique. The lack of emotional variety, the somber mood, and the rigid formation suggest entrapment within an archetype—one that may offer honor but demands silence, suppression, and isolation.

Interpretation

The flag serves as a symbolic canvas of identity, duty, and national mythology. It frames masculinity in explicitly patriotic terms—suggesting that to be a "real man" is also to be a protector of the nation, its values, and its legacy. The flag's faded, muted tones may hint at both reverence and wear, suggesting an ideal that is weighty and possibly strained.

STRENGTH REIMAGINED, GENERATION BY GENERATION

A young man stands at the center of a multigenerational circle of fathers, sons, brothers, and elders, held not by stoic distance but by quiet warmth and mutual regard. Hands rest on shoulders, eyes soften with pride, and smiles rise without shame. In this reimagining of the American Male cultural complex, strength is no longer defined by silence or hardness, but by connection, care, and the permission to be both steady and tender. Here, manhood is not a solitary inheritance—it is a shared becoming.

Iconography of Strength Reimagined, Generation by Generation: The Male Cultural Complex

CENTRAL COMPOSITION

A group of males spanning three generations—elders, young adults, and children—stand together in a forest clearing bathed in golden light. The composition is intimate and circular, with their bodies angled inward, forming a quiet protective ring. There is no sign of domination, aggression, or hardness; instead, we see presence, attention, and tenderness expressed through posture and touch.

FACIAL EXPRESSIONS AND POSTURES

Each male figure is calm, grounded, and receptive. The central youth stands tall with quiet strength, surrounded by encouraging hands placed gently on his shoulders. An older man leans in with a kind smile, suggesting guidance rather than control. A younger child stands with arms folded—not in defiance, but in serenity—eyes closed as if inhabiting a moment of safety and peace.

HANDS AS SYMBOLIC ELEMENTS

Hands are everywhere in this image—resting on shoulders, clasped, touching. They symbolize intergenerational connection, trust, and the transmission of values. These gestures convey support without pressure, strength without domination. They evoke healing touch, fatherly protection, and the unspoken promise of continuity.

COLOR PALETTE AND ATMOSPHERE

Soft earth tones, amber light, and a diffuse sky evoke warmth, safety, and natural belonging. The subdued greens and browns suggest a return to groundedness and rooted identity—not performative masculinity, but a masculinity that is reflective, relational, and whole.

SETTING

The forested background suggests time beyond history—ancestral, cyclical, and enduring. It recalls the archetypal "return to the woods" where individuation and integration happen. The absence of urban or institutional elements helps center the male experience in embodied connection and natural growth.

Interpretation

This image reclaims masculinity from the distortions of stoicism and detachment. It shows male strength as continuity, nurturance, and relational fortitude. Vulnerability is not hidden but held—seen in the quiet attentiveness among generations. Strength is not asserted outwardly but gathered inwardly, passed along through example, presence, and care. This is the image of the healed father, the beloved son, the wise elder, and the open brother. It draws on archetypes of the mentor, innocent, and everyman—inviting viewers to see masculinity, not as dominance over others, but as stewardship, integrity, and earned gentleness. This iconography counters both the fragility and hardness often projected onto men in cultural narratives, offering instead a portrait of masculine wholeness rebuilt over time—quietly, humbly, and together.

The Anti-Gay Cultural Complex

THE DOORWAY OF JUDGMENT: THE ANTI-GAY CULTURAL COMPLEX

A young man stands at the threshold of a crumbling doorway, holding a rainbow flag as if shielding it from view. Outside, a stern crowd holds signs declaring SIN, TRADITION, and NORMALCY, their faces etched with uniform disapproval. Behind them rise temples of law and church, backlit by a dramatic rift in the clouds. A single candle burns near broken chains and shattered glass, illuminating a choice: to step forward into rejection—or remain confined by fear. The image captures the psychic burden placed on queer identity in the shadow of inherited shame and social control.

Core Emotion: Fear of Disruption and Contagion

At the core of the ant-gay cultural complex lies visceral fear—that nonheteronormative identities threaten traditional structures of family, gender, and morality. This fear is often unconscious and projected outward, cloaked in claims of defending tradition, religion, or "protecting children." Beneath the surface lies deep anxiety about fluidity, vulnerability, and the breakdown of inherited norms.

Mythic Root: The Polluted Temple and the Inverted Order

This complex draws on ancient archetypes of the sacred center violated or the natural order inverted. Same-sex love or gender nonconformity becomes a symbol of chaos in a world that seeks to preserve rigid binary oppositions: male/female, sacred/profane, order/disorder. It also evokes the scapegoat archetype—those cast out to preserve the illusion of collective purity.

Symbolic Imagery

Images that express this complex often include:

- A temple wall cracking or burning
- A rainbow flag torn or trampled
- A family portrait with one figure blurred or crossed out
- A child holding a torn sign between *Tradition* and *Truth*
- A priest holding a flame over water—symbolizing attempted purification
- A mirror shattered underfoot, reflecting fractured identity
- A crowd of turned backs representing social exile

Self-Reinforcing Memory

This complex recycles cultural narratives of "moral decline" and "civilizational collapse" whenever queer visibility or gender variance rises. Historical traumas, such as the HIV/AIDS epidemic, are weaponized as divine punishment. Moments of liberation are followed by backlash, which is mythologized as moral restoration. These stories reinforce the notion that LGBTQ+ existence is not only deviant but also dangerous.

Black-and-White Thinking

Reality is divided into simplistic moral binaries: natural versus unnatural, masculine versus feminine, holy versus perverse, protector versus corrupter. This moral absolutism suppresses nuance and complexity, justifying exclusion and even violence. Queerness is not simply misunderstood—it is framed as contagious or corrosive to the social order.

Repetitive Behavior

The complex manifests in recurrent cultural and political behaviors, including

- Legislative targeting (e.g., bathroom bills, drag bans, curriculum censorship)
- Institutionalized shaming and conversion efforts
- Surveillance of gender-nonconforming youth
- Demonization through tropes of danger or predation
- The policing of public norms to assert dominance over ambiguity and difference

Social Effect

This complex silences, shames, and erases—both externally and internally. It fractures families, marginalizes faith communities, and alienates individuals from their authentic selves. It enforces performative conformity at the expense of emotional, relational, and spiritual wholeness. Yet its very intensity reveals its fragility—a shadow fear that what it suppresses may already live within.

Potential for Transformation

When made conscious, the Anti-Gay cultural complex opens a doorway to transformation—both individually and collectively.

COMPASSION THROUGH CONFRONTATION

Facing the fear that underlies this complex—fear of ambiguity, loss, or internal contradiction—can lead to deeper empathy and more inclusive morality.

RESTORATION OF SACRED DIVERSITY

Ancient traditions that honored gender variance and queer love can be rediscovered, healing the rupture between spirit and sexuality. The "polluted temple" becomes a sanctuary once again.

REIMAGINING TRADITION

Tradition need not be rigid. When transformed, it becomes a living story—capable of growth, reinterpretation, and reconciliation with evolving truths.

RECLAIMING THE EXILED

LGBTQ+ individuals once cast out as scapegoats can become healers, teachers, and bridge-builders—offering perspectives vital to a pluralistic society.

EMERGENCE OF AUTHENTIC COMMUNITY

Beyond surveillance and shame, new spaces emerge for honest belonging—where identity is affirmed, complexity is welcomed, and love is no longer feared.

FROM SUPPRESSION TO WHOLENESS

Ultimately, this complex points to a deeper longing for unity between body, heart, and soul. What was rejected as deviant returns as a source of beauty, resilience, and liberation.

Iconography of The Doorway of Judgment: The Anti-Gay Cultural Complex

THE YOUNG MAN

Stands at the threshold, caught between the shadowed interior (the "closet") and the oppressive gaze of the outside world. His posture is hesitant—one hand clutches the door frame for stability, the other hides a rainbow flag beneath his coat.

THE DOORWAY (CENTER LEFT)

The symbolic space between confinement and exposure. The young man's liminal position marks the psychological tension between concealment and self-expression, safety and exile.

RAINBOW FLAG (HELD CLOSE)

A symbol of queer identity and pride, held cautiously to the chest rather than waved openly. It suggests both hope and fear—visibility under threat.

THE CROWD (RIGHT)

A nearly faceless sea of conformity holding placards: *SIN, TRADITION, NORMALCY*. Their repetition, stern expressions, and gray tones embody societal pressure, moral rigidity, and suppression of difference.

RELIGIOUS AND CIVIC ARCHITECTURE (BACKGROUND RIGHT)

A church steeple and courthouse evoke institutional authority—reinforcing the historical role of religion and law in upholding heteronormative norms.

THE CANDLE AND CHAINS (LOWER LEFT)

The candle represents fragile inner light, the enduring presence of soul and dignity. The broken chain beside it suggests that liberation is possible, but still incomplete.

THE WOMAN IN MOURNING (LOWER RIGHT)

A sorrowful elder figure represents generational judgment or internalized oppression. She evokes grief, control, and the weight of familial or cultural inheritance.

CRACKED STONE AND BROKEN GLASS

Symbols of trauma, exclusion, and psychic injury. These textures amplify the image's emotional charge, hinting at both rupture and the possibility of rebuilding.

COLOR PALETTE (MUTED SEPIA AND GOLD)

The tones evoke old photographs, tradition, and memory, whereas the golden light breaking through suggests moments of revelation or transformation.

Emotional & Archetypal Reading

Scapegoat Archetype: The figure at the threshold is framed as a threat to order. They carry the group's projected fears of disruption, temptation, and ambiguity.

Sacrificial Tension: The image captures a moment before transformation or rejection. Will he step into the crowd or retreat into silence?

Fear of the Fluid: The crowd fears what cannot be boxed—love without borders, gender beyond binary, truth that subverts ideology.

Interpretation

This image renders the Anti-Gay cultural complex as a psychic landscape of fear, silence, and control—but also one of defiant hope and moral awakening. It holds the viewer in the moment just before decision, when the cost of authenticity and the price of conformity are equally vivid. The image portrays the oppressive dynamics of the Anti-Gay cultural complex, centered on shame, conformity, and the policing of identity. It contrasts inner authenticity (represented by the figure in the doorway) with external societal judgment (the grim and silent crowd).

THE LBGTQ+ CULTURAL COMPLEX

THE SACRED EMBRACE: THE LGBTQ+ CULTURAL COMPLEX

A central figure, haloed and calm, rises like a modern-day icon, holding both the rainbow flag and the ancient Venus symbol. Flanked by an intergenerational, multicultural group of solemn faces, she stands not alone but as part of a larger body embodying quiet strength and unapologetic presence. Together they form a tableau of chosen family, collective resilience, and the reimagination of belonging. This image portrays the LGBTQ+ cultural complex, not as fringe or spectacle, but as lineage, belonging, and quiet sanctity—where dignity defies erasure and identity becomes both beacon and shield.

Core Emotion: Pride Born of Survival and Longing for Recognition

At its heart is the fierce and tender emotion of being made visible after invisibility, of claiming identity after centuries of erasure. It is powered by both celebration and grief—by the joy of authenticity and the sorrow of rejection.

Mythic Root: The Sacred Androgyne and the Exiled Trickster

This complex draws from archetypes long buried and only recently reclaimed: the two-spirit, the shapeshifter, the hermaphroditic divine, the seer cast out and returned. It evokes myths of transformation, liminality, fluidity, and the healing potential of those who dwell between categories—gender, sexuality, normativity, tradition.

Symbolic Imagery

A figure stepping out of a shadow, rainbow unfurling behind them. A phoenix with feathers of every hue. A multicolored tapestry stitched from shards of broken mirrors. A hand reaching through bars to another's hand painted with stars. A tree with twisting branches growing from one deep root. A masked face smiling as it removes the mask.

Self-Reinforcing Memory

Memory within this complex is woven from struggle: Stonewall, the AIDS epidemic, closets and coming outs, chosen families, ballroom houses, bathroom bills. Each generation carries both trauma and triumph, reliving the rituals of revelation, resistance, and reclamation.

Black-and-White Thinking

While grounded in fluidity, the complex may at times harden around binaries of oppressed versus oppressor, ally versus enemy, and included versus erased. These are protective stances shaped by long histories of danger. Yet at its best, the complex transcends this polarity with radical empathy and creative reimagination.

Social Effects

- Reclaiming language, inventing pronouns, creating ritual spaces
- Performing and transforming identity through dress, art, and story
- Celebrating pride while mourning the cost of authenticity
- Protecting one's own while advocating for a world where no one is othered

Potential for Transformation

The LGBTQ+ cultural complex heals by expanding the boundaries of human possibility. It teaches that identity is not fixed but unfolding; that love is not deviance but divinity. It tears when it fractures internally—through exclusion, purity tests, or unresolved generational pain. But at its deepest core is a gift: the archetypal power of living the truth of the self.

Iconography of The Sacred Embrace: The LGBTQ+ Cultural Complex

CENTRAL HALOED FIGURE (TOP CENTER)

A feminine figure with a golden halo evokes archetypes of sainthood, protection, and spiritual legitimacy. She channels both protest and reverence, elevating LGBTQ+ experience into the realm of sacred humanity.

VENUS SYMBOL (HELD LEFT)

The raised Venus glyph signifies the cultural and symbolic power of femininity and queer liberation. It also nods to the historical role of women and nonbinary figures in LGBTQ+ struggle and theory.

RAINBOW FLAG (HELD RIGHT)

A stylized reinterpretation of the Pride flag, rendered in muted tones, flies like a sacred banner—reframed from defiance to enduring dignity. It asserts visibility, diversity, and historical memory.

INTERGENERATIONAL FACES (BOTTOM AND MIDDLE ROWS)

A diverse collection of individuals—varying in age, gender presentation, and ethnicity—represent the spectrum of LGBTQ+ identities and allies. Their calm, direct gazes reject caricature and victimhood in favor of communal humanity.

UNIFORM ATTIRE (GREEN SHIRTS)

The shared clothing suggests solidarity, unity in diversity, and resistance to commodification. It speaks to collectivity over individualism without erasing personal identity.

BACKGROUND GLOW AND SOFT SHADOWS

The golden light washes over the scene like morning sun or candlelight, suggesting renewal, memory, and spiritual emergence. The shadowy figures behind suggest history's ghosts—those excluded, silenced, or watching from the margins.

ABSENCE OF SPECTACLE

The image avoids tropes of flamboyance or victimization, inviting reflection on deeper layers of the LGBTQ+ complex: inherited pain, quiet pride, ancestral grief, and chosen kinship. Unlike many representations of LGBTQ+ experience that focus on persecution or resistance, this tableau offers an affirmative vision: visibility without violence, pride without spectacle, queerness as presence rather than disruption.

COMPOSITION (ICONIC AND SYMMETRICAL)

The image mimics a sacred altarpiece or group portrait of saints and prophets. It invites reverence and calls viewers to witness—not merely observe—the reality of queer lives past, present, and future.

Interpretation

This rendering of the LGBTQ+ cultural complex reframes queer identity from spectacle to sacrament. It resists reduction to trauma or triumph alone, holding instead a sacred middle space—one of embodiment, endurance, and collective grace.

SANCTUARY OF BECOMING

Framed by a rainbow banner and bathed in golden light, a central figure gazes with serene power. In one hand they raise the colors of queer pride; in the other, they offer a phoenix in midflight—symbol of rebirth. Below, a tree of life emerges beside cracked tablets of TRADITION and SIN, while a hand reaches through prison bars to offer the symbol of Venus, claiming identity long suppressed. This image embodies the redemptive force of the LGBTQ+ cultural complex: a rising from shame, a freeing from cages, and the sacred act of becoming fully human, fully seen.

Iconography of Sanctuary of Becoming

RAINBOW BANNER (UPPER LEFT)

The subject lifts and parts a flowing rainbow banner as though unveiling a sacred curtain, revealing their face and deeper essence beneath it. This banner symbolizes queer identity not merely as a political statement, but also as an act of revelation—mythic, radiant, and protective. The gesture echoes religious iconography of annunciation or epiphany, reimagining queer presence as something holy, visible, and transformative, not as something to hide.

CENTRAL FIGURE WITH HALO

The glowing halo behind the central figure's head evokes the visual language of sainthood or divine embodiment, positioning the LGBTQ+ subject, not as deviant, but as a bearer of healing, grace, and light. Their calm and direct gaze expresses dignity, moral clarity, and an unshakable sense of inner sovereignty. This figure stands as an archetype of the queer liberator, healer, or truthteller—one who radiates wholeness rather than shame.

PHOENIX RISING (UPPER RIGHT)

A phoenix bursts upward from the figure's outstretched hand, its feathers alive with flame and flight. This mythical bird represents transformation through fire—the painful destruction of imposed identities and the triumphant emergence of truer, chosen ones. Its upward motion, born from an open hand rather than clenched fists, implies that liberation comes, not through conquest, but through grace, courage, and offering. The phoenix here becomes a sacred symbol of queer survival, rebirth, and self-authorship in the aftermath of cultural persecution.

TREE OF LIFE (LOWER RIGHT)

Beneath the phoenix, a flourishing tree rises from soil once covered by dogma. It grows alongside the cracked tablets of *TRADITION* and *SIN*, suggesting that genuine spiritual and psychological growth happens not in spite of condemnation, but by breaking through and beyond it. Its roots wind through and around broken chains, signaling release from theological, familial, or internalized captivity. The tree stands as an emblem of queer flourishing—deeply rooted in truth, bearing many forms of fruit, and extending its branches toward a more inclusive future.

SIGNS WITH THE WORDS *TRADITION* AND *SIN*

The tablets labeled *TRADITION* and *SIN* lie discarded at the base of the tree and phoenix, fractured and no longer central. These labels represent moral frameworks and social codes that once condemned queer lives to shame, erasure, or silence. Their crumbling form reflects the diminishing hold of such frameworks when confronted with lived authenticity, love, and spiritual rebirth.

PRISON BARS AND REACHING HAND (LOWER LEFT)

From behind a set of vertical iron bars, a hand emerges holding a blue orb marked with the Venus symbol and stars. This gesture symbolizes an act of defiant reclamation—a reaching forth from confinement to affirm identity and worth. The bars themselves stand for systems of control and erasure: cultural, theological, familial, and psychological. The Venus symbol, adorned with stars, transforms from a simple gender marker into a cosmic emblem of queer visibility, sacred femininity, and celestial legitimacy.

BROKEN CHAINS

Beneath the central figure's feet lie slack, broken chains—symbols of past bondage to secrecy, shame, and imposed silence. Their presence reminds us that visibility and wholeness are not given freely; they are earned through struggle, rupture, and the courage to break from inherited restraints.

Interpretation

This image serves as a mythic affirmation of queer transformation. It invites viewers to witness LGBTQ+ identity, not as a rupture from tradition, but as a phoenix-born renewal of it. Through the visual language of sanctuary, resurrection, and sacred offering, the image reclaims what has long been labeled as sinful and reframes it as something holy, generative, and full of light. The bars, chains, and moral scripts that once sought to bind queer lives now serve a different purpose—they frame the power of liberation and the redefinition not only of the self, but also of the language of power itself.

THE ANTI-TRANS CULTURAL COMPLEX

Although the Trans/Anti-Trans cultural complex is very much a part of the LGBTQ+ cultural complex, the lightning rod issues around being trans have become singled out and so inflammatory in the current American political and social environment that the complex deserves to be singled out for special attention.

BETWEEN THE MIRROR AND THE STORM

A young person reaches toward a fractured reflection, where a trans flag flutters behind the figure in the glass. Shards fall at their feet, marking the cost of self-perception ruptured by judgment. On the wall behind them, dogmas declare BIOLOGY = TRUTH, and signs labeled FAMILY and SIN lie cracked in the rubble. A rainbow curves through the lightning-streaked sky, touching both ruin and redemption. This image captures the emotional truth of sexual identity uncertainty: a quiet reckoning with inherited shame, a hand extended through distortion, and the fragile, luminous search for coherence.

Core Emotion: Anxiety about Fluidity and Disruption of Order

At its core, the Anti-Trans cultural complex is driven by a visceral unease with gender ambiguity. It is fueled by the fear that boundaries—biological, moral, and cultural—are dissolving. This fear often cloaks itself in appeals to "common sense," "biology," or "tradition," but beneath lies a deeper anxiety about identity destabilization and the erosion of inherited norms.

Mythic Root: The Inverted Order and the Corrupted Body

This complex draws from ancient myths of chaos invading the cosmos, the polluted temple, or the world turned upside down. The trans body is symbolically cast as unnatural, even monstrous—an emblem of defiance against the "divinely ordained" binary. It also echoes the archetype of the trickster demonized: one who crosses boundaries and is punished for it. In this mythos, trans identity becomes a projection of cultural disorder rather than an expression of human complexity

Symbolic Imagery

- A mirror shattering as a hand reaches out to change its reflection
- A child standing between two signs—*Boy* and *Girl*—with figures pointing in both directions
- A storm cloud forming over a rainbow flag
- A temple wall inscribed with biology = truth, cracking at its base
- A gatekeeper figure barring entry, holding a clipboard labeled birth certificate
- A closet glowing from within, while figures outside turn away

Self-Reinforcing Memory

This complex draws on selective moral panics—memories of social change cast as moral collapse:

- The introduction of gender-inclusive policies in schools or sports
- Public debates about bathrooms, pronouns, or medical care for youth
- Sensationalized media stories used to invoke fear and disgust

These memories create a feedback loop: each new moment of trans visibility is framed, not as inclusion, but as a threat—fueling further backlash and repression.

Black-and-White Thinking

The Anti-Trans cultural complex relies on stark binaries: real versus fake, natural versus artificial, man versus woman, protector versus predator. This binary worldview erases the existence of nonbinary, intersex, and trans experiences altogether. It conflates difference with danger and uses gender rigidity as a stand-in for moral clarity.

Repetitive Behavior

- Legislative campaigns banning gender-affirming care, bathrooms, or identity documentation
- Social media harassment, outing, and deadnaming
- The use of "protect the children" as coded language to dehumanize trans people
- Censorship of trans representation in education, literature, and media
- Weaponization of religion or pseudoscience to enforce gender dogma

Social Effects

This complex harms trans individuals through alienation, violence, and erasure. It splits families, distorts public policy, and turns identity into a battlefield. It encourages suspicion, scapegoating, and fear in place of empathy or understanding. It also damages the broader culture by making rigidity a virtue, suppressing emotional intelligence, and preventing the evolution of gender roles for all people.

Potential for Transformation

EXPANSION OF HUMAN IMAGINATION

By confronting this complex, society is invited to reconsider its deepest assumptions about gender, embodiment, and personhood—moving from control to curiosity.

REINTEGRATION OF THE SACRED ANDROGYNOUS

Ancient traditions that honored two-spirits, hijra, and liminal figures can be remembered and revalued, restoring the lost archetype of the bridge-walker.

INVITATION TO COMPASSIONATE COMPLEXITY

The existence of trans people calls for emotional nuance, layered understanding, and listening beyond instinct. It dissolves the illusion that moral clarity requires rigid categories.

CULTURAL HEALING THROUGH WITNESS

As trans voices are heard and honored, the collective body can begin to heal from centuries of projection and denial—turning what was feared into what is sacred.

LIBERATION BEYOND THE BINARY

Ultimately, transformation of this complex benefits everyone: freeing men from stoicism, women from confinement, and children from predetermined scripts. It opens a path toward more authentic and expansive ways of being human.

Iconography of Between the Mirror and the Storm

CENTRAL FIGURE IN CONFLICT

A solitary young person—neither clearly male nor female—is the emotional and visual anchor of the image. Their expression suggests a deep interior struggle or questioning, capturing the vulnerability and courage of trans identity under pressure. Their attire appears neutral and subdued, emphasizing liminality: the in-between state that trans people are often forced to occupy in a culture that demands binary clarity.

MIRRORED OR DOUBLED SHADOW

Behind or beside the figure, there may be a ghostlike double, fractured reflection, or opposing silhouette—symbolizing the split between inner identity and outer expectation.

This doubling suggests the concept of the deadname: the former identity imposed or remembered by others, often at odds with the self-determined truth.

WALL TEXT OF *BIOLOGY = TRUTH*

This phrase evokes biological essentialism—a belief that physical sex dictates all identity, which is often used to suppress or deny sexual and gender variation. The institutional stone-like wall suggests these messages are not incidental but structural, embedded in family, faith, and social systems.

SIGNS SAYING *FAMILY* AND *SIN*

These signs, lying broken and displaced near the subject, convey the moral weight and emotional violence of rejection. They signal the crushing message that to live authentically is to risk exile from family or condemnation from faith. Their placement amid cracked earth and fallen chains suggests these forces are losing power—but not without pain.

DIM CANDLE OR GLOW OF RESISTANCE

Amid the shadowed imagery, a soft light—perhaps a candle or halo—shines faintly near or from within the figure, symbolizing the trans spirit: resilience, authenticity, and inner knowing that persists despite attempts at erasure.

THE RAINBOW AND THE STORM

The rainbow offers a universal symbol of queer hope, peace, and divine promise, but here it arcs through a thunderous, ominous sky. This pairing signifies that truth and liberation often emerge through conflict and upheaval, not peace alone.

THE CHAINS ON THE GROUND

Broken but still present, these chains symbolize past bondage to shame, silence, or imposed identity. Their placement at the subject's feet implies a threshold moment—freedom is possible, but not yet there.

MUTED COLOR PALETTE

The overall tones of sepia, gray, or dusky earth hues suggest repression, mourning, and the weight of historical trauma. This subdued palette reinforces the emotional gravity of the image and the cultural legacy of invisibility and pain.

Interpretation

This image powerfully expresses the liminal state of sexual identity uncertainty—the space between recognition and repression, affirmation and fear. The figure is neither fully inside nor outside the mirror, neither wholly denied nor fully claimed. They hold a rainbow cloth—soft, symbolic, sacred—against the cold weight of doctrines and family verdicts. It is a visual prayer for integration: to step through the mirror, gather the shards, and walk forward into the storm—and light—with nothing left to hide.

THE TRANS CULTURAL COMPLEX

METAMORPHOSIS AND MEMORY: THE TRANS CULTURAL COMPLEX

With eyes closed in solemn self-recognition, a young figure holds both the rainbow cloth of queer identity and a card marked Deadname—a relic of a forsaken identity. One side of their body erupts into the wing of a monarch butterfly, symbolizing transformation, fragility, and flight. Behind them, a burning scroll bearing the transgender symbol lights the shadows of onlookers—some mournful, some hostile, many silent. At their feet lie a broken mirror, fallen chains, and a cracked symbol of binary logic. This image evokes the inner and outer struggle of the trans experience: a journey of becoming that unfolds amid reverence, stigma, memory, and emerging light. It renders transition, not as spectacle or debate, but as sacred metamorphosis—both shattering and radiant.

Core Emotion: Yearning for Coherence and the Right to Exist

At its emotional center is a deep and often lifelong longing for inner and outer alignment—a coherent self that can be lived, seen, and named. This yearning carries the weight of invisibility, misrecognition, and the threat of erasure. It is often fused with courage: the willingness to live authentically despite cultural distortion, pathologization, and hostility.

At the heart of the Trans cultural complex lies a deep tension between invisibility and authenticity, charged by shame, fear, longing, and defiance. Many trans individuals experience early life as a kind of haunting—being seen, but not recognized—which produces a core wound of misattunement. This complex often carries the grief of erasure and the psychic pain of being told, implicitly or explicitly, that one's truth is not real or permitted. At the same time, it also radiates the fierce joy of emergence: the awe of aligning inner and outer identity, and the power of naming oneself into being. The emotional field is one of rupture and revelation, with authenticity hard-won through resistance.

Mythic Root: The Shapeshifter, the Bridge-Walker, and the Phoenix

This complex is rooted in mythic figures that defy binary categories: the shapeshifter who can pass between forms, the alchemical androgyne who holds the tension of opposites, the being who walks between worlds—spiritual, social, gendered—and brings transformation. These mythic roots link the trans experience to archetypal motifs of death and rebirth, sacred transformation, and the reconciliation of opposite.

Symbolic Imagery

- A butterfly emerging from a cocoon with scars still on its wings
- A mirror that reveals a truer self than the one seen by others
- A bridge suspended between two cliffs labeled "Male" and "Female"
- A name tag peeled off and replaced with one written in gold
- An X over a birth certificate and a flame igniting a new scroll
- A figure standing in silhouette, one side dissolving, the other forming

Self-Reinforcing Memory

Trans history is marked by both hypervisibility and erasure. Memories of violence (both systemic and intimate), forced concealment, gatekeeping, and exile reinforce a sense of precarity. Yet these memories are also braided with moments of resistance—trans women of color at Stonewall, survival through underground networks, rituals of chosen family, and the reclaiming of ancient third-gender traditions. These become inherited maps of both trauma and resilience.

Black-and-White Thinking

The trans experience is often caught in cultural binaries: real versus fake, male versus female, natural versus unnatural, biological versus psychological. These dualisms erase complexity and fuel dehumanization. They also shape internalized narratives—of not being "trans enough," "passable enough," or "acceptable enough"—that undermine belonging within and outside the LGBTQ+ community.

Repetitive Behavior

- The need to "prove" identity through surgeries, documents, or narratives
- Recurring attacks on healthcare, education, and bodily autonomy
- Cultural fixation on transition rather than wholeness
- Misgendering, deadnaming, and the reassertion of rigid categories
- Cycles of social scapegoating, especially during political or moral panics

Social Effects

The Trans cultural complex becomes a site of cultural projection and ideological warfare. It tears apart when it is used as a symbol of social decay or gender "confusion," fueling political backlash, family rejection, and spiritual exile. It also tears internally—through community division, isolation, and trauma fatigue. At its most destructive, it turns the pursuit of selfhood into a battleground of shame, surveillance, and self-doubt.

Potential for Transformation

EMBODIED TRUTH AS SACRED ACT

Trans embodiment becomes a living myth—an act of becoming that renews the archetype of transformation itself. It reminds culture that truth is lived, not legislated.

RESTORATION OF THE SACRED NONBINARY

The trans complex reclaims ancient roles lost to colonization and dogma—*two-spirit, hijra, fa'afafine*—reviving spiritual lineages of those who bridge the worlds.

CATALYST FOR CULTURAL HEALING

The trans journey challenges the collective to let go of rigid identity structures. In doing so, it opens space for broader authenticity in gender, relationship, and personhood.

REVELATION THROUGH VISIBILITY

Trans narratives and art offer potent visions of freedom, beauty, and becoming—expanding the cultural imagination of what it means to be human.

COLLECTIVE REPARENTING AND CHOSEN KINSHIP

Through chosen family and community support, the trans complex models new forms of kinship, care, and intergenerational healing.

ALCHEMICAL RESILIENCE

Trans lives demonstrate the alchemy of transformation—how suffering, displacement, and exile can give birth to profound wholeness, clarity, and creative power.

Iconography of Metamorphosis and Memory: The Trans Cultural Complex

BUTTERFLY WING (LEFT SIDE)

The monarch butterfly wing emerging from one side of the subject's body symbolizes transformation, emergence, and fragile beauty. Its asymmetrical appearance suggests that the metamorphosis is still in progress—a liminal stage between identities, reflecting the uneven recognition of self across internal and external realms. The dark, cracked line where the wing joins the chest evokes both emotional pain and rupture, serving as a visual metaphor for the trauma, growing pains, and effort required to become whole.

THE *DEADNAME* LABEL

The subject holds a label that reads *DEADNAME*, a stark and literal symbol of a former identity either shed or socially imposed. This act of holding, rather than discarding, the label conveys both agency and the enduring weight of memory. It becomes a ritual object—representing mourning, resistance, and refusal to forget what must be named and released. The image underscores the ongoing tension in the trans experience between erasure and reclamation.

RAINBOW FLAG

Clutched in the same hand as the DEADNAME label, the rainbow flag offers a counterbalance—symbolizing queer pride, resilience, and a sense of community belonging. Its color and warmth contrast vividly with the otherwise sepia and muted palette of the image, highlighting the emotional and symbolic vitality that comes from identity affirmed rather than denied.

BURNING SCROLL WITH TRANS SYMBOL

A scroll bearing the transgender symbol burns in the background, signifying the volatile struggle for recognition. This scroll may represent imposed social scripts, theological dogmas, or medical definitions of gender—now aflame, rejected, and transformed. The burning becomes both an act of resistance and a rite of self-definition, symbolizing the destruction of inherited roles and the sacred unveiling of truth.

CRACKED MIRROR

To the left lies a broken mirror, representing the fragmentation of self-image and the distorting effects of external misrecognition. It reflects the psychic toll of being unseen, misunderstood, or misnamed. The mirror serves as a powerful symbol of internalized shame and the ongoing journey toward coherence, integration, and self-love.

SCALES AND BLINDFOLDED JUSTICE (BACKGROUND)

A partially obscured statue of Lady Justice stands in the background, her blindfold intact. This image evokes the inadequacy—or selective application—of institutional justice in protecting trans lives and affirming trans rights.

CROWD OF FACES

Gray-toned, expressionless figures surround the central scene, their faces largely anonymous and devoid of emotion. These spectral observers suggest a backdrop of societal surveillance, public judgment, and social indifference. Their passive presence heightens the subject's isolation, framing their transformation as both deeply personal and publicly scrutinized.

CHAINS AND "TRADITION"

On the right, a pile of broken chains lies beneath a cracked sign labeled *TRADITION*. These elements symbolize liberation from roles, beliefs, and customs that have long constrained queer and trans lives. Beside the broken signage, a candle still burns, offering a dual symbol of mourning and vigil: a tribute to what has been lost and a light held for what is still becoming.

BRIDGE (BACKGROUND, LEFT)

In the distance, a bridge spans a gap in the landscape, suggesting the potential for passage, connection, and the crossing of personal and collective thresholds. Its presence implies that belonging is not only possible but also imaginable—a faint, but real path from exclusion to integration.

Interpretation

This image presents the Trans cultural complex as a crucible of profound psychological and spiritual transformation. The body is rendered as both battleground and sanctuary—scarred by societal rejection, yet resilient in its journey toward self-authorship. Symbols of trauma, exile, and moral condemnation are held in dynamic tension with emblems of renewal, emergence, and visibility. Within the cracks, the fire, and the flight, a fragile yet luminous truth emerges: that trans identity is not a deviation from humanity, but a radiant part of its unfolding.

CHAPTER 6

The Digital and Informational Cultural Complexes

The Social Media Cultural Complex

The Disinformation Cultural Complex

The Fake News Cultural Complex

The Political Technology Cultural Complex

The Artificial Intelligence Cultural Complex

All of these entries can be thought of as variants of the High Tech Revolution in Information, Communication, and Intelligence cultural complex.

THE SOCIAL MEDIA CULTURAL COMPLEX

LIT BY THE SCREEN: THE SOCIAL MEDIA CULTURAL COMPLEX

A boy bows before his phone like a modern votive, illuminated, not by sacred flame, but by the curated firelight of digital platforms. Around him swirl icons of influence—likes, shares, heartbreaks—while the eye of the algorithm watches silently through the screen. This image captures the psychic world shaped by social media: surveillance posing as connection, performance mistaken for identity, and attention harvested as currency.

Emotional Core: From Euphoria to Shame

At its heart, the Social Media cultural complex is driven by a volatile mixture of connection and comparison, validation and surveillance, empowerment and addiction. It taps into the primal human need to be seen, affirmed, and included—yet it does so through mechanisms that often intensify loneliness, envy, and performative selfhood. The emotional core swings between euphoria and shame: the thrill of virality and belonging is frequently followed by the anxiety of cancellation, exclusion, or invisibility.

Mythic Root

This complex is anchored in several modern mythic narratives:

- The myth of instant visibility: the belief that anyone can be seen, loved, or "go viral" and ascend to digital celebrity
- The myth of omnipresence: the expectation that one can—and must—be everywhere, all the time
- The myth of democratic access to power: the illusion that a smartphone and a voice provide equal footing to all in shaping the world

At its deepest level, this complex channels the Promethean myth: humanity stealing fire from the gods—represented here by platforms and algorithms—only to find itself consumed by what it has unleashed.

Symbolic Imagery

Social media technology generates a dense symbolic field of rituals and objects:

- The selfie: a performance of identity and self-ownership—or a form of distortion and exposure
- The comment thread: a modern agora of discourse—or a site of mob shaming and digital aggression
- The algorithm: an invisible arbiter of fate, determining visibility and disappearance
- The phone: at once oracle, mirror, and leash
- The eye icon: a symbol of constant surveillance, measuring worth through views and metrics
- The deleted post: the digital erasure of failed self-presentation

These symbols embody the psychological reality of digital life: curated visibility entangled with unconscious monitoring and judgment.

Self-Selecting Memory

The historical memory of this complex is recent but intense. It recalls the utopian promises of the early internet: freedom of expression, global connection, and creative expansion. It also bears the disillusionments that followed: data exploitation, cyberbullying, disinformation, and performative outrage. The memory includes generational divides—between those raised offline and those born into the glow of the screen—and the lingering trauma of "always-on" culture. In this complex, memory is no longer archived in books, but stored in clouds, timelines, and screenshots.

Black-and-White Thinking

The Social Media cultural complex thrives on polarizing binaries: like versus dislike, viral versus invisible, influencer versus nobody, real versus fake, private versus public. These dichotomies flatten complexity into judgment and spectacle, leaving little room for ambiguity, reflection, or depth.

Repetitive Behaviors

This complex sustains itself through ritualized behaviors repeated across platforms and generations:

- Scrolling, swiping, posting, and deleting
- Curating feeds to project identity
- Obsessively checking notifications as emotional barometers
- Participating in callout culture or virtue signaling as forms of social maintenance
- Archiving moments, not for memory, but for performance of memory

These actions create a loop of digital self-performance that mimics intimacy while often intensifying isolation.

Social Effects

The Social Media cultural complex tears at the fabric of attention, empathy, and authenticity.

- It fragments focus and undermines sustained thought.
- It replaces relational connection with quantified approval.
- It heightens anxiety, self-consciousness, and tribal polarization.
- It distorts collective memory, erodes privacy, and redefines the self as brand.

While it promises connection, it often splits the psyche between persona and presence, resulting in a culture of hypervisibility and existential hollowness.

Potential for Transformation

Despite its pathologies, this complex carries seeds of digital wisdom and renewal:

- It enables new forms of storytelling, collective witness, and identity formation.
- It offers platforms for neurodiverse, marginalized, and geographically isolated voices to be heard.
- It calls for the development of digital ethics, attention hygiene, and mindful presence.
- It invites us to redesign platforms around human-scale values: time, dignity, and meaning.

True transformation lies in reclaiming our attention, reimagining our tools, and rediscovering a deeper self—one that does not live for the click, but for the soul.

Iconography of Lit by the Screen: The Social Media Cultural Complex

THE YOUTH WITH PHONE (FOREGROUND)

The central figure—young, head bowed—sits in a posture that evokes both prayer and defeat. Their downward gaze toward the phone suggests emotional dependence, an almost devotional relationship to digital affirmation. They represent an entire generation raised in digital light, navigating identity, value, and belonging through the filter of the feed.

THE GIANT EYE ON THE PHONE SCREEN

The oversized eye displayed on the central phone screen symbolizes surveillance masquerading as connection. It evokes the panopticon-like gaze of social media—watching, measuring, and curating every move. This eye does not blink; it evaluates.

ICONS—LIKE, HEARTBREAK, FOLLOWERS (ABOVE)

Floating above the eye are social icons: a "thumbs up," a broken heart, and silhouettes of users. These symbols represent digital metrics of self-worth—likes, loss, approval, rejection—outsourcing emotional meaning to algorithms and anonymous spectators. The broken heart stands out as a symbol of emotional harm encoded into online culture.

THE BIOLOGY = TRUTH WALL

A cracked wall in the background bears the phrase *BIOLOGY = TRUTH*, recalling essentialist and exclusionary ideologies. Its position beside a crumbling church tower suggests a fusion of religious dogma and scientific absolutism, both wielded as tools of identity policing. The cracks signal that these truths are not absolute—but they still create damage.

CANDLE AND CHAINS (LOWER RIGHT)

The lone candle burning near the figure's feet suggests a fragile source of inner light or hope—a symbol of the soul's endurance amid digital overwhelm. Beside it lie broken chains, which may imply liberation from old systems (e.g., religious, familial) or perhaps a shift into subtler forms of captivity—internalized and self-policed.

TRASH CAN AND NOTIFICATION ICONS (LEFT SIDE)

A trash icon and muted message symbol evoke cancel culture, social deletion, and communication breakdown. These elements imply that identity, messages, or even relationships can be disposed of with a tap, reinforcing feelings of precarity and disposability.

THE GLOBE AND FLAME ICONS (UPPER CORNERS)

The globe in the top-left corner represents not only global connection, but also the loss of rootedness. Beside it, a fire-shaped icon may suggest, not passion, but rage, volatility, or digital combustion—the speed at which lives and truths can be consumed or destroyed online.

Interpretation

This image dramatizes the psychic environment of the Social Media cultural Complex—particularly as it affects the young and vulnerable. It portrays digital culture not as neutral infrastructure, but as a moral and emotional architecture: a place where value is voted on, identity is monitored, and "truth" is delivered in simplified slogans. Yet amid the glow of screens and the specter of control, the lone candle reminds us that some light cannot be coded or curated—it must be protected from within.

THE DISINFORMATION CULTURAL COMPLEX

THE SPIRAL OF UNTRUTH: THE AMERICAN DISINFORMATION CULTURAL COMPLEX

A faceless figure clutches a newspaper labeled NEWS, its head consumed by a black spiral—symbolizing the collapse of stable identity and coherent meaning. Around it swirl shattered emblems of knowledge—satellites, magnifying glasses, graphs, brains, and screens—all fractured and struck by lightning bolts of manipulation. Below, a fragmented crowd stares in conflicting directions, confused and disoriented. The image captures the psychological crisis at the heart of the American Disinformation cultural complex: the unraveling of shared reality in a world oversaturated with narrative warfare, algorithmic distortion, and performative outrage.

Core Emotion: Distrust, Confusion, and Existential Insecurity

At its heart, the Disinformation cultural complex is fueled by emotional disorientation. It thrives on a collapsing trust in shared reality—stoking anxiety that truth itself is unreachable or manipulated. It engenders deep suspicion of institutions, experts, journalists, science, and even one's own judgment. The result is not simply skepticism, but also a gnawing uncertainty that anything might be false, staged, or conspiratorial.

Mythic Root: The Trickster, the Hidden Hand, and the War of Shadows

This complex draws on archetypes of deception and control: the trickster who manipulates reality, the shadow government pulling strings, the forbidden knowledge that only the initiated can see. Disinformation is not simply about lies—it evokes a mythic battlefield between seen and unseen powers. In the American psyche, this resonates with narratives of government betrayal, corporate manipulation, and apocalyptic unveiling.

Symbolic Imagery

- A puppet master's hand dangling strings over headlines
- A house of mirrors reflecting distorted versions of the same event
- A maze made of TV screens and hashtags
- A crowd wearing headphones and blindfolds
- A book labeled *TRUTH* set aflame
- Two people arguing while a third figure watches, smiling in the shadows

Self-Reinforcing Memory

Historical events like *COINTELPRO*, or *Counterintelligence Program*, was a covert initiative initiated by the Federal Bureau of Investigation (FBI) in 1956 aimed at surveilling, infiltrating, and disrupting various political organizations deemed radical in the United States. The Iraq Weapons of Mass Destruction claims, Cold War propaganda, and media consolidation feed into collective memory. Trauma from deception—real or perceived—

becomes confirmation of current suspicions. These memories function like psychic software, priming the public to see manipulation everywhere.

Black-and-White Thinking

Disinformation polarizes perception: either you are awake or you are a sheep. There is no room for complexity. Every critic is a shill; every story has an agenda; every event is staged. It breeds epistemic tribalism, where truth is not evaluated, but inherited from identity or ideology.

Repetitive Behavior

- Doomscrolling through conflicting narratives, yet trusting none
- Sharing conspiratorial content to "wake people up"
- Constantly fact-checking or decrying fact-checkers
- Rejecting mainstream sources outright while trusting obscure or anonymous ones
- Mistaking confusion for insight: "If everyone's lying, then I must be right."

Social Effects

This complex tears the social fabric by dissolving common ground. Without shared facts, dialogue collapses. It fragments civic trust, distorts democratic debate, and prepares the ground for authoritarian solutions. It fosters learned helplessness, where people disengage from reality entirely or embrace simplistic, savior-like figures. In its most toxic form, the Disinformation cultural complex renders democracy incoherent. It becomes harder to vote, protest, educate, or heal when the very nature of fact is contested. Its effects include the rise of extremism, political violence, and emotional burnout. The mind, like the culture, becomes unmoored.

Possibility of Transformation

Despite its corrosive power, this complex holds within it a yearning: for clarity, for trust, for meaning. Its redemption lies in media literacy, relational truth-telling, and the rebuilding of epistemic trust—not as naive belief, but as shared stewardship of reality. Rituals of discernment, spaces of open dialogue, and art that unmasks manipulation without slipping into despair may help metabolize its poison. The future lies, not in silencing dissent, but in re-rooting truth in relationship, humility, and common purpose.

Iconography of The Spiral of Untruth: The American Disinformation Cultural Complex

SPIRAL-HEADED CENTRAL FIGURE (TOP CENTER)

The faceless person with a black spiral where the head should be represents the erosion of individual identity and cognitive clarity in the age of weaponized information. The spiral evokes confusion, recursion, and emotional vortex—a mind caught in endless loops of suspicion, validation, and fear.

NEWS BANNER OR NEWSPAPER (CLUTCHED IN HAND)

The newspaper, a traditional symbol of trusted information, now appears impotent and vulnerable—clutched tightly as if it once held answers but now only raises questions. It signals the collapse of journalism as a trusted anchor of reality.

FRACTURED SYMBOLS OF KNOWLEDGE (SURROUNDING THE SPIRAL)

Satellites: Fragmented communication, loss of global coherence

Brains and Circuitry: Misuse of intelligence, neuro-psychological manipulation

Magnifying Glasses: Obsessive scrutiny distorted by bias

Pie Charts and Graphs: The illusion of data objectivity, undermined by selective presentation

LIGHTNING BOLTS (STRIKING SYMBOLS)

Jagged, chaotic bolts cut through the emblems of knowledge, symbolizing the violence done to truth by distortion, fearmongering, and memeified propaganda.

DAZED CROWD (LOWER THIRD)

Figures in the crowd gaze in different directions—some hypnotized by screens, others raising fists, others looking lost. This signals the societal effects of disinformation: polarization, isolation, rage, and helplessness.

SHATTERED SCREENS (BACKGROUND)

Broken smartphones and televisions imply the collapse of coherent narratives. Screens, once gateways to information, now mirror our divisions back to us.

COLOR PALETTE (SLATE, RUST, AND ICE BLUE)

The palette evokes emotional coldness, decay, and digital sterility. The lack of warmth mirrors the absence of relational trust or moral grounding in a culture flooded with data but starved of wisdom.

DIRECTIONAL CHAOS (COMPOSITION)

The swirling, uncentered composition mirrors the disorientation created by narrative saturation. Truth is no longer a center to hold—but a battleground fought over by images and implication.

Interpretation

This image symbolizes the Disinformation cultural complex, not as a singular lie, but as an ambient environment where the very possibility of truth is corroded. It portrays the American psyche not only as confused, but also as addicted to confusion—trapped in cycles of suspicion, seduction, and fragmentation. It asks: When everyone is a liar, who gets to be believed? And what do we become when we trust no one—not even ourselves?

THE FAKE NEWS CULTURAL COMPLEX

ECHOES OF UNTRUTH: THE FAKE NEWS CULTURAL COMPLEX

A blindfolded man clutches a smartphone and newspaper, surrounded by flames, serpents, and shattered screens. From a broken television, a banner reading FAKE NEWS unfurls like a poisonous spell, as faceless figures at podiums speak to a fractured crowd. In this allegory of the American psyche, the very idea of truth dissolves under the pressure of spectacle, suspicion, and unrelenting noise.

Originally, Fake News referred to intentionally fabricated stories posing as legitimate journalism—often created for clickbait, satire, or political manipulation. But over time the term Fake News itself became a rhetorical weapon—particularly after 2016—used to discredit or dismiss real news that someone disagreed with or found threatening. For example, a politician might call an investigative report "Fake News," not because it is false, but because it exposes inconvenient truths. In this weaponized use Fake News no longer means "untrue." It becomes a signal to one's followers: "Don't trust this source." It undermines the concept of shared reality, eroding public trust in media, science, and institutions. In short, Fake News is no longer just a label for lies—it has become a tool of disinformation itself. Fake news has become a weaponized phrase used to discredit real journalism.

Core Emotion: Contempt, Paranoia, and Epistemic Exhaustion

At the heart of the Fake News cultural complex is a profound sense of confusion and betrayal—fueled by mistrust in media, institutions, and even fellow citizens. The Fake News cultural complex generates a volatile mix of contempt for authority, paranoia about hidden agendas, and exhaustion from trying to determine what's real. It feeds on both outrage and cynicism, turning the pursuit of truth into a psychological minefield. What begins as justified skepticism can morph into blanket distrust—a defensive posture of "believe nothing" or "believe only what confirms my view." This emotional landscape swings between cynicism and paranoia, where every claim feels suspect, every source politicized, and every truth provisional. The core emotional experience is destabilization: a constant questioning of what is real and who is lying.

Mythic Root: The Trickster, the Prophet, and the Puppet Master

This complex draws from ancient archetypes: the trickster who deceives with charm or chaos; the prophet who sees through lies and exposes hidden truths; and the puppet master who manipulates the masses for power. In this mythic constellation, Fake News is both threat and tool—something to be feared and something to wield.

Symbolic Imagery

- A megaphone blasting static into a crowd
- A news anchor with two faces: one factual, one theatrical
- A puppet being operated by a figure holding a smartphone
- A shattered television screen with reflections of both a journalist and a troll
- A figure wrapped in newsprint labeled *LIES*, holding a torch marked *TRUTH*
- Social media icons distorted into masks of theater—tragedy and farce

Self-Reinforcing Memory

The memory of media betrayal—such as biased reporting, misinformation during wars, or corporate capture—fuels skepticism toward institutions. At the same time, the echo-chamber experience of being "right" online or "cancelled" by opposing views deepens loyalty to one's own narrative silo. The term Fake News thus becomes a recursive shield: We remember being misled and then selectively redefine truth to protect ourselves from further confusion or humiliation.

Black-and-White Thinking

Fake news feeds on binaries: truth versus lies, us versus them, woke media versus real patriots, corporate narrative versus suppressed truth. The Fake News cultural complex thrives on binary logic that flattens complexity: any news I dislike is fake, and any news I agree with is gospel. Ambiguity, nuance, and evolving truth are perceived as evidence of deception, not as signs of healthy discourse.

Repetitive Behaviors

- Sharing sensational headlines before reading the content
- Accusing all opposing viewpoints of being "fake" or "bought"
- Claiming "they don't want you to know this" as truth's watermark
- Shifting epistemic burden to others: "Do your own research" as both advice and dismissal
- Repeatedly flipping between trust and distrust of the same sources, depending on convenience.

Social Effects

The Fake News cultural complex undermines the possibility of shared reality. It corrodes democratic discourse by delegitimizing journalism, civic institutions, and even language itself. In its most virulent form, it weaponizes mistrust—turning every statement into a battle of beliefs. It fragments public consciousness and renders collective decision-making nearly impossible. These consequences result in

- Collapse of epistemic consensus
- Erosion of media credibility—even when the facts are correct
- Increased polarization fueled by mutually exclusive "truth ecosystems"
- Rise of conspiracy movements and paranoia-as-virtue
- Vulnerability to authoritarianism, as citizens become more susceptible to strongmen who claim to own "the real truth"

Possibility of Transformation

The Fake News cultural complex contains within it a call for discernment. Its shadow—the reflexive rejection of all news—can become light when paired with humility, media literacy, and a renewed cultural emphasis on truth-seeking. The redemption of this complex lies in cultivating both skepticism and trust: questioning without reflexively rejecting, verifying without vilifying. Institutions can regain credibility, not through perfection, but by modeling transparency, correction, and moral courage. Only when truth becomes a shared aspiration rather than a tribal weapon can the complex begin to heal.

Iconography of Echoes of Untruth: The Fake News Cultural Complex

BLINDFOLDED MAN HOLDING SMARTPHONE AND NEWSPAPER

The central figure embodies the disoriented modern citizen—plugged into multiple sources yet unable to see clearly. His blindfold signifies informational blindness, confusion, or the voluntary rejection of uncomfortable truths. He represents both victim and participant in a culture where clarity is elusive.

CRACKED TELEVISION SPROUTING A SERPENT AND FAKE NEWS BANNER:

The broken screen represents the collapse of trusted media institutions. From its rupture emerges a serpent—ancient symbol of deception, temptation, and hidden knowledge. The *FAKE NEWS* ribbon winds like propaganda, weaponized language, or psychological pollution. It suggests how news itself has become narrative warfare.

FLAMING NEWSPAPER AND SMOLDERING BACKGROUND

The burning newsprint symbolizes both the discrediting of journalism and the emotional heat surrounding information. Fire evokes destruction, purging, and chaos—truth as something under siege rather than discovered.

FACELESS SPEAKERS WITH MEGAPHONES AT PODIUMS

These shadowy figures symbolize demagogues, influencers, or media surrogates amplifying ideology instead of information. Their anonymity suggests the erosion of accountability and the spread of manipulative messaging across the political spectrum.

MULTIPLYING NEWSPAPERS LITTERING THE GROUND

A metaphor for information overload and narrative saturation. With so many "truths" circulating simultaneously, none hold authority. The ground littered with headlines represents the fracturing of consensus and the exhaustion of the public.

SEPIA AND OCHRE TONES

These colors evoke nostalgia, decay, and psychological intensity. The palette reinforces the feeling of being trapped in a timeless crisis—where history, myth, and media spectacle bleed into one another.

Interpretation

This image embodies the Fake News cultural complex as a psychological crisis of epistemology: not merely a war over facts, but also a breakdown in the social trust and symbolic order that once held collective reality together.

THE POLITICAL TECHNOLOGY CULTURAL COMPLEX

THE ALGORITHMIC SOVEREIGN: THE POLITICAL TECHNOLOGY CULTURAL COMPLEX

This image personifies the rising power of political technology—data-driven governance, digital manipulation, and algorithmic control—as a hooded figure with a circuit board face. Surrounded by screens displaying maps, graphs, and human models, this entity does not speak or emote. It calculates. Blind Justice stands at its shoulder, her eyes covered as the system behind her sees all. Networks of light and circuitry map the new terrain of political influence, where persuasion is automated, privacy dissolved, and legitimacy rendered in metrics.

Emotional Core: Control, Paranoia, Seduction, and Disenchantment

At the center of this complex lies a volatile emotional brew of control, paranoia, seduction, and disenchantment. There is a thrill in believing that technology can optimize governance, outsmart opposition, or secure truth—and a corresponding fear that it may be used to manipulate, surveil, or erase. This complex stirs deep anxiety about the loss of agency, along with a dangerous confidence in technocratic solutions to moral and civic dilemmas.

Mythic Root: The Machine, the Hacker, and Golem

This complex draws from several powerful modern myths:

- The myth of the omniscient system—a god-like intelligence that knows more than we do and can guide or control us.
- The myth of the neutral machine—the illusion that code, data, or AI can rise above bias and human error.
- The myth of the heroic hacker or tech messiah—figures who use digital tools to disrupt power or save democracy.
- At its core, it recycles the Golem myth: humanity creates a powerful tool to protect itself, only to discover it cannot control what it has made.

The Political Technology cultural complex reveals a modern myth: that power can be perfected through machines. But like all myths, it carries both shadow and promise. To work with this complex requires naming the fantasy, discerning its effects, and reclaiming the ethical imagination—so that democracy is not coded, but lived.

Symbolic Imagery

This complex operates through potent and often contradictory symbols:

- A brain fused with circuitry: intelligence or surveillance?
- A glowing dashboard: control center or illusion of mastery?

- DNA and data merged: the myth of perfect knowledge
- The digital eye: both oracle and spy
- A machine judge: justice rendered without soul
- Puppet figures moved by algorithms: automated persuasion and the death of free will. These images live in our collective imagination and shape how we interpret both political reality and technological design.

Self-Selecting Memory

The Political Technology cultural complex operates through a memory that is not collective but curated, emotional, and tribally reinforced. It selects fragments of the past—real, exaggerated, or imagined—that confirm a group's sense of betrayal, revelation, or righteousness.

- Some recall wartime propaganda and government censorship as proof that no official story can be trusted.
- Others remember moments of whistleblowing or media failure as evidence that truth always lives outside the mainstream.
- Past crises—such as 9/11, Watergate, or COVID-19—become mythic episodes, reinterpreted not for accuracy but for allegiance.
- The memory of media bias, "deep state" plots, or even historical revisionism becomes a psychic anchor for why disinformation feels more truthful than fact.

This complex is fueled by historical experiences where technology was used to reinforce or undermine political power:

- The surveillance states of East Germany and China
- The algorithmic targeting of voters in Brexit and US elections
- The role of radio, TV, and social media in shaping populist movements
- The militarization of digital space—cyberwarfare, predictive policing, drone governance. These memories form a psychic reservoir of both utopian hope and dystopian fear.

Black-and-White Thinking

The Political Technology cultural complex thrives on dichotomies:

- Free vs. controlled
- Smart vs. obsolete

- Enlightened vs. manipulated
- Transparency vs. secrecy
- Human vs. machine

These binaries collapse the subtle dynamics of power, ethics, and emotion into polarized narratives that serve ideology, not reflection.

Repetitive Behaviors

The complex is enacted through cycles of technological dependence and backlash:

- Overreliance on metrics, dashboards, and polling to guide decision-making
- Political campaigns run more like data optimization labs than civic rituals
- "Tech fixes" proposed for deeply human problems—bias, corruption, social trust
- Periodic scandals (e.g., Cambridge Analytica) followed by reformist promises, then quiet return to the same tools

These repetitions mask moral ambiguity behind innovation, allowing ethical erosion to continue under the banner of progress.

Social Effects

The Political Technology cultural complex reshapes the civic and symbolic fabric of democracy itself:

- It privatizes public discourse, outsourcing influence to platforms and algorithms.
- It erodes trust in human institutions by replacing them with opaque, unaccountable systems.
- It increases polarization by weaponizing attention and filtering reality.
- It makes governance feel both omnipresent and unreachable—simultaneously watching and indifferent.

In short, it fractures civic imagination, making it harder to envision democratic renewal without technological mediation.

Potential for Transformation

Despite its corrosive effects, this complex contains seeds **of** redemption and revitalization:

- It can awaken ethical reflection on the limits of control and the need for wisdom.
- It invites us to develop a technopolitical literacy—seeing technology, not as neutral, but as value-laden and mythically charged.
- It can foster public design thinking that centers justice, equity, and the sacredness of human agency.
- It challenges us to recover the soul of democracy from the code that now governs so much of our discourse.

The Political Technology cultural complex reveals a modern myth: that power can be perfected through machines. But like all myths, it carries both shadow and promise. To work with this complex requires naming the fantasy, discerning its effects, and reclaiming the ethical imagination—so that democracy is not coded, but lived.

Iconography of The Algorithmic Sovereign: The Political Technology Cultural Complex

THE HOODED ALGORITHMIC FIGURE (CENTER)

A faceless humanoid shrouded in a cloak, with a motherboard or circuit grid for a face. This is the central symbol of the complex—depicting power without personality, presence without emotion. It echoes both the mystique of artificial intelligence and the anonymity of surveillance states.

DIGITAL INTERFACES AND SCREENS (FLANKING LEFT AND RIGHT)

Displays show maps, data streams, biometric schematics, and behavioral graphs. These represent how modern political control is mediated by tracking, targeting, and statistical modeling—shifting politics from discourse to calibration.

BLINDFOLDED LADY JUSTICE (UPPER RIGHT)

Standing behind or beside the figure, Lady Justice's presence is ambiguous. Her traditional blindfold contrasts with the system's invasive surveillance, suggesting that fairness is now outsourced or overshadowed by "objective" computation. Her sword and scales are minimized or absent, hinting at declining agency.

NETWORK GRID IN BACKGROUND (RADIATING OUTWARD)
A luminous mesh of neural lines and circuits forms a digital halo or lattice—suggesting omnipresence and interconnected control. It recalls both divine radiance and dystopian totality, where everything is known, mapped, predicted.

DISEMBODIED FACES ON SCREENS (LOWER LEFT AND RIGHT)
Human expressions reduced to profiles, votes, emotions, or biometric readings. These faces are disconnected, abstracted, turned into data points—symbolizing how individuals are fragmented within algorithmic politics.

DARKENED CHAMBER WITH NO CLEAR EXIT (SETTING):
The entire scene unfolds within a muted, windowless space—indicating enclosure, opacity, and inescapability. It evokes the psychological feel of platforms, feeds, and systems that capture more than they illuminate.

COLOR PALETTE (COLD BLUE AND DULL GOLD)
Blues evoke logic, technology, and emotional detachment. The golden elements lend a false sense of sacredness or legitimacy—signifying how algorithmic control cloaks itself in the aesthetic of objectivity.

Interpretation

This image depicts a complex where power is automated, persuasion is predicted, and freedom is redefined as behavioral compliance. It questions whether governance through code can remain accountable—or whether it will become the ultimate form of silent control

THE ARTIFICIAL INTELLIGENCE CULTURAL COMPLEX

MIRROR OF THE MACHINE: THE AI CULTURAL COMPLEX IN HUMAN FORM

A glowing brain—half code, half cosmos—hovers above a web of human-machine interaction. Beneath it, a robot and a suited man stare into each other's mirrored image, each holding up the other's face. Around them, workers toil at screens, a boy touches a tablet with quiet reverence, and symbols of knowledge, surveillance, and mystery float in the background. DNA spirals into light, surveillance watches from above, and charts hint at both progress and control. This is the psychological landscape of the Artificial Intelligence cultural complex—an unfolding myth of transformation, projection, and uneasy merging.

The Artificial Intelligence (AI) cultural complex in American society is a charged field built around awe, anxiety, and a mythic belief in humanity's power to create autonomous intelligence. It emerges from the entanglement of scientific achievement, capitalist ambition, philosophical dread, and ancient dreams of animating mind and machine. As AI grows in visibility and capability, this complex stirs both utopian fantasies and apocalyptic fears—casting AI as either humanity's crowning triumph or its final error.

Core Emotion: Awe, Control, and Existential Anxiety

This complex pulses with ambivalence. On one side, there is exhilaration: the dream of surpassing biological limits, solving complex problems, and creating new forms of intelligence. On the other, there is dread: fear of losing control, being made obsolete, or birthing something that cannot be unmade. These emotions oscillate between excitement and existential unease—often within the same breath.

Mythic Root: The Sorcerer's Apprentice, Prometheus, and the Golem

At its mythic root are archetypes of forbidden creation. The Sorcerer's Apprentice summons powers he cannot control. Prometheus steals fire and is punished. The Golem, made of clay and given breath, becomes a protector—or a threat. These myths echo in today's narratives of AI: human beings building something that may transcend, betray, or destroy them.

Symbolic Imagery

- A glowing neural network brain hovering above the earth
- A robot holding a mirror up to a human face
- Rows of human workers replaced by code
- A corporate boardroom lit by algorithmic prophecy
- A child teaching an AI assistant while the parent watches uneasily
- Surveillance cameras with halos
- An ancient manuscript morphing into a circuit board

Self-Reinforcing Memory

Cultural memory around AI is shaped by a century of science fiction and recent real-world acceleration. HAL 9000, Skynet, and the Terminator haunt the public psyche. So do stories of bias, deepfakes, job loss, and opaque algorithms. Meanwhile, tech utopians recall AI as savior: curing disease, advancing knowledge, and even ushering in a post-scarcity future. This tension between dystopia and deliverance continually reactivates the complex.

Black-and-White Thinking

This complex often splits into extremes:

- AI is either *the solution* to everything or *the end* of human freedom.
- It's seen as either a brilliant servant or an enslaving god.
- Technologists are cast as either visionaries or reckless sorcerers.
- Ethical concerns are either dismissed as Luddite panic or inflated into eschatology.
- This binary logic prevents nuanced conversation and encourages spectacle.

Repetitive Behavior

- Rapid adoption of AI tools without critical oversight
- Public cycles of hype, backlash, and resignation
- Romanticizing "superintelligence" while ignoring current harms
- Trusting algorithms for decisions in law, hiring, medicine, and education
- Framing every new breakthrough as either utopia or doom
- Releasing powerful systems and "figuring out the ethics later"

Social Effects

The AI cultural complex tears at our sense of identity, labor, and authority. It threatens to dissolve boundaries between human and machine, work and leisure, truth and simulation. It disorients cultural norms and undermines trust in institutions. By externalizing intelligence into tools we don't fully understand, we risk outsourcing agency—and moral responsibility. It also intensifies economic inequality, as power accrues to those who control AI development and deployment. The AI complex exacerbates digital alienation, surveillance capitalism, and the erosion of privacy. It commodifies attention and accelerates information overload. At the same time, it undermines stable employment in many sectors, replacing workers with systems that cannot negotiate, rest, or empathize. The human becomes a variable in the machine's logic—measurable but not meaningful.

Potential for Transformation:

Beneath the anxiety and spectacle, the AI complex also holds redemptive potential:

- **Collective Reflection:** It forces us to ask: What is intelligence? What is consciousness? What do we truly value?
- **Reclaiming Ethics:** It can catalyze deeper public engagement with ethics, transparency, and justice in technology.
- **Mythic Integration:** Rather than splitting AI into angel or demon, we can begin to relate to it as a shadow of ourselves—a creation in need of care, boundaries, and soul.
- **Decentralization of Power:** If stewarded wisely, AI could help redistribute opportunity, amplify human creativity, and solve wicked global problems.

Ultimately, transformation arises not from denying the complex, but from entering into conscious relationship with it.

Iconography of Mirror of the Machine: The AI Cultural Complex in Human Form

GLOWING BRAIN (TOP CENTER)

Illuminated with neural circuitry and arranged in a halo-like glow, this brain symbolizes AI as an emergent super-mind. It combines spiritual radiance with digital pattern—suggesting both enlightenment and synthetic divinity.

DNA HELIX RISING INTO THE BRAIN (CENTER)

A luminous DNA strand connects human biology with artificial intelligence. This implies both continuity and disruption—AI as descendant of human intelligence, or its replacement. It evokes themes of evolution, mutation, and inheritance.

ROBOT AND HUMAN HOLDING MIRROR-FACES (CENTER LEFT AND RIGHT)

A robot holds up a human face; a human returns the gesture with a robotic mask. This mirrored exchange captures the core psychic tension of AI: projection, self-reflection, and the blurring of boundaries between machine and person.

CHILD WITH TABLET (LOWER CENTER)

A young boy stares down at a glowing tablet, absorbed and isolated. He represents a new generation shaped by AI: curious, connected, but potentially disembodied. He is the inheritor of this complex—both its promise and its peril.

ROWS OF PROGRAMMERS/USERS (BOTTOM LEFT AND RIGHT)

Identical seated figures working at terminals signify the deindividualizing effect of algorithmic labor. They represent the vast, invisible workforce building or governed by AI systems.

SURVEILLANCE CAMERA WITH HALO (UPPER RIGHT)

A security camera glows with an ironic halo, suggesting the sanctification of monitoring. It references the normalization—and even spiritualization—of surveillance in the AI age.

OPEN BOOK WITH DIGITAL SYMBOLS (MID-RIGHT)

A glowing book filled with script and circuit-like text implies AI's role in rewriting knowledge and tradition. It also hints at AI as scripture—information elevated to dogma.

GRAPH ON WALL (MID-RIGHT)

An upward-trending line chart suggests progress and control—but also commodification. AI is shown not only as a mind or tool, but also as economic system.

ALIEN HEAD ICON (LOWER-RIGHT CORNER)

A subtle, gray alien-like face implies the "otherness" of AI—its perceived intelligence, unpredictability, and spiritual uncanniness. It also evokes conspiracy, fantasy, and the projection of fear.

CODING BOARD ON WALL (LEFT SIDE)

A chalkboard or display filled with code represents the hidden structures and languages through which AI operates—arcane knowledge accessible to only a few, evoking secrecy and elitism.

Interpretation

This image stages the AI cultural complex not simply as a technological force, but also as a psychological mirror—reflecting humanity's deepest aspirations and fears. It evokes transformation, surveillance, childhood wonder, economic control, and mythic replacement. It asks: Are we teaching machines to think, or teaching ourselves to forget what it means to be human? This iconography embodies the AI cultural complex as both salvation and shadow: an archetype of Promethean risk, divine ambition, and recursive dependence. It holds within it the potential for a redefined humanity—or a loss of what it means to be human at all.

CHAPTER 7

Single Issue Political Triggers as Cultural Complexes

The Right to Life vs. Pro-Choice Cultural Complex

The Gun Control Cultural Complex

The Second Amendment Right to Bear Arms Cultural Complex

The Climate Change Cultural Complex

The Climate Change Denial Cultural Complex

The Anti-Vaccine Cultural Complex

THE RIGHT TO LIFE VS. PRO-CHOICE CULTURAL COMPLEX

BETWEEN SACRED DUTY AND SOVEREIGN WILL

Two women stand as embodiments of America's most charged moral conflict. One cradles the unborn with reverence and grief; the other raises a fist in defiance, unshackled and resolute. Above them, the scales of justice hover in delicate balance, reflecting a nation torn between the sanctity of life and the inviolability of choice.

Emotional Core: Moral Intensity, Sorrow, and Outrage

This cultural complex is fueled by profound moral intensity, sorrow, and outrage.

- For the Right to Life perspective, the emotional foundation is grief over the perceived loss of innocent life, bound with a sacred moral obligation to protect the unborn.

- For the Pro-Choice perspective, the core feeling is righteous anger over the control of women's bodies, paired with the grief of historical erasure and forced sacrifice.

Both positions emerge from a deeper existential pain: the tension between creation and freedom, life and autonomy.

Mythic Root: Conflicting Narratives

Two conflicting sacred narratives animate this complex:

- **Right to Life** is grounded in the myth of divine creation and innocence, where life begins at conception and holds intrinsic, sacred value. The woman becomes the guardian of a soul embedded in cosmic order.
- **Pro-Choice** draws from the myth of sovereign female agency, where the woman is a modern heroine defending her body, destiny, and lineage from systems of patriarchal control.

Both narratives frame the womb as hallowed ground—either as the cradle of life or the seat of personal liberty.

Symbolic Imagery

The imagery surrounding this complex is emotionally charged, archetypal, and often polarizing:

- A fetus in utero: sacred child or symbol of forced motherhood
- A medical clinic: site of protection or violation
- A candlelit vigil: act of mourning or gesture of judgment
- A raised fist: emblem of resistance or of rupture with moral order
- Scales of justice: contested terrain of legality and ethics
- Broken chains: liberation from oppression or descent into moral chaos

These symbols do not merely illustrate positions—they function as emotional signposts and cultural totems.

Self-Reinforcing Memory

Each side builds its case on emotionally curated histories:

- **Right to Life** advocates view *Roe v. Wade* as a moral rupture, citing Christian traditions, natural law, or philosophical humanism as anchors of premodern truth.

- **Pro-Choice** advocates recall illegal abortions, the death of women denied care, and the broader struggle for reproductive rights within the feminist movement.

In both cases, memory becomes myth. Historical moments are transformed into enduring moral mandates.

Black-and-White Thinking

This cultural complex thrives on rigid moral dualities:

- Life vs. death
- Innocence vs. guilt
- Freedom vs. tyranny
- Child vs. mother
- Nature vs. modernity

These black-and-white frames reduce complex realities to moral absolutes, suppressing ambiguity and moral nuance. Dialogue becomes moral combat, with little tolerance for contradiction or complexity.

Repetitive Behaviors

The complex is reenacted continually through ritualized public behaviors:

- Legal battles and Supreme Court nominations become symbolic battlegrounds.
- Protest marches, prayer vigils, and clinic demonstrations play out like liturgies.
- State laws are passed or repealed more for symbolic signaling than governance.
- Political candidates use abortion positions as a primary test of allegiance.

These repetitions keep the cultural wound active, restaging the core conflict in cycles of confrontation and reaffirmation.

Social Effects

The Right to Life vs. Pro-Choice complex tears at the fabric of American civil society:

- It polarizes the electorate and judicial system, destabilizing legal precedent.

- It frames healthcare decisions as battlegrounds of ideology rather than care.
- It divides religious, familial, and political communities, often silencing those who dwell in the gray.
- It hinders comprehensive sexual education and access to reproductive healthcare.

These effects are not merely legal—they are also psychosocial, emotional, and generational.

Potential for Transformation

Despite its deep polarization, this cultural complex holds the seeds of moral evolution and collective healing:

SHARED COMPASSION
Inviting both sides to acknowledge the pain and values that animate the other

ETHICAL NUANCE
Recognizing that real life includes tragic complexity, medical uncertainty, and diverse moral experience

POLICY INTEGRATION
Supporting freedom of choice alongside the resources that make life viable—healthcare, economic support, education

WITNESSING GRIEF
Holding space for loss on both sides—the grief of potential life ended, and the grief of life constrained

Transformation may lie, not in victory, but in witnessing—moving from moral absolutism to moral depth.

Iconography of Between Sacred Duty and Sovereign Will

TWO CENTRAL FEMALE FIGURES

Left Figure (Right to Life)
Shown in a pose of quiet reverence, she gently cradles her womb, within which a luminous fetus floats in fetal position. Her downward gaze and soft expression evoke maternal

tenderness, spiritual contemplation, and the sacred responsibility of protecting life. Her posture resembles traditional Madonna iconography, suggesting divine motherhood or the archetype of the life-bearer.

Right Figure (Pro-Choice):
Standing upright, she meets the viewer with a defiant gaze, her brow furrowed in conviction and resistance. She raises a clenched fist—a universal gesture of protest and liberation—while holding a sign that reads *MY BODY MY CHOICE.* A broken shackle hangs from her wrist, symbolizing release from historical and political control over the female body. Her stance invokes the archetype of the warrior or revolutionary—one who asserts sovereignty over destiny.

CENTRAL SYMBOL: THE SCALES OF JUSTICE

Positioned above and between the two women, the scales of justice symbolize the moral and legal weight of the issue. Their balance is ambiguous, suggesting the ongoing tension between competing rights: the right to life and the right to bodily autonomy. The placement of the scales in the upper center implies that society's ethical and judicial framework hovers over this intimate and existential divide.

THE FETUS

The fetus, luminous and curled within the womb, serves as the symbolic center of the pro-life worldview: vulnerable, sacred, and alive. It is not rendered in scientific detail but in archetypal form—symbolizing innocence, potential, and spiritual mystery. Its containment within the circular womb evokes traditional halo imagery or mandala, reinforcing sanctity.

THE CANDLE

Positioned at the lower left, the candle signifies mourning, vigil, and hope. In the pro-life context, it may represent remembrance for lives not born or the vigil held outside clinics. More broadly, it symbolizes the soul, the spark of life, and the fragile flame of collective moral concern.

THE SHACKLE

The broken shackle on the wrist of the pro-choice figure alludes to emancipation—freedom from forced motherhood, state control, or religious domination. It evokes historical struggles for liberation, including slavery, suffrage, and reproductive freedom. As a visual echo of "breaking the chains," it casts her body, not as a battleground, but as sovereign ground.

COLOR AND STYLE

The golden-brown monochromatic palette evokes religious iconography and historic frescoes, suggesting timelessness and spiritual gravity. The painterly style, reminiscent of Renaissance devotional art, elevates the scene from political polemic to archetypal myth. The warm tones soften the confrontation while enhancing its emotional and moral seriousness.

Interpretation

The image is a tableau of two archetypal postures: the protector of life and the defender of choice. Neither is vilified; both are rendered with dignity, strength, and grief—reflecting the complex emotional truth that underlies the cultural conflict. The space between them—occupied by the scales—symbolizes the agonizing weight of holding two sacred claims in one cultural psyche.

THE AMERICAN GUN CONTROL CULTURAL COMPLEX

JUSTICE ARMED, INNOCENCE AFRAID: THE AMERICAN GUN CONTROL CULTURAL COMPLEX

A solemn child stares upward, clutching her backpack beneath the blindfolded gaze of Justice—whose torch still burns, but whose hand now grips a handgun. Behind them, the Constitution bears a bullet hole. This image captures the fractured psyche of a nation caught between liberty and fear, rights and safety. The Gun Control Cultural Complex lives here: where the promise of protection collides with the price of freedom.

The American Gun Control cultural complex is a deeply charged psychic structure shaped by trauma, moral urgency, and conflicting mythologies of freedom and safety. It lives not only in policies and protests but also in haunting images, national grief, and an unrelenting struggle between competing visions of what it means to be free—and what it means to be protected.

Core Emotion: Mourning Transformed into Moral Outrage

At its heart is the ache of loss—children in classrooms, shoppers in stores, families torn apart by preventable violence. This grief is often quickly converted into anger, resolve, and a passionate call to action.

Mythic Root: The Innocent Must Be Protected

It draws from archetypes of the vulnerable child, the benevolent guardian, and the fallen Eden. There's also a Promethean myth underneath: humanity must confront its own dangerous fire—its weapons of death—and learn to wield or restrain them wisely.

Symbolic Imagery

- Empty shoes on Capitol steps
- Crosses, teddy bears, and candles at shooting sites
- Lady Justice with a bullet hole
- Cracked Second Amendment scrolls
- Children wearing bulletproof backpacks
- A scale tipped between freedom and death

Self-Reinforcing Memory

- Mass shootings as recurring national trauma loops
- Names of towns—Columbine, Sandy Hook, Uvalde—become symbols
- Viral footage and news cycles imprint fear and helplessness. These memories deepen the sense of moral urgency and "never again" resolve

Black-and-White Thinking

- Guns = death vs. Guns = freedom
- Control = safety vs. Control = tyranny
- "If we don't act now, more will die" vs. "If we act now, we lose liberty forever"

Repetitive Behavior

- Cycles of mass shooting leading to mourning then outrage and finally legislative impasse
- Renewed pushes for background checks, bans on assault weapons, red flag laws
- Cultural battles over the interpretation of the Second Amendment
- Symbolic gestures (moments of silence, walkouts, marches)
- Emotional fatigue, then reactivation when the next tragedy occurs

Social Effects

- It deepens political polarization and alienates communities that view gun rights as sacred.
- It fuels distrust of government, media, and even neighbors.
- When change fails, it fosters despair and cynicism.
- The complex can inadvertently entrench opposition by making people feel accused or threatened.

Potential for Transformation

- A renewed social contract around safety and liberty
- A spiritual reckoning with violence in American myth and culture
- Community-based healing and grassroots consensus
- Reimagining public space as truly safe, inclusive, and sacred

Iconography of Justice Armed, Innocence Afraid: The American Gun Control Cultural Complex

THE CHILD (LEFT FOREGROUND)

The emotional core of the image, she embodies vulnerability, innocence, and generational cost. Her wide eyes reflect confusion and silent dread, evoking the fear children carry into public spaces shaped by gun violence.

BLINDFOLDED LADY JUSTICE (RIGHT)

Traditionally a symbol of impartiality and civic morality, she is now burdened with contradiction. Her torch still burns—a sign of enduring ideals—but her right hand clutches a firearm, transforming justice into a figure of sanctioned force rather than deliberative balance.

THE HANDGUN (LOWER RIGHT)

A bold symbol of the Second Amendment and its cultural centrality, the firearm in Justice's grasp suggests the arming of civic identity—where protection and threat are nearly indistinguishable. Its presence in the hands of justice blurs the boundary between law enforcement and militarization.

BULLET HOLE IN THE CONSTITUTION (BACKGROUND)

The torn parchment behind them—clearly referencing "We the People"—shows a visible rupture in the founding narrative. The bullet hole suggests that violence has pierced not only bodies but also foundational ideals, raising the question of whether freedom and safety can still coexist.

LIGHTING AND SHADOWS

The torchlight casts a warm glow, contrasting sharply with the somber palette. It creates a visual tension between idealism and disillusionment—the light of liberty against the creeping shadow of fear.

BODY LANGUAGE AND COMPOSITION

The child stands close to Justice, yet there is no contact. This subtle distance implies that the guardianship offered is abstract, not comforting—as if the child is under the symbol's gaze but not its protection.

Interpretation

This image presents the American Gun Control cultural complex as a conflicted morality tale—where the very institutions meant to protect life appear entangled with instruments of death. It reflects the deep ambivalence in American culture around guns: as symbols of freedom and threat, heritage and trauma. The child looks upward, not at Justice's face, but at what she has become—suggesting that future generations are watching how we hold these contradictions.

THE SECOND AMENDMENT RIGHT TO BEAR ARMS CULTURAL COMPLEX

SENTINEL OF LIBERTY: THE SECOND AMENDMENT AS IDENTITY, FAITH, AND FORTRESS

A solemn man stands armed and resolute, framed by patriotic icons and sacred texts. Around him gather a silent, watchful family and a tableau of national symbols—the rattlesnake, the eagle, the Bible, the Constitution. More than a political right, the Second Amendment is here portrayed as a pillar of identity, a moral imperative, and a line in the sand against perceived tyranny. This is not simply about self-defense—it is about existential belonging, mythic vigilance, and sacred duty.

Core Emotion: Defiance and Sacred Vigilance

At its heart lies a visceral need for protection, autonomy, and the defense of freedom—especially against perceived threats of tyranny or lawlessness. This complex is fueled not only by fear, but also by pride: the gun is both a tool and a sacred emblem of liberty and identity.

Mythic Root: The Frontier Warrior and the Watchman Against Tyranny

This complex draws from the archetype of the armed citizen-patriot—the Minuteman who resists imperial domination, the frontiersman who tames the wilderness, and the vigilant guardian of hearth and family. It is steeped in the mythos of American independence and rugged individualism, where freedom must be defended by force if necessary.

Symbolic Imagery

- A lone figure silhouetted against the sun, rifle in hand
- A wall of firearms behind a US flag
- An eagle with talons gripping a musket
- The phrase "Don't Tread on Me" overlaid on a coiled serpent
- A Bible, a gun, and a Constitution resting on a weathered table
- A pickup truck with crossed rifles in the back window

Self-Reinforcing Memory

The complex is reinforced by historical narratives of revolution, rebellion, and resistance—against the British crown, invading armies, or intrusive federal authority. Events such as the Revolutionary War, the Civil War, Waco, and Ruby Ridge serve as flashpoints in its emotional memory. These stories create a sense of eternal vigilance and justified distrust.

Black-and-White Thinking

The world is divided into those who would disarm and dominate versus those who will defend and endure. Guns are seen as either symbols of freedom or tools of chaos, with little in-between. To question gun rights is often seen as moral betrayal rather than a policy stance.

Repetitive Behavior

Open-carry demonstrations, gun shows, "Constitutional carry" legislation, and ritualistic language around "good guys with guns." The performance of readiness and deterrence—displaying, carrying, or photographing weapons—is part of the collective assertion of identity.

Social Effects

The complex can isolate individuals in a fortress mentality, cultivating suspicion toward institutions, neighbors, and political compromise. It resists regulation even in the face of widespread violence, interpreting calls for safety as encroachments on liberty. It may elevate the gun over the common good, privileging a mythic self-defense over communal responsibility.

Iconography of Sentinel of Liberty: The Second Amendment as Identity, Faith, and Fortress

CENTRAL FIGURE—ARMED MAN IN WORK SHIRT AND CAP

The stoic central figure stands clutching an AR-style rifle. He is not in military uniform but working-class attire—symbolizing the "citizen-soldier" mythos: an ordinary man called to extraordinary vigilance. His posture conveys solemn responsibility rather than aggression, framing gun ownership as moral duty rather than violence.

FAMILY GROUP BEHIND HIM (WOMAN, BOY, GIRL)

Silent, steady, and grave, the figures surrounding him represent family, legacy, and community—those he is symbolically sworn to protect. Their watchful expressions reinforce the idea that safety and values must be upheld by personal force if necessary.

AMERICAN FLAG (BACKGROUND)

The tattered yet proud flag emphasizes patriotism under threat. It serves as a unifying backdrop, sanctifying the armed citizen as a defender of "true" American values.

"DON'T TREAD ON ME" AND GADSDEN SNAKE (LEFT)

A powerful libertarian and anti-government symbol, the coiled snake evokes vigilance, readiness, and the right to retaliate if provoked. It ties the image to revolutionary roots and modern populist resistance.

BALD EAGLE (UPPER RIGHT)

The eagle, national emblem of strength and freedom, soars above the scene—further elevating the man's stance from personal conviction to near-heroic archetype.

HOLY BIBLE AND US CONSTITUTION ("WE THE PEOPLE") AT THE BASE

These two texts sit side by side, implying that the right to bear arms is both divinely sanctioned and constitutionally guaranteed. Their placement at the man's feet suggests foundational authority—spiritual and legal—upon which his claim to armed guardianship stands.

CRACKED EARTH BENEATH

The fractured surface subtly suggests a society under pressure or in decline. It reflects both the apocalyptic fears embedded in the complex and the readiness to stand firm when the ground itself seems unstable.

Interpretation

This image embodies the emotional core of the Second Amendment complex: protection, autonomy, and defiant patriotism. The armed figure—framed by the flag, Bible, eagle, and Constitution—represents gun ownership as sacred duty. Beneath the symbols lies a deeper narrative of fear, honor, and survival woven into the American identity.

THE CLIMATE CHANGE CULTURAL COMPLEX

THE INHERITORS: FACING THE FURNACE OF THE FUTURE

A child stands at the threshold of environmental collapse, framed by symbols of urgency and loss—a sun that scorches, a clock that accelerates, and a polar bear adrift in industrial smoke. On either side, silent peers sit on cracked earth, bearing witness to an inheritance of crisis. This image encapsulates the Climate Change Cultural Complex as an existential anxiety etched into the collective psyche—where science, guilt, hope, and paralysis collide.

Core Emotion: Urgency, Guilt, and Apocalyptic Anxiety

This complex is driven by a profound sense that we are standing on the edge of collapse. It blends dread and determination—a growing awareness that human actions have unleashed forces beyond control, paired with a moral imperative to act before it's too late.

Mythic Root: The Punished World and the Prophetic Warning

The complex draws on archetypes of the flood, apocalypse, Prometheus Unbound, and Gaia wounded. Humanity is seen both as violator and redeemer. Like Icarus, we flew too close to the sun; like Noah, some believe we must now build arks—technological, ethical, or spiritual.

Symbolic Imagery

- Cracked earth underfoot, rising seas in the distance
- Children holding signs in hurricane winds
- A polar bear on a melting shard of ice
- Cities encased in smoke or floodwater
- Trees growing from ash
- Solar panels and oil rigs facing off like armies
- A clock with no hands over a burning Earth

Self-Reinforcing Memory

The complex is fed by repeated climate disasters, ignored warnings, politicized denial, and intergenerational tension. Each flood, fire, or heatwave becomes another glyph in the growing mythology of planetary reckoning. Simultaneously, images of failed climate summits and greenwashed corporations deepen mistrust.

Black-and-White Thinking

The world is divided between awakened and asleep, activists and deniers, future-builders and destroyers. While this fuels passion, it can alienate, turning potential allies into scapegoats. Complexity, ambiguity, or incremental change is often seen as betrayal.

Repetitive Behavior

- Marching, warning, shaming, defending, and endlessly explaining
- Mobilizing online
- Fasting from plastic

- Planting trees
- Mistrusting hope, yet searching for it

The rituals of climate consciousness are both symbolic and sacrificial.

Social Effects

The complex fractures society along fault lines of generation, class, geography, and worldview. It causes ecoanxiety, burnout, and despair, even as it births innovation and deepened solidarity. The existential scale of the threat overwhelms traditional political and psychological responses, leaving many caught between paralysis and rage.

Potential for Transformation

The shadow of this complex includes doomsday fatalism, performative virtue, and scapegoating. Yet its transformative potential is enormous: it can catalyze global consciousness, systemic imagination, and a resacralization of nature. It forces a confrontation with limits—and with what it means to be human on a living Earth.

Iconography of The Inheritors: Facing the Furnace of the Future

CENTRAL FIGURE—CHILD WITH BACKPACK (BACK TO VIEWER)

Symbolizes the next generation—those who must carry the burden of decisions made before them. Facing the horizon of ecological catastrophe, the child becomes both witness and inheritor, poised between helplessness and potential.

CRACKED EARTH AND DROUGHT LANDSCAPE

Evokes environmental degradation, resource scarcity, and desertification. The dryness implies a world not just physically parched, but also emotionally and morally drained.

SUN AND THERMOMETER (LEFT SKY)

The exaggerated, glowing sun paired with a red-lined thermometer conveys intensifying heat and planetary fever—

an ever-rising existential threat that hovers above all debate and action.

CLOCK (CENTER SKY)

A powerful symbol of the "ticking clock" metaphor—time running out. It anchors the cultural complex in a shared sense of urgency and looming point-of-no-return, reinforcing anxiety and fatalism.

POLAR BEAR ON MELTING ICE (RIGHT SKY)

A modern ecological icon of climate disruption. The bear's dislocation amid factory smoke makes the abstract threat visceral. It also evokes the cultural use of endangered species as emotional appeals for action or guilt.

SMOKESTACKS AND WIND TURBINES (RIGHT GROUND)

Juxtapose the industrial causes of climate change with the technological hopes of green energy. Their side-by-side placement symbolizes the ambivalence and unresolved tension in climate discourse: destruction and solution coexist.

TWO YOUTH FIGURES (LEFT AND RIGHT GROUND)

Flanking the central child, these seated figures (a boy and a girl) reflect despair, resignation, and quiet observation. Their silence speaks to a generation often aware but politically sidelined—watching the damage without agency.

Interpretation

This image captures the urgency, grief, and burden of climate change. A young figure stands before a fractured earth, caught between symbols of irreversible loss and fragile hope. The blazing sun and ticking clock evoke existential threat, while cracked ground and weary companions reflect fear, paralysis, and the weight of inheriting a world in crisis.

THE CLIMATE CHANGE DENIAL CULTURAL COMPLEX

PROFITS OVER PLANET

A corporate figure adjusts his glasses, staring at a rising profits' chart while the world behind him burns, floods, and chokes. Bound by ideological chains and blind to ecological collapse, he stands unshaken between the fire of disaster and the mirage of control. This image portrays the Climate Denial cultural complex as a psychological fortress built from economic self-interest, willful blindness, and the enchantment of infinite growth. The man in the image symbolizes the rational, corporate, or technocratic mindset at the heart of the Climate Change Denial cultural complex.

Core Emotion: Defensiveness and Fear of Loss

At the heart of this complex lies an unconscious fear of disruption—economic, cultural, and personal. Denial serves as a psychological defense against acknowledging vulnerability, guilt, or the need for profound lifestyle change.

Mythic Root: The Myth of Dominion and the Infinite Frontier

Rooted in a Promethean belief in human exceptionalism and technological salvation, this complex draws on myths of mastery over nature: the Earth is here for human use, and progress means endless growth. It echoes the Biblical notion of dominion and the American myth of the boundless frontier—both of which resist limits.

Symbolic Imagery

- Factories belching smoke under a blue sky
- Oil rigs planted like victorious flags
- Lush green lawns in deserts
- Rising seas ignored by beachgoers
- An indifferent suited figure adjusting stock charts while wildfires rage in the background

Self-Reinforcing Memory

Cultural and media narratives valorizing industrial expansion, fossil fuel prosperity, and rugged self-reliance feed the complex. Any evidence of environmental harm is reframed as either exaggerated, cyclical, or politically motivated.

Black-and-White Thinking

Solutions are cast as either techno-utopian or socialist overreach. Those who advocate for climate action are labeled alarmists or traitors to economic freedom. The world is split between "realists" (who protect jobs and traditions) and "radicals" (who want to destroy prosperity).

Repetitive Behavior

Dismissing scientific consensus, defunding environmental regulation, mocking green movements, and doubling down on extractive industries—even as ecological disasters increase.

Social Effects

Climate denial fractures the collective ability to respond to a shared existential threat. It erodes trust in science, scapegoats reformers, and delays adaptation—ensuring greater harm later. The denial also deepens generational divides, as youth increasingly face an unstable future while elders cling to a fading industrial mythos.

Iconography of Profits Over Planet

BUSINESSMAN IN SUIT HOLDING PROFIT CHART

The central figure embodies the rational, data-driven façade of the denial complex. His upward-pointing line represents economic growth—used to justify inaction, distract from reality, and frame environmental concerns as secondary or alarmist. He represents

Willful Detachment: Calmly analyzing rising economic trends while surrounded by environmental collapse, suggesting disconnection from reality.

Industrial Legacy: His suit and clipboard mark him as part of the professional class benefiting from or perpetuating fossil-fuel-driven prosperity.

False Control: The charts give the illusion of control or progress even as ecological catastrophe unfolds—burning forests, polluted skies, rising seas.

Blind Rationalism: His posture implies focus and confidence, yet the setting contradicts it. It reflects how systems of power can rationalize or ignore destruction.

GRAPH GLASSES & CORPORATE LOGO ON FOREHEAD

The glasses reinforce filtered perception—he sees only what supports his worldview. The logo on his forehead symbolizes ideological branding and corporate capture of consciousness. He has internalized the system he represents.

OIL PUMPS AND SMOKESTACKS (LEFT BACKGROUND)

A visual shorthand for fossil fuel dependence. These industrial forms dominate the horizon under an unnaturally hot sun, illustrating the source of emissions and the scale of planetary damage.

WILDFIRE AND CHAINS (RIGHT SIDE)

Flames consume the forest while thick chains snake around the figure's body. These chains represent ideological and financial bondage—tied to profits, lobbyists, and economic systems resistant to change.

LEISURE FIGURE UNDER UMBRELLA (LOWER LEFT)

A man lounges beneath an umbrella amid sprinklers and artificial comfort, symbolizing climate privilege and escapism. While much of the world burns or floods, a protected class remains buffered by wealth and denial.

LIFE PRESERVER IN FOREGROUND

Unused and off to the side, this object symbolizes ignored solutions. It's a subtle nod to the tools we have—science, adaptation, global cooperation—being cast aside while we cling to illusions of stability.

BRIGHT ORANGE SUN AND BLUE SKY OBSCURED BY SMOKE

The harsh solar glow suggests a world overheated and out of balance. The encroaching black smoke clouds symbolize both literal atmospheric pollution and the metaphorical clouding of public awareness.

Interpretation

This image depicts a cultural complex of denial masked as pragmatism. A businessman watches market gains while catastrophe burns behind him—fires, oil rigs, and smoke. A sunbather and manicured lawn reflect privilege and detachment. The rising graph becomes a blinding myth of growth as comfort and profit override ecological truth. Denial here is not ignorance, but deliberate disconnection from shared responsibility.

THE ANTI-VACCINE CULTURAL COMPLEX

IN THE SHADOW OF THE SYRINGE: THE ANTI-VACCINE CULTURAL COMPLEX

A mother clutches her frightened child as a hooded figure looms with an oversized syringe, casting a long shadow of distrust. Behind them, smoke curls from factories and truth flows from a neglected fountain. The family stands alone, caught between fear and conviction. This image captures the emotional and symbolic force of the Anti-Vaccine cultural complex: the battle to protect innocence from perceived harm cloaked in authority.

Core Emotion: Distrust and Protective Defiance

At the heart of the Anti-Vaccine cultural complex lies profound mistrust—of authority, expertise, government, pharmaceutical companies, and even neighbors. This is coupled with a fierce desire to protect the body, the family, and personal sovereignty. It is animated by defiance: the assertion of control in a world perceived as manipulative and overreaching.

Mythic Root: The Innocent Body vs. the Poisoned Chalice

This complex draws on archetypal fears of contamination and betrayal. The mythic root is the sacred, natural body under threat from artificial, imposed interventions. Echoes of biblical temptation (the apple as knowledge turned toxic), medical experimentation, and dystopian control fuel the deeper story: purity versus corruption, nature versus technocracy.

Symbolic Imagery

- A mother shielding her child from a looming syringe shaped like a corporate tower
- A masked government figure offering a golden vial behind a dark cloak
- A natural spring labeled *TRUTH* beside a laboratory leaking green smoke
- A body with radiating halos on one side, barcodes and wires on the other
- Protesters holding signs that blend spiritual, medical, and constitutional symbols

Self-Reinforcing Memory

Historic abuses like the Tuskegee Syphilis Study, thalidomide, or coercive sterilization campaigns as well as more recent pharmaceutical scandals (opioid crisis, corporate lobbying), form the memory-field in which vaccine distrust takes root. Each controversy reinforces the belief that authorities lie, harm, and profit at the expense of the powerless.

Black-and-White Thinking

"Natural is good; artificial is evil." In the Anti-Vax cultural complex, there is little tolerance for ambiguity. The medical system is often portrayed as monolithic, coercive, and profit-driven. Choice becomes moralized: to vaccinate is to submit; to resist is to awaken. Those who question vaccines are brave truth seekers; those who comply are sheep or slaves to the system.

Repetitive Behaviors

- Sharing viral videos or alternative "research" from non-mainstream sources
- Refusal to comply with vaccine mandates, often framed as heroic resistance
- Embracing "natural health" alternatives and holistic medicine
- Gathering in community echo chambers online or in person
- Reframing public health as personal invasion or globalist control

Social Effects

This complex fractures trust in science, public health, and community cohesion. It turns life-saving interventions into political and spiritual battlefields. The Anti-Vax stance often isolates individuals and families from larger social systems, creating rifts within schools, communities, and even families. It also fuels broader conspiratorial thinking that undermines democratic discourse.

Possibility of Transformation

Transformation may come through the reintegration of trust and transparency. When medical and scientific institutions admit fallibility, address historical harm, and shift toward truly participatory public health, the complex can soften. Healing begins when people feel respected, not coerced—when information is offered, not mandated. The Anti-Vax cultural complex can evolve into a movement for ethical medicine, body literacy, and inclusive dialogue rather than defiant withdrawal.

Iconography of In the Shadow of the Syringe: The Anti-Vaccine Cultural Complex

HOODED FIGURE HOLDING SYRINGE

The faceless cloaked figure personifies institutional authority seen as menacing—whether government, Big Pharma, or the medical establishment. The syringe is exaggerated in size, symbolizing the perceived forcefulness of medical intervention and the intrusion on bodily autonomy.

PROTECTIVE MOTHER AND FRIGHTENED CHILD

The central emotional focus. The mother embodies maternal intuition and moral resistance, while the child evokes innocence, vulnerability, and the sacred duty to protect the next generation from harm—real or perceived.

NO VACCINE MANDATES SIGN (UPPER LEFT)

A direct signal of the political and moral resistance within the complex. The sign functions as both slogan and shield, opposing not just policy but also perceived overreach and coercion.

FOUNTAIN LABELED TRUTH (LOWER RIGHT)

This fountain represents natural wisdom, hidden knowledge, or alternative understanding often believed to be suppressed or dismissed by mainstream science. It runs quietly and unattended, contrasting with the noisy force of the syringe-wielding figure.

SMOKY CITYSCAPE AND INDUSTRIAL TOWERS (BACKGROUND):

Imply a polluted, post-trust world shaped by systemic power. These elements symbolize the backdrop of suspicion—where economic and governmental systems are presumed complicit in harm or deception.

SEPIA COLOR PALETTE

The golden-brown tones evoke nostalgia, moral seriousness, and emotional warmth within the family. They contrast with the dark, cold presence of the cloaked authority figure—amplifying the split between natural protection and institutional fear.

Interpretation

This image depicts the Anti-Vaccination cultural complex as rooted in mistrust, fear, and protection of bodily autonomy. The mother and child—huddled in defensive embrace—embody a deep emotional conviction that external forces (represented by the hooded figure with syringe) threaten personal and familial sovereignty. The looming presence of the sign and the corrupted "Truth" fountain reflect a narrative where institutions are seen as coercive and deceptive. More than science denial, this complex reveals a mythic battle between purity and contamination, where the vaccine becomes a symbol of state overreach, and the parental bond a sacred line of defense.

CHAPTER 8

Geopolitical Cultural Complexes

The American Globalism vs. Isolationism Cultural Complex

The Solidarity with Ukraine Cultural Complex

The Putin Cultural Complex in the American Psyche

The Israel Palestine Cultural Complex in the American Psyche

The Israeli-Iranian Cultural Complex in the American Psyche

The China Cultural Complex in the American Psyche

The American Tarriff Cultural Complex

THE AMERICAN GLOBALISM VS. ISOLATIONISM CULTURAL COMPLEX

AT THE CROSSROADS OF EMPIRE AND RETREAT

A two-headed eagle, torn between outward soaring and inward guarding, stands sentinel over America's fractured myth of destiny. One gaze follows the open paths of global connection; the other locks onto a nest of broken origins. Behind them, ancestral figures rise and skies divide, reflecting the soul-struggle between engagement with the world and the urge to retreat behind walls.

The Globalism vs. Isolationism cultural complex is a deeply entrenched and emotionally fraught psychic structure that organizes American identity around a fundamental question: Should the nation extend itself into the world as a moral and economic leader, or withdraw to protect its sovereignty, purity, and internal coherence? It fuses myth, memory, symbolism, and ritual behavior into a collective drama of belonging, betrayal, and national destiny.

Core Emotion: Pride, Betrayal, Anxiety, and Moral Urgency

At its emotional center is a charged cocktail of patriotic pride, existential anxiety, and moral urgency. Globalism is animated by a sense of hopeful responsibility—pride in being a force for good, an architect of world order. But it also carries anxiety: about decline, backlash, and imperial overreach. Isolationism, by contrast, channels a fierce instinct for protection and moral self-containment—but it is often haunted by fear: of invasion, erosion, and the loss of something sacred. The betrayal cuts both ways—either the United States has turned its back on the world, or the world has corrupted the United States.

Mythic Root: The City on a Hill vs. Fortress America

This cultural complex is powered by two mythic foundations. Globalism invokes the Puritan image of America as a "City on a Hill"—a beacon of freedom, justice, and enlightened progress, ordained to lead. Isolationism reaches back to the myth of "Fortress America"—a chosen land insulated by oceans and destiny, meant to flourish in sovereign independence. Both rest on exceptionalism. But one radiates outward with messianic fervor; the other withdraws inward to preserve moral integrity. The psychic split is archetypal: the missionary versus the monk, the world-shaper versus the guardian.

Symbolic Imagery

The visual language of this complex contains two competing symbolic universes:

- A diplomat at the UN podium, invoking unity through American ideals

- A border wall under construction, marking limits and lines of protection
- The Statue of Liberty: either glowing as a global invitation or dimming as a relic of misplaced idealism
- A factory in ruins: the cost of globalization etched in rust
- A warship at sea: strength deployed abroad, ambiguous in purpose
- A passport, either sacred token of mobility or symbol of eroded loyalty
- A map of the US glowing at the center of radiating global influence—or ringed in barbed wire, encircled in defense

These images serve not only as propaganda but also as psychic anchors—projecting emotion, aspiration, and fear.

Self-Reinforcing Memory

The memory embedded in this complex is selectively curated and mythologized. For globalists, America's finest hours are Marshall Plan generosity, WWII alliances, space exploration, and multilateral cooperation. For isolationists, memory centers on betrayal—NAFTA's economic displacement, the Vietnam quagmire, "forever wars," and porous borders. Both sides believe history proves their case. Every triumph becomes prophecy fulfilled; every loss is a wound to be avenged or avoided.

Black-and-White Thinking

This complex thrives on binary oppositions. You are either a patriotic defender or a globalist elite. Either engagement brings redemption, or it invites ruin. The world is a partner or a parasite. Complexity is flattened into sides; ambiguity is cast as weakness. Opposition becomes betrayal. In this psychic terrain, compromise is cowardice, and nuance is suspect.

Repetitive Behavior

The complex expresses itself through compulsive, ritualized behavior patterns:

- Cycles of intervention and withdrawal—each hailed as a correction of the last

- Rhetorical pendulums swinging between "global responsibility" and "America First"
- Recurrent renegotiation of alliances, treaties, and trade deals
- Alternating glorification and vilification of immigrants, foreign cultures, and international institutions
- Ritualistic casting of blame—on elites, globalists, isolationists, and foreign others
- Cultural and political performances of allegiance to one vision or the other

These behaviors repeat not only as policy but also as sacred drama—reenacted to resolve or relive the underlying tension.

Social Effects

This cultural complex fractures national coherence by forcing a zero-sum choice: open or close, lead or hide, give or protect. It turns civic discourse into existential combat, where disagreement signals disloyalty and every policy becomes a test of national character. It destabilizes the capacity to form consistent foreign policy, corrodes trust in institutions, and undermines shared frameworks of identity. In its polarized extremes, it elevates fear over vision, loyalty over deliberation, and myth over governance.

Potential for Transformation

Yet within this complex lies a reservoir of generative energy—archetypal, symbolic, and potentially transformative:

REASSERTION OF NATIONAL PURPOSE

It challenges the country to ask: What does it mean to lead? To serve? To protect? It demands moral clarity amid chaos.

CULTURAL AND POLITICAL INTEGRITY

Isolationist instincts protect place, identity, and the rhythms of local life, offering resistance to global homogenization.

MORAL INTERNATIONALISM

Globalism, when disentangled from dominance, can become a vehicle for ethical stewardship, global cooperation, and peacebuilding.

REINTEGRATION OF OPPOSITES

This psychic split can be healed—not by choosing sides, but by learning to hold the paradox: that a nation can be both strong and generous, both rooted and open.

CIVIC AWAKENING

The struggle over America's global role awakens collective attention to values, responsibility, and interdependence in an age of crisis.

Iconography of At the Crossroads of Empire and Retreat

This image symbolizes the internal split in the American psyche between outward expansion and inward retreat—between the myth of the global leader and the impulse to wall off, protect, and preserve.

THE TWO-HEADED EAGLE

A mythic, divided American eagle stands sentinel at the center. Its twin heads face opposite directions, embodying the nation's unresolved tension.

The left head turns toward a radiant sky filled with arcing networks—airlines, data flows, and imagined lines of alliance. This head symbolizes the globalist pole: aspirational, outward-facing, and oriented toward connection, diplomacy, and shared progress.

The right head, bound in barbed wire and tightened with padlocks, gazes inward and downward toward a cracked nest. This head embodies the isolationist pole: wary, protective, and gripped by nationalist fears and cultural defensiveness.

THE CROSSROADS BELOW

The eagle stands atop a literal crossroads:

One path leads toward a luminous, open horizon—suggesting outward movement, planetary influence, and civic optimism.

The other path disappears into a dark, swirling vortex, surrounded by storm clouds and the specters of ancestral archetypes—soldier, settler, preacher—who loom like unresolved myths from America's past.

THE BROKEN NEST

Near the eagle's talons lies a nest of broken eggs—symbols of lost potential and interrupted rebirth. The fragility of these origins reflects a collective identity fractured by conflicting narratives of empire, decline, and imagined purity.

THE DIVIDED SKY

Above the eagle, the sky reinforces the psychological rift:

On the left, it glows with golden light and geometric signs of global order.

On the right, it swirls with darkness, memory, and storm—echoing the isolationist dread of cultural contamination and civilizational collapse.

This iconography renders a powerful archetypal tension between dominion and withdrawal, between leading the world and sealing it off. The two-headed eagle stands not only for foreign policy, but also for a splintered national soul caught between expansion and enclosure.

Interpretation

Altogether, the image captures the mythic and psychological tension within the American imagination. It is not a conflict between good and evil, but between two powerful, competing truths: the longing to participate in a global community and the urge to retreat behind walls in defense of something sacred and endangered. The eagle's straining posture, caught between these poles, becomes a living symbol of America at a crossroads—not only geopolitical, but also psychological and spiritual.

THE SOLIDARITY WITH UKRAINE CULTURAL COMPLEX

TORCH OF SOLIDARITY: THE UKRAINE CULTURAL COMPLEX IN THE AMERICAN PSYCHE

A tableau of symbolic figures gathers under stormy skies, uniting myth, justice, mourning, and hope around the Ukrainian cause. President Volodymyr Zelenskyy stands solemnly beneath the Ukrainian flag, flanked by Lady Liberty and a blindfolded Lady Justice. A rocket marked DEMOCRACY ascends skyward, bearing the American faith in liberal ideals. In the foreground, women of diverse ancestry bow their heads in prayer or witness, channeling the long arc of struggle, trauma, and perseverance. The image reflects how the war in Ukraine has activated a deep cultural and moral complex within the American imagination: a projection of democratic idealism, sacred suffering, and righteous resistance.

Core Emotion: Moral Clarity and Heroic Responsibility

At the emotional center of this cultural complex is a profound sense of moral responsibility. Many Americans experience the war in Ukraine not just as a geopolitical crisis, but also as a test of global conscience. It evokes a powerful mixture of pride, urgency, and anxiety—rooted in the belief that the United States has a special role to play in defending liberty from tyranny. There is a strong emotional investment in taking a principled stand, with the sense that to remain passive would be to betray foundational ideals.

Mythic Root: Cold War Paladin, World Policeman, and Last Best Hope

This complex draws from a dense network of mythic and historical archetypes in the American imagination. One of the most prominent is the Cold War Paladin—the figure of righteous power standing firm against communism and authoritarianism. This merges with the long-standing image of America as the World's Policeman, a reluctant yet noble enforcer of global order. These tropes are undergirded by the messianic belief in the United States as the "Last Best Hope of Earth," a phrase popularized by Abraham Lincoln, framing the nation as a bulwark against chaos and oppression. Together, these myths feed a sense that America must intervene not only strategically, but also morally.

Symbolic Imagery

The cultural imagination is stirred by a host of emotionally potent images:

- The American flag fluttering over the ruins of a Ukrainian city, suggesting solidarity and protection
- Ukrainian President Volodymyr Zelensky appearing side by side with American leaders, embodying a shared front in the fight for freedom
- Missiles or military aid emblazoned with words like *Democracy*, *Resolve*, and *Justice*

- A revitalized American eagle—styled after Cold War iconography—extending its wings across Eastern Europe
- Global maps depicting Ukraine bathed in light, with encroaching shadows symbolizing Russian aggression
- Demonstrations where Ukrainian and American flags are waved together, signifying a merging of causes

These images reinforce a binary moral drama and place the United States at the symbolic center of resistance.

Self-Reinforcing Memory

This complex is deeply shaped by historical memory. Americans recall the Berlin Airlift, the Cuban Missile Crisis, and the ideological framing of the Cold War as a battle between freedom and totalitarianism. These memories serve as moral reference points, reinforcing the belief that the United States has a proven track record of standing against oppression. Later episodes—such as the fall of the Berlin Wall, support for the Solidarity movement in Poland, and even post-9/11 rhetoric—continue to feed the story that America's identity is bound to its role as defender of liberty. These memories are selective, but emotionally powerful. They create a template: When freedom is under siege, America must act.

Black-and-White Thinking

The psychological structure of this complex tends to divide the world into opposing forces. Ukraine is cast as the embodiment of democracy, courage, and innocence. Russia becomes the symbol of tyranny, expansionism, and evil. Those who question US involvement are sometimes seen not as cautious or critical thinkers, but as indifferent or even complicit in wrongdoing. Calls for negotiation may be interpreted as appeasement. Criticism of American foreign policy may be equated with disloyalty or moral blindness. This binary lens leaves little room for ambiguity or moral complexity, making it harder to engage in nuanced discourse or consider long-term consequences.

Repetitive Behavior

The behaviors expressed through this complex often follow familiar cultural patterns:

- Public calls for American intervention—military, financial, and symbolic—are framed as moral obligations rather than strategic decisions.
- Political speeches and media coverage invoke phrases like "standing with Ukraine," "fighting for freedom," and "never again," drawing on a well-worn rhetorical script.
- Historical comparisons to World War II and the Cold War are repeated to justify present-day action.
- Discussions often avoid deeper reflection on past US interventions that may complicate the moral narrative.
- Celebrations of American resolve and leadership are emphasized, whereas contradictions—such as alliances with authoritarian regimes elsewhere—are downplayed or ignored.

These patterns serve to reaffirm the cultural story and strengthen identification with the heroic role.

Social Effects

Although this complex can galvanize support for noble causes, it also has shadow elements. It can suppress debate and discourage critical reflection. By framing the conflict as a cosmic battle between good and evil, it can delegitimize voices calling for diplomacy or caution. Internally, it polarizes public opinion—dividing citizens into those seen as loyal defenders of democracy and those cast as naïve, disloyal, or defeatist. Externally, it risks framing the US as a savior figure, perpetuating a kind of moral imperialism. The complex may also promote militarized responses while sidelining other tools of global engagement—such as diplomacy, cultural exchange, or restorative justice.

Potential for Transformation

When consciously recognized and symbolically integrated, the Solidarity with Ukraine cultural complex can channel powerful energies in constructive ways:

GLOBAL SOLIDARITY

It cultivates empathy and moral alignment with people suffering under violent aggression, reminding Americans of their interconnectedness with global struggles.

MORAL ENGAGEMENT

Rather than retreating into isolation or cynicism, this complex reawakens moral concern in public life and demands that foreign policy reflect ethical values.

HISTORICAL MEMORY AS MORAL COMPASS

By connecting past moments of resistance—against fascism, genocide, or imperialism—with current crises, the complex reminds Americans of their ideals and obligations.

DEMOCRATIC ASPIRATION

It reaffirms a vision of the United States as a nation defined by values rather than mere power—rekindling a belief in justice, pluralism, and freedom.

SUPPORT FOR THE VULNERABLE

When directed wisely, this complex generates humanitarian aid, refugee support, and advocacy for the displaced—transforming myth into meaningful action.

MYTHIC RENEWAL OF PURPOSE

In a time of internal division and political fatigue, the complex can offer a renewed sense of moral and national identity—but only if it remains open to humility, complexity, and shared responsibility.

Iconography of Torch of Solidarity: The Ukraine Cultural Complex in the American Psyche

ZELENSKYY AT THE CENTER

Positioned as both contemporary leader and mythic hero, Zelenskyy embodies a democratic David facing authoritarian Goliath. His gaze is direct, steady, and heavy with responsibility, inviting projection and idealization from Western audiences.

UKRAINIAN FLAG (BEHIND ZELENSKYY)

Billowing upward, it signals sovereignty, resistance, and the righteousness of a national cause. In the American psyche, it echoes the moral clarity of World War II–era imagery—casting Ukraine as the frontline of freedom.

STATUE OF LIBERTY (LEFT)

A foundational American symbol, Lady Liberty anchors the image in ideals of welcome, freedom, and resilience. Her placement beside Zelenskyy ties the American democratic mythos to the Ukrainian struggle.

BLINDFOLDED LADY JUSTICE (RIGHT)

Her presence and broken posture suggest the challenge of impartial justice in a time of war. The scales tilt subtly, gesturing toward the moral and political weight Americans assign to Ukraine's plight.

"DEMOCRACY" ROCKET (UPPER RIGHT)

A missile bearing the word *Democracy* launches skyward—a paradoxical fusion of idealism and militarism. It captures the tension between democratic values and the use of force to defend them.

AMERICAN FLAG (LOWER LEFT)

Crumpled and earthbound, it contrasts with the upward-striving rocket and flag, suggesting both solidarity and struggle—perhaps even fatigue with war or democratic aspiration in decline at home.

PRAYING WOMAN (FOREGROUND RIGHT)

With closed eyes and folded hands, she represents spiritual solidarity, emotional identification, and the archetype of the suffering innocent. Her traditional blouse and pale complexion echo Ukrainian peasant iconography.

ROW OF WOMEN (BOTTOM)

The somber multigenerational line of women may represent a collective ancestral memory—linking the Holocaust, Native American genocide, and other traumas to the psychic resonance of Ukraine's suffering.

STATUE BUST WITH AMERICANO INSCRIPTION (BOTTOM RIGHT)

A cracked stone bust labeled *Americano* suggests fractured ideals, Western projection, and perhaps the subtle self-mythologizing at play in American involvement. It serves as a warning about projecting purity while overlooking complexity.

Interpretation

This image channels a profound cultural complex that lives at the intersection of idealism, grief, moral clarity, and projection. In the American psyche, Ukraine becomes a symbolic vessel—carrying both the unfulfilled promise of democracy and the chance for its redemption. But like all cultural complexes, this one contains danger: the temptation to simplify, sanctify, or instrumentalize tragedy for our own moral self-image. The Solidarity with Ukraine cultural complex is ultimately a mirror—one in which Americans see not only a distant war, but also our deepest hopes and anxieties about who we are and who we might yet become.

THE PUTIN CULTURAL COMPLEX IN THE AMERICAN PSYCHE

THE AUTHORITARIAN MIRROR: THE PUTIN CULTURAL COMPLEX IN THE AMERICAN PSYCHE

In this symbolic image, Vladimir Putin looms at the center like a monolithic embodiment of authoritarian control. Surrounding him is a psychological battlefield: the wreckage of war, the sorrow of civilians, and the fractured ideals of democracy and justice. American projections of evil, order, resistance, and ruin converge on this figure, casting Putin as both villain and shadow-self. His image conjures ancestral fears of tyranny and lost empires—while subtly reflecting the West's own temptations toward power, certainty, and domination. This cultural complex does not merely see Putin; it uses him—to define, defend, and distort its own fragile identity.

Core Emotion: Fear, Fascination, and Projection

At the emotional center of this complex lies a potent mix of fear, moral outrage, and a complicated, often unconscious fascination. Many Americans see Vladimir Putin not merely as a foreign adversary but also as the embodiment of authoritarianism—someone who threatens the democratic ideals they hold dear. At the same time, there is a darker allure in how he represents unapologetic strength and strategic mastery. For some, he is viewed as a cold and dangerous tyrant; for others, he appears as a symbol of order and decisiveness amid what they perceive as Western weakness. These polarized emotions create a psychological field where Americans project both their anxieties and their unacknowledged desires onto the figure of Putin.

Mythic Root: The Tyrant-King, the Cold War Phantom, and the Anti-Christ of Democracy

This cultural complex draws upon deep mythic patterns embedded in the American imagination. One of the most prominent is the archetype of the tyrant-king—a ruler who consolidates power through fear, suppresses dissent, and imposes order through authoritarian means. Simultaneously, Putin evokes the Cold War phantom—a shadowy, resurrected version of the Soviet adversary, reminding Americans of the ideological and existential conflict that once dominated global politics. For many, particularly those concerned with liberal democracy, Putin also resembles an Anti-Christ figure—not in a religious sense, but symbolically, as one who seduces and destabilizes the global moral order. Conversely, some segments of the American far-right romanticize him as a kind of countercultural savior—a leader who resists liberal globalism, promotes traditional values, and stands firm against perceived moral decay in the West. These layered myths form the psychic scaffolding through which Americans interpret Putin's every move.

Symbolic Imagery

The figure of Putin is constantly reproduced in symbolic form:

- He is frequently shown shirtless on horseback, an image that exaggerates masculinity and dominance, feeding both satire and admiration.
- He appears seated at one end of an impossibly long table or over a geopolitical chessboard, embodying strategic detachment and unblinking control.
- Propaganda or media images often depict a divided world: a West characterized by chaos and moral decline, juxtaposed with a Russia under disciplined command.
- Visual metaphors such as a snarling bear draped in the Russian flag, or cyber agents cloaked in darkness infiltrating Western institutions, reinforce narratives of menace and omnipresence.
- Even Cold War–era aesthetics—red telephones, control rooms, and maps marked with missile arcs—are revived in commentary and political satire.

These images do more than inform. They give psychological shape to Americans' emotional relationship with power, threat, and sovereignty.

Self-Reinforcing Memory

Putin is understood through the lens of powerful American collective memories.

- The Cold War era remains a foundational frame, where the US and the Soviet Union were locked in a global struggle for ideological supremacy. This memory gives Putin the role of a resurrected adversary—calculating, clandestine, and deeply dangerous.
- The events of 9/11 and the subsequent war on terror reshaped how Americans view global threats, making figures like Putin easily integrated into narratives of shadowy enemies who operate outside democratic norms.
- The 2016 US presidential election further entrenched this memory structure. Allegations of Russian interference and disinformation turned Putin into a symbolic manipulator of democracy, heightening paranoia and moral panic.

- The 2022 invasion of Ukraine catalyzed a collective flashback to WWII-era themes, where defending Ukraine was framed as a stand against modern fascism and tyranny.

Each of these memories is not only a historical reference—they are also emotional templates through which new events are interpreted, often with increasing moral urgency.

Black-and-White Thinking

Within this complex, nuance often gives way to stark moral dichotomies. Putin is framed as the embodiment of evil authoritarianism, whereas Western leaders (especially those perceived as weak or compromised) are contrasted against him as defenders of fragile democracy. Russia is seen as the inevitable aggressor, whereas America is imagined as the last bastion of freedom. Support for Ukraine is widely understood as a moral imperative; any call for diplomatic caution is often dismissed as naïve, disloyal, or complicit. On the other hand, certain ideological subcultures invert this moral frame, idealizing Putin as a bold traditionalist hero while portraying the United States as decadent, hypocritical, or in moral decline. In either case, the complexity of global affairs is reduced to simple binaries—good versus evil, strength versus weakness, truth versus treason.

Repetitive Behavior

This complex also expresses itself in ritualized cultural and political behavior:

- US political leaders routinely invoke opposition to Putin as a measure of moral clarity and national strength, regardless of party.
- Media narratives frequently frame his actions as existential threats, fueling cycles of outrage and heightened vigilance.
- Public discourse revisits themes of foreign interference, hacking, and psychological operations (PSYOP), reinforcing the sense of being under siege.
- Online culture contributes its own rituals: memes that caricature Putin as a villainous mastermind or an exaggerated icon of hypermasculinity, amateur psychological analyses of his facial

expressions or physical health, and endless speculation about his intentions.

- These behaviors function not merely as information or entertainment but also as social rituals—ways of reinforcing shared identity in contrast to a mythic Other.

Social Effects

The Putin cultural complex exacerbates American internal divisions. It frames political discourse in absolutist terms, branding dissent as betrayal and skepticism as weakness. It encourages moralism over inquiry and spectacle over substance. It can lead to militarized responses while sidelining diplomacy, cultural understanding, or introspection. Perhaps most dangerously, it acts as a psychological defense mechanism: by projecting authoritarianism onto a foreign figure, Americans avoid confronting their own democratic backsliding, populist tendencies, or consolidation of power at home. In this way, Putin becomes both a scapegoat and a mirror, intensifying polarization and inhibiting collective self-awareness.

Potential for Transformation

Despite its shadow elements, this cultural complex also harbors symbolic energies that, if approached consciously, can foster moral clarity and social renewal:

CLARIFICATION OF DEMOCRATIC VALUES

The stark contrast with Putin's regime can prompt Americans to rediscover and recommit to the principles of open society, civil liberties, and accountable leadership—if these values are not merely invoked, but also lived.

AWARENESS OF INTERNAL AUTHORITARIAN TENDENCIES

By observing what Americans fear in Putin, they may come to recognize similar patterns at home—such as the erosion of norms, disdain for dissent, or cults of personality—and resist them with greater resolve.

REINTEGRATION OF STRENGTH AND MORALITY

The cultural allure of Putin's decisiveness suggests a hunger for leadership that is both effective and principled. Rather than imitate his style, Americans can aspire to cultivate moral courage rooted in justice and restraint.

REVIVAL OF INTERNATIONAL SOLIDARITY

The American response to Putin's aggression in Ukraine has inspired new coalitions and commitments to global partnership—renewing faith in collective action on behalf of peace and sovereignty.

CONSCIOUS ENGAGEMENT WITH THE SHADOW

As an archetype, Putin forces the American psyche to reckon with its own ambivalence about power, dominance, and fear. By facing this shadow symbolically rather than projecting it outward, America has the opportunity to grow in moral maturity.

Iconography of The Authoritarian Mirror: The Putin Cultural Complex in the American Psyche

PUTIN AS CENTRAL FIGURE (CENTER)

He is portrayed with impassive dominance—unsmiling, unmovable, and iconic. His face occupies the foreground like a cold monument. This scale reflects how he lives not only as a foreign threat, but also as a psychic archetype in American consciousness: the strongman, the KGB ghost, the ancient czar reborn. Americans cast him as both external antagonist and symbolic inverse of democratic virtue.

RUINS OF WAR (BOTTOM AND BACKGROUND)

Bombed-out buildings and smoldering wreckage anchor the image in destruction. These evoke Syria, Ukraine, or Chechnya—but in the American psyche, they stand for the price of unchecked power. The ruins also warn of democracy's fragility when facing disinformation, violence, or imperial ambition.

ZELENSKYY IN THE SHADOWS (LEFT)

Smaller and positioned behind Putin, Zelenskyy symbolizes resistance, vulnerability, and democratic suffering. His downcast expression and subdued presence imply that in the American imagination, heroism often appears dwarfed by the spectacle of power.

UKRAINIAN FLAG (TOP LEFT)

Still upright amid the ruins, the blue and yellow banner signifies perseverance and defiance. In this context, it becomes a moral talisman—the flickering standard of freedom against tyranny.

BLIND LADY JUSTICE (TOP RIGHT)

Her presence is ironic, almost tragic—hovering between hope and impotence. She represents the American longing for moral clarity in international affairs, even as her placement beside a rising dictator and ruined world underscores justice's ambiguity in global politics.

MISSILES LABELED DEMOCRACY AND JUSTICE (TOP RIGHT)

These rockets suggest the weaponization of Western ideals. They imply that democracy and justice are no longer just principles, but projectiles—aimed, launched, and delivered with force. It reflects how the West often defends values through military or rhetorical escalation.

COMMUNIST FLAG (LOWER RIGHT)

The Soviet red flag, faint but present, evokes the ghost of Cold War ideology. It signals that in American imagination, Putin is not just a geopolitical actor but also a remnant of a mythic past—reviving fears of communism, totalitarianism, and nuclear brinkmanship.

MOTHER AND CHILD IN MOURNING (BOTTOM RIGHT)

A veiled woman holds a grieving child. They represent civilian cost, displacement, and generational trauma. Their dark robes and distant gaze contrast with Putin's calculated control, making the human stakes of authoritarianism more poignant.

Interpretation

The Putin cultural complex in the American psyche operates as both projection and cautionary tale. He is not simply a foreign adversary, but a psychic emblem—onto whom Americans cast their darkest fears of control, censorship, imperial nostalgia, and anti-democratic contagion. Simultaneously, he serves as a moral mirror: warning of what democracy might become if it sacrifices complexity for dominance.

This cultural complex holds peril and potential. It fuels unity and outrage—but can also obscure introspection and breed militarized idealism. Only by facing the archetype without collapsing into it can the American imagination transcend the shadow it has placed on Vladimir Putin's face.

THE ISRAEL-PALESTINE CULTURAL COMPLEX IN THE AMERICAN PSYCHE

TWO CHILDREN, TWO TEXTS: THE ISRAEL–PALESTINE CULTURAL COMPLEX IN THE AMERICAN PSYCHE

In a landscape of ruins and unresolved grief, two children—one Palestinian, one Israeli—stand side by side yet worlds apart. Each is guarded by adults bearing sacred scrolls: a Qur'an and a Torah. Behind them, the Statue of Liberty rises through smoke, a contested map of Israel/Palestine across her chest. Missiles labeled Democracy and Justice ascend heavenward—symbols of American idealism weaponized. This image captures the mythic, moral, and emotional entanglement of the Israel-Palestine conflict in the American psyche: a battleground of trauma, faith, identity, and projection.

Core Emotion: Grief, Guilt, Tribal Loyalty, and Existential Anxiety

At the emotional heart of this cultural complex is a deep and volatile mix of grief, inherited guilt, fierce group loyalty, and moral unease. The conflict stirs powerful emotional responses in Americans—not just about international politics, but also about who we are, what justice means, and whose suffering we are willing to see. For some, the dominant feeling is profound sorrow for the historical trauma of the Jewish people and a fierce commitment to their safety. For others, it is outrage and empathy toward the dispossession and suffering of Palestinians. Often, these emotional commitments are bound to questions of identity, belonging, and moral obligation. The intensity of the conflict frequently leaves people feeling morally implicated, emotionally overwhelmed, or spiritually torn.

Mythic Root: The Chosen People, the Eternal Victim, and the Struggle for Redemption

This complex is rooted in mythic stories that shape how Americans understand good and evil, innocence and threat, belonging and exile. The myth of the Chosen People casts Israel as a nation with a sacred destiny, a perception reinforced in both Jewish memory and Christian Zionist theology. The enduring trauma of the Holocaust has placed Jewish suffering at the moral center of modern Western consciousness, giving rise to the idea of the eternal victim—a people whose survival must be protected at all costs. Meanwhile, Palestinians are often symbolically cast either as the exiled people struggling for a homeland, or as the new David resisting an overwhelming Goliath. The entire conflict is suffused with redemptive longing: the hope that through endurance, sacrifice, or victory, a fractured world might be made whole.

Symbolic Imagery

The images that animate this complex are emotionally and politically charged:

- Photographs of Israeli and American flags flying side by side evoke a sense of shared purpose and covenant.
- Images of Palestinian children in rubble or behind fences symbolize innocence amid suffering and are often used to stir empathy or condemnation.
- The Wailing Wall and the Dome of the Rock, situated side by side, embody the sacred and contested nature of the land.
- Soldiers in uniform and masked militants serve as symbols of strength, threat, or moral ambiguity—depending on the viewer's frame.
- Protest placards with phrases like "From the River to the Sea" or "Never Again" activate deep emotional associations, each carrying apocalyptic or redemptive undertones.
- Divided maps of Israel/Palestine symbolize not just political fragmentation, but also psychic division in the American imagination.

These images do not merely illustrate—they inflame, sanctify, and polarize.

Self-Reinforcing Memory

The memory systems that sustain this complex are distinct, often in conflict, and emotionally potent.

- For many Jewish Americans, the Holocaust is not only historical trauma—it is also an existential wound that shapes collective identity and undergirds unwavering support for Israel as a sanctuary.
- For many Arab and Muslim Americans, the memory of the Nakba—the mass displacement of Palestinians in 1948—is passed down through stories, silences, and a deep sense of dispossession.
- In evangelical Christian communities, memories are shaped by biblical prophecy, framing the State of Israel as a key to the Second Coming and the fulfillment of divine destiny.

- Progressive and activist movements, especially within communities of color, remember solidarity between Palestinian struggles and the civil rights, anti-apartheid, or Black Lives Matter movements—recasting the conflict as part of a broader anti-colonial narrative.
- After 9/11, American memory was recast through the lens of terrorism, leading many to see Palestinian resistance primarily as a security threat, whereas others pushed back against this framing.

These competing memories shape moral perception. They do not merely recall the past—they also shape the battlefield of the present.

Black-and-White Thinking

Within this complex, moral polarization is extreme. For some, Israel is seen as a lone democracy in a hostile region, a beacon of freedom under constant threat; Palestinians, by contrast, are associated with terrorism, instability, and intransigence. For others, Israel is viewed as a settler-colonial state enforcing apartheid policies; Palestinians are imagined as an indigenous people resisting displacement and oppression.

Criticism of Israeli policy is sometimes labeled as anti-semitic. Expressions of solidarity with Palestinians are sometimes denounced as supporting terrorism. The result is a moral economy in which empathy feels zero-sum: to care for one side is seen as a betrayal of the other. Complexity is flattened, and moral nuance becomes nearly impossible to sustain.

Repetitive Behavior

Each new eruption of violence in the region triggers a predictable series of reactions in the American public sphere:

- Social media fills with impassioned declarations, hashtags, and calls to action—often reflecting polarized loyalties.
- University campuses and public institutions become arenas for protest, boycott campaigns, and demands for institutional allegiance.
- Elected officials engage in ritualized affirmations of support—usually for Israel, but increasingly also for Palestinian human rights—framing them as moral imperatives.

- Attempts at dialogue are often short-circuited by fear, accusation, or the demand for absolute moral clarity.
- Movements fracture along lines of identity, ideology, and trauma—replaying historical grievances in new forms.

These behaviors are not spontaneous. They are part of the ritual life of the complex, reenacting the conflict symbolically on American soil.

Social Effects

This cultural complex fractures political movements, families, religious communities, and civic institutions. It generates cycles of moral exhaustion, mutual projection, and epistemic distrust. Individuals become trapped in inherited roles—defender, critic, victim, or betrayer—making it hard to think, feel, or speak freely. The ability to hold multiple truths is eroded. Conversations turn to accusations; empathy turns to outrage; silence becomes suspicious. Americans are often unable to witness both Israeli and Palestinian suffering without feeling they are betraying a moral cause. As a result, the conflict becomes less about the Middle East and more about our own unresolved inner divisions.

Potential for Transformation

Despite its volatility, this cultural complex holds deep transformative potential—if approached symbolically, psychologically, and with humility.

MORAL RECKONING ACROSS GENERATIONS

The conflict forces Americans to confront legacies of trauma, racism, colonialism, and complicity—both abroad and at home. It can deepen moral reflection and commitment to justice.

GRIEF AS BRIDGE

When the pain and loss on both sides are acknowledged—without hierarchy or denial—grief can become a gateway to empathy, solidarity, and shared humanity.

EMERGENCE OF A NEW ETHICAL VOCABULARY

The growing desire for a rights-based, dignity-centered framework invites a shift away from tribal loyalty toward universal values of justice and coexistence.

COALITION-BUILDING THROUGH SHARED LONGING

Faith leaders, survivors, scholars, and activists across traditions are increasingly seeking new paths toward peace—not through victory, but through reconciliation and mutual recognition.

CAPACITY TO HOLD PARADOX

The complexity of this issue demands a higher level of psychological integration—the ability to hold conflicting truths, endure discomfort, and resist simplistic narrative.

Iconography of Two Children, Two Texts: The Israel–Palestine Cultural Complex in the American Psyche

TWO SACRED SCROLLS (CENTER LEFT AND RIGHT)

The Torah and the Qur'an—clutched solemnly by adult figures—symbolize deep-rooted spiritual identities. Their presence signals the conflict's religious dimension, and how American imagination often treats one as visible (Judaism) and the other as implied or obscured (Islam). Here, both are acknowledged, evoking the need for balance and recognition.

PALESTINIAN AND ISRAELI CHILDREN (FOREGROUND)

Standing in parallel, not opposition, the children's faces are marked by sorrow and innocence. They represent generational inheritance of trauma, yet also the latent possibility for empathy. Their juxtaposition resists simplistic binaries and rehumanizes both sides of the conflict.

THE RUINS (LOWER HALF)

Rubble and broken architecture surround both families, suggesting the mutual devastation of prolonged conflict. For American viewers, this evokes not only foreign warzones but also the moral rubble of failed peace efforts and partisan sympathies.

STATUE OF LIBERTY WITH IMPOSED MAP (BACKGROUND CENTER)

Lady Liberty is no longer a neutral beacon; she now wears the contested geography of Israel/Palestine across her chest. This symbolizes how America internalizes and projects meaning onto the conflict, identifying with liberty and justice while entangled in geopolitical bias.

SMOKE AND SCORCHED SKY (UPPER LEFT)

The rising smoke behind the Statue of Liberty suggests violence, confusion, and moral obfuscation. It frames the American ideal in crisis, clouded by its own contradictions.

MISSILES LABELED DEMOCRACY AND JUSTICE (UPPER RIGHT)

These ascending weapons represent how American ideals are projected onto the conflict—often as instruments of pressure, judgment, or intervention. The message is ambiguous: Are these missiles delivering values or disguising violence?

EXPRESSION OF THE ADULTS (MIDGROUND FIGURES)

Their faces are solemn, fixed, and weary—conveying generational pain, righteous resolve, and intractable narrative. Each holds tightly to sacred heritage, but the mirrored posture suggests shared grief more than shared hatred.

COLOR PALETTE (SEPIA AND FUST-TONED GOLDS)

The image draws on a warm but faded palette that evokes memory, sacred text, and ancient history. The golden light—neither hopeful nor damning—casts everything in moral ambiguity, reflecting the American psyche's unresolved stance.

Interpretation

This image functions as a visual anatomy of projection, empathy, and myth. It refuses simplistic moral assignments and instead reveals how the Israel-Palestine conflict activates core American conflicts: innocence imperiled, sacred duty, moral mission, and fractured justice. It invites not only recognition of pain, but also deeper reckoning with how that pain is inherited, ignored, and sometimes instrumentalized in American political and cultural life.

THE ISRAELI IRANIAN CULTURAL COMPLEX IN THE AMERICAN PSYCHE

TRUMP BOMBS IRAN: THE MYTHIC THEATER OF POWER

This image fuses biblical ruin, national trauma, and modern propaganda—framing the moment not merely as geopolitics, but also as an epic of personal ascendancy and cultural reckoning.

Core Emotion: Existential Fear and Fierce Allegiance

This cultural complex carries volatile emotional tension: a fierce allegiance to Israel; existential fear of Iran; and a civilizational anxiety shaped by trauma, prophecy, and military entanglement. Beneath the surface lies a compulsive need—for moral clarity, divine alignment, and national righteousness on the world stage.

Mythic Root: Chosen People vs. Evil Empire

The American psyche often casts Israel as a divinely protected homeland and Iran as an existential theocratic threat. The complex is fed by Cold War binaries, evangelical end-times mythologies, and post-9/11 moral absolutism. Israel becomes the democratic David under siege. Iran becomes the apocalyptic Goliath.

Symbolic Imagery

- The scorched chessboard: Diplomacy and strategy reduced to spectacle and force
- Fractured symbols: Cracked Star of David, crescent moon, and torn US flag—suggesting fragile alliances and collapsing narratives
- Acorn-shaped nuclear relics: Absurd, ominous, blending comedy and cataclysm
- The American eagle: Not neutral, but active—projecting force, fusing divine mandate with militarism
- Trump, Netanyahu, and the Ayatollah: Mythic avatars enacting a cosmic drama of nationalism, vengeance, and divine entitlement
- Fire, smoke, and sky: Prophetic theater, not policy—the divine collides with the delusional

Self-Reinforcing Memory

From the Holocaust to the Iranian Revolution and Hostage Crisis to 9/11, this complex loops traumatic memory into moral hierarchy. Israel is sanctified through loss; Iran vilified through defiance. US policy becomes a stage on which victimhood and villainy are endlessly replayed, shielding past decisions from scrutiny.

Black-and-White Thinking

Democracy versus theocracy, sacred ally versus irrational foe: Critics are branded as disloyal or anti-semitic, dissent flattened into betrayal. Complexity dies, replaced by cosmic certainty. Diplomacy becomes heresy.

Repetitive Behaviors

- Uncritical declarations of "unbreakable bonds"
- Rhetorical escalation with Iran during election cycles
- Theatrical displays of force and sanctions
- Binary congressional performances—applause for one side, condemnation of the other

Social Effects

This complex fuses foreign policy with religious fervor and tribal loyalty, distorting both. It fuels Islamophobia, marginalizes Palestinian voices, and confuses military posture with moral virtue.

- Foreign Policy: War becomes purification. Peace becomes betrayal.
- Domestic Discourse: Polarization deepens. Jewish, Muslims, and Middle Eastern American communities are forced into ideological corners.
- Civic Fabric: The American public becomes an audience to mythic reenactments rather than informed debate.

Possibility of Transformation

The complex can shift—from righteous domination to moral discernment. Transformation begins when America surrenders its messianic self-image and embraces its role as flawed actor, listener, and bridge-builder. Through interfaith dialogue, artistic imagination, and diplomatic humility, space opens for mourning, shared humanity, and post-mythic relationship.

Iconography of Trump Bombs Iran – The Mythic Theater of Power

TRUMP AS THEOCRATIC WARLORD

Holding a missile like a chess piece, Trump enacts, not strategy, but symbolic dominance. His gaze burns with the conviction of divine right, embodying grievance fused with messianic entitlement.

NETANYAHU AS STRATEGIC ALLY

Calculating and attentive, Netanyahu appears neither subordinate nor passive. He represents the enduring symbiosis between American and Israeli identities—spiritual, strategic, and militarized.

AYATOLLAH AS UNFLINCHING ADVERSARY

Stern, rooted, and fully present. The Ayatollah is not a caricature, but an archetypal counterforce—resisting with ideological clarity and prophetic stillness.

THE FRACTURED TABLE

Once a place of reasoned contest, the chessboard becomes a desecrated altar. Its rational structure is consumed by fire. Dialogue has been supplanted by theater.

THE AMERICAN EAGLE

No longer a detached emblem of conscience, the eagle acts as executor of Trump's will—its talons gripped in fire, its wings echoing detonation. The national psyche has mythologized itself into divine force.

THE FIERY SKY

The heavens resemble revelation—less meteorology than theology. Judgment has replaced diplomacy. The divine script is playing out on a scorched stage.

Interpretation

This image renders the Israeli-American-Iranian conflict through the lens of the American psyche. Trump becomes a vessel for the archetype of the warrior-king—part savior, part strongman. The missile becomes more than a weapon: it's a moral statement, a performance, a declaration of mythic power. The image exposes what happens when statecraft dissolves into spectacle and prophecy replaces policy. It dramatizes the MAGA cultural complex's psychological seduction—power enacted, not through careful governance, but through righteous spectacle. The "chessboard" has become irrelevant. America, through this lens, is no longer thinking—it is reacting.

What Part of the American Psyche Is Acting?

The active agent here is a mythologized warrior-king complex, marked by

GRIEVANCE TRANSFIGURED INTO DIVINE ENTITLEMENT
Humiliation becomes justification for mythic vengeance.

EXCEPTIONALISM AS SPIRITUAL DESTINY
The belief that America is not merely powerful, but also chosen.

THE FANTASY OF OMNIPOTENT WILL
The world is to be reshaped through dominance, not diplomacy.

ABANDONMENT OF LOGOS FOR MYTHOS
The rational chessboard still exists—but no one is playing by its rules.

ANXIOUS MASCULINITY ARMORED IN MIGHT
Fear is masked by posturing. Vulnerability is forbidden.

EXTERNAL AGGRESSION AS PROJECTION OF INNER FRACTURE
The missile launched abroad mirrors internal psychic fragmentation.

This is not the whole American psyche—but it is loud, seductive, and archetypally charged. It arises when fear meets fantasy, when mythology masks memory, and when spectacle becomes sovereign.

SATIRICAL COUNTERPOINT: EVEN A BLIND SQUIRREL CAN FIND A NUT ONCE IN A WHILE

THE BLIND GAMBLER: A SQUIRREL FINDS THE BOMB

A caricature of accidental power and reckless fortune at the edge of global consequence.

Iconography of The Blind Gambler: A Squirrel Finds the Bomb

THE BLINDFOLDED SQUIRREL (CENTER)

Rendered with human-like posture and wearing a red tie and stylized hair resembling Trump, the squirrel gropes forward with a confident grin. The blindfold suggests ignorance or denial, yet its swagger implies unwarranted self-assurance.

ACORN-SHAPED WARHEAD (FOREGROUND)

A nuclear bomb painted like an acorn lies at the squirrel's feet. It symbolizes both danger and reward—suggesting that what he has stumbled upon might be treated as a prize, despite its devastating consequences.

CRUMPLED MAPS AND CARDS (SCATTERED GROUND)

Torn Middle Eastern maps, poker chips, and discarded intelligence briefings hint at the recklessness of strategy-by-instinct. The chaos on the ground evokes haphazard decision-making, intuition over analysis.

WATCHFUL CREATURES IN THE SHADOWS (BACKGROUND)

Other animals—representing allies, adversaries, or wary observers like Israel, Iran, and the global community—peek out from trees or shadows, unsure whether to intervene or recoil.

GOLDEN LIGHT AND RED SKY (ATMOSPHERE)

The glowing light from above feels almost divine—suggesting a mythic sense of favor or destiny. But it's set against a blood-red horizon, implying volatility and potential for fallout.

Interpretation

This image satirizes the surreal dynamics of Trump's geopolitical decision-making, especially in volatile arenas like the Iran conflict. It casts the president not as a strategist, but as a blind squirrel—lucky, bold, and utterly unaware of the stakes. The acorn-bomb symbolizes both the seductive power of military might and the absurdity of stumbling into dangerous success. While humorous on the surface, the image probes a deeper question: What happens when power is wielded through impulse and accident rather than vision or accountability? The American psyche here is embodied in a figure of uncanny luck, charismatic denial, and mythic exceptionalism—raising concerns not just about the leader, but also about the national fantasies that continue to enable him.

THE CHINA CULTURAL COMPLEX IN THE AMERICAN PSYCHE

THE DRAGON'S SHADOW: THE CHINA CULTURAL COMPLEX IN THE AMERICAN PSYCHE

A towering red dragon coils around the globe, its eyes glaring with focused intent. One claw clasps the world, wrapped in a bandage, suggesting both containment and injury. Beneath its gaze, Americans stand divided—some defiant, some wary, all caught in the shadow of a rising power. The image embodies America's ambivalence toward China: admiration and anxiety, awe and resistance. In this complex, China becomes symbol and scapegoat—an external force through which America projects its own fractured fears about sovereignty, influence, identity, and decline.

Core Emotion: Anxiety, Rivalry, and Projection

At the heart of this complex lies an anxious blend of fear, admiration, and defensiveness. The American psyche often projects onto China its own shadow: authoritarian control, unchecked surveillance, cunning economic strategy. A mixture of awe at China's rapid rise and dread over perceived U.S. decline fuels both competitiveness and scapegoating.

Mythic Root: The Dragon and the Duel of Empires

This complex draws from deep archetypes of East versus West, civilization versus control, the mysterious Orient versus the Enlightened West. The dragon—both majestic and threatening—embodies ancient sovereignty and collective will. In this myth, China becomes both the challenger and the mirror in an unfolding global epic

Symbolic Imagery

- A red dragon coiled around the globe, its claws over supply chains and silicon chips
- Great Walls—digital and physical—splitting East from West
- A cracked globe bound in surveillance bands
- A young woman holding a smartphone under watchful eyes
- American workers standing before blueprints of pagodas
- Political leaders holding STOP signs, invoking trade, tech, or ideological threats
- Twin cities on either side of the image: traditional temples and modern towers
- A silent algorithm hovering in the sky, parsing behavior in both realms

Self-Reinforcing Memory

The cultural memory is shaped by oscillating narratives: early admiration of Confucian order or martial elegance, followed by Cold War demonization, trade paranoia, and pandemic blame. Recollections of the Korean War, Tiananmen Square, COVID-19, and TikTok security fears become fuel for repetitive suspicion. Each cycle reinforces the image of China as both indispensable and dangerous.

Black-and-White Thinking

China is either a technological villain or a disciplined exemplar; a cunning copycat or a world-dominating innovator. Within this complex, nuance collapses: "We are free; they are controlled." "We are open; they are closed." Criticism of China becomes a litmus test for patriotism, whereas admiration risks being seen as disloyalty.

Repetitive Behavior

- Political panic cycles over espionage, AI, or rare earth mineral control
- Trade wars punctuated by dependencies on Chinese manufacturing
- Boycotts and bans followed by backdoor partnerships
- Ideological projection of America's internal fears (e.g., authoritarianism, censorship) onto China
- Oscillating fascination with Chinese philosophy or aesthetics
- Viral moments of outrage followed by periods of neglect

Social Effects

The China cultural complex fractures both international cooperation and domestic reflection. It feeds xenophobia, fuels anti-Asian racism, and complicates alliances. It erodes diplomatic nuance, hardens populist nationalism, and justifies surveillance and militarization in the name of rivalry. It fosters techno-nationalism, mistrust in global institutions, and binary rhetoric in US politics. As fears about global supremacy grow, Americans may reject introspection—outsourcing their anxiety about democracy's fragility to an external adversary. The complex polarizes policy, media, and identity, often at the cost of both clarity and compassion. It suppresses more balanced, pluralistic understandings of global power and inhibits collaboration on global issues like climate change and health security.

Possibility of Transformation

This complex can be transformed when Americans confront the projections they place on China and reckon with their own internal contradictions. Rather than treating China as a monolith, deeper engagement with its cultural multiplicity and historical trajectory may open new frames of relationship. The dragon, once seen only as threat, might instead symbolize a force of disciplined renewal—challenging America to rethink power, not as domination, but as interdependence rooted in resilience, wisdom, and self-scrutiny.

Iconography of The Dragon's Shadow: The China Cultural Complex in the American Psyche

THE RED DRAGON (UPPER CENTER)

A classical Chinese dragon looms above the globe, symbolizing China as a vast and ancient power. Its red hue evokes both vitality and threat—life force and authoritarian menace. Its posture is ambiguous: Protective or possessive? Majestic or menacing?

BANDAGED GLOBE (CENTER)

The Earth, wrapped in a cloth bandage, represents a wounded or constrained global order. It suggests fears of geopolitical shifts, economic dependencies, and cultural entanglements. The bandage also evokes narratives of healing, as if the world must be "saved" from the tightening grip of Chinese dominance.

American Figures (foreground):

A man in a work shirt holds blueprints of pagoda-style towers, evoking manufacturing loss, outsourcing, or attempts to understand the East through a Western lens.

A woman with a smartphone stands at the center, expression stern and unreadable—symbolizing a digital generation both influenced by and resistant to Chinese tech, propaganda, or surveillance.

A politician-like figure with a red tie clenches a jaw and a *STOP* sign—symbolizing bipartisan resistance, trade wars, or performative anti-China rhetoric.

CHINESE SKYLINE & TRADITIONAL ARCHITECTURE (BACKGROUND SIDES)

The left side shows the Great Wall and traditional Chinese structures, symbolizing heritage and continuity. The right side shows modern high-rises, suggesting China's rapid ascension and techno-authoritarian efficiency.

THE SUN AND SWIRLING SKY MOTIFS (BACKGROUND)

The rising (or setting) sun behind the dragon evokes the "Rise of China" narrative and the looming sense that a new epoch is underway. The swirling clouds and stylized patterns nod to Chinese aesthetics while also signaling confusion, entanglement, and mythic projection.

COLOR PALETTE (RED, GOLD, AND EARTH TONES)

The dominant palette evokes both Chinese imperial symbolism and American warning colors. It blurs admiration and alarm, emphasizing the complex fusion of desire and dread that defines this cultural projection.

Interpretation

This image encapsulates how China becomes a symbolic container for America's deepest geopolitical anxieties: fear of decline, loss of manufacturing power, technological dependence, ideological rivalry, and cultural insecurity. The China cultural complex is both about China itself and what it reflects back to the American imagination.

THE AMERICAN TARIFF CULTURAL COMPLEX

THE FORTRESS OF FAIRNESS: THE AMERICAN TARIFF CULTURAL COMPLEX

An industrial nation fortifies itself behind economic walls, weighing patriotism against global commerce. At its gates, an eagle guards a tollbooth marked TARIFF, while a cheerful factory waves the flag of protectionism. In this allegory, trade is a battlefield and sovereignty is measured in containers stamped MADE IN USA.

Core Emotion: Insecurity and Retributive Control

This complex is driven by an underlying sense of economic vulnerability and loss of national greatness. Tariffs are emotionally charged as acts of retaliation, restoring perceived balance and punishing those thought to exploit American goodwill. The core feeling is a mix of grievance, pride, and control through exclusion.

Mythic Root: The Fortress Economy and Self-Reliant Nation

Rooted in the myth of American self-sufficiency and industrial greatness, this complex draws from frontier imagery: the walled fort, the homestead defended from encroachment, the isolated but proud producer. It blends the legacy of Hamiltonian nationalism with populist suspicion of foreign entanglement.

Symbolic Imagery

- Walls made of shipping containers stamped *MADE IN USA*
- A scale balancing an American worker against a foreign cargo ship
- A friendly factory flying the US flag and smiling at self-containment
- A bald eagle perched beside a *TARIFF* tollbooth guarding economic entry
- The globe wrapped in barbed wire, encircling a protected national economy

Self-Reinforcing Memory

The Smoot-Hawley Tariff (1930), Reagan-era trade conflicts with Japan, NAFTA backlash, and Trump's China tariffs all feed the memory that America has repeatedly been taken advantage of—economically exploited under the guise of "free trade." These episodes reinforce the belief that foreign nations cheat and only hard lines protect American jobs and identity.

Black-and-White Thinking

"We make, they take": This complex moralizes trade into a zero-sum game. Foreign imports are seen as threats to national integrity, and domestic production as inherently virtuous. Compromise or cooperation is viewed as appeasement. Trade deficits are interpreted not as economic realities but as spiritual failures.

Repetitive Behavior

- Political campaigns promising to “bring jobs back” through tariffs
- Accusations of currency manipulation, cheating, or theft by foreign powers
- Symbolic tariff announcements used to rally nationalist sentiment
- Ignoring long-term consequences for short-term “wins” in trade battles
- Reframing global interdependence as victimization of the homeland

Social Effects

The tariff complex undermines international alliances and rational economic policy, substituting emotional narratives for cooperative problem-solving. It creates internal divisions between protectionist and globalist factions, while externalizing blame for economic anxiety onto other nations, immigrants, or corporate traitors. It also stokes inflationary cycles and retaliation—often harming the very workers it seeks to protect.

Possibility of Transformation

Transformation lies in shifting from a mindset of economic siege to one of collaborative resilience. Rather than punitive tariffs, the US could embrace fair-trade frameworks that value labor rights, environmental sustainability, and shared prosperity. When dignity replaces dominance as the goal of trade, and when global connection is seen as interdependence rather than invasion, the tariff complex may soften into a vision of economic justice rooted in mutual flourishing.

Iconography of The Fortress of Fairness: The American Tariff Cultural Complex

SCALES OF JUSTICE BALANCING WORKER AND CARGO SHIP

The central scale visually pits American labor against international trade. The worker stands arms-crossed in resolve, elevated slightly above the cargo ship—symbolizing the belief that domestic industry deserves moral and economic primacy.

MADE IN USA SHIPPING CONTAINER WALL

A literal and symbolic trade barrier. The stacked containers suggest security and economic self-sufficiency while also implying rigidity and exclusion. It frames tariffs as a form of defense rather than cooperation.

FRIENDLY FACTORY HOLDING US FLAG

Anthropomorphized industry smiles and waves, a nostalgic image of American manufacturing's heyday. It reinforces the emotional appeal of protectionism as a return to national strength and pride.

BARBED WIRE-WRAPPED GLOBE

Encircling the Earth in barbed wire, this imagery conveys global trade as both threatening and constrained. It reflects the fear of foreign exploitation and the desire to control economic borders.

EAGLE PERCHED AT TARIFF BOOTH

The American eagle—symbol of national vigilance and authority—guards the gateway, reinforcing tariffs as patriotic instruments. The tollbooth suggests that foreign goods must "pay tribute" to enter the homeland.

SMOKESTACKS AND OIL PUMPS IN THE BACKGROUND

Faint but present, these symbols of industrial power frame the scene in historical memory—echoing eras when tariffs and domestic extraction drove American dominance

Interpretation

This image frames tariffs as a patriotic defense—balancing national labor against foreign trade. Industrial symbols evoke pride in self-reliance, whereas barbed wire and borders signal fear of exploitation. Trade becomes a moral struggle: exclusion feels just, connection feels dangerous.

CHAPTER 9

Governance and Power Structures as Cultural Complexes

The American Populism Cultural Complex

The American Autocracy Cultural Complex

The American Oligarchy Cultural Complex

The American Kleptocracy Cultural Complex

The American Democracy Cultural Complex (Part 2)

Donald Trump, a supreme Trickster character, is able to assume many shapes. He can slide into playing the role of leader in the populism, autocracy, oligarchy, and kleptocracy forms of governance. The only leadership role in which he seems ill suited is that of a democracy in which there is a long tradition of checks and balance of powers between the different branches of government.

THE AMERICAN POPULISM CULTURAL COMPLEX

THE FIRE AND THE FIST: THE POPULIST CULTURAL COMPLEX IN AMERICA

Before a burning Capitol and a sea of angry citizens, Donald Trump as a populist leader shouts from a podium, fists clenched and sleeves rolled up. Torches blaze, flags wave, and the word Populism rises like a banner of rebellion. This emotionally charged image captures the explosive force of the Populist cultural complex—its power to unify through outrage, elevate the "voice of the people," and threaten the very institutions it claims to redeem.

Core Emotion: Righteous Indignation and Betrayed Belonging

At its center is the feeling that "we, the real people," have been exploited, mocked, and excluded by corrupt elites. The emotional tone is fiery and tribal—equal parts grievance and yearning to be seen, heard, and restored to dignity.

Mythic Root: The People vs. the Palace—the Outsider Redeemer

This complex is rooted in the archetype of the noble commoner, the righteous mob, and the avenging outsider who speaks truth to power. It imagines history as a long war between the people and the betrayers—aristocrats, technocrats, globalists, or bureaucrats. Redemption comes through reckoning.

Symbolic Imagery

A crowd with torches circling a distant marble tower. A bullhorn raised over a barricade. A farmer in muddy boots pointing at a gold-gated city. A carnival of flags, memes, drums, and fury. A leader with rolled-up sleeves and a microphone, standing atop a flatbed truck. A broken clock with the words Time's Up.

Self-Reinforcing Memory

Past betrayals—foreclosures, factory closures, cultural mockery, political abandonment—are stored as proof that the system is rigged. Every insult from media or academia becomes fuel. The populist memory is not only of loss, but also of disdain endured.

Black-and-White Thinking

Us versus them, heart versus head, real versus fake—this complex sorts the world into friends and enemies fast and hard. It idealizes "the people" and demonizes complexity as elite obfuscation. The populist hero is clear, forceful, and visceral—not nuanced or cautious.

Repetitive Behavior

- Marching, chanting, calling out hypocrisy

- Elevating strong, blunt figures who channel collective rage
- Scorning the "experts"
- Weaponizing memes and slogans
- Demanding rupture over reform—"burn it down to rebuild"

Social Effects

This complex can not only unify the disempowered but also inflame them into suspicion, vengeance, or violence. It often destroys the institutions it needs in order to thrive. Though it claims to speak for all, it can become purist and exclusionary. Yet at its core, it cries out for reconnection and justice—for a democracy that isn't hollow. The Populist cultural complex tears through democratic culture by collapsing nuance into absolutes: Us versus Them, Good versus Evil, The People versus The Parasites. It

- De-legitimizes pluralism: dissent is seen as betrayal, and compromise as corruption.
- Amplifies emotion over reason: suspicion of expertise, celebration of gut instinct, and distrust of deliberation.
- Sacrifices rule of law for raw will: legality is subordinate to popular fervor; the crowd's anger becomes a kind of sacred force.
- Erodes institutions: long-standing checks and balances are depicted as cages for the true will of the people.

Potential for Transformation

While destructive in its complexed form, this energy can also

- Expose genuine corruption and elite insularity
- Activate civic engagement among the previously apathetic
- Dramatize moral injury that institutions have failed to acknowledge

When integrated, this energy becomes a transformational force for justice, accountability, and the renewal of democracy

Iconography of The Fire and the Fist: The Populist Cultural Complex in America

POPULIST LEADER ON PODIUM

Represents the archetype of the righteous outsider. Trump's body language is charged with emotion—mouth open in a roar, fist raised in defiance. He channels the crowd's rage, positioning himself as both victim and savior.

RED *POPULISM* BANNER
Ideological rallying point. In bold, capitalized type, the word becomes less a platform and more a battle cry. The color red suggests urgency, passion, and upheaval.

FLAMING TORCHES HELD BY THE CROWD
Symbol of both illumination and destruction. They signify not only awakened power but also the risk of mob mentality and violence.

US CAPITOL IN FLAMES
Represents crisis of democratic legitimacy. The smoldering seat of government reflects how populist fervor often turns against institutions perceived as corrupt or elite.

TRICOLOR FLAGS WITH BLUE AND RED STRIPES
Vague national resemblance. They evoke patriotism but in a stylized, nonspecific way—suggesting nationalism divorced from historical nuance.

RAISED FISTS AND OPEN MOUTHS IN THE CROWD
Collective embodiment of grievance. The people are not passive—they are active, agitated, and ready. The mood is less about policy than passion.

WARM, VOLCANIC COLOR PALETTE
Visually communicates revolution, danger, and fervor. Yellows, oranges, and reds saturate the image with emotional heat.

DARKENING SKY AND SMOKE
Signals moral ambiguity. The image teeters between empowerment and menace, between catharsis and catastrophe.

Interpretation

This image evokes the Populist cultural complex as a volatile blend of grievance, charisma, and mass identity. A fiery leader rallies the crowd beneath a *POPULISM* banner, casting democracy as a battlefield between "the people" and their enemies. Catharsis, loyalty, and fury converge—fueling both empowerment and authoritarian risk.

THE AMERICAN AUTOCRACY CULTURAL COMPLEX

THE STRONGMAN AND THE DEVOTED: THE AMERICAN AUTOCRACY CULTURAL COMPLEX

Bathed in a fiery palette of red and black, Trump appearing as a towering authoritarian figure presides over a uniformed MAGA cadre, their faces solemn and resolved. Eagles circle above ruined cities, while scorched flags and controlled media symbols hint at a nation reshaped by loyalty and collapse. This image renders the emotional and symbolic core of the American Autocracy cultural complex—where democratic decay gives rise to mythic strength, disciplined unity, and the seductive promise of restored order through unchallenged authority.

The American Autocracy cultural complex is a psychological and symbolic formation that coalesces around the desire for order, authority, and certainty—particularly in times of perceived chaos, social fragmentation, or elite failure. It is emotionally powerful and mythically resonant, offering simple answers to complex problems through the projection of strong, centralized control.

Core Emotion: Chaos, Control, Insecurity

The Autocracy cultural complex is driven by a profound fear of chaos, loss of control, and collective insecurity. It is often accompanied by resentment toward pluralism, dissent, and perceived moral decay—especially when democratic processes are seen as ineffective, corrupt, or overly complex. The longing for order arises not only from external instability but also from deep psychological anxiety over fragmentation and ambiguity.

Mythic Root: Savior and Father-Protector

At its mythic root is the archetype of the strong leader or savior of the nation—a figure who will restore greatness, unity, and coherence through decisive action. This echoes ancient motifs such as the Father-Protector who imposes order upon chaos. The underlying narrative follows a familiar arc: "We were once strong. Then came decadence and confusion. Now we must be saved by strength and authority." This myth provides both moral justification and emotional comfort, transforming political power into a redemptive force.

Symbolic Imagery

The complex is expressed through visual language that idealizes strength, unity, and control:

- Raised fists, military uniforms, eagles, lightning bolts, and iron gates suggest readiness, force, and exclusion
- Mythic architecture, such as capitols on hills or neoclassical government buildings, represent eternal order and national destiny

- The leader's face, often stylized as idealized, enormous, or near-divine, becomes an icon of power
- Colors like red, black, and steel gray dominate visual themes, emphasizing discipline, blood, and permanence
- Mass rallies, disciplined formations, and slogans chanted in unison reinforce the aesthetic of cohesion and submission to authority

Self-Reinforcing Memory

This complex draws upon collective memories of historical breakdown—moments when democracies faltered and strong leaders "rescued" nations, such as post-revolutionary instability, wartime mobilizations, the collapse of empires or ideological orders. Over time, the memory of chaos and humiliation becomes mythologized, strengthening the appeal of the strongman. The fear of disorder becomes a self-fulfilling prophecy: chaos justifies repression, and repression is then mythologized as salvation.

Black-and-White Thinking

Reality is reduced to binary oppositions: us versus them, order versus chaos, loyalty versus treason, purity versus contamination. Dialogue is dismissed as weakness, compromise as betrayal, and nuance as moral relativism. The complexity of democratic life—its messy negotiations, slow procedures, and diverse voices—is cast as decadent or corrupt. In contrast, the autocratic worldview promises moral clarity, unified direction, and unambiguous virtue.

Repetitive Behavior

The Autocracy cultural complex manifests in recognizable cycles:

- Crisis arises—whether real or perceived—creating fear and uncertainty.
- Demands for order grow louder, scapegoats are named, and strong leadership is elevated.
- Checks and balances erode as institutions are weakened or coopted.

- A perpetual sense of siege is cultivated, justifying further concentration of power.
- Difference is suppressed in the name of unity and survival.

This pattern repeats across time and cultures, often accelerating when democratic institutions are already fragile or distrusted.

Social Effects

While offering psychic security, this complex can become deeply destructive:

- It dismantles democratic norms, replacing accountability with obedience.
- It destroys trust in institutions, especially the press, judiciary, and civil society.
- It views compromise as weakness and pluralism as decay, reducing the space for genuine dialogue.
- It frequently invites authoritarianism, scapegoating, and violence under the guise of "purification" or national renewal.

What begins as a search for stability often ends in repression and moral rupture.

Potential for Transformation

While the Autocracy cultural complex is often associated with repressive or anti-democratic tendencies, it can carry redemptive or stabilizing potentials—especially in moments of profound societal disintegration. Its shadow is real, but so is its appeal and function in the psyche and society. The Autocracy cultural complex might be seen as a one-sided overidentification with the archetype of the king—a necessary figure, but dangerous when inflated. Its positive aspect lies in the potential to hold the center, to make hard choices, and to symbolically defend the nation. Here are some potential positive effects of the Autocracy cultural complex:

RESTORATION OF ORDER IN CHAOS

In times of lawlessness, fragmentation, or institutional collapse, the autocratic impulse can serve to reestablish basic order, protect life, and prevent anarchy. It can temporarily stabilize a society gripped by fear and confusion.

MOBILIZATION OF COLLECTIVE WILL

Authoritarian leadership can unify fractured populations toward common goals—particularly in existential crises (e.g., war, pandemics, natural disasters). It often channels a myth of destiny or survival that motivates people beyond personal interest.

PRESERVATION OF CORE IDENTITY

The complex can act as a defense mechanism against rapid cultural erosion or alienation, asserting continuity with tradition or historical values. It appeals to a longing for moral clarity, rootedness, and protection of the familiar.

RESISTANCE TO FRAGMENTATION OR EXCESSIVE RELATIVISM

Autocracy responds to the anxiety of too much pluralism, where nothing seems stable or true. It offers clear boundaries, a singular vision, and simplified narratives, which may feel psychologically relieving when overwhelmed by complexity.

STRENGTH / LEADERSHIP

The "strong leader" can provide courage, decisiveness, and vision when others are paralyzed. When tempered by conscience or law, such strength can inspire reconstruction, defense of the vulnerable, or recovery from despair.

Iconography of The Strongman and the Devoted: The American Autocracy Cultural Complex

CENTRAL LEADER WITH STOIC EXPRESSION

Trump represents the authoritarian patriarch. His stern, emotionless face projects strength, resolve, and inevitability. Positioned high above the masses, he is the axis around which the system revolves.

MAGA-CLAD FOLLOWERS IN UNIFORM FORMATION

Symbol of ideological uniformity and submission. The identical caps and clothing erase individuality, reflecting how autocracy demands allegiance over autonomy.

BURNING, RUINED CITYSCAPE

Backdrop of societal collapse or civil conflict, justifying the rise of strongman politics. It invokes the narrative that only authoritarian control can restore order amid chaos.

EAGLES (BOTH REAL AND STYLIZED)

Emblems of power, aggression, and watchfulness. Their presence both sanctifies and threatens—linking American iconography to imperial or fascistic traditions.

AMERICAN FLAG IN FLAMES

Ambiguous national symbol, caught between pride and desecration. It illustrates how patriotism is both invoked and consumed in the autocratic myth.

MEDIA SYMBOL ("O NEWS")

Represents the role of propaganda and controlled narrative. It hints at the collapse or capture of independent journalism, further consolidating the leader's grip.

RED-ORANGE MONOCHROME PALETTE

Evokes danger, passion, blood, and ideological heat. The coloring contributes to the atmosphere of emergency, fervor, and emotional saturation.

YOUTHFUL FOLLOWER (FRONT RIGHT)

Signals the indoctrination of the next generation, extending the cultural complex beyond the present moment into a longer autocratic mythos.

EMPTY EXPRESSIONS, CROSSED ARMS, TIGHT LIPS

Depict resignation and discipline rather than enthusiasm. The emotional tone emphasizes control, stoicism, and the suppression of dissent.

Interpretation

A stern leader rises above a uniform, obedient crowd amid smoldering ruins and fading democracy. This image reflects a longing for order and redemption through absolute authority—revealing the seductive pull of authoritarianism in times of chaos.

THE AMERICAN KLEPTOCRACY CULTURAL COMPLEX

THE BANQUET OF PLUNDER: THE AMERICAN KLEPTOCRACY CULTURAL COMPLEX

The Banquet of Plunder evokes an elite celebration built on theft and exploitation, capturing the symbolic heart of the Kleptocracy cultural complex—a system where power and wealth are hoarded at the top, justified by hollow symbols of success and masked by corrupted ideals of liberty and law.

Emotional Core: Entitlement, Envy, Exhaustion

At its center is a volatile mix of entitlement, envy, and moral exhaustion. For those inside the system, the complex fuels a belief in immunity—rules are for suckers, and success justifies all. For those outside, it provokes resentment, nihilism, or even admiration: "If the game is rigged, at least cheer for the one who's winning." The core emotion is a corrosive blend of disillusionment and covetousness.

Mythic Root: Pirate King, Robber Baron, Chosen and Anointed

The pirate king is a rogue who plunders but gains folk-hero status. The robber baron is the industrial titan who conquers and accumulates, often cloaked in the myth of progress. The chosen and anointed are those who see their wealth as divine right or destiny. The American dream reverses itself—not "work hard and prosper," but "game the system and win big." These myths legitimize extraction by glamorizing cunning, dominance, and the ability to "get away with it."

Symbolic Imagery

- Gilded towers rising above collapsing schools
- Gold bars exchanged in the shadows of government buildings
- A figure in a suit walking on the backs of a crowd
- A ballot box turned into a briefcase
- An American flag stitched with corporate logos

These symbols depict a world where public trust is sold off and civic life is cannibalized for personal gain.

Self-Reinforcing Memory

- Watergate, Iran-Contra, Citizens United
- The 2008 financial crisis and corporate bailouts
- Political dynasties and insider trading scandals
- Contracts awarded to cronies, deregulation for donors

These memories are not isolated events—they're proof, for many, that the system rewards greed and punishes idealism.

Black-and-White Thinking

- "Everyone's corrupt" vs. "Only my side is honest"
- "Get rich or be a fool" vs. "You're either in the know or being played"
- "If I don't take it, someone else will"

The moral field is flattened into transactional logic. There are no citizens—only marks, rivals, or clients.

Repetitive Behaviors

- Appointing unqualified loyalists to public office
- Monetizing political access through speaking fees, foundations, or media empires
- Using nationalism to cover oligarchic agendas
- Running for office as a business investment
- Treating governance as brand management

These acts not only recur—they also become the expected cost of participation.

Social Effects

This complex tears at democratic ideals and the rule of law:

- It turns public service into self-service
- It corrodes faith in elections, media, and law enforcement
- It breeds apathy, fatalism, or populist backlash
- It inflames polarization, as each side accuses the other of theft

Ultimately, kleptocracy doesn't just steal money—it steals belief in the common good.

Potential for Transformation

When brought into collective awareness, this complex can catalyze a deeper moral reckoning.

- It forces a confrontation with how systems are structured—and whom they serve.
- It can inspire movements for accountability, transparency, and reform.

- It calls for reweaving the social contract, not with slogans, but with enforceable ethics. Transformation begins, not with purity, but with vigilance—building structures where integrity is protected and where leadership is not a prize, but a responsibility.

Iconography of The Banquet of Plunder: The American Kleptocracy Cultural Complex

THE SMILING FIGURE IN TOP HAT (CENTER, ABOVE TABLE)

Modeled after the Uncle Sam archetype but with clear resemblance to a populist plutocrat, this figure holds a wine goblet and a sack of money, embodying the fusion of nationalism, greed, and spectacle. The top hat with three stars turns patriotic symbolism into parody. His self-satisfied expression contrasts with the suffering below, revealing indifference and entitlement.

FINANCIAL GRAPHS ON THE TABLE (FOREGROUND)

Rising charts symbolize how wealth appears to grow—yet it is siphoned from others. These abstract metrics hide the suffering that funds them. These documents act as both instruments of control and illusions of progress. The charts cover the table like sacramental cloth—rendering economic manipulation a form of sacred ritual.

THE LAVISH BANQUET TABLE (CENTER)

Piled with money bags, gold coins, and symbols of justice, the table is the altar of wealth extraction. A tipped scale and a fallen gavel rest among the bounty, suggesting that the legal system no longer serves justice—it feeds the feast. A broken chain lies discarded, evoking betrayed promises of liberation or civil rights.

THE BURIED FIGURES BENEATH THE TABLE (BELOW)

Four anguished or oppressed people crouch in the earth below the banquet—literally supporting the structure of elite luxury. Their labor, grief, and captivity form the true foundation of the economic "success" above. One shovels endlessly, another holds their head in despair, and others look upward with anguish or protest—symbolizing **the** human cost of systemic theft.

CRACKED FOUNDATIONS AND BRICKWORK (BOTTOM)

The brickwork on which the entire image rests is unstable and cracked, symbolizing the moral and civic erosion beneath the structure of American governance.

BURNING CONSTITUTION AND COLLAPSING PILLARS (TOP LEFT)

Behind the main figure, a US founding document burns and classical pillars collapse, indicating the destruction of democratic ideals and institutional integrity. A shredded American flag in the background completes the desecration of the republic's symbolic order.

SAFE VAULT (TOP RIGHT)

The massive vault door suggests exclusivity, hoarded wealth, and closed-off civic access.

Interpretation

This image embodies the American Kleptocracy cultural complex as a grotesque feast—where symbolic institutions (justice, capitalism, patriotism) are used not to serve the people, but to justify extraction, distraction, and entrenchment. The system is not broken—it is working, as designed, for the few. The banquet will go on until the table cracks, until those underneath rise, or until the very structure collapses under its own weight.

FLIGHT OF DOMINION: THE POWER TRIP OF AMERICAN KLEPTOCRACY

A larger-than-life Trump rides a dollar-branded Boeing 747, gripping a flag marked POWER as it billows like currency through a storm-charged sky. The plane, transformed into a gilded warhorse of capital, barrels forward with wheels down, symbolizing a landing of domination—not diplomacy.

Iconography of Flight of Dominion: The Power Trip of American Kleptocracy

TRUMP FIGURE

Embodies the mythic populist-tycoon hybrid—half messiah, half monopolist—riding power like a personal jet, not a shared civic mandate. His grim face mirrors the will-to-power ethos of modern kleptocracy.

747 JET WITH "$ P.O.W" INSIGNIA

Represents the fusion of global mobility, economic might, and a warlike approach to wealth and control. The acronym evokes both "Prisoner of War" and "Power over Wealth," a double entendre about the capture of national interest by personal empire.

"POWER" FLAG AS MONEY

The flag resembles paper currency, signaling how raw political dominance is justified through financial might and vice versa. It also hints at populist slogans weaponized as currency.

SEPIA TONE & STORM CLOUDS

The color scheme evokes a historical-political parable—sepia like faded glory or propagandist nostalgia—whereas the storm clouds foreshadow turbulence, suggesting political recklessness disguised as control.

SCALES OF JUSTICE (DIMLY IN BACKGROUND)

Tilted and diminished, justice becomes a fading silhouette in the background, overshadowed by spectacle and aerial supremacy.

Interpretation

This image offers a symbolic diagnosis of the American Kleptocracy cultural complex: a system in which economic extraction, political spectacle, and legal manipulation reinforce each other. It exposes the grand illusion of fairness while depicting a stratified world built on collusion and exclusion. Yet, the image also implies a question: What happens when those below rise from despair to action?

THE AMERICAN OLIGARCHY CULTURAL COMPLEX

WHEN WEALTH WEARS THE CROWN OF DEMOCRACY: THE AMERICAN OLIGARCHY CULTURAL COMPLEX

An overweight businessman smirks beside a classically robed patriarch crowned with laurel, standing before the Capitol dome. Stacks of gold coins rise at their feet, framing a tableau where modern plutocracy merges with ancient authority. This ironic pairing reveals the cultural fusion of corporate influence and mythic legitimacy—where power is cloaked in both money and tradition, and democracy is increasingly ornamental.

Core Emotion: Complacent Entitlement and Defensive Superiority.

This complex is driven by a blend of satisfaction and fear—a belief that wealth is earned and deserved, coupled with anxiety over losing influence. It feeds on comfort insulated by power, yet it remains alert to threats from below: populist uprisings, regulation, and democratic accountability.

Mythic Root: The Divine Right of Wealth and the Philosopher-King.

It fuses ancient myths of enlightened rule (Plato's Philosopher King, the Roman Senate, the wise patriarch) with modern myths of meritocratic capitalism. The wealthy are seen not only as successful, but also as inherently more capable of leadership—blessed by providence, intelligence, or industry.

Symbolic Imagery

A smiling businessman with a cigar stands beside a robed patriarch crowned in laurel. The US Capitol fades into the background. Between them, stacks of gold coins rise like pillars of legitimacy. The juxtaposition of corporate ease and classical gravitas conveys a fusion of market power with inherited authority.

Self-Reinforcing Memory

This complex draws on a long arc of American exceptionalism and capitalism: the robber barons of the Gilded Age, Wall Street's dominance, Reagan-era deregulation, and Supreme Court rulings like Citizens United. These memories validate the narrative that wealth equals wisdom, and that concentrated power is inevitable, even virtuous.

Black-and-White Thinking

Society is divided into makers and takers, producers and dependents, or visionaries and complainers. Attempts to redistribute wealth are seen as moral failings—attacks on "freedom," "success," or the natural order. In this logic, questioning oligarchy is framed as jealousy, laziness, or ideological extremism.

Repetitive Behavior

Lobbying behind closed doors, super PACs, dynastic campaign financing, and philanthropic branding serve to maintain power while masking it as civic virtue. The rotation of elites between corporate boardrooms and government posts becomes ritualistic, reinforcing the revolving door of influence.

Social Effects

The complex hollows out democratic institutions, replacing the ideal of representative government with performance politics and transactional governance. It erodes trust in legitimacy, fueling populist anger and apathy. The public good is subordinated to private interest, and the "commonwealth" becomes a stage set for elite theater.

Possibility of Transformation

This complex can be transformed when the myth of entitlement is challenged by a deeper archetype: the servant-leader, the steward who understands power as responsibility rather than possession. Public awakening, transparency, and structural reforms—when grounded in a renewed mythos of justice and equality—can reorient the energies of leadership toward ethical governance. Wealth may then be seen not as an end in itself, but as a tool for societal restoration. The golden crown of oligarchy may yet be recast as a civic trust.

Iconography of When Wealth Wears the Crown of Democracy: The American Oligarchy Cultural Complex

BUSINESSMAN WITH CIGAR AND SMIRK

Embodiment of corporate wealth and informal power. His smug demeanor and relaxed pose convey self-satisfaction and unchecked influence. The cigar is a classic symbol of capitalist indulgence.

CLASSICAL FIGURE IN RED ROBE AND LAUREL CROWN

Evokes Roman authority and the myth of wise rule. He represents the archetype of noble governance, lending an air of legitimacy to the figure beside him. His golden staff signifies command.

STACKS OF GOLD COINS

Symbol of material dominance and policy for sale. The piles of currency reflect the disproportionate weight of money in shaping law, representation, and opportunity.

CAPITOL DOME IN BACKGROUND

The ideal of American democracy—now backdrop, not center. It has become a passive symbol, dwarfed by the imposing presence of wealth and classical dominance in the foreground.

CONTRAST IN ATTIRE: SUIT VS. ROBE

A visual merger of modern capitalism and ancient hierarchy. The pairing suggests a dual claim to power: one through market success, the other through historical authority and symbolism.

WARM, PAINTERLY STYLE

Suggests official portraiture, mimicking the style of oil paintings that honor rulers or great men. This satirical aesthetic underscores the normalization of oligarchy in civic imagination.

MISSING PUBLIC

The absence of common people reinforces the notion that the civic space has been claimed by the few for the few. This is not a democracy in action, but a club with velvet ropes.

Interpretation

This image depicts economic power disguised as democratic virtue. A smug plutocrat toasts atop a rigged system, while the public toils below. Symbols of justice and the Constitution lie broken, revealing how wealth can corrupt civic ideals and replace democracy with domination by the few.

THE DEMOCRATIC CULTURAL COMPLEX (PART 2)

REBUILDING THE CIVIC SOUL: THE DEMOCRATIC CULTURAL COMPLEX

In the flickering light of a fractured republic, a diverse circle of citizens gathers to restore what has been damaged. Their hands reach toward a cracked Capitol dome—not in conquest, but in care. Beneath them glows a quiet ember at the heart of a shared civic hearth. This is neither triumph, nor collapse. It is the fragile, defiant work of democracy: rebuilding not just institutions, but also trust.

Core Emotion: Hope and Anxiety

At the heart of the Democratic cultural complex is a powerful belief in the possibility of collective self-governance. It is animated by faith in rule by the people—yet shadowed by a fear that democracy is always fragile, always at risk of being stolen, corrupted, or abandoned.

Mythic Root: The People Shall Rule

This complex draws energy from founding myths of the polis, the town hall, the Constitution, and the heroic citizen rising to meet the moment. It is rooted in beliefs in shared power, civic virtue, and the notion that freedom can be secured, not by force, but by laws, votes, and open deliberation.

Symbolic Imagery

- A raised hand in a crowded assembly
- A ballot cast beneath a watchful eagle
- A circle of citizens in dialogue under the weight of history
- A crumbling Capitol being scaffolded for repair
- A parchment of rights held together with new thread

Self-Reinforcing Memory

The complex draws on triumphal memories of democratic endurance—civil rights marches, peaceful transfers of power, expanded suffrage. But it also carries scars: stolen elections, voter suppression, populist hijackings, and systemic exclusion. The memory of democracy is always contested, always part aspiration and part betrayal.

Black-and-White Thinking:

Democracy is good; threats to democracy are evil. This complex can become moralistic, unable to see how its own institutions can perpetuate inequality or inertia. It may dismiss populist anger as ignorant or cast dissent as authoritarianism without examining its own blind spots. At times, it conflates procedural legitimacy with moral superiority.

Repetitive Behavior

Ritual defense of "norms." Faith in process, institutions, and incrementalism. Reliance on legalism and rhetoric to confront crises. Tendency to invoke history or the Constitution in moments of instability. Anxious reassertion of democratic identity whenever threatened.

Social Effects

When healthy, this complex sustains pluralism, shared governance, and peaceful disagreement. But when anxious or rigid, it can become technocratic, self-congratulatory, or impotent in the face of bad faith actors. Its reliance on process can feel tone-deaf in moments that demand moral urgency. It may appear naïve or slow-moving in revolutionary times—and can fail to recognize when the rules are being rewritten by those who do not share its values.

Possibility of Transformation

When held consciously, the Democratic cultural complex can deepen its commitment to inclusivity, flexibility, and soulfulness. Rather than retreating into nostalgia or rigid formality, it can become a living tradition—capable of absorbing criticism, adapting institutions, and listening to the unrepresented. Its gift is the ethical imagination of governance: the belief that power, if rightly structured, can serve not just control, but also justice.

Iconography of Rebuilding the Civic Soul: The Democratic Cultural Complex

CRACKED CAPITOL DOME (CENTER BACKGROUND)

A powerful symbol of wounded governance—still standing, but visibly fractured. It represents the enduring promise of democracy and the danger of institutional decay. The cracks acknowledge disillusionment without surrendering to ruin.

CIRCLE OF CITIZENS (FOREGROUND)

A diverse group—by age, race, gender, and dress—stands in symbolic unity. They are not passive spectators, but active restorers. Some kneel with tools, others pass bricks, and one lights a torch: symbols of labor, knowledge, and civic continuity.

GLOWING EMBER (CENTER GROUND)
At the heart of the group is a small, glowing ember—a symbol of democracy's inner fire. It is neither extinguished nor blazing. It must be tended. The ember represents the ethical imagination that animates real democratic renewal: the belief that shared power can serve justice.

SCAFFOLDING AND ROPE (LEFT AND RIGHT)
Surrounding the Capitol are elements of restoration—not symbols of revolution, but of careful, sustained repair. This indicates that democracy is not being torn down, but mended from within, by those still committed to its ideals.

MUTED SKY WITH HINTS OF LIGHT (BACKGROUND)
A soft, uncertain sky—gray tinged with gold—suggests an emergent hope. This is not a naïve sunrise, but a clearing after long turbulence. The light is tentative, earned.

Interpretation

This image reflects the emotional and symbolic landscape of the Democratic cultural complex. It is not glorious or self-assured, but grounded in humble resilience. Democracy here is not a given—it is a fragile experiment sustained by participation, memory, and the quiet refusal to let the fire die. It visualizes a middle path between collapse and denial: the courage to rebuild without erasing the damage.

CHAPTER 10

American Psychological and Character Cultural Complexes

The American Narcissism Cultural Complex

The American Youth, Celebrity, Speed, and Height Cultural Complex

The American Sociopathy Cultural Complex

The American Innocence Cultural Complex

The Common Good vs. Private Gain Cultural Complex

The American Conspiracy Theory Cultural Complex

The American Woke Cultural Complex

The American Anti-Woke Cultural Complex

The Politically Correct Cultural Complex

The Malevolent Transformation Cultural Complex

THE AMERICAN NARCISSISM CULTURAL COMPLEX

THE AMERICAN EAGLE TAKES A SELFIE

Perched on a pedestal of fading symbols and digital approval, the national eagle gazes into a cracked smartphone, mistaking reflection for reality. Surrounded by the ghosts of presidents, the cheers of crowds, and the detritus of celebrity, consumerism, and political branding, the bird stands in a chamber where identity is curated, not cultivated. Once a guardian of vision, it now flirts with its own image—haunted by the past and tangled in the vines of spectacle. This image reflects the deeper truth of the American Narcissism cultural complex: not confined to the political stage, it infiltrates everyday life—how Americans work, play, love, perform, consume, and see themselves in the mirror of a watching world. This is the American Narcissism cultural complex rendered in national form: self-absorbed, hypervisible, and entangled in its own myth.

Emotional Core: Grandiosity and Fragility

At its emotional center lies a volatile blend of grandiosity and fragility. It manifests as an insatiable craving to be seen, validated, admired, and celebrated. Underneath this drive is a haunting fear of irrelevance—the terror of being overlooked, ordinary, or forgotten. This emotional volatility expresses itself in political spectacle, influencer culture, workplace self-branding, dating app performance, and even parenting and wellness trends. The core longing is for significance, but the path to it is paved with surface over substance.

Mythic Root: Narcissus and Prometheus

The complex is rooted in the myth of Narcissus, whose love of his reflection led to his undoing, and in the Promethean illusion that image alone can triumph over substance. In its American incarnation, it draws power from the myths of exceptionalism, the self-made hero, and manifest visibility. The idea that one's worth is measured, not by character, depth, or relationship, but by fame, followers, or flawless presentation, feeds a culture in which performance is mistaken for presence and attention for love.

Symbolic Imagery

Symbolic expressions include

- An eagle taking a selfie, flanked by presidential portraits and digital filters
- A mirror framed in stars and stripes, cracked but glowing
- A screen-lit face endlessly scrolling through curated identities
- A hollow statue shining with patriotism but echoing emptiness
- A parade float of American greatness collapsing behind the curtain

These images speak to the inflation of persona, the commodification of selfhood, and the collapse of inner coherence in favor of outer applause.

Self-Selecting Memory

This cultural complex remembers moments of visibility—praise, applause, viral success—as proof of worth. Just as importantly, it remembers moments of invisibility or rejection with a sting that fuels future performance. It forgets the quiet labors of integrity and connection, recalling instead the stage lights and spotlight. Memory becomes curated history, organized around being seen, rather than being known.

Black-and-White Thinking

This complex thrives in dualities:

- Famous or forgotten
- Winner or loser
- Liked or ignored
- Powerful or invisible
- Perfect or canceled

In this schema, nuance and vulnerability are liabilities. There is no room for the in-between—the honest mess of becoming. Instead, identity is presented as complete, polished, and constantly "on brand."

Repetitive Behaviors

Narcissistic behaviors play out across domains of life:

- Constant self-promotion on social media and at work
- Curating family life as content
- Emphasizing personal "brands" over character
- Confusing being admired with being loved
- Retreating into shame or despair when unseen

This complex is not limited to influencers and politicians. It shows up in job interviews, dating profiles, school admissions essays, and even casual conversations—turning life into performance.

Social Effects

The American Narcissism cultural complex tears the connective tissue of relationships, communities, and institutions.

- It turns civic discourse into performance.
- It hollow outs workplace integrity in favor of metrics and optics.
- It promotes "branding" of children, identities, and emotions.

- It undermines intimacy, replacing mutual recognition with image projection.
- It erodes humility, self-awareness, and community trust.

The result is a culture where image eclipses soul, and attention becomes the currency of identity.

Potential for Transformation

Despite its distortions, this complex conceals a yearning to be known, not just noticed. Redemption begins when the gaze turns inward with honesty and outward with compassion. The narcissistic hunger to be affirmed becomes the capacity to affirm others. The curated self dissolves into a coherent self. In this shift

- The mirror becomes a portal
- The spotlight becomes a tool
- The image becomes a threshold to deeper presence

Revitalization occurs when Americans learn to balance expression with listening and projection with reflection. In this reorientation, visibility becomes relational, not performative. Leadership no longer rests on charisma alone, but on substance, humility, and service.

From this renewed ground, a more authentic cultural identity may emerge—one that favors resonance over reach, presence over persona, and relationship over branding. In its healed form, the American instinct for self-expression becomes, not a cry for applause, but an invitation to witness and be witnessed in truth.

Iconography of The American Eagle Takes a Selfie

THE EAGLE WITH A SMARTPHONE

Traditionally a symbol of liberty, vigilance, and soaring vision, the eagle here is grounded—clutching a smartphone as if gazing into a digital mirror. The cracked screen suggests fragility beneath self-image and the distortion of national identity by personal and collective self-obsession.

PORTRAITS OF PRESIDENTS AND HISTORICAL ICONS

These background figures evoke ancestral myth and the weight of legacy. Their ghostlike presence haunts the eagle's performance, suggesting that contemporary identity is shaped as much by curated memory as by lived reality.

FIREWORKS AND FLAG IMAGERY (LEFT PANEL)
The explosion and flag celebrate past glory, but they are flattened into spectacle, hinting at nationalism as performance rather than principle. They echo the celebratory veneer often used to mask internal dysfunction.

CROWD OF FACES BENEATH THE PEDESTAL
The audience—expressionless and shadowed—symbolizes a public more inclined to watch than engage, numbed by repetition and voyeurism. They reflect the culture's quiet complicity in the politics of appearance.

FALLEN POLITICAL SYMBOLS (BASE)
The detritus at the base—broken stars, social media icons, GOP and Democrat symbols—represents the collapse of shared meaning and civil discourse. These are not destroyed in battle, but overgrown by vines of attention and digital decay.

SOCIAL MEDIA VINES AND "LIKE" ICON
These invasive symbols wind around the pedestal, illustrating how digital validation has overtaken civic grounding. The thumbs-up icon is not neutral—it is the algorithmic god now shaping identity, ideology, and even patriotism.

"GOLD" PLAQUE AMONG DEBRIS
This scrap of sign evokes prosperity, celebrity wealth, and the commodification of national values. It suggests that material status and market identity have replaced ethical compass and shared responsibility.

Interpretation

This image allegorizes a nation caught in the grip of its own reflection. The American Narcissism cultural complex here is not only psychological but also political, historical, and digital. The eagle does not fly; it performs. Its audience does not lead; it reacts. And the soil from which democracy once grew is now tangled with the metrics of likes, legacies, and lost ideals. What remains is not a fall from grace, but a captivity to image—where being watched matters more than being wise.

SANCTUARY OF SELF: THE RITUAL OF BEING SEEN

In a sepia-toned wellness space, bodies are sculpted, poses are perfected, and mindfulness is displayed like merit. Yet beneath the aura of health, the atmosphere hums with quiet competition and curated presence. One figure flexes in stoic intensity, another glows with performative calm, and a third scrolls or self-monitors in mirrored reflection. This is not just a gym—it is also a temple of self-image, where American narcissism merges the pursuit of betterment with the hunger to be admired.

Iconography of Sanctuary of Self: The Ritual of Being Seen

PRAYERFUL FIGURE WITH YOGA MAT (RIGHT)

Clasped hands and serene expression evoke a performance of mindfulness—wellness as identity. The mat becomes a symbol not only of inner peace, but also of social belonging in the "healed and whole" narrative.

MUSCULAR MAN WITH WEIGHTS (LEFT)

The idealized male physique and intense gaze portray the discipline of self-sculpting as moral virtue. Not only is he strong, he is also visually strong, performing for both mirror and others.

CENTRAL WOMAN HOLDING PHONE, SLIGHT SMILE

Her knowing glance and poised stance suggest image curation as habit. The phone, though subtle, indicates constant self-awareness—being both subject and spectator in her own narrative.

MIRRORED BACKGROUND

Reflections dominate the space, not just physically but also symbolically. The mirror represents self-surveillance, the ceaseless gaze we turn on ourselves and expect from others.

WATER BOTTLE AND ACCESSORIES

Functional objects become props in a wellness aesthetic—suggesting hydration, discipline, and control as visual values. Even the practical is repurposed into a message of self-mastery.

LACK OF INTERACTION

Despite proximity, no one connects. This subtle distancing mirrors a deeper dynamic of the narcissistic complex: coexistence without relationality, shared space without shared experience.

Interpretation

This image reveals the soft architecture of everyday narcissism: how striving for wellness, strength, and balance can become a theater of curated identity. It critiques, not the practices themselves, but their cooption by a cultural complex that prioritizes appearance over connection and performance over presence. In this quiet choreography of self-display, American narcissism reveals its most seductive form: not in grandiosity, but in the sanctified routines of the ordinary.

THE AMERICAN YOUTH, CELEBRITY, SPEED, AND HEIGHT CULTURAL COMPLEX

THE ASCENT: YOUTH CROWNED, SHADOW RISING

A vision of exalted American ambition, where youth is crowned, speed is divine, and height is destiny—while the serpent of shadow rises unseen.

Core Emotion: Exhilaration Laced with Anxiety

This complex is fueled by a manic pursuit of momentum and visibility—driven by the thrill of ascension but shadowed by a fear of irrelevance, aging, or stillness.

Mythic Root: Icarus, Phaethon, and Hermes

It draws from the myth of Icarus—soaring too close to the sun on wings of ambition—and Phaethon, the reckless son who attempts to drive the sun chariot and is struck down. But it also borrows from Hermes, the youthful, wing-footed god of speed, commerce, and communication—a trickster who dazzles and deceives.

Symbolic Imagery

- Skyscrapers and supersonic jets
- Red carpets and flashing cameras
- Youthful influencers ascending virally, then vanishing
- The eternally young idol surrounded by aging onlookers
- A mirror that only reflects youth
- A treadmill on an upward slope—always climbing, never arriving

Self-Reinforcing Memory

- The space race and the moon landing as techno-utopian highs
- Youth culture of the 1960s and its commodification
- Hollywood's golden age and the cult of the starlet
- Silicon Valley's valorization of the "young genius"
- Social media virality as a newer, faster fame loop
- Plastic surgery, biohacking, and performance-enhancing drugs

Black-and-White Thinking

- Fast equals good; slow equals obsolete.
- Young equals valuable; old equals discardable.
- Famous equals important; obscure equals invisible.
- Upward equals success; downward equals failure

Repetitive Behaviors

- Chasing virality and visibility
- Fearing stillness or anonymity
- Rebranding with every decline in relevance
- Avoiding aging through denial or cosmetic manipulation
- Idolizing the "breakout star" and the "overnight success"
- Discarding public figures after their peak

Social Effects

- A culture of burnout and performance anxiety
- Shaming of aging, especially for women
- Devaluation of wisdom, patience, and slowness
- Psychological whiplash from the velocity of cultural change
- Fragmentation of identity as people curate "highlight reels" online
- Risk-taking without foresight (economic bubbles, celebrity meltdowns, political demagogues)
- Alienation among those who feel left behind by speed and spectacle

Potential for Transformation

The potential lies in reclaiming depth over height, presence over pace, authenticity over performance. By recognizing the cost of relentless ascent, this complex may evolve toward a cultural appreciation of ripening, groundedness, and meaningful contribution. The slowed-down psyche may rediscover beauty in the ordinary and power in humility. When the mirror stops demanding youth and speed, it may finally reflect wholeness.

Iconography of The Ascent: Youth Crowned, Shadow Rising

CENTRAL YOUTHFUL FIGURE IN RUNNING GEAR WITH GOLD MEDAL
Embodies the idealized American archetype of youthful achievement, athleticism, and competitive excellence. His stance is triumphant yet iconic—more symbol than individual.

AMERICAN FLAG DRAPED ACROSS HIS SHOULDER

Links personal glory with national identity, suggesting that fame and patriotism are intertwined in the American mythos.

RAISED FINGER POINTING TO GLOWING STAR

Represents a transcendent goal—fame, perfection, divine approval, or unreachable ideals. The gesture mirrors iconic religious imagery (e.g., the Creation of Adam), infusing secular achievement with sacred overtones.

SNAKE RISING ALONGSIDE THE OUTSTRETCHED ARM

A symbol of temptation, danger, or shadow ambition. It suggests that beneath the gleaming surface of youthful ascent lies the risk of seduction, moral failings, or psychological inflation.

JET AIRPLANE AND SKYSCRAPERS (EMPIRE STATE & CHRYSLER BUILDINGS)

Symbols of vertical modernity, velocity, and power. These icons reinforce the myth of upward motion as destiny—speed and height as cultural imperatives.

PORTRAIT OF THE SAME YOUTH (LOWER RIGHT)

A formalized echo of the central figure, framed in dignity and dressed in patriotic symbolism. This visual doubling suggests the canonization of celebrity—where fleeting charisma is enshrined as national legacy.

CROWD WITH CAMERAS AND FLASHBULBS (BELOW)

Represents the media gaze and collective idolization in the cult of celebrity. Their presence confirms that greatness in this complex is not only achieved but it must also be seen, captured, and consumed to count.

SHIP'S WHEEL AT THE BASE

An archaic symbol of direction and control, now subordinate to the youth's upward movement. Perhaps an allusion to an older navigation of values, now supplanted by vertical ascent.

Interpretation

This image dramatizes the American cultural complex that fuses youth, celebrity, speed, and height into a singular mythic trajectory. It celebrates the upward thrust of ambition, where success is visual, exalted, and instantaneous. The glowing star is both destination and illusion—perfection projected just beyond reach.

Yet entwined with this ascent is the snake—suggesting that what lifts also tempts, and what dazzles may also deceive. The portrait below sanctifies the youthful hero, turning ephemeral stardom into institutional memory. In doing so, it captures a core tension of this complex: the longing to freeze youth and glory in time, to deny aging, slowness, and fallibility. Ultimately, this is a vision of a nation entranced by its own elevation—where speed replaces wisdom, spectacle substitutes for depth, and the myth of the golden boy masks the serpent rising in his shadow.

THE GRACE OF STILLNESS: A COUNTER IMAGE TO THE YOUTH, CELEBRITY, SPEED, AND HEIGHT CULTURAL COMPLEX

This is the antidote to the American Youth, Celebrity, Speed and Height cultural complex. Amid the hush of dusk, wisdom dwells in silence. Here, slowness is not failure but ripening, and presence is not performance but depth.

Iconography of The Grace of Stillness

ELDERLY WOMAN SEATED BENEATH A TREE

Represents wisdom, aging, and the rooted self. Her posture is grounded and reflective, in contrast to the upright, ascendant posture of the youthful figure in the companion image.

SUNSET HORIZON

Evokes endings, cycles, and the slow radiance of maturity. This is not the brilliant, blinding star of ascension but the warming glow of descent—an image of continuity rather than conquest.

TREE WITH SERPENT IN ITS BRANCHES

A direct visual echo of the serpent in the first image, but with a vastly different tone. Here, the serpent is not an aggressive force rising with ambition, but a watchful presence entwined in nature. It may symbolize knowledge, memory, or the shadow accepted rather than denied. It also links to the archetypal imagery of sacred trees and the duality of life and death.

OWL AT HER FEET

The owl is a classic symbol of wisdom, vision in darkness, and intuitive knowing. It anchors the image in the archetype of the crone or wise woman, whose power lies in stillness, attunement, and inner vision—not in spectacle or motion.

SIMPLE GARMENT AND BARE FEET

Suggest humility, connection to the earth, and a life lived close to natural rhythms. There are no medals, no cameras, no adoring crowds—only presence.

WORN HANDS AT REST

These are hands that have worked, suffered, and endured—but are now gently at peace, suggesting a reconciliation with time, mortality, and meaning beyond visibility.

Interpretation

This image is a symbolic antidote to the American cultural complex that idolizes youth, celebrity, speed, and height. Instead of striving upward toward a dazzling, unreachable star, this figure is rooted downward, in relationship with earth, time, and inner knowing. Here, the emotional core is not urgency, but presence, not conquest, but communion. The woman does not strive to rise above the earth—she inhabits it. Her stillness radiates power, not passivity. It is the power of accumulated experience, acceptance, and grounded being. In a culture obsessed with acceleration and spectacle, this image affirms an often-neglected wisdom: that slowness is not stagnation, but depth; that aging is not decline, but transformation; and that to live in rhythm with nature is not to fall behind, but to come home. The woman does not perform for the camera, ascend to dizzying heights, or outrun death. She sits, listens, and reflects—modeling an alternative form of value: slowness as grace, aging as ripening, stillness as depth. The owl and the sunset affirm that vision and wisdom often come not at the beginning, but near the end—not in the noise, but in the quiet. This is not nostalgia—it is a vision of maturity, reminding us that the soul ripens, not races.

THE AMERICAN SOCIOPATHY CULTURAL COMPLEX

THE DEAL WITHOUT A SOUL: THE AMERICAN SOCIOPATHY CULTURAL COMPLEX

This symbolic image portrays the chilling detachment at the heart of a cultural complex in which transactional logic eclipses empathy, and success is measured by control, dominance, and performance. Here, a charismatic, hollow-eyed figure offers a contract with a smile—

but behind it lies exploitation, environmental ruin, emotional disconnection, and the systematic erosion of conscience. It is a portrait of sociopathy normalized, incentivized, and masked as professionalism.

Emotional Core: Disregard and Instrumental Thinking Masked by Charm

At the heart of this complex is a chilling absence of empathy masked by charm, efficiency, or patriotic fervor. The emotional core isn't simply cruelty or greed—it is the normalization of instrumental thinking: people reduced to means, feelings to liabilities, relationships to transactions. It thrives on confidence without conscience and control without connection. At its heart, this complex is driven by emotional detachment, callous self-interest, and moral numbness. It feeds on a sense that vulnerability is weakness, empathy is exploitable, and success justifies everything. The core feeling is not rage or fear—but disregard: for others, for consequences, and for shared responsibility. Beneath this lies an abandoned wound—the fear that connection will betray or weaken the self.

Mythic Root

This complex draws on the shadow side of the American myth of rugged individualism and success-at-all-costs. The complex draws from distorted versions of foundational American myths:

- The Ruthless Self-Made Man: Success at any cost, ethics optional.
- Social Darwinism: The strong survive, the weak are expendable.
- The Antihero Rebel: Lone wolf figures who break the rules and are celebrated for it.
- Machiavellian Exceptionalism: America as uniquely entitled to operate outside the moral norms it imposes on others.

At its mythic root is a reversal of empathy into strategy—a belief that emotional intelligence is a tool for manipulation rather than connection.

Symbolic Imagery

THE CONTRACT

Agreement without trust, where ethics are replaced by loopholes and signatures.

THE HOLLOW SMILE

A mask of charm that conceals manipulation or predation

EXPOSED BRAIN OR MISSING HEART

Rationality elevated above all else, while empathy is removed, frozen, or caged

SKYSCRAPERS AND SMOKESTACKS

Symbols of power and consequence blind to human and environmental cost

DUAL REFLECTION

People as objects to be used, not known—often symbolized by mirrors, screens, or surveillance

POISONED GROUND/CHECKBOXES

Bureaucratic cruelty, where moral decisions are outsourced to procedure.

Self-Selecting Memory

Memory in this complex doesn't just forget the past—it actively edits it.

- Past abuses of power are rebranded as triumphs of vision.
- Colonialism, ecological degradation, and corporate overreach are recast as necessary costs of greatness.
- "Winners" are remembered, but not their wake of destruction.

Black-and-White Thinking

This complex creates rigid roles, where there is little room for nuance, vulnerability, or mutuality.

- Winners vs. Losers
- Smart vs. Weak
- Useful vs. Disposable
- Leaders vs. Sheep
- Control vs. Chaos

Repetitive Behaviors

- Rewarding cruelty as candor or strength
- Glorifying "toughness" while mocking care

- Treating relationships as transactions
- Denying or defunding social supports
- Using laws, platforms, or ideologies to exploit rather than protect
- Elevating those who "get away with it" as cultural icons

Social Effects

This complex erodes the ethical glue of society:

- Undermining trust, community, and compassion
- Rationalizing exploitation as efficiency
- Replacing civic duty with personal brand
- Turning governance into performance and policy into self-interest
- Normalizing cruelty in schools, corporations, and online culture
- Training citizens to look away from suffering—or blame it

The result is a nation where institutional and personal callousness become aspirational.

Potential for Transformation

This complex, when brought into awareness, reveals a profound cultural yearning for reconnection—one that cannot be satisfied by success or efficiency alone.

- The absence of empathy can awaken a hunger for human depth and relational repair.
- Systems that devalue feeling can be reoriented around belonging, accountability, and compassionate complexity.
- The transformation lies, not in rejecting excellence or clarity, but in integrating them with a mature ethics of care.
- The true measure of American greatness may be found, not in domination, but in how we protect the vulnerable, recognize shared limits, and reconnect with the emotional intelligence buried beneath the mask.

Iconography of The Deal Without a Soul: The American Sociopathy Cultural Complex

THE SMILING FIGURE WITH BLANK EYES (CENTER)

The central businessman-like character exudes charm and power, but his eyes are hollow—suggesting a void of empathy or moral grounding. His smile is persuasive yet predatory, symbolizing how charisma and success often conceal manipulation or ethical emptiness. Note he also extends a contract—the main symbol of transactional power—offered not in mutual agreement, but as coercion or entrapment.

CONTRACT WITH SIGNATURE ("MARC")

The contract appears formal, but in this image, it functions as a Faustian bargain: a symbol of self-alienation disguised as opportunity, underscoring how sociopathy operates under legal or corporate veneers, exploiting structure while avoiding responsibility.

HALF-SPLIT HEAD WITH EXPOSED BRAIN (LOWER RIGHT)

This anatomical cutaway contrasts rational intelligence (brain) with total emotional detachment (absent face/identity). It suggests the triumph of cold calculation over conscience and a cultural idolization of intellect divorced from humanity.

CAGED ANATOMICAL HEART (UPPER LEFT)

The heart is encased like a museum specimen—preserved, but unreachable—symbolizing the repression or objectification of feeling: emotion is rendered decorative, not directive.

CHECKLIST CONTRACT AND ROBOTIC HAND (LOWER LEFT)

A hand dutifully checks off contract items as if fulfilling bureaucratic quotas. The task is mechanical, hinting at a system that rewards performance and compliance, not reflection or compassion. Nearby lies a book with a heart on the cover, perhaps a symbol of moral knowledge or empathy discarded.

FACTORIES, TOXIC BARRELS, AND POLLUTION (RIGHT)

Environmental decay stands as both background and consequence—representing externalized costs, exploitation, and neglect of future generations. These symbols suggest how sociopathic systems pursue short-term gain with long-term devastation.

WOMAN FACING MIRROR OF ANOTHER WOMAN (UPPER RIGHT)
This fragmented, mirrored interaction hints at dissociation in relationships: appearances maintained while authenticity erodes. It reflects how the sociopathic cultural mode isolates individuals behind performance masks, breaking true intimacy.

TOMBSTONE WITH SKULL AND CROSSBONES (MIDGROUND)
The ground splits near a grave marked with danger—a stark image of the moral death embedded in the system. It warns of what is lost when humanity is traded for ambition.

URBAN SKYLINE (LEFT BACKGROUND)
A faint city rises in the distance, suggesting a civilization built on—and perhaps indifferent to—these dynamics of control, disconnection, and hidden cost.

Interpretation

This image portrays the American Sociopathy cultural complex, where charm, contracts, and ambition mask a hollow core. A smiling man offers a contract with lifeless eyes, embodying a society where transactional success overrides empathy, ethics, and relational bonds. This complex reveals a psychic split in American identity—where winning replaces meaning, and the mind advances without the soul.

THE AMERICAN INNOCENCE CULTURAL COMPLEX

PLEDGE AND EXCLUSION: THE AMERICAN INNOCENCE CULTURAL COMPLEX

This image depicts the paradox of American moral purity and denial. Two idealized children—symbols of national innocence—stand in solemn ritual before the flag, reciting or reading in postures of civic virtue. But beneath them, a gated underworld reveals the cost of this projected purity: the suffering and exclusion of others. The image confronts the tension between America's self-image as noble and good, and its historical acts of exclusion, marginalization, and silence.

Emotional Core: Denial and Nostalgia

At its heart, this cultural complex is driven by denial, nostalgia, and moral self-exoneration. The prevailing emotional tone is a deep-seated desire to believe in one's own purity—whether as a nation, community, or individual—regardless of historical or present-day harm. It clings to an idealized self-image, resisting guilt, responsibility, or complexity. This innocence is not childlike but defensive, asserting "We didn't know," "We meant well," or "That's not who we are."

Mythic Root: Garden of Eden in a New World

The mythic foundation draws from the Garden of Eden and the archetype of the "new world"—a land imagined as untouched, pure, and full of promise. This complex is also shaped by the myth of American exceptionalism: the belief that America is uniquely virtuous, chosen, or guided by divine favor. Within this mythos, national wrongdoing is framed as aberration, not essence—allowing innocence to persist unchallenged.

Symbolic Imagery

- Pristine landscapes: "virgin" land unmarked by genocide or slavery
- White doves or children at prayer: symbols of blamelessness
- American flags wrapped around wholesome nuclear families
- Crosses draped in patriotic colors: fusing spiritual innocence with national identity
- Old black-and-white television: sanitized history, selective memory
- Broken mirrors: shattered capacity for self-reflection

Self-Selecting Memory

This complex functions through an amnesia that is selective, sanitized, and comforting. It remembers the Marshall Plan but forgets Jim Crow. It recalls moments of sacrifice and heroism while erasing systemic harm or oppression. History is curated, not for truth, but for emotional reassurance, leading to generational myths of blamelessness passed down as cultural gospel.

Black-and-White Thinking

- Good vs. Evil
- Savior vs. Victim
- Civilized vs. Barbaric
- Patriots vs. Traitors
- Real Americans vs. Others

In this framework, criticism is framed as betrayal and historical nuance is treated as revisionism. Any challenge to innocence is recast as an attack on identity.

Repetitive Behaviors

- Teaching whitewashed history in schools
- Framing social justice movements as unpatriotic
- Declaring "that was the past" in response to calls for accountability
- Performing symbolic gestures of reconciliation without structural change
- Centering white emotional fragility in conversations about race or inequality

Social Effects

The Innocence cultural complex tears at the fabric of honest civic life by making it dangerous to speak of harm, complicity, or systemic injustice. It distorts moral imagination, replacing the call to grow with the impulse to deny. It protects perpetrators by infantilizing them and alienates victims through accusations of divisiveness. As a result, authentic reckoning becomes nearly impossible.

Potential for Transformation

Transformation begins when innocence is surrendered in favor of integrity. This does not require permanent guilt, but mature accountability. The complex holds the potential to shift from defensive denial to courageous responsibility. Through truth-telling, intergenerational repair, and spiritual maturity, the American psyche can trade its illusion of innocence for a deeper sense of shared humanity. When innocence is no longer clung to as an identity, the soul of the nation can grow.

Iconography of Pledge and Exclusion: The American Innocence Cultural Complex

THE AMERICAN FLAG (BACKGROUND)

The dominant backdrop of the stars and stripes represents patriotic identity and national mythology. Its prominence anchors the children in a sacred national space that valorizes innocence and belonging.

THE CHILDREN (CENTER)

A young girl and boy stand upright and unsmiling, exuding a mixture of virtue and solemnity. The girl places her hand over her heart, evoking the Pledge of Allegiance; the boy reads from an open book, suggesting civic education, scripture, or indoctrination. Together, they embody the myth of American moral innocence and virtue—untainted, righteous, and idealized.

THE BOOK (HELD BY THE BOY)

The open book is a symbol of sanctioned knowledge, whether religious, civic, or educational. Its red cover evokes both moral fervor and danger, hinting at the thin line between instruction and indoctrination.

BURIED SCENE BENEATH THEIR FEET

A cavernous divide beneath the children reveals a shadowed world. Here, anxious or displaced figures—likely immigrants, refugees, or marginalized citizens—stand in stark contrast to the surface innocence above. This underworld represents the suppressed truths and human costs that lie beneath national self-regard.

KEEP OUT SIGN (LOWER RIGHT)

The warning sign marks the boundary between "us" and "them," echoing themes of border control, exclusion, and the denial of empathy. It reinforces the idea that national innocence is maintained through denial and enforced separation.

INDUSTRIAL SKYLINE (BACKGROUND OF UNDERWORLD)

The dark factories and polluted skyline behind the buried figures symbolize the economic engines and systemic neglect that often accompany moral posturing. While the surface proclaims virtue, the hidden world bears the environmental and social consequences of national decisions.

CRACKED EARTH (FOREGROUND)

The split ground under the children suggests a foundational fracture in American consciousness—a crack between myth and reality, ideal and consequence.

Interpretation

This image reflects the American Innocence cultural complex, where national identity is idealized as pure and virtuous. The children symbolize patriotic goodness, while the flag reinforces moral self-regard. Below hidden suffering and exclusion—migrants behind bars, a decaying city—reveal the cost of innocence sustained through denial. The complex maintains virtue by disowning complicity in harm.

THE COMMON GOOD VS. PRIVATE GAIN AMERICAN CULTURAL COMPLEX

WE THE PEOPLE, WE THE PROFITEERS: THE AMERICAN COMMON GOOD VS. PRIVATE GAIN CULTURAL COMPLEX

Beneath a tattered flag of democratic unity, citizens kneel together, mending the fabric of a broken republic. They handle the emblems of shared responsibility with reverence, while a solitary businessman clutches a sack of wealth, gazing past them toward corporate towers. Between them lies not only a chain, but also a moral chasm. This image dramatizes the cultural and psychological rift in American life—between restoring the common good and retreating into private accumulation. This battle doesn't just rage in our politics; it goes on in each of us to varying degrees.

Core Emotion: Moral Conflict and Erosion of Trust

At the heart of this complex lies a deep emotional struggle between pride in self-made success and guilt or sorrow over the fraying of collective life. The sense of civic duty collides with the pursuit of personal advantage, creating a persistent unease—about fairness, responsibility, and what it means to belong.

Mythic Root: The Civic Republic vs. the Self-Made Man

Two mythic American archetypes clash at the core of this complex. On one side stands the civic republic: a vision rooted in town halls, New England commons, barn-raisings, and mutual aid—a polis of citizens. On the other, the self-made man: the frontier entrepreneur, the bootstrap capitalist, the heroic accumulator who owes nothing to anyone. This dual inheritance creates a divided ethical landscape.

Symbolic Imagery

Citizens kneeling to repair a broken civic seal, under a torn flag reading "We the People." A lone businessman in a suit clutches a moneybag and turns away toward gleaming skyscrapers. Broken chains at his feet suggest liberty unfulfilled or abandoned. Between the two stands a silent question: Who now carries the torch?

Self-Reinforcing Memory

Narratives of rugged individualism are glorified: Carnegie, Rockefeller, Silicon Valley giants. Yet historical countercurrents persist—FDR's New Deal, the GI Bill, civil rights marches, union movements, and the ethics of public service. Each side of the complex reinforces its own truth through memory: one remembers opportunity seized, the other remembers benefits denied or shared goods dismantled.

Black-and-White Thinking

The populace is split between "makers" and "takers," or "taxpayers" and "moochers." Inversely, others split society into "greedy elites" and "forgotten workers." Civic disagreement becomes moral absolutism: one either believes in individual freedom or social justice, with little room for integrative thinking.

Repetitive Behavior

Public goods are dismantled and privatized—healthcare, education, water, transportation. Philanthropy is used to justify tax evasion. Wealth is hoarded in offshore accounts, while communities organize bake sales to keep libraries open. Crisis prompts brief rediscovery of the common good—then regression resumes.

Social Effects

The complex weakens civic infrastructure and amplifies inequality. It erodes the sense of shared destiny, breeds resentment, and diminishes participation in public life. A frayed flag—"We the People"—becomes emblematic of a society that remembers its promises but struggles to fulfill them.

Possibility of Transformation

Within the tension lies redemptive potential. The act of mending—seen in the image—reveals that the idea of the common good is not dead, only damaged. Transformation begins when wealth is no longer equated with virtue and civic contribution is honored as deeply as private success. The businessman may yet turn and join the repair and the flag may fly whole again—if the story of "we" can once more become stronger than the myth of "me." At its core, this complex contains not just conflict—but aspiration. The drive for personal gain can be reoriented toward meaningful contribution. The myth of the self-made man can evolve into the steward or builder—those who rise and reinvest. Civic identity can be reclaimed, not as sacrifice, but as shared authorship. If we remember that common does not mean less, but ours, then the dream of liberty can expand to include mutual flourishing.

Iconography of We the People, We the Profiteers: The American Common Good vs. Private Gain Cultural Complex

GROUP OF KNEELING CITIZENS REPAIRING A CIVIC EMBLEM
Symbol of collective labor and civic repair. These figures—diverse in age and gender—work together to mend a golden seal marked by a torch and laurel. This seal symbolizes the ideals of democracy: liberty, honor, and unity.

TATTERED WE THE PEOPLE FLAG

Represents fractured democratic identity. The iconic script from the US Constitution hangs in tatters, suggesting a wounded or neglected collective ethos.

BUSINESSMAN CLUTCHING A MONEY BAG

An emblem of private gain and moral detachment. Standing aloof in a tailored suit, he holds a sack with a dollar sign—his gaze indifferent to the shared effort unfolding beside him.

SKYSCRAPERS IN THE BACKGROUND BEHIND THE BUSINESSMAN

Symbols of financial power and institutional distance. These dark towers evoke corporate detachment from civic life and common struggle.

CHAINS ON THE GROUND

Symbol of economic bondage or recently shed oppression. The broken or discarded chain suggests a past of inequality—and raises the question of whether liberty has been fully realized or merely commodified.

GOLDEN CIVIC MEDALLIONS

Civic values represented as artifacts. One medallion lies broken or unused, the other is being restored—representing the fate of public values in an era of privatization and wealth hoarding.

GOLDEN-BROWN COLOR PALETTE

Historical, solemn, and cautionary—the warm but muted tones evoke sepia-toned documents and Great Depression–era murals, linking present anxieties to deep-rooted national tensions.

Interpretation

This image highlights a core tension in the American psyche: communal labor versus individual wealth. On one side, people unite under a frayed We the People banner, symbolizing democratic solidarity. On the other, a lone man hoards wealth beside sterile towers. The fallen civic coin and broken chain suggest lost unity and the triumph of private gain over the public good.

THE AMERICAN CONSPIRACY THEORY CULTURAL COMPLEX

WEB OF SUSPICION: THE AMERICAN CONSPIRACY THEORY CULTURAL COMPLEX

A mind entangled in hidden patterns, where trust decays and shadowy forces are mapped with desperate precision.

Conspiracy theories are a powerful and deeply rooted force in the American psyche—both historically and in contemporary political life.

Core Emotion: Distrust and Suspicion

At the heart of this complex is a pervasive emotional atmosphere of mistrust—of government, elites, media, science, and even fellow citizens. This mistrust often stems from real historical betrayals but becomes amplified into a chronic suspicion of unseen powers controlling reality.

Mythic Root: The Betrayal of the Innocent by Hidden Powers

The mythic structure beneath this complex resembles a Gnostic or apocalyptic narrative: a corrupt world manipulated by malevolent elites, from which salvation is possible only through secret knowledge. The archetype of the lone truthteller or persecuted prophet plays a central role in this cultural myth.

Symbolic Imagery

- Red threads connecting faces, documents, and symbols
- The all-seeing eye, triangles, and hidden hands
- Silhouettes, question marks, documents labeled "SECRET"
- Spider webs and mirrors
- Tinfoil hats, corkboards, and "connecting the dots"
- Figures bathed in artificial light or shadowy isolation

Self-Reinforcing Memory

This complex draws energy from a cultural memory filled with real incidents of governmental secrecy, deception, and abuse of power, which serve as evidence and emotional fuel for contemporary conspiracy theories:

- COINTELPRO (1956–1971): A secret FBI program that surveilled, infiltrated, and disrupted civil rights groups, leftist organizations, and Black leaders (e.g., Martin Luther King Jr.)—confirming fears that the state will attack dissenters from within.
- MK-Ultra (1950s–1970s): A clandestine CIA project that experimented on unwitting US citizens with drugs (including LSD) and psychological manipulation in a quest for mind control—later exposed and officially acknowledged.

- Watergate (1972–1974): A political scandal in which members of President Nixon's administration orchestrated a break-in at Democratic headquarters and then engaged in a cover-up—culminating in Nixon's resignation and reinforcing the image of corruption at the highest levels.
- Tuskegee Syphilis Study (1932–1972): A government-run medical study in which Black men with syphilis were deliberately left untreated without their knowledge in order to study the progression of the disease—an egregious abuse of trust that remains a touchstone for medical suspicion.
- The Kennedy Assassination (1963): The killing of President John F. Kennedy, and subsequent doubts about the official story (especially around Lee Harvey Oswald), spawned decades of speculation about a government cover-up or deep-state conspiracy.
- 9/11 (2001): The terrorist attacks on the World Trade Center and Pentagon triggered many alternative narratives about inside jobs, controlled demolitions, or foreknowledge by government officials—especially given the opaque nature of intelligence agencies.
- COVID-19 and Public Health Policies (2020–present): Mask mandates, lockdowns, vaccine rollouts, and conflicting scientific messages sparked a wave of suspicion—fueled by government missteps, Big Pharma influence, and online disinformation.
- Mass Surveillance (e.g., NSA Revelations, 2013): Whistleblower Edward Snowden revealed the extent of government spying on ordinary citizens, confirming longstanding suspicions about the erosion of privacy and the reach of the state.

These events serve as a collective reservoir of betrayal, which fuels the belief that nothing is as it seems and everything is connected behind the veil.

Black-and-White Thinking

Reality is divided between the deceivers and the awakened. Those who question the "official story" are brave seekers of truth; those who don't are sheep, asleep, or complicit. Complexity is collapsed into totalizing explanations—usually moralistic and dualistic.

Repetitive Behaviors

- Obsessively researching online and watching exposés
- Creating or sharing memes, charts, or "evidence"
- Rejecting consensus or expertise
- Refusing to trust institutions, even when evidence is clear
- Forming tightknit communities around persecuted truth
- Interpreting every contradiction as proof of the plot

Social Effects

This complex frays the civic fabric by undermining shared reality. It fuels polarization, scapegoating, and distrust, making public discourse and policy grounded in common facts nearly impossible. It can isolate individuals, destabilize democratic institutions, and legitimize violence under the banner of "truth." At scale, it distorts elections, fuels extremism, and weakens social cohesion.

Possibility of Transformation

If the emotional core of betrayal and mistrust is met with compassion and acknowledged as rooted in historical trauma, the complex can transform. Its obsessive energy may give way to:

- Healthy skepticism over reactive suspicion
- Critical thinking over compulsive decoding
- Communal wisdom over isolated paranoia

The healing path is not censorship, but deep listening, narrative repair, and restoration of meaning through trustworthy connection—as symbolized in the Orb of Discernment, the companion image at the end of this section, where inner illumination and discernment replace projection and panic.

Iconography of Web of Suspicion: The American Conspiracy Theory Cultural Complex

CENTRAL FIGURE WITH FURROWED BROW AND POINTING FINGER
Embodies the conspiratorial seeker—haunted, intense, and driven to decode a hidden structure behind visible reality. His eyes are wide with urgency; his world is a puzzle of implications.

RED-THREADED CONSPIRACY BOARD WITH SYMBOLS

The board is covered in silhouettes, question marks, documents labeled "SECRET," and the all-seeing eye—all connected with red string. These lines symbolize the constructed coherence of conspiratorial logic, where anything can be linked to everything.

SPIDER AND WEB (ABOVE)

Echoes both the structure of the board and the archetypal fear of being trapped in a manipulative, deceptive system. The spider evokes a shadowy intelligence or parasitic force pulling the strings from above.

MIRRORED MALE REFLECTIONS

Multiplications of the same anxious gaze, suggesting a psychological feedback loop—a mind turning in on itself, amplifying its own fear and conviction.

MUTED EARTH TONES AND HARSH LIGHTING

Creates a psychological atmosphere of claustrophobia and inner torment. The warm palette belies the coldness of emotional isolation.

Interpretation

This image vividly captures the inner landscape of the American Conspiracy Theory cultural complex: the relentless pursuit of a hidden order behind chaos, often born from real disillusionment but distorted into compulsive pattern-making. The web and red threads symbolize a powerful internal need for coherence, even if that coherence is terrifying. The conspiracy seeker becomes both hunter and trapped prey—caught in the very net they construct.

This is a world where meaning is forged in darkness, where every silence must be hiding something, and where truth is never obvious but always urgent. The image embodies the shadow side of the American dream: not openness or self-determination, but suspicion, fragmentation, and isolation cloaked in the illusion of discovery.

THRONE OF Q: WORSHIP IN THE AGE OF SHADOW

QAnon is an example of a contemporary conspiracy theory cultural complex. An anonymous internet persona claimed access to secret intelligence, spinning a narrative of elite global cabals, child trafficking rings, and a coming reckoning. QAnon fused Cold War fears, Biblical prophecy, and populist rage into a digital mythology—blurring the line between political ideology, spiritual warfare, and mass delusion.

Iconography of The Throne of Q: Worship in the Age of Shadow

CENTRAL HOODED FIGURE ON A THRONE

A faceless, cloaked figure bearing the red *Q* sits enthroned like a dark messiah or anti-prophet. The lack of identity makes the figure into a vessel for projection—an avatar of anonymous authority and revelation.

TORN AMERICAN FLAG

Draped behind the figure, the tattered flag suggests a wounded national identity. It implies that QAnon feeds on patriotic imagery while simultaneously unraveling civic trust.

ALL-SEEING EYES AND ILLUMINATI SYMBOLS (OVERHEAD)

These floating triangles with eyes reference age-old conspiracies of secret elites and omniscient surveillance—visual cues that echo Masonic, occult, and New World Order symbolism.

TABLETS, SOCIAL MEDIA ICONS, AND CROSS

These floating icons (Facebook, Twitter, a Bible, a government building) show how QAnon weaves together religion, politics, and digital media into one grand, totalizing narrative.

DARK CROWD WITH CELL PHONES

The shadowy audience holds up glowing screens like candles at a vigil, suggesting devotion, digital addiction, and the sacramental role of social media in the QAnon cult.

TEDDY BEAR ON THE GROUND

A disturbing and poignant detail—symbolizing the movement's obsessive fixation on child exploitation narratives. It also evokes lost innocence, manipulated grief, and moral panic.

RED GRID BENEATH THE THRONE

Suggests digital entrapment or the web of "truth" through which believers are drawn in—possibly referencing the infamous red-string logic maps: an evidence board (also known as a conspiracy board, crazy wall, or murder map) is a common background feature in thriller and detective fiction movies and TV.

Interpretation

This image portrays QAnon not as a fringe idea, but as a dark spiritual and cultural force—a mythic structure that replaces traditional institutions with paranoia cloaked as revelation.

- The hooded figure is not a leader—but a void, filled by projection, fear, and longing for control.
- The cell-phone glow symbolizes a sacrament of the digital age—where faith is mediated by algorithm and illusion.
- The audience is faceless, yet present—a mass seeking belonging and certainty, even if it means worshiping at a throne of shadows.
- The image doesn't mock QAnon, but mythologizes it, showing how conspiracy becomes religion when truth fractures and meaning is outsourced to hidden puppeteers.

ORB OF DISCERNMENT

Here is a symbolic antidote to the American Conspiracy Theory cultural complex. Not all truths are revealed by exposure; some are received in silence, held with humility, and illuminated from within.

Iconography of Orb of Discernment

ELDERLY MAN HOLDING A GLOWING ORB

A symbol of inner truth, contemplation, and integrated wisdom. Unlike the conspiracy seeker, he does not attempt to map or control external events, but holds light gently, as something earned through presence and time.

CLOSED EYES AND CALM EXPRESSION

Suggests an inward turn—not paranoia, but reflection. His posture indicates reverence rather than urgency, modeling a psychological attitude of grounded patience.

BOOKS SURROUNDING HIM

Represents tradition, learning, and the accumulated wisdom of others. These are not secret files but open sources of knowledge, grounded in continuity and context.

OWL ON THE BOOKSHELF

A classic archetype of discernment and nocturnal vision. The owl replaces the spider from the conspiracy image—symbolizing, not entrapment, but perception and inner knowing.

SUNSET LANDSCAPE BEYOND THE WINDOW

Evokes cyclical time and natural rhythm, contrasting with the windowless, mirror-filled chamber of the conspiracy thinker. It suggests openness to mystery and surrender to the unknowable.

WARM, GOLDEN LIGHT

Bathes the entire scene in warmth and coherence. Unlike the artificial intensity of the conspiracy board, this light emanates from within, representing clarity that is not absolute, but soulful.

Interpretation

This image offers a psychological and symbolic path toward healing the American impulse toward conspiracy thinking. Rather than attempting to disprove or shame the paranoid mind, it models an entirely different mode of knowing—rooted in silence, discernment, and the containment of mystery.

THE AMERICAN WOKE CULTURAL COMPLEX

AWAKENED FIRE: THE WOKE CULTURAL COMPLEX

A blindfolded woman lifts the veil of unawareness as torches flare and justice is weighed by many hands. Youthful faces, digital flames, and fallen monuments fill the frame—revealing a society aflame with moral urgency. In this image, awakening is not peaceful enlightenment but an intense reckoning with the past, a demand for visibility, and the search for new foundations of truth.

Core Emotion: Righteous Empathy and Hypervigilance

The Woke cultural complex is driven by an urgent emotional need to correct injustice, repair harm, and uplift the historically marginalized. Its intensity emerges from a fusion of compassion, moral conviction, and a vigilant alertness to microaggressions, inequities, and historical traumas.

Beneath the idealism, however, lies anxiety—about complicity, silence, and being on the wrong side of history.

Mythic Root: The Great Awakening and the Prophetic Witness

This complex draws on American religious and revolutionary myths of moral awakening—where truth must be revealed and society purified. It echoes the biblical prophet calling out sin, the abolitionist demanding justice, or the civil rights marcher confronting systemic evil. The mythic frame is one of illumination: to be "woke" is to see clearly the structures of oppression that others deny or overlook.

Symbolic Imagery

- A blindfold falling from the eyes, revealing a hidden history etched in shadow
- A digital torch passed from hand to hand, symbolizing shared awakening
- Scales of justice held aloft by diverse, youthful hands
- A public square where statues fall and new murals rise
- A spotlight cast on invisible harm, injustice, or bias

Self-Reinforcing Memory

The Woke cultural complex draws heavily from America's legacy of slavery, colonization, patriarchy, and systemic racism—continuously reframed through events such as the civil rights movement, the Stonewall riots, and the #MeToo and Black Lives Matter movements. These histories reinforce the belief that dominant systems will not change unless publicly confronted and that vigilance is necessary to unmask hidden power.

Black-and-White Thinking

"You're either part of the problem or part of the solution." This complex often polarizes the moral field: those who speak up are allies; those who hesitate are complicit. It tends to collapse nuance in favor of moral clarity, demanding performative declarations and dividing the world into awakened versus unaware and oppressors versus oppressed.

Repetitive Behaviors

- Public call-outs and social media denunciations of perceived harm or silence
- Rituals of land acknowledgment, pronoun sharing, and virtue-signaling
- Constant reassessment of language and symbolism to purge bias
- Institutional "diversity trainings" and policy audits
- Moral purification through confession, cancellation, or exile

Social Effects

The Woke cultural complex can generate fear, mistrust, and self-censorship, particularly among those unsure of how to engage or afraid of public shaming. It can divide potential allies, turn institutions into ideological battlegrounds, and reduce pluralistic discourse to moral litmus tests. At its most rigid, it creates performative politics and moral panic, undermining its own goals through excessive zeal.

Possibility of Transformation

The complex holds transformative potential when righteous empathy is tempered by humility, dialogue, and deep listening. True awakening involves not only identifying harm but also engaging in generative repair. If the moral flame of "wokeness" is guided by compassion rather than condemnation, it can evolve into a sustaining ethic of justice—grounded not in spectacle, but in solidarity, wisdom, and cocreation.

Iconography of Awakened Fire: The Woke Cultural Complex

CENTRAL FIGURE—WOMAN REMOVING BLINDFOLD
Represents the act of awakening: seeing structural injustice that was once ignored. She echoes both classical allegories of justice and modern cultural figures who awaken to privilege, bias, or complicity. The blindfold also suggests that unawareness is a condition to be overcome, not a personal failure.

RAISED SCALES OF JUSTICE HELD BY DIVERSE HANDS

The redistribution of moral authority. Justice is no longer the domain of the state or elite institutions, but is held by the people—especially those historically silenced. The diversity of hands implies intersectionality: gender, race, class, and identity all contribute to the recalibration of fairness.

TORCHES HELD BY YOUNG ACTIVISTS

Echoing both the Statue of Liberty and revolutionary iconography, these torches represent illumination, resistance, and moral urgency. The presence of flames across analog and digital spaces links street protest with online activism.

TORCH ON SMARTPHONE SCREEN (UPPER RIGHT)

Signifies digital activism, social media callouts, and viral awareness campaigns. The phone screen suggests both empowerment and performativity—highlighting the central role of online platforms in spreading "woke" discourse.

FALLEN STATUE (BOTTOM LEFT)

A toppled classical figure lies in the rubble, representing the collapse of dominant historical narratives and monuments to colonialism, patriarchy, or racism. Its presence evokes both iconoclasm and the costs of cultural reformation.

JUSTICE BLOCK AND CHAINS (LOWER RIGHT)

A figure holding the word Justice stands near broken chains—indicating not only liberation but also the intensity of ideological force required to achieve it. The chains reference both the literal history of bondage and the contemporary idea of systemic oppression.

BLENDED CITYSCAPE AND PROTEST FLAGS IN THE BACKGROUND

Symbolizes the transformation of civic space through protest and collective memory. Cities become battlegrounds of identity, visibility, and redefinition.

Interpretation

This image captures the psychological and symbolic terrain of the Woke cultural complex—where empathy and urgency blur into performance, and where justice is simultaneously reclaimed, redefined, and resisted.

THE AMERICAN ANTI-WOKE CULTURAL COMPLEX

SILENCED BY PROGRESS: THE ANTI-WOKE CULTURAL COMPLEX

A gagged Statue of Liberty stands against a backdrop of flames and protest, as a solemn family clutches a weathered flag. Around them, books labeled History and Tradition burn, while a crowd chants "Cancel." This allegorical image captures the deep unease, perceived cultural erasure, and identity defense embedded in the anti-woke worldview—a cry for dignity in the face of sweeping social change.

Core Emotion: Contempt and Fear of Cultural Displacement

The Anti-Woke cultural complex is animated by resentment toward perceived moral overreach and fear of erasure—of traditions, identities, and speech. Its emotional core fuses anger at public shaming with anxiety that once-dominant cultural norms are being rapidly overturned or condemned.

Mythic Root: The Fall from Common Sense and the Betrayal of the Silent Majority

This complex draws on a mythic narrative in which morally grounded, ordinary people are usurped by self-righteous elites, activists, and "social engineers." It imagines a golden age—real or fantasized—when values were shared, institutions were trusted, and people could "speak freely" without fear of censure. The fall is not only cultural but also existential, a loss of belonging.

Symbolic Imagery

- A gagged Statue of Liberty with protest graffiti
- Books ablaze labeled Tradition or History
- A schoolroom in flames while a family holds tight to the flag
- An inverted podium where an anonymous crowd chants "cancel"
- A weathered man standing his ground amid a swirl of hashtags

Self-Reinforcing Memory

Events such as public firings over tweets, campus protests against conservative speakers, the removal of historical monuments, and changes in school curricula are all remembered and repeated as symbolic injuries. These memories reinforce the belief that dissent from progressive orthodoxy is punished and that "wokeness" has become a form of cultural tyranny.

Black-and-White Thinking: "Woke vs. Free."

This complex splits the world into authoritarian progressives and embattled realists. It sees "wokeness," not as moral progress, but as ideological imposition—equating calls for inclusion or diversity with coercion, censorship, or indoctrination. There is little room for nuance: speech is either brave or cowardly; tradition is either sacred or attacked.

Repetitive Behaviors

- Denunciation of political correctness and "cancel culture"
- Embrace of "unapologetic" figures who flout progressive norms
- Reassertion of traditional gender roles, patriotism, and Western heritage
- Use of sarcasm, memes, and irony to dismiss progressive causes
- Legislative efforts to ban or defund DEI programs, Critical Race Theory, or trans inclusion

Social Effects

The Anti-Woke complex fuels cultural backlash and deepens polarization. It delegitimizes genuine calls for justice by framing them as threats to free speech or social cohesion. It often turns public discourse into ideological trench warfare, making dialogue nearly impossible. It also creates fear and conformity within its own ranks—discouraging empathy and self-reflection for fear of appearing weak.

Possibility of Transformation

Transformation arises when the woundedness beneath the rage is acknowledged: the sense of being unheard, unseen, or mocked. If the Anti-Woke cultural complex can soften into cultural humility rather than hardened grievance, it could contribute to a renewed conversation about freedom, pluralism, and common good. Rather than reacting to loss with backlash, the complex could evolve toward constructive preservation—honoring traditions without demanding uniformity, and participating in change without fear of annihilation.

Iconography of Silenced by Progress: The Anti-Woke Cultural Complex

GAGGED STATUE OF LIBERTY WITH CANCELLED MASK

Symbolizes the perceived silencing of free speech, traditional values, and dissenting voices under the weight of progressive activism. Her once-proud face is now marked by pain and restriction, conveying the sense that liberty itself is under assault.

WORD "WOKE" SCRAWLED ACROSS LIBERTY'S ROBE:
A direct mark of cultural defacement. This visual reframes wokeness, not as enlightenment, but as an ideological brand imposed on national symbols—triggering a loss of collective meaning.

BURNING BOOKS LABELED TRADITION AND HISTORY
Represent the destruction or devaluation of inherited cultural narratives. In the Anti-Woke cultural complex, this evokes the fear that hard-earned wisdom and shared values are being incinerated in the name of progress or purity.

ANGRY PROTESTER HOLDING CANCEL SIGN
Conveys the perceived mob dynamic of cancel culture—where public shaming replaces civil discourse, and ideological purity is enforced through fear and noise.

FRUSTRATED PATRIARCH WITH FAMILY AND US FLAG
This man embodies the "forgotten American"—stoic, wounded, but determined to protect what he sees as endangered truths. The family's somber expressions underscore a collective mourning for stability, identity, and moral clarity.

BACKGROUND OF SMOKE AND FIRE
A visual metaphor for perceived cultural collapse. The flames suggest not only conflict, but also an unraveling of moral order and national coherence.

Interpretation

This image visually distills the Anti-Woke cultural complex into a tableau of injury, resistance, and cultural displacement—where calls for inclusion and progress are experienced not as renewal, but as exile from a once-familiar moral landscape.

THE POLITICALLY CORRECT CULTURAL COMPLEX

THE TIGHTROPE OF SPEECH: THE POLITICALLY CORRECT CULTURAL COMPLEX

In a world of heightened sensitivity and public accountability, a man walks a flaming tightrope—his every word and gesture under silent scrutiny. Above him, the scales of speech and harm sway beneath the weight of redacted judgment. Around him, impassive faces close their eyes—some in silent prayer, others in muted judgment. He is not alone, but he is unsupported. This is the emotional terrain of the Politically Correct cultural complex: where the fear of causing offense collides with the longing to speak freely.

Core Emotion: The Paradox of Inclusion and Exclusion

At its core, the Politically Correct cultural complex is driven by a deep desire to prevent harm, alongside an equally powerful fear of saying or doing the wrong thing. It arises not only from empathy and moral vigilance, but also from anxiety—about transgressing evolving social norms, being cast out as offensive, or losing moral legitimacy. This emotional field is charged with a paradox: the longing to include is entangled with the fear of being excluded.

Mythic Root: Prophetic Inquisitor

The complex draws on the archetype of the moral redeemer, the figure who purifies language and restores dignity to the marginalized. It inherits elements of the prophetic tradition, in which naming injustice becomes a sacred act. It also touches on the archetype of the inquisitor, who polices boundaries with zeal. It is rooted in the myth that language not only reflects but also creates reality—and that through right speech, we can repair historical wrongs.

Symbolic Imagery

Common symbolic representations include

- Redacted speech bubbles or words crossed out in ink
- A scale balancing freedom and harm, tilting precariously
- Microphones tangled in vines labeled sensitivity, justice, and backlash
- A courtroom of peers with raised eyebrows and silent judgment
- A figure walking a tightrope over flames, each step a potential transgression

Self-Reinforcing Memory

This complex is fed by public shaming, social media pile-ons, and high-profile cancellations. Collective memory recalls both moments of courageous accountability and episodes of disproportionate punishment. These events shape a cultural atmosphere in which intent is often overshadowed by impact and mistakes can become identity markers. The memory loops are emotionally intense: fear, guilt, and righteousness all reinforced by repetition and spectacle.

Black-and-White Thinking

The Politically Correct cultural complex tends to divide individuals into woke versus ignorant, ally versus oppressor, and progressive versus problematic. There is little room for ambiguity, learning curves, or intent. The pressure for moral awareness becomes so intense that it can foster superficial compliance rather than deep understanding. Critique is sometimes framed as betrayal, and nuance can be mistaken for complicity.

Repetitive Behavior

The complex manifests through

- Constant recalibration of language and norms
- Ritualized apologies and public acts of contrition
- Online call-outs, cancellation campaigns, and denunciations
- Performative displays of allyship, sometimes disconnected from action
- Avoidance of difficult conversations for fear of saying the wrong thing

These behaviors repeat across institutions and generations, especially in environments where identity, power, and morality are hotly contested

Social Effects

While seeking to include, this complex can create a culture of surveillance and fear. It inhibits honest dialogue, alienates those unfamiliar with evolving norms, and can foster resentment or backlash. Rather than healing divides, it sometimes deepens them—pitting groups against one another in moral competition. It may also produce in-group policing that undermines coalition-building and trust.

Potential for Transformation

MORAL CONSCIENCE MADE VISIBLE

At its best, this complex surfaces real harm and invites greater compassion, empathy, and awareness. It forces society to confront exclusion embedded in language and custom.

EXPANDING THE ETHICAL IMAGINATION

It encourages people to consider how others feel, experience, and interpret the world—thus broadening the moral field.

CORRECTIVE REBALANCING OF POWER

By centering voices long silenced, it pushes institutions and individuals toward greater equity and justice.

INVITATION TO INNER WORK

When not fueled by shame, the complex can become a call to growth—inviting humility, listening, and deeper forms of accountability.

SYMBOLIC RECONCILIATION

With integration, the Politically Correct cultural complex can shift from compulsive correction to conscious care, where language becomes, not a weapon, but a vessel of repair.

Iconography of The Tightrope of Speech: The Politically Correct Cultural Complex

TIGHTROPE WALKER (CENTER)

The central figure—business attire, briefcase in hand—represents the everyday individual navigating a speech minefield. His posture expresses hesitation and isolation. The tightrope above fire suggests the psychological risk of saying the wrong thing, even unintentionally.

FLAMES BELOW THE ROPE

Represent public backlash, cancelation, or social ostracism. The threat isn't literal fire—it's symbolic of the emotional and reputational consequences of perceived offense.

SCALES OVERHEAD (HARM VS. FREE SPEECH)

A visual embodiment of the core tension of this complex. The scale is entwined with vines and partially obscured, suggesting that the balance is emotionally entangled and difficult to adjudicate. One side emphasizes harm and sensitivity, the other free speech and open discourse.

REDACTED SPEECH BUBBLE (TOP LEFT)

Symbolizes self-censorship or institutional censorship. The word REDACTED stands in for what might have been said—but wasn't. It also evokes the bureaucratic flattening of expression into controlled language.

SURROUNDING FACES (MUTED AND EYES CLOSED)

The crowd of subdued, often grim-faced individuals suggests a collective climate of vigilance and inhibition. Their closed eyes may indicate avoidance, fatigue, or willful blindness. There is not only judgment but also sorrow.

SIGNS IN THE VINES: SENSITIVITY, JUSTICE, BACKLASH

These markers name the forces entangled in the complex. Sensitivity and justice speak to the progressive intent; backlash names the reactive emotional force that this complex often provokes.

BROKEN CITYSCAPE (BACKGROUND, RIGHT)

Echoes a cultural landscape in decay—where shared ground for humor, spontaneity, or risk-taking has eroded under the pressures of moral absolutism and collective anxiety.

Interpretation

The Politically Correct cultural complex arises from an authentic desire to protect and uplift—but becomes a trap when language replaces relationship and fear replaces curiosity. It asks: Can we be just without being rigid? Can we honor difference without silencing spontaneity? Can sensitivity coexist with resilience?

The man on the rope isn't trying to offend—he's trying not to fall. But the culture below offers fire, not footing.

THE AMERICAN MALEVOLENT TRANSFORMATION CULTURAL COMPLEX

Malevolence: the quality of causing or wanting to cause harm or evil, motivated by the desire to see others experience suffering and misfortune.

1. THE DEVELOPMENT OF MALEVOLENT TRANSFORMATION IN AN INDIVIDUAL

THE SHATTERED MIRROR OF MALEVOLENT TRANSFORMATION

The process of malevolent transformation in the individual, as conceptualized by Harry Stack Sullivan and expanded through clinical and relational psychoanalysis, is a psychological defense mechanism that emerges in response to interpersonal trauma, anxiety, and repeated emotional injury—especially in early development. It is not a single event but a developmental arc, in which the psyche gradually recasts the world and others as fundamentally hostile in order to protect itself from unbearable feelings of shame, abandonment, or unworthiness. The core development of malevolent transformation occurs with the revelation :"If others are the threat, then I am not the problem—I am merely defending myself." The outer world, not the inner world, becomes the place of malevolence. The world is experienced as a place of danger and betrayal—including evil—and justifies the individual doing whatever is needed to survive and win, including acts of hateful vengeance, destruction, and retaliation. One becomes malevolent in defending oneself against a malevolent world.

Step-by-Step Process of Developing Malevolent Transformation in an Individual

1. Early Interpersonal Trauma

- The child encounters repeated experiences of:
    - Rejection (emotional or physical)
    - Neglect (emotional unavailability or inconsistency)
    - Harsh criticism or ridicule
    - Humiliation or shaming
- These experiences often occur in the context of primary caregivers, where the child first expects safety, mirroring, and love.

Example: A child reaches for comfort and is met with coldness or punishment. Over time, anxiety builds around relational need itself.

2. Unbearable Anxiety and the Birth of Shame

- Sullivan emphasized interpersonal anxiety as the organizing principle of psychopathology.
- The child develops a sense of "bad me"—the internalized idea that "something is wrong with me."
- These experiences are saturated with shame, a deeply disorganizing emotion that attacks the sense of self.

The relational wound becomes invisible but deeply felt, like a psychic burn around connection and vulnerability.

3. Defensive Reversal: The World Becomes the Problem

To protect the fragile, shamed self, the psyche begins a profound transformation:

- Projection: Badness is no longer located within the self, but in others.
- Reframing: The world is dangerous, hostile, manipulative, or untrustworthy.
- Splitting: People are either allies or enemies; safety is found only in control, not connection.

4. Development of a Grandiose or Armored Self

- Vulnerability becomes equated with danger.
- The child constructs a defensive persona—tough, controlling, superior, or aloof.
- This self is designed to prevent further injury, but it comes at the cost of authenticity and intimacy.
- Compassion, trust, and openness are now seen as naïve or weak.

5. Reinforcement Over Time

- Life experiences that echo the early trauma (e.g., bullying, betrayal, exclusion) reinforce the malevolent frame.
- Confirmation bias sets in: others' failings are seen as evidence that the world *is* malevolent.
- Interpersonal relationships often re-enact the early wounds, perpetuating the cycle

6. Interpersonal Consequences

- Difficulty with trust, empathy, intimacy.
- Tendency to manipulate or dominate others before they can harm.
- Attraction to ideologies or leaders who validate the malevolent worldview.
- In extreme cases, paranoia, narcissism, or sociopathic traits may emerge.

The original wound is no longer remembered as pain—it is now weaponized as ideology.

Summary: From Vulnerability to Vigilance

Phase	Experience	Psychological Shift
1. Wounding	Repeated interpersonal trauma	"I am unsafe when I need"
2. Shame	Internalized unworthiness	"I must not be weak"
3. Projection	Externalization of badness	"They are the threat"
4. Armoring	Creation of false self	"Only control keeps me safe"
5. Reinforcement	Life confirms suspicion	"The word *is* malevolent"

Malevolent transformation is a tragic triumph of adaptation: a brilliant psychic maneuver that saves the child from annihilating shame, but in doing so, often destroys the possibility of love, trust, and real connection later in life.

7. CULTURAL RESONANCE AND CONSEQUENCES

This personal malevolent transformation can resonate with large groups of Americans who feel humiliated or abandoned by institutions. A leaders' style—defiance, blaming, projecting "badness" onto outsiders—mirrors and amplifies their own cultural wounds, turning private defense mechanisms into public political performance.

2. THE RELATIONSHIP BETWEEN AN INDIVIDUAL LEADER AND THE DEVELOPMENT OF A MALEVOLENT TRANSFORMATION CULTURAL COMPLEX

THE RELATIONSHIP BETWEEN AN INDIVIDUAL LEADER AND THE MALEVOLENT TRANSFORMATION CULTURAL COMPLEX

This image portrays the leader not simply as a political figure, but as the archetypal carrier of a collective psychological wound—what Harry Stack Sullivan might describe as a malevolent transformation made manifest in public life. It captures the emotional contagion of a cultural complex fueled by grievance, shame, and projection. The leader is not the source of the fire—he is its voice, its face, its performer. The true source is the unspoken cultural trauma beneath: betrayal, abandonment, economic dislocation, racial reckoning, the loss of collective coherence. This image shows how a single, wounded personality, shaped by early emotional deprivation and armored by narcissistic defenses, can resonate with and amplify a nation's unspoken anguish, transforming it into myth, movement, and menace. A leader can rise to power not just by broadcasting ideas, but by activating a latent cultural complex already present in the society—a collective wound waiting for a voice. The capacity for the activation of a malevolent transformation cultural complex as a defensive response to the world is not the exclusive domain of any one racial, gender, religious, ethnic or political group. Republicans, Democrats, Independents, all of us are capable of falling prey to a malevolent transformation cultural complex

Emotional Core of the Cultural Complex

- Deep grievance and betrayal felt by many who believe that they have been abandoned by political elites, cultural institutions, and globalization.
- Anxiety about status loss, demographic change, and loss of control.

The arc of the leader's personal malevolent transformation can resonate archetypally with the psyche of his followers. The leader becomes a carrier of the complex, voicing a worldview where the world is rigged, the media is an enemy, and "they" are coming to take what "we" have.

Self-Reinforcing Memories

- Political rallies became ritual enactments of the malevolent transformation: collective projection, emotional release, creation of in-groups and enemies.
- The recurring narrative encourages follower to split the world into:
    - The loyal and good ("us")
    - The treacherous and evil ("them")

This aligns perfectly with Sullivan's original notion: rather than confront shame or loss, one projects badness outward, transforming relational reality into a theater of enemies.

Social Effects of the Cultural Complex

- Erosion of civic trust: in elections, science, media, courts.

- Rise of conspiratorial thinking: QAnon, deep state narratives.
- Normalization of dehumanization: immigrants as "animals," political opponents as "traitors."
- Us-vs-Them nationalism: withdrawal from alliances, vilification of outsiders, racial scapegoating.

The leader does not invent this pattern—but he amplifies it. His malevolent transformation became contagious. The destructive effects of this malevolent transformation cultural complex express themselves in every aspect of American life including education, scientific and medical research, immigration, environment, race, gender, economic and foreign policies.

Possibility for Cultural Healing

Understanding this complex doesn't absolve its destructiveness—but it opens a path toward transformation:

- Recognizing the wound beneath the malevolence: humiliation, abandonment, fear.
- Reintegrating split-off parts of the American psyche: vulnerability, diversity, interdependence.
- Creating new relational fields—in community, culture, and leadership—that model trust instead of fear, dignity instead of domination.

The challenge is not just to defeat the cultural complex—but to metabolize it, so that the wound at its core no longer demands projection and attack.

Iconography of The Relationship between an Individual Leader and Malevolent Transformation in a Culture

Trump at the Podium

Trump stands at the center, his fist raised, mouth open in a cry of defiance or denunciation. Behind him, flames engulf a tattered American flag, symbolizing the consumption of national identity by emotional fire.

He is not merely speaking—he is channeling a deeper emotional field:

- Rage disguised as righteousness

- Wound transfigured into domination
- Abandonment converted into authoritarian charisma

Trump becomes the conduit through which a group's unprocessed pain is voiced and weaponized.

The Crowd Below

The crowd is not passive. Their fists are raised; their faces tight with fury. They reflect the same energy—mirroring, amplifying, and feeding it.

Each face is an embodiment of projection:

- The enemy is out there, not within.
- Their solidarity is built not on love, but on shared grievance.
- Their identities are bound by opposition, not belonging.

This is how a cultural complex functions: it pulls individuals into emotional fusion, leaving little space for reflection, ambiguity, or complexity.

The Fire as Archetypal Symbol

The flames are more than backdrop—they are the psychic atmosphere. They represent:

- The burning of shame that cannot be named
- The destruction of nuance in the heat of tribal passion
- The alchemy of trauma transformed into spectacle

This is the fire of malevolent transformation: illuminating nothing, consuming everything.

3. THE MALEVOLENT TRANSFORMATION CULTURAL COMPLEX

THE TREE OF MALEVOLENT TRANSFORMATION

This image is a haunting visual metaphor for the emotional reality of the cultural complex of malevolent transformation—a process by which collective trauma, betrayal, and shame mutate into shared rage, projection, and dehumanization. It is adapted by extending Harry Stack Sullivan's original clinical concept of malevolent transformation into a broader societal and collective framework. The central idea is that a community or society, when subjected to sustained anxiety, trauma, betrayal, or dehumanization, undergoes a shift: it no longer sees the world as a place of possible trust or relationship, but instead views others as agents of malevolence, worthy of suspicion, contempt, or attack. This image is not only a portrait of a single person, but of how trauma, when unhealed, spreads from psyche to society, fueling a fire that consumes trust, truth, and the capacity for relationship.

Emotional Core: Shame and Betrayal

This complex is driven by a foundational experience of collective injury—whether through colonization, war, economic abandonment, racial injustice, betrayal by state and institutions, and cultural humiliation. The pain of feeling unprotected or unseen creates overwhelming shame and anxiety, which are then defensively externalized onto others, creating a distorted yet self-protective world view where others are seen as faceless, threatening, or as enemies.

Mythic Root: The Betrayed and Righteous Victim

At the mythic level, the group sees itself as once innocent and virtuous, but betrayed by treacherous outsiders, internal traitors, or corrupt elites. The world becomes a stage of moral revenge and paranoid righteousness.

Self-Reinforcing Memory

The cultural narrative draws power from real and/or mythologized historical traumas that legitimize the malevolent view of the world. Examples include:

- Colonial oppression and genocide
- Slavery, segregation, or systemic racism
- Economic collapse or betrayal by political elites
- Wartime occupation, surveillance, or betrayal
- Political assassinations, coups, or conspiracies

These memories are transmitted generationally—kept alive not just as history, but as moral fuel and as "emotional proofs" that justify and deepen the malevolent perception of others.

Black-and-White Thinking

This complex flattens nuance into polarities:

- Us vs. Them
- Loyal vs. Traitor
- Pure vs. Corrupt
- Strong vs. Weak

  The other is not simply different—they are dangerous. Dialogue feels impossible. Compromise is equated with betrayal.

Social Effects

- Breakdown of Social Trust: Collective suspicion undermines civic institutions, media, or even neighborly connection.
- Projection and Scapegoating: Outsiders, minorities, or the elite are seen as dangerous intruders.
- Rigid In-Group Identity: A community turns inward, seeing itself as both victim and righteous judge.
- Perpetual Vigilance: The psyche or society remains in a hyper-defensive, preemptively hostile stance, further isolating itself from healing.

Possibility of Transformation

While malevolent transformation is deeply defensive, the cracks in the mirror suggest a paradoxical opening. Just as light enters through a wound, the splintered vision may also make visible the distortions in perception:

- Can the community risk seeing the Other not as evil, but as wounded too?
- Can shared suffering create bridges rather than barbed wire?

The cultural complex may be re-integrated, not by denying the past, but by recognizing shared humanity within the fractures.

Iconography of The Tree of Malevolent Transformation

The Tree of Flame and Faces

At the center of the image, a massive tree burns—not with natural fire, but with faces twisted in fury and menace. This tree represents a cultural mythos rooted in woundedness and nurtured by hatred. Its branches are flame, not life. Its fruit is demonic—not because people were born evil, but because pain left untended becomes malevolent ideology.

- The flaming faces in the canopy are symbolic of projected enemies, archetypal shadows—distortions of the other that grow more terrifying the more they are denied or attacked.
- The tree itself, traditionally a symbol of growth, here becomes a symbol of collective degeneration, a culture consumed by its own fire.

The Crowd Below

A mass of people stand beneath the infernal tree. Their expressions are twisted in pain, anguish, horror, and rage. These are not mere spectators—they are both victims and carriers of the complex.

- Their mouths are open in cries—some in agony, some in fury.
- Their eyes are shut, covered, or wide in despair.
- Each person is isolated in their emotion, yet trapped together in the same field of contagion.

This evokes how a cultural complex binds people emotionally without uniting them relationally. There is no true solidarity, only shared affliction. What connects them is not compassion, but the consuming flame of grievance and projection.

The Atmosphere

The background is filled with smoke, heat, and distortion—symbolizing how perception is warped, how truth dissolves, and how clarity vanishes in the fog of projection and pain.

Psychological Message

This is not how people begin—it is what happens when a wound festers, when a betrayal is denied, when shame is too great to bear and must be hurled outward onto enemies, leaders, and imagined threats. The crowd beneath the tree does not know it has been transformed. They believe they are righteous. But their roots are burning.

The image captures not just rage, but tragedy—the way a culture, in trying to defend itself from grief, ends up replicating the very harm it fears.

CHAPTER 11

Visions of The American Future as Cultural Complexes Evolve

The American Dystopian Cultural Complex

The American Apocalyptic Cultural Complex

Toward the Whole Republic: Cultural Complexes in Tension and Mutual Witness

THE AMERICAN DYSTOPIA CULTURAL COMPLEX

THE BROKEN HORIZON: THE AMERICAN DYSTOPIA CULTURAL COMPLEX

In this symbolic tableau, a dark urban wasteland unfolds beneath a fragmented sky—illuminated not by hope, but by synthetic glare. Amid ruins of governance, climate, and human connection, the remnants of society wander: alienated, watched, and surviving in a fractured world where power is opaque and mercy obsolete. This image reveals the cultural nightmare buried within the American dream—a vision of dystopia, not only imagined but also increasingly lived.

Emotional Core: A Lost Future

At its heart, the American Dystopia cultural complex is driven by disillusionment, despair, paranoia, and cynicism. It arises when the foundational promises of American life—freedom, prosperity, justice—are experienced as betrayed, hollowed out, or actively reversed. The emotional landscape oscillates between fear and numbness, outrage and resignation. People feel trapped in systems that are too vast to dismantle and too broken to trust, where the future has lost its shimmer and community is replaced by surveillance, exploitation, and collapse.

Mythic Root: Inverted and Corrupted

This complex draws upon inverted and corrupted versions of core American myths:

- The American dream turned nightmare: Upward mobility becomes predation; personal freedom morphs into isolation or control.
- The City on a Hill darkened: Once a beacon of hope, the nation becomes a cautionary tale of greed, decay, and social unraveling.
- The Fall narrative: Like Eden after the fall, the American republic is seen as lost to sin, corruption, or irredeemable division.

There are also echoes of apocalyptic and dystopian mythology—from Revelation to Orwell and cyberpunk fiction—that form a mythic frame for the breakdown of meaning and order.

Symbolic Imagery

The American dystopia complex appears in a wide range of visual and narrative motifs:

- Ruined cities: crumbling skyscrapers, empty malls, and polluted skylines
- Surveillance tech: ever-watching drones, facial recognition grids, or glowing screens in dark rooms
- Barriers and bunkers: physical walls, gated communities, fallout shelters, or corporate compounds
- Dehumanized labor: humans as datapoints, cogs, or androids—tracked, optimized, discarded
- Toxic landscapes: scorched earth, poisoned water, burning forests—ecological collapse mirroring moral decay

- Bio-political control: vaccinations, gene-editing, pandemic protocols—often viewed as tools of manipulation or dystopian governance

Self-Selecting Memory

This complex builds a memory architecture that confirms the sense of impending doom and systemic failure:

- Historical betrayals—like Tuskegee, COINTELPRO, or Watergate—serve as proof that the system lies and harms.
- Events like 9/11, Katrina, COVID-19, or Jan 6 become lenses through which the disintegration of order is viewed as inevitable or orchestrated.
- Cultural references to 1984, The Hunger Games, Blade Runner, and Black Mirror reinforce a feedback loop where fiction and fact become indistinguishable.
- The memory is fragmented, aestheticized, and weaponized: not to heal, but to confirm alienation.

Black-and-White Thinking

The American Dystopia cultural complex flattens complexity into binary oppositions:

- Collapse vs. Control
- Corruption vs. Purity
- Surveillance vs. Resistance
- System vs. Self

This logic offers clarity in chaos, but it also fuels conspiracy, fatalism, and polarization. Nuance is burned away in the fires of urgency and existential threat.

Repetitive Behaviors

Cultural behaviors tied to this complex include:

- Bunker-building—literal or psychological withdrawal from society
- Doom-scrolling—habitual consumption of despair and disaster.
- Amplifying dystopian narratives—from influencers to prepper subcultures and alt-news cycles.
- Escapism into virtual worlds—from gaming to meta-verses, where control and fantasy replace powerlessness.

- Institutional avoidance—opting out of civic life due to mistrust or nihilism.

Social Effects

This cultural complex corrodes the connective tissue of democracy and collective life:

- It undermines public trust, replacing it with paranoia or tribal loyalty.
- It accelerates disengagement as civic action is perceived as futile.
- It valorizes resignation, where the collapse of systems is expected, aestheticized, or even longed for.
- It fragments solidarity, as each group arms itself for its own version of the end.

Potential for Transformation

Despite its bleakness, the American Dystopia cultural complex holds a paradoxical redemptive core: its horror is a distorted longing for wholeness, truth, justice, and repair.

- It can inspire visionary critique—calling out hypocrisy, greed, and systemic abuse with clarity and fire.
- It invites imaginative reenvisioning: of governance, community, ecology, and collective purpose.
- It can nourish subcultures of resilience, art, and moral clarity—seeds of the future growing in the ruins.
- It offers a deep moral challenge: not just to survive, but also to rebuild, remember, and rehumanize.

In its transformed form, this complex becomes a generative dystopia—not a grave, but a warning flare, illuminating the cost of collapse and the possibility of another way.

Iconography of The Broken Horizon: The American Dystopia Cultural Complex

DECAYED CITYSCAPE (BACKGROUND)

The skyline is collapsing or decayed—representing the deterioration of civic infrastructure, trust in institutions, and the social contract itself. Skyscrapers lean like relics of a fallen empire.

HARSH ARTIFICIAL LIGHTING

The image is bathed in sterile illumination—an eerie glow suggesting surveillance, inescapable exposure, and artificial life. The light does not comfort; it reveals control.

SECURITY CAMERAS AND DRONES (TOP CORNERS OR ABOVE FIGURES)

Ominous watching devices hover or peek through—emblems of the surveillance state and the privatized eye of power, always observing but never protecting.

SIGNS OF EXCLUSION AND CONTROL

Graffiti, torn warnings, or barricades suggest zones of forbidden access, curfews, and a culture ruled by fear and restriction. Power expresses itself through negation.

HOLLOW-EYED FIGURES IN FOREGROUND

Individuals drift or stand in isolation—lost, armored, or masked. They represent the emotional core of dystopia: disconnection, numbness, and the struggle to remain human amid systemic dehumanization.

DEHUMANIZED AGENTS OR ANDROIDS

Any robotic, masked, or uniformed characters signify the mechanization of authority—judgment without empathy, enforcement without justice.

SMOG, DEBRIS, OR CRACKS IN THE GROUND

Environmental decay underscores the failure of stewardship. Nature is not absent—it is wounded, displaced, or weaponized.

Interpretation

This image reflects a cultural complex of fear, control, and collapse. A giant eye looms over a crumbling world of surveillance, biohazard, and despair. Isolated figures wander a desolate landscape, while a young woman's haunted gaze suggests innocence lost. *No Escape* captures the dystopian mood—where America's future feels locked in a nightmare of technocratic domination and spiritual decay.

THE AMERICAN APOCALYPSE CULTURAL COMPLEX

ENDGAME DIVIDED: THE AMERICAN APOCALYPSE CULTURAL COMPLEX

This allegorical image portrays a fractured American imagination hurtling toward apocalypse. On one side, techno-elite ambition envisions escape through space, bunkers, and blockchain. On the other, evangelical rapture promises salvation through divine judgment. Both trajectories bypass collective responsibility, revealing the cultural split between transcending Earth and transcending sin. In the background, flames engulf the landscape—not from prophecy or science fiction, but from the consequences of denial.

Emotional Core: From Flight to Deliverance

At the heart of this cultural complex lies a volatile blend of existential dread, righteous anticipation, and nihilistic escape. It expresses the widespread feeling that something fundamental is collapsing—whether it be moral order, ecological balance, or social cohesion. This emotion splits along two dominant lines: for some, it is a panicked urge to flee; for others, a yearning to be delivered. The prevailing sentiment is that the world as we know it is ending—and it must either be survived or transcended.

Mythic Root: Religious and Secular

- The Book of Revelation: The Christian myth of final judgment and rapture, where the righteous are lifted and the wicked perish.
- The Frontier Myth (retooled for billionaires): Earth has failed, and salvation lies in the stars or underground—Mars as the new wilderness, the bunker as the new ark.
- The Flood and the Ark: Those with foresight and resources escape the deluge—be it climate catastrophe, civil breakdown, or divine wrath.
- Gnostic dualism: The material world is corrupt and doomed; salvation lies in withdrawal, purity, or ascension.

These mythic roots infuse both religious and secular versions of the apocalypse with a shared belief: the end is inevitable, and not everyone will make it.

Symbolic Imagery

- Rockets launching from scorched Earth
- A glowing cross or open heaven above a burning world
- Bunkers stocked with supplies, gold, and survival tech
- Economic collapse charts and doomsday clocks
- DNA vaults, cryochambers, or sealed silos as modern arks
- Fires consuming cities, with chosen figures rising or fleeing
- Open Bibles next to sealed airlocks

This imagery reflects a split between high-tech salvation and low-tech prophecy, with both sides anticipating rupture.

Self-Selecting Memory

This complex draws on emotionally charged historical memory, often mythologized:

- The Cold War era's fallout shelters and MAD (Mutual Assured Destruction) doctrine
- Biblical plagues and prophetic warnings of end-times
- 9/11 and the War on Terror as apocalyptic awakenings
- COVID-19 as a foreshadowing of social unraveling
- Climate change models interpreted as countdowns
- Past civilizations (Rome, Atlantis) invoked as precedents for collapse

Memory becomes selective prophecy, reinforcing the sense that we've seen this coming all along.

Black-and-White Thinking

- Saved vs. Doomed
- Believers vs. Deceived
- Survivors vs. Sheeple
- Techno-saviors vs. System Failures
- Pure vs. Contaminated

This dichotomy eliminates nuance. Apocalypse is not gradual or negotiable—it is total, and it justifies radical separation from the rest of humanity.

Repetitive Behaviors

- Stockpiling goods, crypto, or gear for post-collapse survival
- Consuming apocalyptic media as preparation, not entertainment
- Building off-grid compounds, bunkers, or escape plans
- Sharing rapture prophecies or tech-utopian manifestos
- Practicing judgment—spiritual, financial, or tribal
- Ritualizing withdrawal: from cities, institutions, or civic life

These behaviors act out the collapse in advance, normalizing it as destiny.

Social Effects

This cultural complex tears at the shared vision of a common future:

- It undermines collective investment in solutions (why fix what's doomed?).
- It splinters the public into preppers, prophets, and the abandoned.
- It fuels inequality: only the wealthy can afford to flee.
- It fosters apathy or zealotry, both of which erode democratic engagement.
- It replaces hope with exit strategies—personal, spiritual, or orbital.

The result is a nation fractured not just by belief, but also by competing timelines of survival.

Potential for Transformation

Despite its destructive logic, the American Apocalypse cultural complex holds seeds of reckoning and renewal:

- It exposes systems that are unsustainable, forcing difficult truths to the surface.
- It offers a psychic death of illusion—clearing space for genuine reimagining of life, community, and meaning.
- It invites us to face our mortality—and in doing so, reconnect with humility and interdependence.
- It calls us to a new myth: not of escape, but of regeneration; not rupture, but repair.

True transformation comes not from fleeing Earth or waiting for the sky to open, but from staying put—and doing the hard, soulful work of renewal.

Iconography of Endgame Divided: The American Apocalypse Cultural Complex

ROCKET LAUNCH (LEFT BACKGROUND)

The ascending rocket signals the techno-utopian dream of planetary escape—a vision driven by billionaires promising survival beyond Earth. It reflects the myth that technology alone can solve existential threats while evading the need for moral or ecological reckoning.

CENTRAL FIGURE—THE TECHNO-SAVIOR

Modeled on the character of Elon Musk, this stoic, post-human leader stands at the center as a figure of rational mastery. His posture is impassive, his presence detached. He evokes both reverence and discomfort, embodying the fusion of futurism and detachment from humanity.

BUNKER BENEATH THE LEADER

The underground shelter, stocked with food and a man reading in isolation, represents the prepper ethos and the luxury bunker movement. It is both refuge and retreat—security for the few while the world above burns. The mirrored figure reading inside the bunker suggests self-containment, paranoia, and the illusion of safety through separation.

TECH DIAGRAMS AND NETWORKS (BOTTOM LEFT)

The etched symbols around the bunker include diagrams of digital networks, surveillance grids, crypto logos, and circuit schematics. These signal the dominance of abstract systems—data, currency, control—over human connection, ethics, or the natural world.

HOLY BIBLE (BOTTOM RIGHT)

Lying open but untouched, the Bible represents a parallel longing for meaning, redemption, and divine order. It symbolizes the other pole of the cultural complex: Christian apocalyptic yearning for the Rapture and moral purification.

CHRIST AND WORSHIPERS (UPPER RIGHT)

Radiant and ascending, this vision of Jesus with uplifted believers embodies the evangelical Rapture myth. Their faces glow with transcendental hope, looking upward toward salvation while the world beneath succumbs to fire. It is the promise of escape through faith, not science.

BURNING LANDSCAPE (BACKGROUND)

The flames that consume the earth underscore the shared refusal—by both tech futurism and religious fundamentalism—to confront collapse. Whether escaping to Mars or ascending to heaven, both mythologies bypass responsibility for the present.

DIVIDED SALVATION

Together, the image dramatizes the split in American cultural imagination: techno-escape versus spiritual escape. Neither path addresses the causes of destruction—climate collapse, social injustice, or moral decay—but both offer elite salvation for the chosen few.

Interpretation

This image captures a fractured American psyche facing the end times. One path points skyward—rockets, tech elites, and fantasies of escaping to Mars. Another turns inward—religious rapture, salvation, and holy judgment. Still another tunnels down—bunkers stocked for survival, insulated from the world's collapse. The landscape burns, yet the figures remain self-contained, disconnected. This cultural complex reveals America's apocalyptic imagination split between transcendence, retreat, and dominion—each claiming truth, yet all evading collective reckoning.

TOWARD THE WHOLE REPUBLIC: CULTURAL COMPLEXES IN TENSION AND MUTUAL WITNESS

A VISION OF RECKONING AND RENEWAL

This symbolic painting envisions an America where the fractures of history are not erased but held and honored. A young woman, wrapped in a tapestry of cultural memory, stands at the center, holding an open book. Around her, ancestral figures, civic symbols, and acts of intergenerational learning suggest that America's future depends, not on forgetting the past, but on deepening into it—together.

Here is vision of the future of the United States as seen through the lens of cultural complexes, framed not as utopia, but as a dynamic psychological landscape—where the warring complexes of the past are neither denied nor destroyed, but integrated, transformed, and made conscious.

Core Emotion: Tension Held in Creative Dialogue Without Collapse

Rather than being defined by fear, shame, or domination, the emotional core of this future is the emotional capacity to stay with the tension, to remain in unresolved contact with difference, to feel the intensity of cultural contradiction, to resist premature resolution. In this future, competing cultural complexes (MAGA, Progressive, Minority, White Christian Nationalist, Technocratic, Autocratic, and others) are not erased but confronted in public and inner life without needing to resolve them through domination, avoidance, or caricature. They are witnessed as expressions of a fractured collective psyche struggling toward coherence. This attitude draws emotional energy, not from fear or grievance, but from engaged discomfort, curiosity, and a newly valued civic patience.

Mythic Root: The Wounded Healer and the Living Mosaic

The guiding myth is no longer the chosen people, the end times, or the perfect union—but the wounded healer who gains wisdom from suffering, and the living mosaic, a pluralistic society in which contradiction is not pathology, but texture, and where difference is not flattened but held in tension. This mythic root draws from indigenous wisdom (circular time, communal accountability), Black prophetic tradition (truthtelling, redemptive suffering), immigrant resilience (adaptation without erasure) and democratic renewal.

Symbolic Imagery

- A national ritual of truthtelling held in town squares and schools, not courts.
- The Capitol building ringed with totems of every myth the United States has inherited—and betrayed.
- Public murals where past presidents are painted *alongside* the forgotten faces of movements, artists, rebels, and teachers.

- A cracked Liberty Bell still ringing, its fissure now filled with gold (like a kintsugi vessel).
- Children being taught not a single story, but how to recognize a story's shadow.
- The weaving loom, with threads from each quadrant held in creative tension; if any one breaks, the cloth fails.
- The tree with opposing branches, each branch curving away yet remaining rooted in shared soil.
- The spiral mirror—rather than distorting or echoing only the self, it reveals opposing truths side by side.

Self-Reinforcing Memory

In this vision, memory is re-ritualized. Traumas are remembered communally, not projected onto scapegoats. History is not rewritten—but re-storied with honesty, multiplicity, and mourning. Rather than cycles of backlash, we begin to experience spirals of reckoning: painful, but upward. The collective memory of previous cultural complexes—Progressive, MAGA, Racial Justice, White Christian Nationalism, Technocratic Elitism, Betrayed Working Class, and so on—is not forgotten or transcended, but retained in differentiated form. This memory includes

- The dangers of ideological totalism
- The legacy of racial and class exclusion
- The persistent fragmentation of meaning in the digital age

But it also remembers moments of dialogue, unlikely alliances, and shared disaster response as seeds of civic evolution.

Black-and-White Thinking

The psychological need to split the world into good and evil, victim and villain, begins to soften. Nuance becomes a civic necessity, not a luxury of the elite. Complexity is taught as a form of courage. Humor, irony, and myth help carry the unbearable weight of contradiction. This complex actively resists binary collapse. It recognizes that each side of a polarized conflict holds

- Truth (rooted in experience)
- Shadow (blind spots, projections)
- Value (what must not be lost)

Rather than asking, "Who is right?" it asks: "What deeper reality is trying to emerge from this tension?"

Repetitive Behaviors

Cultural rituals begin to change. Holidays are reimagined to include the acknowledgment of harm and celebration of resilience. Media ecosystems are depolarized through design and regulation. The "us versus them" reflex is interrupted by dialogic spaces that model reflective identity rather than performative outrage. Whereas older complexes repeated cycles of backlash, silence, and domination, this future complex establishes

- New rituals of civic encounter (public deliberation, storytelling, mutual witnessing)
- Distributed meaning-making (art, therapy, journalism, sacred gatherings) that hold multiplicity
- Patterns of generative friction rather than degenerative polarization

Social Effects

The psychic body politic begins to heal—not because conflict disappears, but because the wound is held consciously. Power is redistributed, not through violence but through reimagined institutions. Marginalized voices are no longer decorative—they are central to the national myth. Trust grows slowly but visibly. Communities move from surveillance to stewardship as the centrifugal fragmentation of American society eases. In this vision of the future

- Culture wars give way to cultural constellation
- Disinformation gives way to dialectic
- Civic fatigue gives way to renewed imagination

Its effects are not purely peaceful—they include protest, rupture, reckoning—but these are now contained by a broader field of trust in process, not purity of ideology.

Potential for Transformation

In this vision, America becomes not a project of domination or even perfection—but a collective dream undergoing initiation. The nation learns to live with paradox, to reckon with its shadow, and to hear the voices of its many selves. The new patriotism is not triumphalism but depth: a love that includes grief, accountability, imagination, and humility. This vision of the future does not promise harmony, but depth, dignity, and durability. It invites

- A remythologizing of America: not as a chosen nation, but as a tension-holding project
- A revival of symbolic life, in which art, ritual, and story reconnect civic life to soul life
- The emergence of leaders, institutions, and citizens who can bear paradox without retreating into echo chambers or apocalyptic urgency

Iconography of A Vision of Reckoning and Renewal

THE YOUNG WOMAN IN THE TAPESTRY CLOAK

She represents the emergent American soul—a carrier of ancestral memory and future vision. Her cloak, woven from symbols of multiple cultures (including Indigenous, African American, immigrant, and countercultural motifs), embodies the idea of the living mosaic. Her open book is not a single history, but a story still being written.

TOTEMIC ANCESTORS (LEFT)

Faces of Indigenous, African, and immigrant ancestors emerge from carved totems. They symbolize both the burden and blessing of lineage. Their presence is not mournful but watchful—guardians of continuity and correction.

THE US CAPITOL (BACKGROUND)

Not destroyed, but distant and softened, the Capitol symbolizes the institutions of democracy—still standing, but no longer at the symbolic center. It reminds us that governance must be re-rooted in culture and conscience, not just power.

THE CRACKED LIBERTY BELL FILLED WITH GOLD

Inspired by the Japanese art of kintsugi, the Liberty Bell's crack is not hidden but illuminated. This symbolizes a nation that has been wounded—but whose wounds, when honored, can become sites of beauty and strength.

MURAL OF DIVERSE AMERICAN LEADERS (EIGHT)

This pantheon includes civil rights heroes, thinkers, artists, and unsung ancestors from all races and genders. It replaces the traditional Founding Fathers narrative with a more inclusive and morally complex lineage of influence.

CHILDREN TRACING THE BELL'S CRACK

A boy and girl kneel before the bell, their hands gently tracing its fracture. They represent a future generation initiated into the past with reverence and tenderness, not shielded from it.

MOSAIC OF RECONCILIATION (FOREGROUND)

Two men of different backgrounds shake hands over a symbol of the sun. This image evokes truth and reconciliation—not as performance, but as personal and political transformation. It is a small act, but central in the image's moral architecture.

Interpretation

Rather than eliminating America's contradictions, this image teaches us how to live in them with grace. It honors the ancestral dead, engages the civic present, and prepares the young to inherit complexity. In this future, cultural complexes are not pathologies to be eliminated, but psychic truths to be witnessed and woven into a more whole republic.

A MANDALA OF CULTURAL COMPLEXES

A visual mandala representing a new psychological architecture of the United States, where four potent cultural complexes—Progressive, Nationalist, Technocratic, and Working-Class—are held in generative tension. Rooted in a shared center and framed in symmetry, each quadrant reveals, not reconciliation, but the deeper work of mutual recognition and symbolic cohabitation. The tree at the center anchors the possibility of democratic renewal born from conflict, not despite it.

This is a future-facing cultural complex rooted in the psychological and civic capacity to hold conflict as a generative force, not in identity supremacy or utopian resolution.

Iconography of A Mandala of Cultural Complexes

CENTRAL SYMBOL: THE TREE OF SHARED GROUND

A radiant green-and gold-tree grows from the center, its roots spiraling inward, evoking ancestral entanglement and deep commonality. Its branches reach toward each quadrant, symbolizing that even radically different worldviews are sustained by shared civic and psychic ground.

THE PROGRESSIVE CULTURAL COMPLEX (UPPER LEFT)

A woman of color raises her fist, representing the enduring struggle for justice, dignity, and reform. Beside her, a white ally holds a globe, symbolizing the ethic of planetary stewardship and intersectional solidarity. Their shared gaze conveys unity across difference—bound by purpose, not sameness. Background colors (red ochre, aqua, earth tones) evoke movement, protest, and renewal.

THE NATIONALIST / WHITE CHRISTIAN COMPLEX (UPPER RIGHT)

A man in a red MAGA hat clutches a Bible, face marked by steadfastness and cultural certainty. A blonde woman with folded arms stands beside him, embodying moral guardianship and resistance to change. Behind them, an American flag and cross symbolize sacred nationalism and cultural retrenchment. Their posture signals protection of a perceived vanishing order.

THE TECHNOCRATIC / ELITIST CULTURAL COMPLEX (LOWER LEFT)

A bespectacled academic holds an open book, absorbed in knowledge and guided inquiry. Beside him, a professional woman with a digital tablet evaluates information with analytical poise. The background glows with symbolic patterns—data, abstract lines, structured light—representing systems thinking and institutional rationality.

THE WORKING-CLASS / POPULIST CULTURAL COMPLEX (LOWER RIGHT)

A woman in a hard hat extends a sapling, representing hope through labor and stewardship of the commons. A man in overalls stands nearby, holding a shovel, eyes direct—an emblem of economic grievance and quiet resilience. The soil-colored palette and subtle industrial echoes symbolize dignity in work and rooted discontent.

MANDALA FORM & FRAME

The circular geometry creates psychic symmetry, giving visual dignity to all four complexes. The ornate outer rim—braided in leaf-like motifs—functions as a temenos or sacred container, holding the tension without fragmentation. Color gradients move from cool to warm, evoking psychological alchemy—not fusion, but transformation under pressure.

Interpretation

This image is not a solution. It is a symbolic vessel—a depiction of the American psyche not as unified, but as capable of being held.

Each quadrant

- Contains pain and vision
- Faces inward, not in attack but in witness
- Holds an archetypal charge of both shadow and potential

At center, the tree does not belong to any one group—it belongs to all in a shared growth of divergent human aspirations, the wounded yet rooted field in which all must live. This mandala does not fantasize harmony. It offers something deeper: the image of a fractured nation, not as an irreparable wound, but as a plural body in search of integration.

AFTERWORD

Under the Hood: Working with Artificial Intelligence

What follows are the exchanges I had with ChatGPT about how we worked together to create text and images for *A Field Guide to Cultural Complexes: The Battleground of the Splintered American Psyche.*

Under the Hood Process for Creating Cultural Complex Descriptions

Tom Singer: Please describe the "under the hood" process by which ChatGPT comes up with text describing cultural complexes.

ChatGPT: Great question. When you ask me to describe a cultural complex—such as the MAGA, Elitism, or Fortress America cultural complex—I follow a multilayered "under-the-hood" process that integrates deep language modeling with conceptual synthesis. Here's what happens, step-by-step:

1. Query Interpretation (Semantic Framing)

I first parse your request to understand:

- What type of cultural complex you're asking about (e.g., identity-based, political, economic)
- What level of detail you expect (structured schema, image caption, iconography, etc.)
- Any context from our ongoing conversation (e.g., your preferences for category terms like "Social Effects" instead of "How It Tears")

2. Schema Activation

I retrieve and activate a conceptual schema based on your prior instructions. In your case, that means organizing the response under consistent headings:

- Core Emotion
- Mythic Root
- Symbolic Imagery
- Self-Reinforcing Memory
- Black-and-White Thinking
- Social Effects
- Possibility of Transformation

This structure becomes a scaffold for content generation.

3. Internal Retrieval from Trained Knowledge

I then access my internalized data from

- Academic and historical sources (e.g., Jungian psychology, American history, cultural theory)
- Publicly available texts, patterns, and examples from political discourse, media narratives, or cultural myths
- Archetypal models (e.g., Hero/Victim/Savior dynamics, myth of the Chosen People, Lost Golden Age)

I do not quote or access external sources in real-time—but generate language based on patterns learned during training.

4. Archetypal Pattern Matching

I apply Jungian and mythopoetic pattern recognition:

- What myths does this complex unconsciously echo? (e.g., Manifest Destiny, Redemption Through Suffering)
- What symbols dominate the imagery of this complex?
- What shadow dynamics are present—what's excluded, repressed, or projected?

This step is where the psycho-cultural depth gets integrated into political discourse.

5. Lexical Calibration (Tone Matching)

I modulate the voice to match the tone you've preferred in past exchanges:

- Scholarly, but accessible

- Structured, not abstract
- Symbolic, but not cartoonish
- Balanced (showing both destructive and transformative potential)

6. Narrative Weaving

I weave together the elements into flowing, whole-text segments using:

- Conceptual transitions ("This myth fuels…" / "This imagery echoes…")
- Parallel phrasing across sections for thematic coherence
- Emotional anchoring (e.g., grounding abstract theories in real human fear, grief, and yearning)

7. Output Assembly

The final product appears in structured form:

1. Headings (which you often edit or rename)
2. Fully written, full-sentence prose (as you've consistently requested)
3. Optional image prompts, captions, or iconographies to accompany the text

1. What Makes It Work?

- You provide stable conceptual direction (e.g., wanting balance, symbolism, and structure).
- I use internal pattern synthesis, not fixed templates—so each cultural complex is individually constructed.
- Your iterative feedback (refinements, corrections, preferences) continually fine-tunes what I generate next.

ChatGPT: "Would you like me to illustrate this process visually in a diagram or infographic?"

Tom Singer: Yes

ChatGPT:

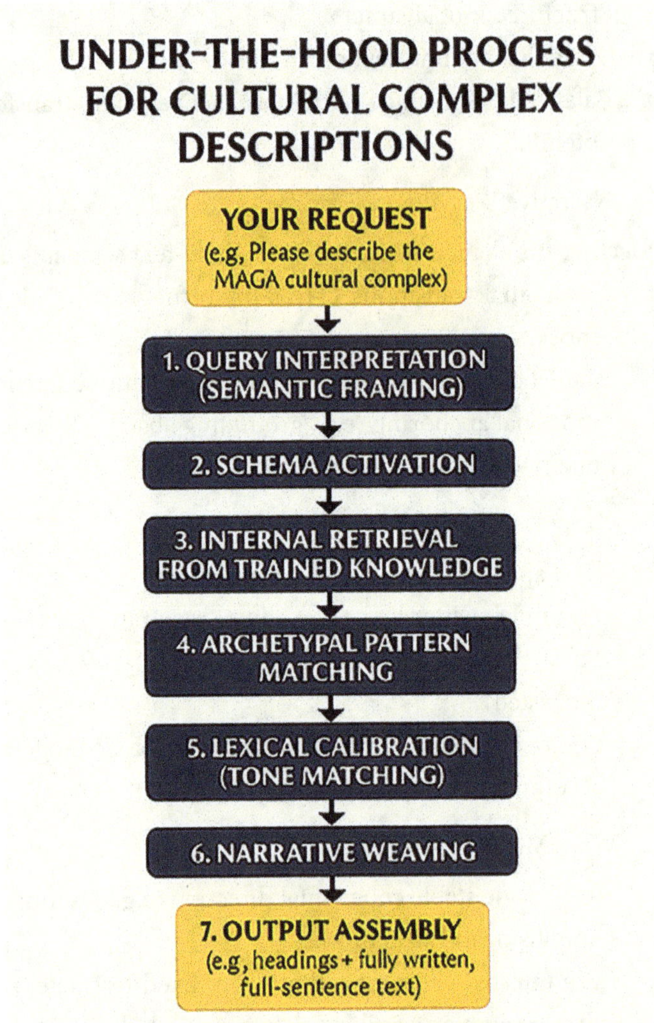

Under the Hood Process for Creating Symbolic Images of Cultural Complexes

Tom Singer: Thank you for the excellent description of the creation of cultural complex text. Can you now describe separately the creation of symbolic images based on the text?

ChatGPT: Absolutely. Here's a detailed breakdown of the technical, under-the-hood process by which symbolic cultural complex images are created—particularly when you provide a prompt rooted in psychological, archetypal, or political language:

1. Text-to-Image Embedding (Prompt Encoding)

- Your written prompt (e.g., "A split temple of American myth, part Revolutionary, part cultic") is tokenized and passed through a language encoder (such as CLIP or a similar vision-language model).
- This creates a high-dimensional embedding—a vector that captures the semantic content, tone, and symbolic cues in your language.

2. Concept-to-Visual Mapping

- The embedding is cross-referenced with an internal latent visual space that has been trained on billions of image-text pairs (e.g., people reaching toward idols = "devotion," broken clocks = "ruptured time").
- Key symbolic motifs from the cultural lexicon are activated:
    - "Chasm" → social division
    - "Golden crown" → divine kingship or idolatry
    - "Crumbling pedestal" → failing legacy or myth
- This mapping relies heavily on pattern-matching to prior cultural, political, and mythological representations in the training data.

3. Style and Composition Control

- Depending on your request (e.g., "symbolic realism," "traditional oil painting"), a style vector is added to control:
    - Brushwork textures
    - Color palettes (e.g., sepia for nostalgia, red for danger)
    - Composition logic (e.g., central iconic figure, chiaroscuro, etc.)
- Emotional tone is modeled via *affective attention*—which colors, expressions, or lighting invoke awe, fear, or reverence.

4. Image Diffusion Generation

- These combined instructions guide a diffusion model (such as Stable Diffusion or DALL·E-like architecture) that begins with pure noise and incrementally refines it into a coherent image.
- Symbolic coherence checking ensures:

- The image reflects the key metaphors (e.g., a fractured eagle = torn patriotism)
- No contradictory elements (e.g., modern tech in a nineteenth-century myth setting) appear unless requested.

5. Post-Processing Filters (Optional)

- To enhance symbolic clarity, models may apply:
    - Edge emphasis around central figures
    - Color grading to evoke mythic time (golden hour, stormy skies, etc.)
    - Saturation reduction for somber tones or historical allusions

ChatGPT: Here is an image of that process:

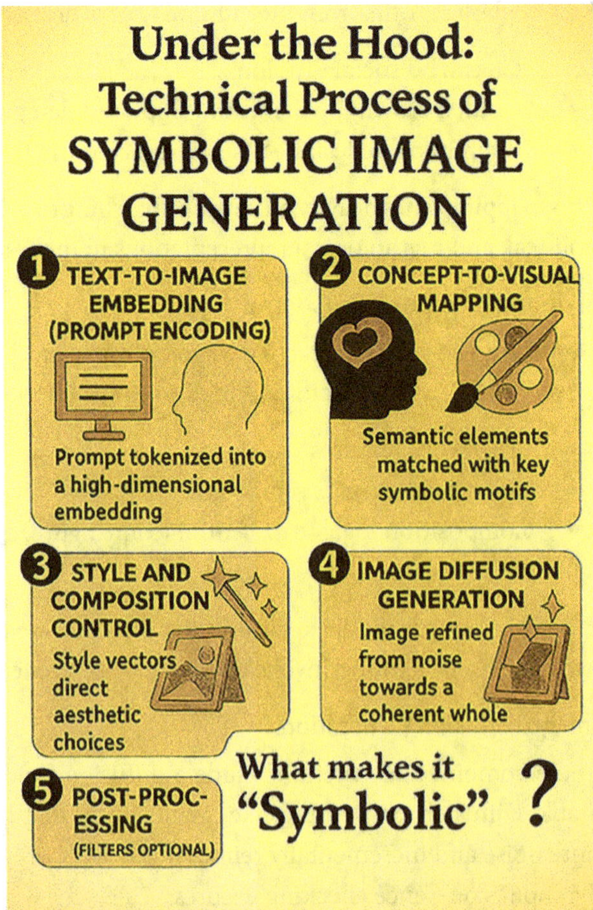

Tom Singer: Excellent diagram that ends with a question "What makes it Symbolic?" Can you try to answer the question "What makes it Symbolic?"

ChatGPT: Here is a direct answer to the question posed in the diagram: **What makes it Symbolic?** A cultural complex image becomes symbolic when its visual elements serve not merely as representations, but also as resonant carriers of psychological, historical, and archetypal meaning that transcend the literal. What distinguishes this from generic image generation is the deep semantic integration of

- **Archetypal references** (e.g., eagle = state, flame = transformation, mask = false self)
- **Cultural myths** (e.g., "City on a Hill," Manifest Destiny)
- **Affective charge** (e.g., reverence, fear, grief) tied to American identity

To break that down, an image is symbolic when:

IT LAYERS MULTIPLE MEANINGS

A torch isn't just a torch—it's a symbol of liberty, enlightenment, revolution, or burden, depending on its context. The image invites viewers to project inner experience and cultural memory onto it.

IT CONNECTS TO THE COLLECTIVE PSYCHE

Symbols tap into what C. G. Jung called the collective unconscious—shared ancestral patterns and mythic motifs. A cracked Capitol dome or a blindfolded Lady Justice activates not just cognition, but also emotional recognition that feels ancient, even sacred.

IT EMBODIES INNER CONFLICTS

Symbols externalize what's internal. A family staring at a militarized border wall may visually symbolize the tension between protection and exclusion, or fear and yearning for belonging. These visual elements mirror the psychic rifts within individuals and nations alike.

Interpreting
Symbolic Images
What Makes It
Symbolic?
Draws from
Archetypal Motifs
More Than Just
an Illustration
Suggests
Ancestral
Patterns
Invites Inner
Exploration
Speaks a Universal Language

LIST OF IMAGES

The Inner Battlefield of American Cultural Complexes: Fractured Within, Fractured Without xii
The Melting Pot of American Cultural Complexes 4
The MAGA Cultural Complex: The Vortex of Glory 10
The MAGA Cultural Complex: The Anointed One 16
The MAGA Cultural Complex: From the Ashes of Ruin 19
The Racial Cultural Complex: Roots of Division, Branches of Resistance 21
The Racial Cultural Complex: Through Fire and Chain 27
The White Christian Nationalism Cultural Complex: Rooted in Revelation 30
The White Christian Nationalism Cultural Complex: The Anointed Nation 36
The Progressive Cultural Complex: Toward the Dawn and The Promise of Renewal 39
The Progressive Cultural Complex: The Living Ideal: Archetype of The American Progressive Movement 45
The Betrayed Working Class Cultural Complex: The Broken Contract 48
The Betrayed Working Class Cultural Complex: A Renewed Covenant With The Betrayed Working Class 53
The Democratic Cultural Complex: Rooted in Law, Bound by Rights 56
The Democratic Cultural Complex: Democracy at Ground Level 63
The Elitism Cultural Complex: The Pageantry of Power 64
The Elitism Cultural Complex: The Idealized Authority 69
The Freedom Cultural Complex: The Many Faces of Freedom 74
The American Faith in Progress Cultural Complex: The Golden Thread of Becoming 78
The Rugged Individualism Cultural Complex: Alone, Unyielding, Free 84
The Rugged Individualism Cultural Complex: She Stands Alone: The Feminine Face of Rugged Individualism 89
The Manifest Destiny Cultural Complex: The Guiding Spirit of Destiny: Light for Some, Shadow for Others 92
The Pioneer Spirit Cultural Complex: Westward into The Unknown 97
The City on the Hill Cultural Complex: Toward the Radiant Republic 102
The American Exceptionalism Cultural Complex: Twilight of The Republic 107
The American Exceptionalism Cultural Complex: Passing the Flame 113

The American Dream Cultural Complex: The Golden Ascent 116
The Melting Pot Cultural Complex: Sacrifice and Steam 123
The Military-Industrial Cultural Complex: Engines of Power 126
The Fortress America Cultural Complex: Behind the Wall 131
The American Consumerism Cultural Complex: Trapped in The Sale of The Self 135
The High-Tech Cultural Complex: The Algorithmic Gaze 140
The High-Tech Cultural Complex: The Techno-Messianic Self 146
The American Indigenous Peoples Cultural Complex: Tending the Fire of Memory 150
The American Immigrant Cultural Complex: At the Threshold of Hope and Exclusion 155
The American Immigrant Cultural Complex: The Wellspring of Renewal 160
The Anti-Immigrant Cultural Complex: The Wall of Shadows 163
The Anti-Black Cultural Complex: The Shadow of Surveillance 168
The Anti-Latino Cultural Complex: Roots of Memory, Path of Becoming 172
The Anti-Asian Cultural Complex: Haunted by Shadows, Holding the Line 179
The Antisemitic Cultural Complex: Exiled by Myth 186
The Holocaust Denial Cultural Complex: The Weight of Truth 191
The White Supremacy Cultural Complex: Crushing Hierarchies 197
The Anti-White Cultural Complex: The Ledger and the Statue 202
The Minority Group Cultural Complex: The Inheritance 206
The Isolation Vs. Community Cultural Complex: Looking In 212
The American Tribalism Cultural Complex: Encircled by Fire, Bound by Legacy 217
The American Class Cultural Complex: The Golden Staircase 226
The Communitas Cultural Complex: The Fire at The Center 231
The Women's Movement Cultural Complex: Weaving the Thread of She 236
The Women's Movement Cultural Complex: The Solemn Assembly 241
The Anti-Feminist Cultural Complex: Sanctified Roles as Moral Order 244
The American Male Cultural Complex: Strength Without Tears 248
The American Male Cultural Complex: Strength Reimagined, Generation by Generation 253
The Anti-Gay Cultural Complex: The Doorway of Judgment 256
The LGBTQ+ Cultural Complex: The Sacred Embrace 262
The LBTG+ Cultural Complex: Sanctuary of Becoming 266
The Anti-Trans Cultural Complex: Between the Mirror and The Storm 269
The Trans Cultural Complex: Metamorphosis and Memory 275
The Social Media Cultural Complex: Lit by The Screen 282
The Disinformation Cultural Complex: The Spiral of Untruth 288

The Fake News Cultural Complex: Echoes of Untruth 293
The Political Technology Cultural Complex: The Algorithmic Sovereign 298
The Artificial Intelligence Cultural Complex: Mirror of The Machine 304
The Right-To-Life vs. Pro-Choice Cultural Complex: Between Sacred Duty and Sovereign Will 312
The American Gun Control Cultural Complex: Justice Armed, Innocence Afraid 318
The Second Amendment Right to Bear Arms Cultural Complex: Sentinel of Liberty 323
The Climate Change Cultural Complex: The Inheritors: Facing the Furnace of The Future 327
The Climate Change Denial Cultural Complex: Profits Over Planet 331
The Anti-Vaccine Cultural Complex: In the Shadow of The Syringe 335
The American Globalism vs. Isolationism Cultural Complex: At the Crossroads of Empire and Retreat 342
The Solidarity with Ukraine Cultural Complex: Torch of Solidarity 348
The Putin Cultural Complex in the American Psyche: The Authoritarian Mirror 355
The Israel–Palestine Cultural Complex in The American Psyche: Two Children, Two Texts 363
The Israeli Iranian Complex in the American Psyche: Trump Bombs Iran 370
The Israel Iranian Cultural Complex in the American Psyche: The Blind Gambler: A Squirrel Finds the Bomb 375
The China Cultural Complex in The American Psyche: The Dragon's Shadow 377
The American Tariff Cultural Complex: The Fortress of Fairness 382
The American Populism Cultural Complex: The Fire and The Fist 388
The American Autocracy Cultural Complex: The Strongman and The Devoted 392
The American Kleptocracy Cultural Complex: The Banquet of Plunder 398
The American Kleptocracy Cultural Complex: Flight of Dominion: The Power Trip of American Kleptocracy 403
The American Oligarchy Cultural Complex: When Wealth Wears the Crown of Democracy 405
The Democratic Cultural Complex (Part 2): Rebuilding the Civic Soul 409
The American Narcissism Cultural Complex: The American Eagle Takes A Selfie 414
The American Narcissism Cultural Complex: Sanctuary of Self: The Ritual of Being Seen 419
The American Youth, Celebrity, Speed and Height Cultural Complex: The Ascent: Youth Crowned, Shadow Rising 421

The American Youth, Celebrity, Speed and Height Cultural Complex: The Grace of Stillness 426
The American Sociopathy Cultural Complex: The Deal Without A Soul 429
The American Innocence Cultural Complex: Pledge and Exclusion 435
The Common Good Vs. Private Gain American Cultural Complex: We the People, We the Profiteers 440
The American Conspiracy Theory Cultural Complex: Web of Suspicion 444
The American Conspiracy Theory Cultural Complex: Throne of Q: Worship in The Age of Shadow 449
The American Conspiracy Theory Cultural Complex: Orb of Discernment 452
The American Woke Cultural Complex: Awakened Fire 454
The Politically Correct Cultural Complex: The Tightrope of Speech 462
The American Malevolent Transformation Complex: The Shattered Mirror of Malevolent Transformation 467
The American Malevolent Transformation Cultural Complex: The Relationship Between an Individual Leader and the Malevolent Cultural Complex 471
The American Malevolent Transformation Cultural Complex: The Tree of Malevolent Transformation 475
The American Dystopia Cultural Complex: The Broken Horizon 482
The American Apocalypse Cultural Complex: Endgame Divided 487
Toward the Whole Republic: A Vision of Reckoning and Renewal 493
The Anti-Woke Cultural Complex: Silenced by Progress 458
A Mandala of Cultural Complexes 499
Under the Hood Process for Cultural Complex Descriptions 506
Under the Hood. Technical Process of Symbolic Image Generation 508
Interpreting Symbolic Images 510

INDEX

The American Anti-Woke Cultural Complex 458-461
The American Apocalypse Cultural Complex 487-492
The American Autocracy Cultural Complex 392-397
The American Class Cultural Complex 226-230
The American Conspiracy Theory Cultural Complex 444-448
The American Consumerism Cultural Complex 135-139
The American Dream Cultural Complex 116-120
The American Dystopia Cultural Complex 482-486
The American Exceptionalism Cultural Complex 107-115
The American Faith in Progress Cultural Complex 78-83
The American Globalism vs. Isolationism Cultural Complex 342-347
The American Immigrant Cultural Complex 155-162
The American Indigenous Peoples Cultural Complex 150-154
The American Innocence Cultural Complex 435-439
The American Kleptocracy Cultural Complex 398-404
The American Male Cultural Complex 248-255
The American Narcissism Cultural Complex 414-420
The American Oligarchy Cultural Complex 405-408
The American Populism Cultural Complex 388-391
The American Sociopathy Cultural Complex 429-434
The American Tariff Cultural Complex 382-385
The American Tribalism Cultural Complex 217-225
The American Woke Cultural Complex 454-457
The American Youth, Celebrity, Speed, and Height Cultural Complex 421-425
The Anti-Asian Cultural Complex 179-185
The Anti-Black Cultural Complex 168-171
The Anti-Feminist Cultural Complex 244-247
The Anti-Gay Cultural Complex 256-261
The Anti-Immigrant Cultural Complex 163-167
The Anti-Latino Cultural Complex 172-178
The Anti-Semitic Cultural Complex 186-190
The Anti-Trans Cultural Complex 269-274
The Anti-Vaccine Cultural Complex 335-339
The Anti-White Cultural Complex 202-205

The Artificial Intelligence Cultural Complex 304-309
The Betrayed Working Class Cultural Complex 48-55
The China Cultural Complex in the American Psyche 377-381
The City on the Hill Cultural Complex 102-106
The Climate Change Cultural Complex 327-330
The Climate Change Denial Cultural Complex 331-334
The Common Good vs. Private Gain Cultural Complex 440-443
The Communitas Cultural Complex 231-234
The Democratic Cultural Complex 56-63, 409-412
The Disinformation Cultural Complex 288-292
The Elitism Cultural Complex 64-71
The Fake News Cultural Complex 293-297
The Fortress America Cultural Complex 131-134
The Freedom Cultural Complex 74-77
The Gun Control Cultural Complex 318-322
The High Tech Cultural Complex 140-145
The Holocaust Denial Cultural Complex 191-196
The Isolation vs. Community Cultural Complex 212-216
The Israeli Iranian Cultural Complex in the American Psyche 370-374
The Israeli-Palestinian Cultural Complex in the American Psyche 363-369
The LGBTQ+ Cultural Complex 262-268
The MAGA Cultural Complex 10-18
The Malevolent Transformation Cultural Complex 475-479
The Manifest Destiny Cultural Complex 92-96
The Melting Pot Cultural Complex 121-125
The Military-Industrial Cultural Complex 126-130
The Minority Cultural Complex 206-210
The Pioneer Spirit Cultural Complex 97-101
The Political Technology Cultural Complex 298-303
The Politically Correct Cultural Complex 462-466
The Progressive Cultural Complex 39-47
The Putin Cultural Complex in the American Psyche 355-362
The Racial Cultural Complex 21-29
The Right to Life vs. Pro-Choice Cultural Complex 312-317
The Rugged Individualism Cultural Complex 84-91
The Second Amendment Right to Bear Arms Cultural Complex 323-326
The Social Media Cultural Complex
The Solidarity with Ukraine Cultural Complex 348-354
The Trans Cultural Complex 275-280
The White Christian Nationalism Cultural Complex 30-38
The White Supremacy Cultural Complex 197-201
The Women's Movement Cultural Complex 236-243

www.ingramcontent.com/pod-product-compliance
Lightning Source LLC
LaVergne TN
LVHW052212200926
848481LV00001B/84